Mentoring in Formal and Informal Contexts

A volume in
Adult Learning in Professional, Organizational, and Community Settings
Carrie J. Boden-McGill, *Series Editor*

Mentoring in Formal and Informal Contexts

edited by

Kathy Peno
University of Rhode Island

Elaine M. Silva Mangiante
Salve Regina University

Rita A Kenahan
DePuy Synthes Institute

INFORMATION AGE PUBLISHING, INC.
Charlotte, NC • www.infoagepub.com

Library of Congress Cataloging-in-Publication Data

A CIP record for this book is available from the Library of Congress
http://www.loc.gov

ISBN: 978-1-68123-461-8 (Paperback)
        978-1-68123-462-5 (Hardcover)
        978-1-68123-463-2 (ebook)

Printed in the United States of America

CONTENTS

PART I

MENTORING IN HIGHER EDUCATION

PART II

MENTORING IN K–12 TEACHER EDUCATION

PART III

MENTORING IN HEALTHCARE

PART IV

MENTORING IN MULTIPLE CONTEXTS

PREFACE

Thomas D. Cox
Adult Higher Education Alliance

Following in the tradition of the AHEA book series, the editors and authors of this year's book entitled *Mentoring in Formal and Informal Contexts* used a pragmatic approach to this very important topic. The authors explore the significance of the mentoring in a variety of contexts and offer insights into successful mentoring practices.

The scope of this book truly encapsulates one of the purposes of AHEA, and that is to serve as a vehicle for cooperative consultation and collaboration among professionals in the field. Whether individuals' work is in higher education, K–12 teacher education, health care, or a host of other contexts for mentoring, this book serves as a valuable tool to build or strengthen the relationships mentors and those they support.

On behalf of AHEA I would like to thank your Series Editor, Dr. Carrie Boden-McGill for her dedication to our efforts to publish the book annually. I would also like to thank this year's book editors, Drs. Kathy Peno, Elaine Silva Mangiante, and Rita Kenahan, for their commitment to the book, many hours of editing and collaborating with the authors, and genuine interest in the mission of AHEA.

For such an effort as this to be successful, it cannot be done in a silo. It takes an open atmosphere of collegiality and collaboration. So I am very appreciative to all the authors who completed this important work and chose

Mentoring in Formal and Informal Contexts, pages ix–x
Copyright © 2016 by Information Age Publishing
All rights of reproduction in any form reserved.

the AHEA book series as an outlet for their ideas and contributions. The AHEA book series has evolved into an important contribution to the field of adult and higher education, and it is my hope that it continues to gain ground as the organization continues to grow.

My hope is that you enjoy reading the book and keep it close at hand as a reference you will pick up time and time again.

FOREWORD

Stuart E. Dreyfus
Professor Emeritus
University of California at Berkeley

As the reader no doubt knows, mentoring can and should profitably accompany a great number of educational opportunities. This book attests to the variety of situations and issues that good mentoring raises.

Here, I would like to address my own pet situation and issue. I would like to consider the situation where the mentee, after considerable formal academic education in a skill domain, is now learning in the presence of a mentor to cope successfully with the real world of that skill. I naturally assume that the mentor has had considerable experience in the domain including the kind of situation that has just occurred or is occurring during a mentoring session.

The road to real-world skill is the subject of a five stage model of skill acquisition with which I am associated. According to the model, an adult learner of a new skill, when at stage one *novice*, needs rules for decision-making that involve isolated features of the skill domain recognizable even by an inexperienced beginner. The learner becomes at stage two *advanced beginner* when a teacher, coach, or mentor points out features of the skill domain that are useful in decision-making rules, but which themselves can only become available to the learner based on examples in the skill domain. The experiential learning from examples, such as significant visual

Mentoring in Formal and Informal Contexts, pages xi–xiii
Copyright © 2016 by Information Age Publishing
All rights of reproduction in any form reserved.

phenomena or sounds or smells etc., is important for the issue I wish to address in this foreword since learning must be intuitive. I shall return to this topic shortly. By pointing out this fact to a mentee, the mentor will be paving the road to later advancement. Stage three, *competence*, occurs when the learner, becoming overwhelmed by the available number of features, is taught to choose the most important ones and to develop a plan for achieving a decision-making goal. These are all analytic stages (with the exception of the intuition involved at stage two) requiring thinking and choosing. Stage four, *proficiency*, is the subject of my remarks to follow. While an employer of a mentor may feel that the job is done when the mentee is competent, I believe that the most important learning event is now at hand. This involves the transformation of the mentee from an analytical thinker into an intuitive *sense-maker*. Many skill-learners fail to take this leap. Stage five, *expertise*, completes that transformation into an intuitive *doer*.

Returning to the mentoring situation described before my one paragraph digression, a less than expert mentor, whose skill by the way should itself develop experientially through the above stages, might be tempted to ask or tell the mentee what should be done in an observed situation because, after all, the ultimate goal of the training is expert *action*.

However that would be premature. In this case, my hypothesized mentor who is a skill-domain expert will inevitably be intuitively seeing the current situation from a particular perspective, meaning that certain sights and sounds and perhaps smells and other stimuli will stand out as salient, while many other aspects of the situation will not even be noticed. Using the terminology of the psychologist, J. J. Gibson, the situation for the mentor "affords" some particular goal-directed orientation, some sense-making of the situation as well as what action should then ensue. I assume that this is not the case for the mentee who may be overwhelmed by the apparent complexity of the observed situation. What should the mentor productively do and, equally importantly, not do?

It would be helpful at this point if the mentor reminds the mentee of the recognitional ability he or she has acquired intuitively as an advanced beginner. Furthermore, if the mentor has gotten to know a bit about the mentee's outside interests and skills, it should then be possible for the mentor to be prepared to point out one or more situations where the mentee effortlessly uses experiential perception to experience and respond to an affordance with no conscious use of reasoning or rule-following. The current situation, the mentor could explain, should be seen as a step, perhaps the first, toward attaining experiential perception in the current learning domain.

The mentor should point out what he or she considers to be the salient aspects of the current situation. Prior educational experiences of the mentee all too often put its emphasis on what to *do* in particular situations rather than how to recognize the *affordance* of a particular situation. In the situation that I have hypothesized, the mentor should call attention to the fact that he or she was once in the position of the mentee of experiencing an overwhelming number of things going on rather than just what really mattered. The mentor should explain that an effortless intuitive sense-making perceptive ability comes about only through sufficient experience with a particular type of situation, so the inexperienced mentee should feel no guilt at this stage of education for lacking it. Hopefully, the mentee will envy the easy sense-making of the mentor and will desire to become intuitive. If so, he or she will later emotionally replay the current situation and what it afforded to the mentor. Then the mentee's brain, with no conscious effort on the mentee's part, will begin its experiential learning concerning the particular type of situation.

It is likely, due to the mentee's fact-and-rule-based prior educational experiences that he or she will ask how the mentor recognized what stimuli mattered when determining the issue at hand. Here, I believe, the mentor will be unwittingly inhibiting the mentee's progress if he or she attempts to answer that question other than by saying that with enough experience it will just naturally happen. Again, the mentor might have prepared an example where the mentee, perhaps before attaining linguistic abilities and certainly before acquiring abstract-reasoning skills, has experientially by trial-and-error, even without the presence of a mentor, acquired some particular skill.

In summary, there will be times when the mentor's challenge will be to move a mentee beyond the difficult but comfortable analytical mode of competence so compatible with the style of most formal academic education into the ultimately effortless and superior mode of intuitive expertise. A necessary way-station of this journey, easily overlooked when skilled *action* is the ultimate goal, is the intuitive *perception* of what stimuli impinging on the mentee matter and what goal they afford.

I realize that some mentoring scholars writing or reading this important book may well have gone far beyond my ruminations on this topic. I applaud them and simply wish to call attention to this somewhat elusive but crucial topic for some who might profit from being introduced to it.

ACKNOWLEDGMENTS

Collaborating on a project of this magnitude requires the support of many dedicated professionals, and this is no exception. We first wish to recognize the AHEA Board for sponsoring this work and for providing support along the way. Most notably, Carrie Boden-McGill provided hours of detailed information about the process, the minutiae, and reflections on her experiences of editing a book like this. Her pearls of wisdom provided great insight when they were needed the most.

We are particularly grateful to Thomas Cox and the rest of the AHEA Board for coordinating the book and the 2016 conference in order to provide an opportunity for rich discussion and learning in the area of mentoring adult learners. We also wish to thank Fred Prashun, who handled all of the behind-the-scenes business details and developed the logo for the book. We extend a special thank you to David Quinn at the University of Rhode Island for providing technical and editorial support.

One of the highlights of our professional lives has been the opportunity to meet Stuart Dreyfus and discuss the work he and his brother, Hubert, did in developing the Novice to Expert Skill Acquisition Model. To have Stuart write the Foreword for this book is an honor of the highest degree. The Dreyfus and Dreyfus model has provided a strong conceptual framework for research in the fields of medicine and education. In fact, several authors in this book refer to the Skill Acquisition Model in their chapters. Dreyfus and Dreyfus continue to inspire our thinking and our research, and we hope we will honor them through our work as well.

Mentoring in Formal and Informal Contexts, pages xv–xvi
Copyright © 2016 by Information Age Publishing
xv

We also would like to thank Victoria Marsick, who was instrumental in the identification of potential authors for this book, as well as Lois Zachary, who has written extensively on mentoring herself, for helping us identify key writers in the field.

Finally, we appreciate and are very grateful to the chapter authors who kindly shared their work with us and responded to our many requests for edits and information. You were a joy to work with! We appreciate every single one of you!

INTRODUCTION

Kathy Peno
University of Rhode Island

Elaine Silva Mangiante
Salve Regina University

Rita Kenahan
DePuy Synthes Institute

The editors are pleased to present this book that offers multiple perspectives on formal and informal mentoring in multiple contexts. Mentoring is of critical importance to the development of individuals and groups in many fields and, when lacking, can be a detriment to performance, acculturation, promotion, and the ability to feel productive and balanced in the pursuit of educational goals, careers, and other personal contexts. The chapters in this volume offer a look at both formal and informal mentoring research and practice in a variety of settings.

The book is divided into four sections: Part I, Mentoring in Higher Education, is further subdivided into Faculty and Student Mentoring. Part II, Mentoring in K–12 Teacher Education, focuses mainly on mentoring preservice teachers of general and special education. Part III, Mentoring in Healthcare, provides a look at mentoring in academic medicine as well as nursing and, Part IV, Mentoring in Multiple Contexts, examines mentoring

Mentoring in Formal and Informal Contexts, pages xvii–xix
Copyright © 2016 by Information Age Publishing
All rights of reproduction in any form reserved.

in both business and higher education settings as well as in post-higher education contexts in diverse geographical locations.

The book begins with an overview by Chandler, Murphy, Kram and Higgins who provide an historical view of mentoring research and elaborate on their developmental network perspective in both formal and informal contexts. Many authors in this book have cited the seminal work of Kram (1985) and other works by these authors; therefore, the editors felt this chapter would provide a meaningful overview for the book.

In Part I, Mentoring in Higher Education, Mandell and Coulter provide an introduction to mentoring in higher education as they critically examine the role of faculty as mentors in academic settings. Within the Higher Education subsection, Mentoring Faculty, Ciccomascolo and Seitsinger provide a frame of the multi-modal approach they use for providing faculty mentoring opportunities in their college at The University of Rhode Island. Sedivy-Benton, Chavkin and Boden-McGill offer personal stories to explore their own mentoring experiences in their different disciplines of practice while navigating different stages of their own careers.

In the Mentoring Graduate Students subsection of Part I, King presents a unique model of virtual mentoring. She draws on her years of experience to provide effective strategies for utilizing technology to mentor doctoral students, in particular. Hansman explores the research and literature as well as practical mentoring models which inform faculty about effective strategies for mentoring graduate students given the many barriers both mentors and mentees bring to bear. Dickerson, Agosto, Dickerson, and Dove provide insights into the use of developmental mentoring networks in a Black Greek Letter Organization (BGLO). They focus their discussion on both formal and informal methods used to prepare and support collegiate advisors that work with student members of the BGLO housed at their university. Alston explores age as a factor in faculty-student mentoring. In particular, she examines how age was experienced by young female faculty engaged in a mentoring dyad with older female doctoral students.

In Part II, Mentoring in K–12 Education, Silva-Mangiante and McAuliffe provide the results of a study that examines the experiences of both university clinical educators and school field-based clinical educators as they implement newly acquired mentoring skills to supervise pre-service teachers. Moore and Semnoski provide insight into the mentoring needs of pre-service teachers in the field of special education as they suggest ways to connect teacher candidates with authentic learning experiences to prepare them for interacting with families of children with special needs. Silva-Mangiante and Peno further explore the use of their mentoring model, the Purposeful Ongoing Mentoring Model (POMM), with field-based clinical educators and their student teachers in elementary science classrooms. In this case, they use the model to develop a tool for clinical educators to use when mentoring their student teachers in planning for and implementing reform science teaching practices.

In Part III, Mentoring in Healthcare, three perspectives are offered on mentoring in academic medicine and nursing. Aminololama-Shakeri and Seritan examine various mentoring models utilized in academic medicine: dyad, network, peer, and reverse mentoring. Additionally, they make suggestions for thinking about mentoring differently as the needs of learners change over time. Carter, Brock, Fulco, Garber, Hemrajani, Lee, Matherly, Miller and Pierce explore the influence of mentors and role models on both teaching and learning in academic medicine. Authors provide reflections of salient mentoring episodes and the effect on their own practice. Criscitelli looks at informal mentoring in nursing as a way to enhance skill development and provide a continuum of lifelong learning support. Utilizing the two different models, she looks at strategies for informal mentoring support for nursing students, novice nurses, and experienced nurses as well.

In Part IV, Mentoring in Multiple Contexts, Langer provides a description of a program at Columbia University that uses formal and informal mentoring in concert with business and industry to develop future technology executives. Langer explores the ways that the program collaborates with organizations to provide students with experiential activities in the field and access to an IT Executive as their mentor. Concluding this section is Kenahan, Lim-Williams, Liu Wong, Mondo, Tiu-Wu, and Watson as they describe the collaborative mentoring process they used during their graduate program and post-graduation to achieve both personal and professional goals.

In conclusion, we present this volume to provide further insight and meaning into the various modalities for mentoring that can be used in multiple contexts. It is our hope that these chapters will inspire readers to consider various mentoring approaches to promote the continued development of professionals in their respective fields. We trust that you will find some pearls of wisdom from these authors to challenge you toward a more enriched understanding and relevant use of mentoring in your practice.

CHAPTER 1

BRIDGING FORMAL AND INFORMAL MENTORING

A Developmental Network Perspective

Dawn E. Chandler
Queens University of Charlotte

Wendy M. Murphy
Babson College

Kathy E. Kram
Boston University

Monica C. Higgins
Harvard Graduate School of Education

In this chapter, we offer the notion of a developmental network as a concept that bridges formal and informal mentoring to serve as a vehicle for career advancement, as well as adult development and learning. Initially introduced into the corporate work context about 15 years ago (Higgins & Kram, 2001), little attention has been given to the importance of develop-

Mentoring in Formal and Informal Contexts, pages 1–20
Copyright © 2016 by Information Age Publishing
1

mental networks for individuals in contexts like education and health care where they are equally relevant to practitioners and the organizations that employ them. We describe how a developmental network, a set of people from various social spheres who advance a focal individual's (protégé's) personal and professional growth, can include formally assigned and informally cultivated relationships. In addition, we assert that developmental networks offer a realistic depiction of how individuals actually experience mentoring in numerous contexts.

Personal and professional growth encompasses skill building and career advancement, as well as broader and deeper indicators of adult development that manifest in transformation of attitudes and thought processes. Just as the original work on mentoring illuminated how a traditional mentoring relationship could transform ways of thinking, feeling, and behaving to prepare individuals for positions of greater responsibility and career advancement, it also highlighted how these relationships could lead to fundamental transformations in self-esteem, self-efficacy, and identity (Kram, 1985; Ragins & Kram, 2007; Dobrow & Higgins, 2005). When we consider the potential benefits of developmental networks, we are referring to all of these foregoing positive outcomes.

We assert that developmental networks are holding environments for adult development that have the prospect of offering various types and levels of support to individuals. Holding environments are contexts that enable individuals to develop as adults; they are like petri dishes in many respects, allowing for safe experimentation at one's learning edge (Bowlby, 1988; Kegan, 1982). Our chapter offers a review of the evolution of the mentoring literature away from its historical emphasis on a single, dyadic relationship between a senior mentor and junior protégé toward a network of developers and provides examples in different contexts. It also provides a brief review of conceptual and empirical studies related to developmental networks to date and explains the types of developers and the diverse support they can provide to a focal individual. Next, we discuss how members of developmental networks can exhibit holding behaviors like confirmation, contradiction, and continuity that aid growth and, as a set of developmental relationships, can provide a productive holding environment for personal and professional growth (McGowan, Stone, & Kegan, 2007).

We explain that developmental networks are relevant both for individuals who nurture them for their personal and professional development and for organizations and their capacity to adapt to changes in the external environment (e.g., trends of increasing diversity, fast technological change, and increasingly volatile economic conditions in sectors that include and extend beyond the corporate context, such as health care and education). We identify several institutional/organizational barriers and opportunities that can shape the nature of developmental networks as well as the context in which they are embedded. We consider the implications of our ideas for how individuals in corporate settings, in education, and in health care, among other contexts, might use networks to address their developmental needs as well as the constraints and enablers they may face in their contexts.

MENTORING AS A VEHICLE FOR ADULT DEVELOPMENT AND LEARNING

Levinson first introduced mentoring as a means of facilitating a young man's quest to "become his own man" in his and his colleagues' seminal book on adult development (Levinson, Darrow, Klein, Levinson, & McKee, 1978). Building on this work, Kram's classic qualitative study defined "traditional" mentoring as a relationship between a senior, more experienced individual—the mentor—and a less experienced, junior protégé (or mentee) within the same organization (Kram, 1985). Kram found that mentors provided two types of developmental functions, career and psychosocial support. Career support is instrumental in nature including sponsorship, coaching, exposure and visibility, challenging assignments, and protection; whereas, psychosocial support includes acceptance, counseling, friendship, and role modeling. Later studies empirically validated these functions as relevant to a range of industries and contexts (Noe, 1988; Ragins & McFarlin, 1990; Scandura & Ragins, 1993).

Since Kram's seminal work introducing mentoring into the modern literature, mentoring has received significant attention and empirical scrutiny as a vehicle for personal and professional growth. Research has focused on antecedents (e.g., personality, age, gender, and race), outcomes, processes, the complexities and opportunities associated with cross-race and cross-gender relationships, types of relationships and support, and more recently, developmental networks (importantly, the latter research to date is focused almost exclusively on the corporate context) (e.g., Allen & Eby, 2007; Ragins & Kram, 2007). Mentoring has been found to be associated with numerous positive outcomes in various industries (e.g., workforce, health care, education, and military), including objective outcomes such as total compensation and promotion rates (Whitely, Dougherty, & Dreher, 1991), reduced turnover and exit of the profession (Payne & Huffman, 2005; Smith & Ingersoll, 2004), and heightened personal learning (Lankau & Scandura, 2002), as well as subjective outcomes such as enhanced career satisfaction (Fagenson, 1989), organizational commitment (Payne & Huffman, 2005), increased involvement at work and self-esteem (Koberg, Boss, & Goodman, 1998), and job satisfaction (Bahniuk, Dobos, & Hill, 1990). Although some evidence exists that informally cultivated relationships may be viewed more positively than formally assigned ones (Ragins & Cotton,

1999), other research suggests that the quality of the relationship (i.e., satisfaction with it) plays a stronger role in determining resultant career attitudes (Ragins, Cotton, & Miller, 2000). In the first two decades after Kram's study, most research was aimed at understanding single relationships between individuals and, in particular, the traditional mentoring relationship (Chandler & Kram, 2007).

A Reconceptualization of Mentoring as a Developmental Network

Today's career context is shaped by a number of factors that undermine the likelihood that a person will be able to have all of his or her needs met by one person (Higgins & Kram, 2001). Individuals transition between roles with greater frequency (Arthur, 2008; Arthur & Rousseau, 1996; Bidwell & Briscoe, 2010; Briscoe, Hall, & Mayrhofer, 2012). Technological advancements allow for geographically distant relationships to form and globalization increases their likelihood (Ensher & Murphy, 2007). Organizational membership has altered developmental needs and opportunities for relationships with individuals whose backgrounds are different than the focal individual (Blake, 1999; Kram & Hall, 1996) among other shifts. Taken together, today's career environment across contexts favors the likelihood that people rely upon multiple developers who provide varying types and levels of developmental support (Higgins & Kram, 2001; Murphy & Kram, 2014).

Recognizing that individuals are likely to receive support from a network of individuals as opposed to a single individual, Higgins and Kram (2001) applied a social network perspective to mentoring, introducing the concept of a "developmental network" as a set of people a protégé names as taking an active interest in and action to advance the protégé's personal and professional growth by providing developmental assistance" (cf., Higgins and Kram, 2001, p. 268 for original definition; see Dobrow, Chandler, Murphy, & Kram, 2012 for a recent review). A developmental network consists of developers that are named by a protégé as assisting with his or her personal and professional development. It need not be bound by any particular organization; it can bridge informal and formal mentoring, as a person's network might include a formally assigned developmental relationship at work (e.g., a senior-ranking assigned mentor) or outside of work (e.g., an executive coach), as well as one or more developmental relationships nurtured informally over time (e.g., a family member, friend, peer at work, a subordinate). *As such, we suggest that a developmental network is a unifying concept to integrate formal and informal mentoring across a variety of contexts.* Figure 1.1 shows a depiction of a developmental network with the various social spheres from which developers can stem.

Figure 1.1 Potential relationships in a developmental network. *Source:* Adapted from Murphy & Kram, 2014.

Primary and Secondary Network Dimensions

The original application of social network theory to mentoring focused on two dimensions: *strength of tie* and *diversity* (Higgins & Kram, 2001). Strength of tie refers to the level of affect, trust, rapport, and frequency of communication that exists between the focal individual (protégé) and the person's developers. Relationships between a protégé and each of his or her developers can range from weak—characterized by less frequent contact and a lesser degree of developmental assistance—to strong—characterized by frequent contact and mutual motivation to interact and provide reciprocal benefits (Granovetter, 1973).

Diversity as a dimension can refer to any number of differences between a focal person and his or her developers or between the developers themselves (e.g., gender, race, nationality, functional backgrounds or education). As it has been empirically examined to date, diversity has been operationalized in one of two ways in relation to the number of non-redundant ties a person gains from his or her developers: (a) the range of social spheres and identity groups represented in a person's network; or (b) the density (or interconnectedness) of relations among the developers (Brass, 1995; Higgins, 2001). A low range network includes relatively few social spheres (e.g., work employer and home) while a high range network includes several or more (e.g., work employer, community organization, family, and religious organization). A high-density network would be one in which the developers all know one another, thus likely resulting in the provision of highly redundant information and resources. At the same time, a high-density network enables developers to coordinate their assistance to a particular protégé. On the other hand, a low-density network, in which few, if any, developers know each other, would result in novel and non-redundant support, enabling richer development and growth.

Over time, researchers have proposed other dimensions relevant to understanding developmental networks, including size (Higgins, 2000), multiplexity (the extent to which developers provide more than one function or serve more than one role) (Cotton, Shen, & Livne-Tarandach, 2011), developmental initiation (Higgins, Chandler, & Kram, 2007), and inner-outer core (Cummings & Higgins, 2006). (Table 1.1 offers a brief description of each dimension.) For example, Cummings and Higgins (2006) longitudinal research on networks' stability found an inner-outer core in which the inner core that remained stable over time was characterized by high psychosocial support and low career support, suggesting the importance of examining how networks evolve structurally in response to people's growth and changing needs over time.

Types of Developers and Functional Support

In addition to a traditional mentor who provides high levels of career and psychosocial support, a developer can be any number of people who provide varying types and levels of support at different points in time (Shen, Cotton, & Kram, 2015). Recent developmental network research identified six types of advisors of which a "full service" mentor is one of three types in the "inner circle," which is characterized by greater closeness and strength

TABLE 1.1   Developmental Network Dimensions

Developmental Network Dimensions	Description
Tie Strength	Closeness of the relationships (e.g., affect, trust, rapport and frequency of communication)
Diversity	Range and density, as well as important differences among developers, including experience, expertise, social context, and background
Size	Number of developers in a network
Developmental Initiation	Developmental-seeking behaviors exhibited by a focal individual
Multiplexity	The extent to which a single tie provides receipt of more than one type of support or plays more than one role (as would be the case when a developer is a friend and ally)
Inner–Outer Core	Ties providing high psychosocial support and low career support populate the inner core.

Source: Adapted from Murphy & Kram, 2014.

of tie; a "personal advisor" is a close, non-work relationship involving the provision of psychosocial support, while a "career advisor" is a close relationship that provides career support. In the "outer circle" are the "personal guide" and "career guide" who provide limited psychosocial and career support, respectively. Also in the outer circle is a "role model," whose interaction is one-way (in that the focal individual watches and emulates the role model or chooses to act in ways counter to an "anti-role model," yet the latter is either passive or interactions are non-existent) (Shen et al., 2015). Developmental networks can include formal and informal relationships, and can be with a number of different types of people, including friends, supervisors/managers, family members, peers at work, individuals with community or religious organizations, and subordinates/junior team members (Cotton et al., 2011; Kram, 1985; Murphy & Kram, 2010; Shen & Kram, 2011, among others).

What We Know about Developmental Networks

Over the last 15 years, scholars have completed a number of empirical studies to clarify the antecedents of effective developmental networks, as well as the outcomes associated with various network structures. Here we offer a brief overview of studies that have explored several important antecedents and consequences of particular developmental network structures including the types and amount of support provided.

Network antecedents. Among the antecedents that have been conceptually and empirically explored are developmental needs (Higgins, 2007), personality (Dougherty, Cheung, & Florea, 2008), relational savvy (Chandler, Hall, & Kram, 2010), and fit between developmental needs and support provided (Shen, 2010; Shen et al., 2015). First, research suggests that an individual's network structure is contingent upon his or her developmental needs (Higgins, 2007). Certain personality traits (e.g., introversion, extroversion, and conscientiousness) have been predicted to affect relative proactivity in seeking out developmental interactions (Dougherty et al., 2008). A person's relative relational savvy, that is his/her adeptness with developmental relationships, predicts network diversity and size wherein savvier individuals have larger and more diverse networks (Chandler et al., 2010). Lastly, the degree of fit between the support an individual receives and his/her needs predicts whether a network results in positive outcomes (Shen et al., 2015).

Consequences of amount of support. Numerous studies have examined the relationship between the amount and type of developmental support an individual receives and outcomes such as optimism (Higgins, Dobrow, & Roloff, 2010), extraordinary career achievement (Cotton et al., 2011), career self-efficacy (Higgins, Dobrow, & Chandler, 2008), salary, and career and life satisfaction (Murphy & Kram, 2010). For example, early career support was associated with optimism later in life, and the amount of psychosocial support one received was associated with optimism (Higgins et al., 2010). Greater psychosocial and career support from a wide range of communities was found to be associated with extraordinary career achievement (Cotton et al., 2011). Career support provided by one's network was positively related to perceptions of success and career self-efficacy (Higgins et al., 2008). Support from non-work developers was positively associated with life and career satisfaction, and support from work developers was positively related with salary (Murphy & Kram, 2010).

Consequences of network structure. A number of studies have also explored and found positive consequences of network structure, including clarity of career identity (Dobrow & Higgins, 2005), extraordinary career performance (Cotton et al., 2011), changing careers, confidence to overcome obstacles (Higgins, 2001), and promotion (Higgins & Thomas, 2001). Denser networks—in which the most or all of the developers know one another and thus do not tend to provide novel or varied information—were negatively related with career identity clarity, signaling the value of a diverse network (Dobrow & Higgins, 2005). Larger, more diverse and multiplex networks were associated with extraordinary career performance (Cotton et al., 2011). Greater diversity of psychosocial ties was associated with confidence to overcome obstacles, and greater diversity of career-related ties led to greater likelihood of changing careers. Lastly, the relative senior status of developers positively influenced promotion (Higgins & Thomas, 2001).

Although most of the empirical research on developmental networks has found positive effects of particular network dimensions, notably diversity, studies suggest that a "dark side of mentoring," in which negative interactions like sabotage, deception, neglect, and harassment perpetrated by the mentor and/or protégé (Eby, 2007; Eby & McManus, 2004; Scandura, 1998) can occur between the two. In the network sub-literature, for example, one study found that maintaining elite graduate ties in one's network over time was negatively associated with perceptions of success (Higgins et al., 2008), due to a person's tendency to compare one's standing to others. This and other studies highlight the importance of nurturing a network that includes developers with whom one can have satisfactory relationships.

Developmental networks have received substantial attention in corporate settings but little attention in other contexts to date, including education and health care. We assert here that developmental networks are relevant across various industries as the types of mentoring support provided by developmental networks are important for adult learning and growth and reflect most practitioners' realities in managing their careers. To illustrate the power of developmental networks and the practical reality of their significance, we offer the following anecdote.

Jordan Wright and Her Developmental Network. Jordan Wright began her career as a general ledger accountant with a medium-sized high technology company in Silicon Valley. Taking the advice of a professor who urged the importance of having multiple mentors at work, Jordan immediately began to build relationships with those around her and worked diligently to signal her competence, thus heightening the likelihood that they would be attracted to her as a protégé. The company's Chief Financial Officer and her supervisor, the accounting manager, both evolved into developers for her, the former being a "career guide" who offered advice on long-term career strategies and feedback on how she was perceived by others in the organization, and the latter being a "career advisor" who gave her numerous challenging assignments, visibility by introducing her to middle- and senior-level employees in other departments, who sponsored her for a financial analyst job reporting to his counterpart, the finance director.

Jordan also nurtured a mutually beneficial developmental relationship with two peers with whom she brainstormed career strategies, navigated sensitive political situations, and exchanged information. They also coached each other in various ways. For example, one peer coached her on the company's accounting system; she coached him on certain obscure GAAP conventions, leveraging her accounting degree. Ultimately, Jordan and the two peers became friends; they provided her with psychosocial support in the form of caring and sharing at and beyond work, which heightened her job satisfaction. Outside of work, Jordan relied upon her parents and boyfriend, her "inner core," for psychosocial support by affirming her identity, career, and life choices.

Three years after starting with the company, Jordan had been twice promoted, landing an early senior financial analyst position. She completed her master's degree with a prestigious program and later successfully passed the CPA exam, and she felt accomplished and satisfied with her career. She perceived herself as on a successful long-term path toward a dream of becoming the most senior financial officer of a small to medium-sized organization. She credited her developmental network as a key vehicle for her success.

Developmental Networks as Holding Environments

We propose here that a network of developers can, as a collective, act as a holding environment for adult learning and development. The idea of a holding environment is rooted in constructive developmental theory (CDT), which brings together the constructive perspective—that individuals engage in an active process of constructing reality—and the developmental perspective—that individuals evolve through alternating periods of growth, stability, and change (Kegan, 1982; McGowan et al., 2007). From a constructive developmental perspective, developers' use of holding behaviors, including confirmation, contradiction, and continuity, enable individual growth (Chandler & Kram, 2005; Ghosh, Haynes, & Kram, 2013). Importantly, the notion of a developmental network has largely been viewed as a vehicle for career development. Integrating its original conception with CDT brings to the fore the idea that networks can also be viewed as nurturing adult development. In any context, both career and adult development are critical to any one person as the two go hand in hand.

It is important to recognize that supportive behavior in any developmental relationship will vary based on the needs and development of the focal individual. As McGowan, Stone, and Kegan (2007) explain, "Good mentoring can involve good 'holding' (confirmation), good 'letting go' (contradiction), or reliable 'sticking around' as the relationship is reconstructed as one between colleagues (continuity) or all three" (p. 406). A good holding environment is consistently supportive, thus providing the individual with a solid relational foundation during times of transition, job or organizational uncertainty, and through life changes.

In addition, particular developmental functions—both career and psychosocial support—that characterize mentoring and other developmental relationships, can be viewed as sources of confirmation, contradiction, or continuity, depending on where the focal individual is in his or her developmental journey. Early in one's career, for example, sponsorship, coaching, and challenging assignments are likely to be experienced as providing confirmation for who the young adult is becoming in the professional context. Later on, in an unfolding career and life, those same functions might be viewed as challenging an individual's current path by opening doors that were not yet considered. Similarly, the developer whose actions provide continuity and support for the young adult just launching a career may at a later stage offer friendship in order to transform the relationship into more of a peer friendship as the focal person transitions to a more complex stage of development.

Ghosh, Haynes, and Kram (2013) suggest characteristics of developers who could serve as part of a holding environment for an emerging leader. First, developers should be at a more advanced level of adult development than the focal individual in order to recognize that person's limitations and help them to overcome them (see also, Chandler & Kram, 2005). Second, developers should be adept at relational coordination, which includes facilitating mutual respect and creating shared goals and knowledge (see also, Gittell, 2002). Finally, developers should foster high-quality relationships characterized by high emotional carrying capacity (i.e., expressing a broad range of varying emotions), tensility (i.e., flexibility and resilience), connectivity (i.e., generative and openness), sense of positive regard, and mutuality (i.e., both parties are actively engaged) (Dutton & Heaphy, 2003; Dutton & Ragins, 2007). Developmental networks that serve as holding environments for adult development may occur across various contexts and industries, including healthcare and education. For example:

Ben Sullivan's Inability to Delegate. Ben Sullivan's rise to Principal of Westmont High School largely rested on his can-do and would-do anything approach. Having risen in the teaching ranks at Westmont and then moved into the assistant principal role, Ben excelled because he was viewed as someone who could successfully juggle and complete many tasks and projects simultaneously.

When he was promoted to the Principal's role, however, Ben found himself stretched beyond his limits. His many responsibilities required that he begin to delegate more, which, in spite of his best efforts in the past, he was unable to do; he continued to tackle too much and beyond to burn out. He reached out to his father and wife, a former middle school principal and manufacturing executive, respectively, and asked for help with his problem. Both acknowledged the challenge of delegation and acknowledged that they, too, experienced similar issues in the past (*confirmation* behavior, that is, behavior that made Ben feel safe and validated).

Each offered him behavioral strategies related to delegation and asked what he planned to do. In addition, his father asked him what he was afraid he was losing if he did actually delegate to his assistant principal, committees, and teachers (*contradicting* behavior that caused him to reflect upon his own behavior and perspective). His father's coaching sparked a realization that he feared losing his identity as a "star," someone who could do everything successfully and more often than not, better than everyone else. As Ben pondered what to make of the revelation that actually delegating to others posed a personal threat to him, a third developer in his network, a friend from a school leadership development program who was an assistant principal, offered the suggestion that he take small actions toward delegating and track the effects on his sense of self.

Ben's father, wife, and friend committed to being sounding boards for him as he moved along a new journey with the aim of a new identity (*continuity* behaviors), that of a coach of others as they tackle responsibilities. His new approach required that he smartly delegate and then be a resource and guide to others in tackling new responsibilities and projects.

While Jordan Wright's story exemplifies how support from developmental network aids career development and associated positive outcomes such as early promotion, Ben's story urges consideration of a network's impact on adult development, in Ben's case, the period of reconstructing his work approach and mindset during a period of instability and change. Ben's network collectively served as a holding environment for him, offering confirmation, contradiction, and continuity behaviors, all of which helped him take on a new identity at a critical juncture in his career. Applying a constructive developmental perspective to developmental networks offers a richer vantage point to view them.

Institutional Contexts and Developmental Networks

Considering Jordan's and Ben's developmental networks in isolation from the larger context in which they are embedded misses the latter as an important factor that affects the former. Several institutional/organizational barriers and opportunities can shape the nature of developmental networks and the level of developmental initiation within a given context (Fletcher & Ragins, 2007; Murphy, 2011; Shen, Cotton, & Kram, 2015; Wanberg, Welsh, & Hezlett, 2003). Such factors include the extent to which the reward system and senior leadership acknowledge and encourage helping behavior; the overall organizational culture as it pertains to collaboration, mentoring, feedback, and employee development; the level of interdependent interactions and teamwork within an organization; and the extent to which leadership development practices provide opportunities for individuals to develop the relational skills required of developmental relationships (Fletcher & Ragins, 2007).

If strong developmental networks are to flourish in an organizational setting, then individuals must be rewarded for help-seeking and help-giving behaviors. Performance management systems that incorporate coaching as a leadership competency expected from managers are more likely than those that do not to encourage coaching of subordinates. Using such criteria as a basis for succession planning is critical for effectively promoting leaders with a developmental approach who will reinforce this aspect of the workplace culture (Murphy & Kram, 2014). Leaders' championing of others' efforts to mentor and mentoring others themselves will signal the importance and value of mentoring across the organization. Jordan Wright's network was shaped by an organizational context in which her manager was explicitly evaluated on the degree to which he mentored others, and the company's chief executive officer espoused the value of mentoring and encouraged it within the organization.

An organization's culture has a significant impact on the shape of developmental networks, as employees' beliefs about the value of collaboration, of seeking and giving feedback, mentoring, and employee development will impact the degree of developmental support individuals offer each other. For example, certain organizational contexts (e.g., workplace environments that are team-based and collaborative) are more conducive to nurturing diverse networks than those that are more competitive and hierarchical. The latter may present obstacles due to norms and practices that undermine effective relationship building among individuals who might be able to help one another.

Indeed, these barriers stemming from culture may operate at the professional level as well. Professional norms are very strong in some contexts, such as education, for example—a context in which the need for change is dire and yet the conditions to do so are trying. In the teaching profession, the dominant professional norms are egalitarianism, autonomy, and independence (Donaldson et al., 2008; Lortie 1975); teachers have come to value the egg crate structure of schools in which they can, essentially, close their own classroom doors and do their own work (Donaldson et al., 2008; Lortie 1975).

In this kind of traditional school structure and the strong norms that envelop it, teachers refrain from help-giving and help-receiving and, more generally, oftentimes refrain from fully engaging in their own and others' professional development. They lack the resources, such as time to do so, but also, the norms of the profession run counter to sharing best practices as well. Further, as education researchers have described, given the current high-accountability environment that envelops public schools in the United States, teachers often do not feel psychologically safe speaking up or asking for help regarding their work (e.g., Higgins, Ishimaru, Holcombe, & Fowler, 2012).

Consequently, the constraints of this context make the conditions necessary for the cultivation of informal and formal developmental relationships particularly challenging— although, at the same time, especially needed. Ben Sullivan may have felt compelled to seek out assistance beyond the school—all three of his developers were extra-organizational—due to a lack of help-seeking norm within his school, something that he, as the school's leader, could consider striving to change as he acclimated to his new role.

Still, and despite the larger pressures that constrain organizations and the cultures in which people work, recent research suggests that under certain conditions, organizations are and can become "deliberately developmental" (Kegan, Lahey, Fleming, & Miller, 2014). Deliberately developmental organizations are unique in that unlike in most organizations, employees feel comfortable exposing their vulnerabilities and discussing their weaknesses in a constructive manner. The underlying assumptions are that people grow in the process of doing their work and that identifying and overcoming debilitating behavioral patterns is part of doing their job well (Kegan, Lahey, & Fleming, 2014). In order to do so, leaders must communicate and model these practices as well as place people in roles that cause "constructive destabilization," that is, in roles that are manageably "over their heads." Critical components of this destabilization include: (a) intentionally matching people with stretch assignments that connect to what is meaningful to them; (b) tracking competencies and using this information to facilitate peer mentoring; (c) setting expectations for learning as part of succession planning; and (d) providing a supportive team environment in which giving and receiving feedback is everyone's responsibility (Kegan et al., 2014). For example:

> *Peer mentoring circles at Brigham and Women's Hospital.* At Brigham and Women's Hospital in Boston, several initiatives existed to foster the training and mentoring of new physicians. In assessing this supportive culture, administrators realized that there were some master mentors among their senior faculty; yet, there was not a good mechanism for sharing insights and learning among the mentors themselves. The hospital created the Faculty Mentoring Leadership Program (FLMP) specifically for senior faculty to enhance their skills as mentors and to grow as leaders. Participants had to be nominated as "experienced mentors with impact" and get a letter of support from their department chair or supervisor to participate. (Tsen, et al., 2012)

Cross-departmental peer mentoring circles met for nine one-and-a-half hour lunchtime sessions to discuss cases based on participants' experiences as mentors. Each circle had two facilitators who served as co-participants rather than instructors since case materials were created by participants. In these meetings, mentors furthered their development through discussion of challenging, complex, and controversial issues. More importantly, they developed peer mentoring relationships with one another, building cross-specialty relationships and expanding each participant's developmental network in the organization.

The Brigham & Women's Hospital initiative is an example of a formal program designed to foster a more deliberately developmental organization (Murphy & Kram, 2014). By design, active participation in the program generated a shared learning experience that enhanced mentors' capacity to develop others and provided them with a network of development-oriented colleagues (Tsen et al., 2012). Since these were all senior faculty and the program has been rolled out to new participants, the institution continues to benefit from the extension of these active developers' knowledge and skills and the informal mentoring they provide to each other and their less experienced colleagues.

IMPLICATIONS FOR INDIVIDUALS AND ORGANIZATIONS

Developmental networks are important both for the individuals who nurture them for their personal and professional development and for the institutions in which they work. Institutions can shape the cultivation of both informal and formal relationships and so, the holding environments in which individuals develop. Thus, in addition to considering the role that individuals play in cultivating effective and multiple mentoring relationships, it is critical to consider the role that organizations play in shaping the environments in which mutually beneficial and truly developmental relationships can emerge.

Even in strong professional contexts, such as the teaching profession, in which the norms against sharing best practices are rampant, recent research shows that it is possible to create those organizational contexts conducive to learning. In a recent study of New York City schools, for example, research has found that some schools do have cultures in which teachers feel psychologically safe (Childress, Higgins, Ishimaru, & Takahashi, 2011). Although not yet examined, we would expect that in these kinds of cultures, it is especially likely that individual workers, such as teachers, would feel that through their help-seeking and help-giving on the job, they could turn these advice-giving and receiving relationships into those that are developmental in nature. Further, and if it is the case that these kinds of relationships begin to flourish, then it is also likely, we expect, that there will be positive spillover effects between these kinds of relationships and those of others in the building, such as staff workers. We contend that as developmental relationships are cultivated, over time, it is likely that individuals will feel more comfortable taking steps to thoughtfully and intentionally build the kinds of support networks that they feel will be most valuable to their own personal and professional development.

As a final consideration, it is important to note that while developmental networks may be useful in a variety of contexts, they are not universally useful to all who may cultivate them. That is, no one particular network structure is best. As individuals have different developmental needs and goals—whether that be to advance to a certain job position, as in our first anecdote or to balance work and family (or to more effectively delegate), as in our second anecdote—so, too, may they need different kinds of support in their personal and professional development (Higgins, 2007). As a result, certain kinds of organizational contexts and certain types of networks may be more or less suitable, given individuals' particular developmental needs and the ways these needs evolve over time. Indeed, individuals' networks should be expected to evolve, just as one's personal and professional developmental goals can be expected to evolve (Cummings & Higgins, 2006). The two should, ideally, move in tandem. Further, and as they do so, it is likely, as the education sector description suggests, that the organization itself may change. That is, as people become both developers and protégés—as they recognize the needs of their colleagues and their own evolving needs as an adult—the organizational context may become more conducive to meeting the diverse needs of its employees. Of course, evolving in this way will require specific skills such as relational savvy (Chandler et al., 2010) and perhaps even entrepreneurial behavior (e.g., to break existing norms and speak up and ask for help) (Murphy & Kram, 2014), but we are hopeful that understanding the significance of crossing boundaries to cultivate developmental networks will spur these kinds of behaviors that can benefit both the organization and the individuals who work within it.

CONCLUSION

In this chapter, we argue that a developmental network approach matches practitioners' realities as they navigate a turbulent career environment. Various contexts pose both constraints and opportunities through which developmental networks can serve as holding environments for adult learning and development. Further, we consider the role that organizations can play in creating the conditions for the cultivation of effective developmental networks. We view the notion of a developmental network as an integrating concept that helps bridge formal and informal relationships and is relevant to multiple contexts, including the corporate context, healthcare, and education among them. This chapter is relevant to practitioners who would shape networks based on their unique developmental needs and goals to organizations and institutions that would nurture environments conducive to strong developmental alliances between people with varying developmental needs and goals.

REFERENCES

Allen, T. D., & Eby, L. T. (2007). *Blackwell handbook of mentoring: A multiple perspectives approach.* Oxford, England: Blackwell Publishing.

Arthur, M. B. (2008). Examining contemporary careers: A call for interdisciplinary inquiry. *Human Relations, 61*(2), 163–186.

Arthur, M. B., & Rousseau, D. M. (1996). *The boundaryless career: A new employment principle for a new organizational era.* New York, NY: Oxford University Press.

Bahniuk, M. H., Dobos, J., & Hill, S. K. (1990). The impact of mentoring, collegial support, and information adequacy on career success: A replication. *Journal of Social Behavior & Personality, 5*(4), 431–452.

Bidwell, M., & Briscoe, F. (2010). The dynamics of interorganizational careers. *Organization Science, 21*(5), 1034–1053.

Blake, S. (1999). At the crossroads of race and gender: Lessons from the mentoring experiences of professional Black women. In A. J. Murrell, F. J. Crosby, & R. J. Ely (Eds.), *Mentoring dilemmas: Developmental relationships within multicultural organizations* (pp. 83–104). Mahwah, NJ: Erlbaum Associates.

Bowlby, J. (1988). *A secure base: Clinical applications of attachment theory.* London, England: Routledge.

Brass, D. J. (1995). A social network perspective on human resources management. *Research in Personnel and Human Resources Management, 13,* 39–79.

Briscoe, J. P., Hall, D. T., & Mayrhofer, W. (2012). *Careers around the world: Individual and contextual perspectives.* New York, NY: Routledge.

Chandler, D. E., & Kram, K. E. (2007). Mentoring and developmental networks in the new career context. In H. Gunz, & M. Periperl (Eds.), *Handbook of career studies* (pp. 241–267). Thousand Oaks, CA: Sage.

Chandler, D. E., & Kram, K. E. (2005). Applying an adult development perspective to developmental networks. *Career Development International, 10*(6/7), 548–566.

Chandler, D. E., Hall, D. T., & Kram, K. E. (2010). A developmental network and relational savvy approach to talent development: A low-cost alternative. *Organizational Dynamics, 39*(1), 48–56.

Childress, S., Higgins, M., Ishimaru, A., & Takahashi, S. (2011). Managing for results at the New York City Department of Education. In J. Oday, C. Bitter, & L. Gomez (Eds.), *Education reform in New York City: Ambitious change in the nation's most complex school system* (pp. 87–108). Cambridge, MA: Harvard Education Press.

Cotton, R. D., Shen, Y., & Livne-Tarandach, R. (2011). On becoming extraordinary: The content and structure of the developmental networks of Major League Baseball Hall of Famers. *Academy of Management Journal, 54*(1), 15–46.

Cummings, J., & Higgins, M. C. (2006). Relational instability at the core: Support dynamics in developmental networks. *Social Networks, 28*(1), 38–55.

Dobrow, S., & Higgins, M. C. (2005). Developmental networks and professional identity: A longitudinal study. [Special Issue on Mentoring]. *Career Development International, 10*(6/7), 567–587.

Dobrow, S. R., Chandler, D. E., Murphy, W. M., & Kram, K. E. (2012). A review of developmental networks: Incorporating a mutuality perspective. *Journal of Management. 38*(1), 210–242.

Donaldson, M., Moore Johnson, S., Kirkpatrick, C., Marinell, W., Steele, J., & Szczesiul, S. (2008). Angling for access, bartering for change: How second-stage teachers experience differentiated roles in schools. *The Teachers College Record, 110*(5), 1088–1114.

Dougherty, T. W., Cheung, Y. H., & Florea, L. (2008). The role of personality in employee developmental networks. *Journal of Managerial Psychology, 23*(6), 653–669.

Dutton, J., & Heaphy, E. (2003). Coming to life: The power of high quality connections at work. In K. Cameron, J. Dutton, & R. Quinn (Eds.), *Positive organizational scholarship* (pp. 263–278). San Francisco, CA: Berret-Koehler.

Dutton, J. E., & Ragins, B. R. (Eds.). (2007). *Exploring positive relationships at work: Building a theoretical and research foundation.* Mahwah, NJ: Erlbaum.

Eby, L. T. (2007). Understanding relational problems in mentoring. In B. R. Ragins & K. E. Kram (Eds.), *The handbook of mentoring at work* (pp. 323–344). Thousand Oaks, CA: Sage.

Eby, L. T., & McManus, S. E. (2004). The protégés role in negative mentoring experiences. *Journal of Vocational Behavior, 65*(2), 255–275.

Ensher, E. A., & Murphy, S. E. (2007). E-mentoring: Next generation research strategies. In B. R. Ragins, & K. E. Kram (Eds.). *The handbook of mentoring at work: Theory, research, and practice* (pp. 299–322). Thousand Oaks, CA: Sage.

Fagenson, E. A. (1989). The mentor advantage: Perceived career/job experiences of protégés versus non-protégés. *Journal of Organizational Behavior, 10*(4), 309–320.

Fletcher, J., & Ragins, B. R. (2007). Stone center relational cultural theory: A window on relational mentoring. In B. R. Ragins & K. E. Kram (Eds.), *The handbook of mentoring at work: Theory, research, and practice* (pp. 373–399). Thousand Oaks, CA: Sage.

Ghosh, R., Haynes, R. K., & Kram, K. E. (2013). Developmental networks at work: Holding environments for leader development. *Career Development International, 18*(3), 232–256.

Gittell, J. H. (2002). Coordinating mechanisms in care provider groups: Relational coordination as a mediator and input uncertainty as a moderator of performance effects. *Management Science, 48*(11), 1408–1426.

Granovetter, M. S. (1973). The strength of weak ties. *American Journal of Sociology, 6,* 1360–1380.

Higgins, M. C. (2000). The more, the merrier? Multiple developmental relationships and work satisfaction. *Journal of Management Development, 19*(4), 277–296.

Higgins, M. C. (2001). Changing careers: The effects of social context. *Journal of Organizational Behavior, 22,* 595–618.

Higgins, M. C. (2007). A contingency perspective on developmental networks. In J. E. Dutton & B. R. Ragins (Eds.), *Exploring positive relationships at work: Building a theoretical and research foundation* (pp. 207–224). Hillsdale, NJ: Erlbaum.

Higgins, M. C., Chandler, D. E., & Kram, K. E. (2007). Developmental initiation and developmental networks. In B. R. Ragins & K. E. Kram (Eds.), *The handbook of mentoring at work: Theory, research, and practice* (pp. 349–370). Thousand Oaks, CA: Sage.

Higgins, M. C., Dobrow, S. R., & Chandler, D. E. (2008). Never quite good enough: The paradox of sticky developmental relationships for elite university graduates. *Journal of Vocational Behavior, 72,* 207–224.

Higgins, M. C., Dobrow, S. R., & Roloff, K. S. (2010). Optimism and the boundaryless career: The role of developmental relationships. *Journal of Organizational Behavior, 31*(5), 749–769.

Higgins, M. C., Ishimaru, A., Holcombe, R., & Fowler, A. (2012). Examining organizational learning in schools: The role of psychological safety, experimentation, and leadership that reinforces learning. *Journal of Educational Change, 13*(1), 67–94.

Higgins, M. C., & Kram, K. E. (2001). Reconceptualizing mentoring at work: A developmental network perspective. *Academy of Management Review, 26*(2), 264–288.

Higgins, M. C., & Thomas, D. A. (2001). Constellations and careers: Toward understanding the effects of multiple developmental relationships. *Journal of Organizational Behavior, 22*(3), 223–247.

Kegan, R. (1982). *The evolving self: Problem and process in human development.* Cambridge, MA: Harvard University Press.

Kegan, R., Lahey, L.L., & Fleming, A. (2014, January 22). *Does Your Company Make you a Better Person?* HBR Blog. Retrieved from http://blogs.hbr.org/2014/01/does-your-company-make-you-a-better-person/

Kegan, R., Lahey, L., Fleming, A., & Miller, M. (2014). Making business personal. *Harvard Business Review, 92*(4), 44–52.

Koberg, C. S., Boss, W. R., & Goodman, E. (1998). Factors and outcomes associated with mentoring among health care professionals. *Journal of Vocational Behavior, 53*(1), 58–72.

Kram, K. E. (1985). *Mentoring at work: Developmental relationships in organizational life.* Glenview, IL: Scott Foresman.

Kram, K. E., & Hall, D. T. (1996). Mentoring in a context of diversity and turbulence. In E. E. Kossek & S. A. Lobel (Eds.), *Managing diversity: Human resource strategies for transforming the workplace* (pp. 108–136). Cambridge, MA: Blackwell Business.

Lankau, M. J., & Scandura, T. A. (2002). Mentoring and personal learning: Content, antecedents and outcomes. *Academy of Management Journal, 45,* 779–790.

Levinson, D. J., Darrow, C. N., Klein, E. B., Levinson, M. H., & McKee, B. (1978). *The seasons of a man's life.* New York, NY: Knopf.

Lortie, D. (1975). *Schoolteacher: A sociological study.* London, England: University of Chicago Press.

McGowan, E. M., Stone, E. M., & Kegan, R. (2007). A constructive-developmental approach to mentoring relationships. In B. R. Ragins & K. E. Kram (Eds.). *The handbook of mentoring at work: Theory, research, and practice* (pp. 401–425). Thousand Oaks, CA: Sage.

Murphy, W. M. (2011). From e-mentoring to blended mentoring: Increasing students' developmental initiation and mentors' satisfaction. *Academy of Management Learning & Education, 10*(4), 606–622.

Murphy, W. M., & Kram, K. E. (2010). Understanding non-work relationships in developmental networks. *Career Development International,* 15, 637–663.

Murphy, W. M., & Kram, K. E. (2014). *Strategic relationships at work: Creating your circle of mentors, sponsors, and peers for success in business and life.* New York, NY: McGraw-Hill.

Noe, R. A. (1988). An investigation of the determinants of successful assigned mentoring relationships. *Personnel Psychology, 41*(3), 457–479.

Payne, S. C., & Huffman, A. H. (2005). A longitudinal examination of the influence of mentoring on organizational commitment and turnover. *Academy of Management Journal, 48*(1), 158–168.

Ragins, B. R., & Cotton, J. L. (1999). Mentor functions and outcomes: A comparison of men and women in formal and informal mentoring relationships. *Journal of Applied Psychology, 84,* 529–550.

Ragins, B. R., Cotton, J. L., & Miller, J. S. (2000). Marginal mentoring: The effects of type of mentor, quality of relationship, and program design on work and career attitudes. *Academy of Management Journal, 43*(6), 1177–1194.

Ragins, B. R., & Kram, K. E. (Eds.) (2007). *The handbook of mentoring at work: Theory, research, and practice.* Thousand Oaks, CA: Sage.

Ragins, B. R., & McFarlin, D. B. (1990). Perceptions of mentor roles in cross-gender mentoring relationships. *Journal of Vocational Behavior, 37*(3), 321–339.

Scandura, T. A. (1998). Dysfunctional mentoring relationships and outcomes. *Journal of Management, 24*(3), 449–467.

Scandura, T. A., & Ragins, B. R. (1993). The effects of sex and gender role orientation on mentorship in male-dominated occupations. *Journal of Vocational Behavior, 43*(3), 251–265.

Shen, Y. (2010). *Developmental networks of expatriates: A person-network fit perspective.* Unpublished dissertation, Boston University, Boston, Massachusetts.

Shen Y., & Kram, K. E. (2011). Expatriates' developmental networks: Network diversity, base, and support functions. *Career Development International, 6*(6), 528–552.

Shen, Y., Cotton, R. D., & Kram, K. E. (2015). Assembling your personal board of advisors. *MIT Sloan Management Review, 56*(3), 81.

Smith, T. S., & Ingersoll, R. M. (2004). What are the effect of induction and mentoring on beginning teacher turnover? *American Educational Research Journal, 41*(3), 681–714.

Tsen, L. C., Borus, J. F., Nadelson, E. W., Seely, A., Hass, A. L., & Fuhlbrigge, A. L. (2012). The development, implementation, and assessment of an innovative faculty mentoring leadership program. *Academic Medicine, 87*(12), 1–5.

Wanberg, C. R., Welsh, E. T., & Hezlett, S. A. (2003). Mentoring research: A review and dynamic process model. *Research in Personnel and Human Resources Management, 22,* 39–124.

Whitely, W., Dougherty, T. W., & Dreher, G. F. (1991). Relationship of career mentoring and socioeconomic origin to managers' and professionals' early career progress. *Academy of Management Journal, 34,* 331–351.

PART I

MENTORING IN HIGHER EDUCATION

CHAPTER 2

ACADEMIC MENTORING AS PRECARIOUS PRACTICE

Alan Mandell
Xenia Coulter
SUNY Empire State College

At Empire State College, as at a number of other institutions that emphasize individual education, a new faculty role has evolved—that of a mentor. These faculty mentors carry out a complex role more characteristic of the undergraduate teacher of 40 years ago before education became compartmentalized into subdisciplinary specialists, counseling specialists, placement specialists, and student activities specialists. In the mentor role, these functions are brought back together. The faculty mentors are responsible, both individually and collectively, for the design, approval, and implementation of each student's degree program and for each specific study plan (or contract) undertaken in fulfillment of that degree program . . . The role is highly facilitative.

—James W. Hall, President of Empire State College (1971–2000)

DEFINITIONS

Those of us in higher education who call ourselves mentors as distinct from professors rarely question that designation. That what we do with students in a mentoring relationship might be problematic to those who mentor in other contexts is not often recognized. Nor do we wonder how it is that

Mentoring in Formal and Informal Contexts, pages 23–42
Copyright © 2016 by Information Age Publishing
23

the concept came to be applied in a setting where an ordinary student can successfully graduate from college without any significant contact with an individual professor at all. It is true that many colleges, driven by concerns about retention, have sought out innovative ways of promoting greater faculty-student contact. However, for most colleges, mentoring as a way of teaching is not a model that immediately comes to mind as a likely, or scalable, solution.

Moreover, as adult educators, we also tend not to inquire about the assumption that academic mentoring is uniquely designed for adult learners. Exactly how this restricted meaning came about is not clear. As far as we can piece it together, mentoring as a distinctive mode of college instruction was popularized at Goddard College during the presidency of Royce S. Pitkin (1936–1969). Students needed individual guidance, particularly with the introduction in the early 1960s of a low-residency program for adults who, of necessity, mostly studied away from the college on their own. The term, "mentor," is not part of the written record (e.g., Benson & Adams, 1987, Davis, 1996), although it seems to have been brought from Goddard in Vermont to Empire State College in New York in the early '70s by Arthur Chickering (Bonnabeau, 1996). Age did not seem to be the primary determinant as much as mode of instruction, namely, the extensive use of guided independent study. Chickering, a psychologist, may also have been influenced by Carl Rogers (e.g., Chickering & Associates, 2014) who promoted a similar method of teaching that he applied, without hesitancy, to preschool and elementary school children, college students, and adults (Rogers, 1969). That academic mentoring today has come to be associated only with adults may be simply because independent study, which requires mentor-like advisement, encouragement, and intellectual guidance is, for many working adults, the only practical way they can attend college.

More puzzling, however, is the close association of academic mentoring with the philosophy of progressive education. According to Jackson (1990), John Dewey, who developed and popularized progressive ideals, dreamed of a school:

> . . . in which old divisions had been overcome or otherwise disappeared. Gone were to be the airtight compartments of work and place, thought and action, cognition and volition and all the other dichotomies we so commonly use to categorize and ultimately isolate the polarities of human experience. (p. x)

Given that the very essence of mentoring rests upon an explicit divide between the mentor-as-expert and the mentee-as-supplicant, the assignment of the term "mentor" to individual faculty in those colleges that seek to incorporate Dewey's progressive views (e.g., 1916/1966) seems strange, even ironic. With such a clear hierarchical foundation, a typical academic mentoring relationship is, at least at first glance, an oddly inappropriate and potentially precarious way by which to reduce the distance between teacher and student.

Mentoring As Commonly Understood[1]

The mentor-mentee relationship, however, is defined by more than a difference in status. It also involves a significant engagement between two individuals. Not unusually, mentor and mentee meet together on a regular basis, for example, to exchange views, set goals, and discuss matters of common concern, through one-on-one conversations. Much then depends upon the ordinary rules of social interaction to help the mentor and mentee achieve the explicit expectations such relationships are designed to meet. The atmosphere is usually friendly and relaxed enough that the lines of authority that would ordinarily divide the participants are rendered much more permeable.

In the business world, mentoring, a growing enterprise (e.g., Insala, 2015), is seen as a way of helping newly hired employees "learn the ropes" and to become successfully integrated into the organization's culture. Workplace mentors provide information, give advice, coach their mentees' activities, and, when appropriate, advocate on their behalf. They undertake these tasks because they sincerely want their mentees to fit well in their new surroundings, to succeed as fellow members, and perhaps even to become future leaders in the same organization. Even in the educational workplace, experienced teachers behave similarly when mentoring their inexperienced colleagues (e.g., Cox, Boettcher, & Adone, 1997). Although workplace mentors tend to be older and more seasoned than their mentees, both participants are adults and share a common background and interest in their work. Thus, the only truly significant distinction between them is that the workplace mentor is presumed to have professional knowledge and skills—expertise—that the mentee lacks.

In the world of social services, however, adults often serve as mentors for teenagers—particularly those at risk in school or those moving in what are deemed socially unacceptable directions (see, e.g., Freedman, 1993; Shiner, Young, Newburn, & Groben, 2004). Although these age-based mentoring relationships are often arranged within a school setting, mentors are not typically part of the formal teaching staff, and age difference does not alter the basic purpose of the relationship. The mentors are expected, as usual, to know what the mentees do not know—in this case about how they can become productive members of society. As in the workplace model, these community-based mentors take on multiple roles in helping their mentees; and they must have a deep personal interest in them as individuals.

However, in this situation, mentors often do not share a common background with their mentees who may hold unfamiliar values and experience pressures and expectations that are unknown to those, not only from another segment of society but perhaps even more importantly, another generation. Although it is not always made explicit, information delivery in such intergenerational mentoring relationships is necessarily highly bi-directional. It's just not possible to adequately guide, advise, or coach someone with whom you have little in common without a good knowledge of their specific desires, interests, hopes and fears. As many mentors have observed (e.g., Herman & Coulter, 1998), new learning is not just for the mentee, but for the mentor as well.

Already we can see some hidden complexities with these two mentoring models. There are always questions of match between mentor and mentee in terms of gender, race, culture, and personality. Moreover, in the workplace, the mentor role may uncomfortably overlap with that of management or the functions of the human resource department. Unless the mentor is the president of the organization, she does not have ultimate authority, and her ability to help her mentee, particularly in terms of advancement, will be limited to the degree she can maneuver within the complex political structure in many larger workplaces. At its heart, the mentor's job is to help the mentee develop as an employee, but only in such a way as to successfully fit into the existing culture. Lines must also be drawn in the range and depth of a mentor's personal feelings about the mentee. In the community, while working with teens, mentors are in many instances playing the role of substitute parent, and they must be very careful not to become an actual replacement. They must also make sure that their advice and coaching do not run counter to school rules and regulations or to those social mores that often the mentor is expected to model. However, helping a teenager become a good citizen is much more open-ended than helping an adult become a good employee. The community-based mentor has to be careful to give the mentee enough room to develop in directions consistent with that mentee's own interests and dispositions, not just those of the mentor. In sum, the path a mentor walks, even in these relatively common settings, is narrower and more difficult to navigate than it might at first appear (e.g., Head, Reiman, & Thies-Sprinthall, 1992).

Mentoring as an Academic Activity

It becomes an interesting question to ask how these key features of mentoring relationships are represented in higher education, a context that is quite unlike the workplace or the world of troubled teens (Cohen, 1995; Cohen & Galbraith, 1995; Parsloe & Wray, 2000; Zachary, 2000). In terms of expertise, of course, the distinction between teacher-as-mentor and student-as-mentee is not markedly changed. Conventional professors, however, see themselves as instructors—deliverers of an area of knowledge in which they are experts—who are hardly expected to know each student individually, much less have a personal interest in or concern for each one. Occasionally, some professors do reach out and provide extra advice and assistance for individual students who seem to share their own interests. As a result, their "protégés" soon come to see them quite explicitly as their mentors. In this situation, just as in the workplace, because the mentor and student have much in common, the bi-directionality so important with teenagers is not a necessity. Of course, if the relationship lasts long enough, a true give-and-take, a friendship, can certainly develop, but it is not a requirement of these special cases.

However, when *every* student is assigned a mentor, a central feature of instruction at Goddard, Empire State, and other similar colleges, the situation begins to resemble the mentoring conditions for teenagers. The professor-mentor, for example, can no longer just instruct but must also advise, coach, advocate, solve problems for, and motivate his or her student-mentees and personally care about and be committed to their development and success on their educational journey (Daloz, 1999). To do all this, academic mentors must apprehend (and hopefully appreciate) the many ways the interests and goals of their mentees do not match their own. In other words, such mentors must do what does not necessarily come naturally to traditional college professors: Instead of imparting what they know, they must listen carefully to what their mentee-students believe or desire, regardless of whether such beliefs or desires are similar, or even relevant, to their own. As Schein (2013) argues, authentic listening runs counter to our culture's "rules about status" (p. 54) and in effect requires professors to "reinvent" themselves as guides (Chen, Fortunato, Mandell, Oaks, & RyanMann, 2001) whose primary purpose is to help their mentees find and develop their own intellectual paths (e.g., Herman & Mandell, 2004).

Many professors do not have the disposition or desire to become mentors; nor do they believe such a model is appropriate in an institution of higher education that strives to strengthen the minds of students through disciplinary study. Others, however, who see the traditional instructional model to be highly demotivating for many students—particularly those who are academically at risk—have been much more open to the mentoring approach. They embrace their own transformation from subject matter experts into multifaceted academic guides—true mentors—because they welcome the roles and responsibilities not ordinarily feasible for classroom teachers. And they approve, and indeed they advocate for, the opportunity to similarly transform students from passive recipients of expert information into active seekers of knowledge that is relevant and important to them. Although "mentoring" was not even mentioned as an explicit part of Dewey's progressive philosophy, any mentoring model that focuses on mentees' lives and concerns seems to provide exactly those conditions that Dewey sought to introduce into the classroom.[2] It is perhaps for this reason that mentoring in academia is closely tied to the ideals of progressive education.

How are such student-centered conditions so conducive to good mentoring established? When the teacher-as-mentor and student-as-mentee meet alone in order to talk with each other (in sharp contrast to the classroom where teachers talk *at* their students), the mentor is exposed to questions and problems that arise from her mentees' immediate personal, professional, social, and educational experiences. As mentor and mentee consider these experiences together, it becomes increasingly real to the mentor that the usual ways of "just in case" instruction (Collins & Halverson, 2009, p. 48), in which students learn one discipline after another so as to be prepared for real life once the educational phase is over, is disconnected from the average student's preoccupations and is an ineffective way of developing important intellectual skills. The mentor recognizes instead that her mentees are already well into the world, that education neither begins nor ends in school, and that, as Dewey argued (1938/1997), the situations and observations that matter to students offer rich opportunities for intellectual development. Disciplinary knowledge, the "past products" (Dewey, 1916/1966, p. 211) of academic investigations, can be made relevant and useful when it is introduced "just in time" (Collins & Halverson, pp. 14–15) to bear upon conditions the students actually experience. Thus, the teacher-mentor in collaboration with the student-mentee effortlessly comes upon potential learning experiences that arise directly out of the mentee's concerns, rather than from the disciplinary affiliation of the mentor.

But this entire process raises a key question. If the mentor's discipline is not what drives the mentoring relationship, what then is the particular expertise the mentor brings to the situation? Why would any student wish to be such a person's mentee? A quick answer is that the academic mentor has "an inquiring mind" (Houle, 1961), or the disposition to be curious about the world and a mastery of the intellectual skills needed to act upon that curiosity. Academic mentors know how to ask good questions, locate good information, help select what is appropriate and evaluate it; they also know how to sort through and organize what is discovered in relation to a particular question or hypothesis. That they are an expert in a particular discipline is also important, not because they have mastered that subject area, but as a measure of their ability to organize and carry out serious investigations.

The presumption in mentoring—also in higher education—is that if a person knows how to do something, he or she will automatically know how to teach it. But here, the workplace model offers some additional insights: Armed with skills of inquiry, the mentor does not need to instruct. Instead, mentors use these skills not to tell and show, but to guide and assist their mentees as they engage in work about which the mentees already have some prior knowledge. The same can be said for mentors in an academic mentoring relationship. Just as Pallas Athene, goddess of wisdom, "took Mentor's form so as to guide, counsel, and enable both Odysseus and his son Telemachus through their journey and return home" (Roberts, 1999, p. 3), the academic mentor, already aware of her mentee's situation and purposes, is able to prepare him for, and even guide him along, his own intellectual path (Daloz, 1999).

The workplace model also suggests another reason why, in higher education, the mentoring model has seemed especially appropriate for the adult student. If traditional-aged college students are not without prior learning, but come to college with a developed sense of self along with questions and opinions about the way the world works, surely adult students do too, but even more so. While adult students may need guidance negotiating the world of academia, they are already capable self-directed learners in life (Coulter & Mandell, 2016). As far back as 1926, Eduard Lindeman offered a heart-felt and thorough argument for the knowledge and persistence of adult learners, and more recently Kett (1994) has provided ample historical evidence to that effect. In addition, Houle (1961) and Tough (1979) presented a range of empirical evidence supporting claims by both Dewey and Lindeman that continuous learning is a natural and common part of life. The increasingly popular trend to now award adults credit for what they have learned on their own—at home, as community activists, and at work— similarly testifies to that fact (e.g., Andersson & Harris, 2006; Michelson, 2015), even when such learning does not necessarily match any particular college course. Thus, adult learners are particularly well prepared to make use of the mentor's guidance, not only for pursuing their specific interests and professional goals, but also for deepening their understanding of and appreciation for their own life experiences.

Academic Mentoring in Practice

How does this model play out in practice? Here, in broad strokes, is a typical scenario: For continuing students (who are familiar with the process),[3] the mentee meets his mentor for an hour or more at the end of a term to discuss what the mentee has in mind for his next set of studies. Together, they identify and begin to shape a study plan in which they articulate the purpose of the study, the anticipated learning activities that would be required, and the criteria to be used in evaluating what the student has learned when the study is over. This plan is recorded in a written "learning contract" (see e.g., Knowles, 1975), which is reviewed by an appropriate administrator. When the next term begins, the mentor and mentee plan to meet on a mutually acceptable schedule (such as every few weeks). At each meeting the mentee describes what has been accomplished so far, answers the mentor's questions, and shares various previously agreed-upon learning "products" (e.g., journal entries, reviews, essays, interview summaries). Most of all, the two engage in a lively dialogue about the subject of study, its current direction, and any implications, revelations, and any other issues that bear upon what the mentee is hoping to accomplish (see e.g., Herman & Mandell, 2004). Usually, at the end of the term, the mentee completes some kind of project or produces a written document that may summarize, illustrate, critique, or draw conclusions about what he learned relative to his original purpose.

On the face of it, the replacement of the classroom with self-directed independent studies that are guided and monitored by a mentor would appear to be the best possible approach for busy adult college students. For faculty who prefer to focus on strengthening and developing student intellectual skills and habits of inquiry rather than on insuring that their students receive proper coverage of conventional subject matter, academic mentoring is an ideal form of education. However, just as with the workplace and social service mentoring models, it turns out that in practice, things are not so simple. In addition to the ambiguities inherent in all mentoring situations, the academic model introduces its own new complexities and issues that are specific to its educational mission. Incomplete or inaccurate interpretations of their mentees' academic needs, sudden changes in institutional policies, inadequate or missing educational resources, all this, and more, can sabotage the best intentions of any mentor. And ever present at every turn, mentors are unceasingly pressured—by their own unacknowledged tacit assumptions, by the conflicting demands of students, by institutional imperatives, and even by cultural expectations—to revert back to what the world typically expects of faculty in college: to exert their well-earned authority and assume their proper role as teacher.

As we see it, one important source of difficulty for the mentor is the uncertain meaning of the word, "guidance." How much authority should the mentor give to the expressed wishes of the mentee? When does advice become instruction? Obviously, it depends upon the nature of the actual goals themselves, and the details of the plans the mentee has in mind. In addition, many adult college students do not come to college to strengthen their intellectual skills; they come to earn a degree or to prepare for work. A few may have in mind a particular academic major, but their plans sometimes do not extend beyond finding enough time to engage in college-level studies that, at least early on, they cannot fully imagine. If, at the outset, the mentor asks how they propose to achieve such goals, a new student might understandably point out that she is looking to the institution—to the mentor—to tell her how to proceed. A teacher, even an advisor, would have no difficulty doing so (indeed most may see this as their job), but a mentor has to push further in an effort to better discern—that is, uncover, and help the mentee express—what, precisely, she hopes to accomplish. Yet, clearly, both actions, whether making a course suggestion or asking open-ended questions (Vella, 2008) until the student is able to articulate what she wants to learn, are legitimate forms of guidance. If the former is not appropriate for a mentor, but the latter is, what is the distinction? One might argue that it does not advance the mentee's skills of inquiry to tell her what to do. On the other hand, if the answer is too difficult to determine, or it is essentially out of the mentee's reach, it also does not help advance a mentee's skills if she is overwhelmed by the question and cannot succeed. On what basis, then, does the mentor make these judgments?

Schneider et al. (1981) conducted an extensive investigation comparing effective and successful mentors and teachers to those who were deemed less so. The results produced a list of competencies common to the best mentors and teachers that are very similar to what we have described so far as inherent in academic mentoring. However, the major conclusion that the researchers drew was that ultimately good mentoring was a "balancing act." As they described it:

> ... we found the faculty interviewed for the study attempting to hold in balance two different roles, each of which appeared central to his or her actual effectiveness in working with adult students. On the one hand, the faculty members' own reports on their interactions with students revealed a pervasive student-centeredness, which meant, in simple terms, a determination to respond to adult students as persons, as individuals—in short, as adults—with their own legitimate needs, perspectives, and concerns. On the other hand, the faculty members were clearly balancing their student-centeredness with highly directive and prescriptive roles as well. It was their ability to hold these two elements together that made a difference.... (p. 66)

While we might argue with the *level* of prescriptiveness described above as indicative of good mentoring, we fully acknowledge the conflicting impulses, and the never fully certain resolution, that plays out at almost every stage of the mentoring relationship.

Take, for example, the selection of subject matter. To start with, not every student interest is readily translatable into an academic investigation. One mentee, for instance, already absorbed in the teachings of Edgar Cayce, wanted to design a learning contract that would enable him to build an apparatus to physically measure auras. The mentor, a psychologist, unable to accept even the most basic of Cayce's premises, also wanted the contract to include an investigation into why the academic world largely rejects Cayce's ideas. She saw this condition as a form of compromise; the student saw it as an attack on his thinking; and in the end, no contract was ever developed. The resolution of the conflicting mentor roles, in this case, was unsuccessful. It could be that the mentor did not trust that the student would "discover" the limitations of Cayce's theory on his own. Or, perhaps she did not know exactly how to create learning activities that would "guide" the mentee to question Cayce's theory himself without her having to tell him at the outset the outcome that she desired. Whatever the reason, the underlying problem was not in what the mentee wanted to learn, but in what the mentor perceived to be academically appropriate. For Dewey, the line that separates students as active agents in their own learning from those who are the passive recipients of knowledge deemed by the teacher as best for them, was glaringly obvious; however, for this mentor, the line was elusive at best and virtually impossible to draw. The elusiveness of this distinction is regularly experienced by academic mentors and, indeed, by any teacher who holds a student-centered philosophy.

The mentor not only has her own sense of academic quality to guide her thinking, but she must fulfill institutional and public expectations as well. Matthew Arnold's (1869) exhortation that the major purpose of education is to teach students "the best that has been thought and known in the world current everywhere" (preface, para. 3) is accepted rather enthusiastically at many educational institutions. Even though in the twenty-first century it is obvious that such a goal makes little sense, given not only the amount of knowledge we have accumulated, but the speed at which old knowledge is being continually overturned, academics still find it difficult to give it up completely. Hence, with the best of intentions, students are expected to cover a set of "general education" disciplines without regard to whatever their own educational purposes might be. Thus, the student-directed nature of the mentoring relationship is severely challenged when, for example, an adult student reluctantly returning to school, expresses an interest in comparing the behaviors of young children dropped off for day care without breakfast to those already fed, and then discovers that learning to quantify and statistically compare those behaviors is not enough to meet the "general education" requirement in mathematics as stipulated by her institution. Instead, she must still take a specific required course in algebra that she has already unsuccessfully tried and which, at this point, seems totally disconnected from her own concerns.

Setting subject matter aside, there are any number of interpersonal pitfalls that can arise between mentor and mentee. That an academic mentor has a PhD and fervently wants to help guide his students through the world of academic scholarship, does not guarantee that the mentor will also be able to deal with differences in personality, gender, race, or culture (e.g., Hansman, 2003). One bright, interested, knowledgeable and White mentor, who was intimately familiar with the history of IQ testing and the flawed (and indeed fraudulent) research that indicated significant racial differences in intelligence between African Americans and Caucasians, was eager to introduce his Black mentees to the faulty data and poor reasoning that promoted these false claims and to show how the record came to be corrected. The mentor not only did not realize that his own revelation was a foregone conclusion for his mentees, but that to engage with the history of the so-called "IQ controversy" was extremely painful for them. The mentor's misjudgment persisted until one of his mentees—after weeks of apparent procrastination—told him: "I just can't stand reading this stuff." Although his mentees were no doubt interested in investigating issues related to race in America, the mentor, so captivated by his own knowledge, became obsessed with "telling" rather than "listening" to what his mentees really wanted to know. He assumed their interests coincided when, in fact, they were worlds apart.

Such incidents should, but do not always, remind us that the mentor-mentee relationship, no matter how rewarding, nonetheless rests upon limited knowledge of our students. It is easy to forget that our understanding of the needs and motivations of our mentees is totally dependent upon what they choose to tell us. In addition, our own intuitions and interpretations, biased as they are by our own past experiences, can easily block even the best of mentors from hearing what their mentees actually are, and are not, telling them. Ironically, this selective deafness is apt to occur particularly with older students. In our experience, even though they come to college already armed with considerable knowledge, they are easily intimidated, and often silenced, by the academic world. Mentors in their eagerness to acquaint their new mentees with the fruits of relevant scholarly knowledge may be too impatient to appreciate that their mentees are not blank slates. So, for example, fearful that her knowledge is not of value, an experienced social worker, now a mentee, may not tell her mentor that she is a state-wide consultant on family issues when the mentor, hearing only that she is interested in families, suggests that she take an introductory course in Marriage and the Family.

Then, there is the overriding problem of time (Giddens, 2003). As in all mentoring models, adult mentees with regular work, family, and social responsibilities have limited time to spend with their mentor. Indeed, for many an adult college student, the academic mentoring model is initially attractive because of the many fewer hours needed for mentor meetings than for regularly scheduled weekly classes. However, unlike the case of workplace or community mentoring, much of the work of both the academic mentor and mentee takes place outside their individual meetings. Mentees must read, investigate, develop projects, write reports; mentors must prepare for their mentee meetings, engage in myriad forms of bureaucratic exercise, and pursue their individual scholarly commitments. Moreover, the specific requirements of the learning contracts that emerge from the mentor-mentee planning must be completed within a fixed and very short time frame, the ubiquitous 15-week semester, or at some institutions even shorter "accelerated" terms (Wlodkowski & Kasworm, 2003). Not only do these term limits unduly restrict the range and direction of mentee-driven intellectual inquiries, they also become significant obstacles for adult mentees whose lives cannot be so conveniently scheduled. A sick child, an urgent business trip, a broken furnace or car, or a sudden crisis in the family or at work, can totally disrupt the process and intent of academic mentoring, unlike the more traditional mentoring models where the asynchronous rhythms of the participants' lives can be more easily accommodated.

Mentees too are in a hurry: They want that diploma or new job as quickly as possible. The need for speed and efficiency, however, can seriously impact the breadth and depth of the investigations the mentor and mentee decide are necessary for the student to achieve her goals. The kind of engagement in learning that academic mentoring is designed to encourage can come to be perceived by a busy adult as demanding far more time and energy than pre-designed courses (increasingly available online) with clearly demarked temporal segments and little call for student agency and initiative. Such perceptions can only be effectively addressed by mentors who are able to stay focused, not just on short-term content goals, but on those long-term plans for strengthening a mentee's intellectual skills that continue well beyond the limits of a 15-week term. Such a focus is particularly difficult to sustain because it requires that the mentor relinquish a reliance on well-established disciplinary content and trust his ability to respond imaginatively to a mentee's needs, while still meeting high academic standards. Once again, the balancing act, the precariousness of practice, is clearly in evidence.

Time pressure, indeed the human imperative for efficiency, affects the mentoring relationship in other ways as well. For example, it makes it very difficult for a mentor to patiently wait for mentees to discover some truth, rather than to simply tell them what they need to know, when the latter takes so much less time. Once a learning contract is painstakingly constructed to meet one student's needs, it becomes all too easy to hand over the same already developed contract to another student with similar needs. Then, if several students seem to have the same interests, it seems only natural not only to use that same contract, but to meet these three or four mentees together as a group. The slide from a small group of mentees to regularly scheduled classes is not hard to imagine. Thus, it requires explicit effort and constant vigilance by the individual mentor to resist such seemingly insignificant moves and to remain committed to respecting and promoting the active engagement of the mentee, despite the extra time it may take. Unfortunately, the mentoring relationship itself contains no internal constraints that might help the mentor resist these pressures. Indeed, the presumptive (lower) status of mentees, who might ordinarily prefer a more flexible schedule, makes it difficult for them to speak up when a busy mentor engages in various shortcuts. In other words, without some kind of external support to counteract such pressures for efficiency, the mentoring relationship will always be pushed in a direction that undermines its student-centered purpose.[4]

The Precarious Nature of Academic Mentoring

As adult educators, however much we might cherish our own understanding of mentoring's deeply dialogical values, and however much we might imagine that mentoring presents a significant and critical alternative to teaching and learning as it has become embedded in academic life in America, we also need to recognize that it is a precarious practice. That is, however loudly we call its name, hope for it to hold sway and gain legitimacy, or expect that mentoring programs (and they are indeed plentiful these days) will succeed in wrenching us away from what faculty and students take for granted, we need to recognize that there always is more to do. Change is difficult, and the power of entrenched institutional and pedagogical interests is indeed great and often at odds with the heart of mentoring.

Put in another way, within mentoring practice itself and between mentoring and an institution that supports it, there is much that must be seen, considered, attended to and worked with. In particular, as we have sought to describe, there are abiding tensions at both the microscopic and macroscopic levels that must be acknowledged if mentoring is to become anything more than a term of endearment. Certainly a first step, which we attempt in this chapter, is to bring out into the open the inherent features of academic mentoring that make it so precarious and difficult to sustain. Only if we are able to articulate in detail these tensions, conflicts, even contradictions, will we be able to take the next necessary steps that may help us to successfully maintain mentoring practices despite their precarious nature. Let us list and summarize, as comprehensively as possible, the issues that arise within the mentoring relationship, that is, at the micro-level, and then at the institutional or macro-level.

First, the micro-level.

A Mentor's Expertise

We need to ask: What is the particular expertise that the mentor possesses? What are the tensions between the mentor expertise needed for realizing a progressive view of education and the mentor expertise with which most faculty already identify: his or her disciplinary affiliation? Might the history and the pull of such disciplinary expertise ever win the day? Can it be otherwise?

A Mentor's Attitude

We need to ask: Is there a proper mentoring attitude? What are the tensions between the mentor's need to listen and build upon the student's ideas, questions and interests and the mentor's impulse to yield to the long-standing academic practice of teaching-by-telling? Should the pull to profess be dampened? If so, how can this ever take place?

A Mentor's Academic Focus

We need to ask: How do we contend with the tensions that arise between the championing of studies that consist of individual and idiosyncratic combinations of resource materials and studies that reflect the promotion of typically disciplinary studies that are routinely required? Can both kinds of studies; can both kinds of curricula be given equal academic weight? Or, as Dewey (1916/1966) and Lindemann (1926) have argued, should disciplinary study be invoked only after the mentee, not the mentor, comes to demand it?

A Mentor's Knowledge of a Mentee

We need to ask: How do we acknowledge that the mentor's knowledge of her mentee is necessarily limited by time, context and attitude? How do we step aside and evaluate the mentor's confidence that the knowledge she has gleaned from mentoring conversations is complete? How do the tensions between being complete and being sufficient play out in practice?

A Mentor's Comfort With a Mentee; A Mentee's Comfort With a Mentor

We need to ask: Should any academic institution be concerned about whether the mentor and mentee feel personally comfortable with each other? Should there be some kind of effort to find a match between the mentee and mentor based upon academic interests? Is it sufficient that the mentee trusts that the mentor has the necessary expertise to recognize and appreciate the student's strengths and interests, and that that mentor trusts that the mentee has the potential to succeed merely by virtue of having enrolled in college? What are the limits of "comfort" as a criterion for a good match?

A Mentor's Time

We need to ask: What are the on-going tensions between the need to wait and take time in every step of the mentor-student relationship and the need (at both the individual and institutional levels) to be more efficient, to push ahead and to take short-cuts? Who has the time to do what?

A Mentor's Judgments

We need to ask: Are we motivated to identify and correct clear misunderstandings and errors in a face-to-face mentor-mentee meeting? Or, as in the ordinary rules of everyday conversation, are we more regularly inclined to look for points of agreement? What judgments should a mentor be making and how should they be constructively communicated to the mentee?

And now, the macro-level.

On Basic Definitions

We need to ask: If the work of the mentor is complex, varied, and demanding, and if the term itself must become more than our public embrace of an emotionally loaded and culturally valued notion that suggests that caring must be a significant element of teaching and that student anonymity and alienation thwart learning, how exactly is mentoring defined at any particular institution? What are the specific roles that come with that institution's mentoring terrain? Who is responsible for carrying out work that ensures that mentoring becomes more than only a part of a too easily intoned institutional marketing strategy?

On Time and Compensation

We need to ask: If the mentoring of adult learners is a labor intensive activity, not only who has time for such work, but how is such time compensated? Can mentoring be integrated into the daily responsibilities of a faculty member so that mentoring becomes much more than the admirable personal sacrifice of a faculty member to work well beyond the expectations of one's course load? How do institutional priorities and policies respond to such very basic issues? Who will pay for what?

On Process and Content

We need to ask: The "complex role" of the mentor referred to by Hall (1976) (see our opening page) consists of integrating both "process" (learning to understand the nature of the mentee's intentions) and "content" (the actual courses and program of study the student engages). For the institution, however, the former is virtually invisible. How then, can an institution be designed so as to provide support, not only for learning contracts, degree programs, and grades, but for the mentee's educational journey that shapes those outputs? How, indeed, can the institution be made to acknowledge the critical dependence of good outcomes upon seemingly ineffable input processes? Is there any way that institutional priorities can be better aligned with those of their mentors? In other words, as mentors struggle daily to find the right balance between process and content, can institutional policies be developed that represent—and similarly seek to balance—these two essential components of student learning?

On the Evaluation of Learning

We need to ask: Are letter grades appropriate for evaluating a kind of student learning that encompasses much more than mastery of fact? Should society's current obsession with accountability be permitted to dictate that student learning must be easily quantified? Should narrative evaluations, which *can* capture the complex learning outcomes in situation- as opposed to discipline-based studies, be eliminated solely for reasons of institutional convenience?

On Students as Mentees

We need to ask: If faculty are mentors, students are mentees. Putting aside "mentee" as a rather uncomfortable and quite contrived term, do all of our students come to college expecting to become mentees? Do they wish to be mentored? How, in a world in which practical considerations of job, professional preparation, salary, and schedule overpower many other wishes, are students expected to behave in their mentee roles? How do we prepare students for such a new experience as authors of their own learning, especially if this is far from what they ever expected to be doing in college?

On Learning to be a Mentor

We need to ask: Mentoring work is not only difficult and labor intensive; it requires new learning, regular engagement, and ongoing critical reflection. As a theory and practice of teaching and learning that raises basic questions about how professors teach and how students learn, and as a significantly different way to understand the expression of expertise, we cannot assume that we can all know how to mentor nor that every faculty member will unambivalently dive into mentoring work. How do faculty learn? What plans are in place for ongoing faculty development in which, together, faculty take on difficult issues about their teaching and about their students' learning? How can faculty development become more than periodic informational get-togethers or top-down training sessions? Can faculty development ever be experienced as part of the very core of faculty work and as an institutional investment in the creation of a true mentoring learning community in which everyone has a stake?

On Institutional Change

We need to ask: Mentoring is about change; it is about altering the expectations that most of us internalized in our own schooling and that are cemented into institutional ways. If change is going to come about, how can mentoring ripple through an institution and lead to significant change at every level of institutional life, from counseling to course and curriculum development to faculty compensation and criteria for review to participation in day to day and major institutional decisions? What would an institution committed to mentoring actually look like and what would a plan and a strategy need to include in order to reach such a goal?

IN CONCLUSION

We have tried to identify some of the roots of mentoring in academia, particularly with adult students, in order to elucidate the ways in which mentoring itself is a precarious practice. While we have focused exclusively upon academic mentoring, it is possible that at least some of the micro and macro issues we have noted may pertain, regardless of setting, to all mentoring relationships. Once the many concerns, risks, even threats, are openly acknowledged and better understood, perhaps a broader view of mentoring may suggest new and different ways of addressing these challenges. It may also be that new ideas, if not also additional support and assistance, may come from various progressive educational institutions which share mentoring's student-centered focus. Even more helpful may be the reflections of those adult alumni who have already experienced and benefited from a mentored education. However, no matter how much we are able to improve its sustainability in higher education, no matter how it may be better defined, explained, or investigated, mentoring itself will never be a routinized, safe, or easy enterprise. Nonetheless, what does remain clear and steadfast is its great potential for strengthening and deepening habits of lifelong learning, the importance of which is beyond question.

NOTES

1. We are aware that Jacobi (1991) has observed "the absence of a widely accepted operational definition of mentoring" (p. 505), a concern that Crisp & Cruz (2009) reiterated more than 25 years later: "[M]entoring research has made little progress in identifying and implementing a consistent definition and conceptualization of mentoring..." (p. 526). Thus, we identify here certain commonly accepted features of mentoring, not as a claim or argument, but simply as a useful heuristic.
2. Dewey never referred to his students as "at risk" yet the Vermont students he originally taught and who stimulated the development of his philosophy certainly fit that profile,
3. New students, however, learn that over time they will create with their mentors their entire curriculum, not unlike at conventional colleges that offer "individualized major programs" (e.g., Egan, 2014)—but with advisors, which is part of a movement to engage student advisors more seriously in the university's academic agenda (e.g., Hemwall & Tracte, 2005). Egan says it is a "dialogic and iterative" process that helps students "make connections...and...[think] through the way compelling curricula are constructed, both sequentially...and

complementarily." The advisor "plays a role with respect to a student's entire curriculum that is analogous to the role that the excellent teacher plays with respect to the content of a single course" (Lowenstein, 2005, abstract). Both roles, we argue, are fulfilled by the academic mentor.

4. Unfortunately, institutional "support" tends to exacerbate this problem. What mentor would not seek shortcuts if, instead of being responsible for 20 mentees, he is assigned 100?

REFERENCES

Andersson, P., & Harris, J. (Eds.). (2006). *Re-theorising the recognition of prior learning.* Leicester, England: NIACE.

Arnold, M. (1869). Culture and anarchy [Gutenberg Adobe Editions]. Retrieved from www.gutenberg.org/cache/epub4212/pg4212.html.

Benson, A. G., & Adams, F. (1987). *To know for real: Royce S. Pitkin & Goddard College.* Adamant, VT: Adamant Press.

Bonnabeau, R. F. (1996). *The promise continues: Empire State College the first twenty-five years.* Virginia Beach, VA: Donning Company/Publishers.

Chen, J. R., Fortunato, M. V., Mandell, A., Oaks, S., & Ryan Mann, D. (2001). Reconceptualizing the faculty role: Alternative models. In B. L. Smith & J. McCann (Eds.), *Reinventing ourselves: Interdisciplinary education, collaborative learning, and experimentation in higher education* (pp. 328–339). Bolton, MA: Anker.

Chickering, A. W., & Associates (2014). *Cool passion: Challenging higher education.* Washington, DC: NASPA (Student Affairs Administrators in Higher Education).

Cohen, N. H. (1995). *Mentoring adult learners: A guide for educators and trainers.* Malabar, FL: Krieger Publishing Company.

Cohen, N. H., & Galbraith, M. W. (1995). Mentoring: New strategies and challenges. *New Directions for Adult and Continuing Education, 66,* 5–14.

Coulter, X., & Mandell, A. (2016). Rediscovering the North American legacy of self-initiated learning in prior learning assessments. In M. Keppell, S. Reushle, & A. Antonio (Eds.), *Open learning and formal credentialing in higher education* (pp. 34–56). Hershey PA: IGI Global.

Collins, A., & Halverson, R. (2009). *Rethinking education in the age of technology: The digital revolution and schooling in America.* New York, NY: Teachers College Press.

Cox, M. D., Boettcher, C. K., & Adone, D. S. (Eds.). (1997). *Breaking the circle of one: Redefining mentorship in the lives and writings of educators.* New York, NY: Peter Long.

Crisp, G., & Cruz, I. (2009). Mentoring college students: A critical review of the literature between 1990 and 2007. *Research in Higher Education, 50*(9), 525–545.

Daloz, L. (1999). *Mentor: Guiding the journey of adult learners.* San Francisco, CA: Jossey-Bass.

Davis, F. K. (1996). *Things were different in Royce's day: Royce S. Pitkin as progressive educator: A perspective from Goddard College, 1950–1967.* Adamant, VT: Adamant Press.

Dewey, J. (1916/1966). *Democracy and education.* New York, NY: Free Press.

Dewey, J. (1938/1997). *Experience and education.* New York, NY: Touchstone Press.

Egan, K. D. (2014). Empowerment through advising: Academic advising in individualized major programs. *The Mentor: An Academic Advising Journal.* Retrieved from https://dus.psu.edu/mentor/2014/07/empowerment-through-advising/

Freedman, M. (1993). *The kindness of strangers: Adult mentors, urban youth, and the new volunteerism.* San Francisco, CA: Jossey Bass.

Giddens, A. (2003). *Runaway world: How globalization is reshaping our lives.* New York, NY: Routledge.

Hall, J. W. (1976). The faculty and the future. *Alternative Higher Education, 1*(2), 99–110.

Hansman, C. A. (2003). Reluctant mentors and resistant protégés: Welcome to the "real" world of mentoring. *Adult Learning, 14*(1), 14–16.

Head, F. A., Reiman, A. J., & Thies-Sprinthall, L. (1992). The reality of mentoring: Complexity in its process and function. In T. M. Bey & C. T. Holmes (Eds.). *Mentoring: Contemporary principles and issues* (pp 5–24). Reston, VA: Association of Teacher Educators.

Hemwall, M. K., & Trachte, K. C. (2005). Academic advising as learning: 10 organizing principles. *NACADA Journal, 25*(2), 74–83.

Herman, L., & Coulter, X. (1998, Fall). John and Maria: What mentors learn from experiential learning. *All About Mentoring, 15*, 21–25.

Herman, L., & Mandell, A. (2004). *From teaching to mentoring: Principles and practice, dialogue and life in adult education.* New York, NY: Routledge.

Houle, C. O. (1961/1993). *The inquiring mind: A study of the adult who continues to learn* (3rd ed.). Norman, OK: Oklahoma Research Center for Continuing and Professional Higher Education.

Insala. (2015). *Mentoring benchmarking survey report.* Retrieved from: http://www.insala.com

Jackson, P. W. (1990). Introduction. In J. Dewey, *The school and society/The child and the curriculum.* Chicago, IL: University of Chicago Press.

Jacobi, M. (1991). Mentoring and undergraduate academic success: A literature review. *Review of Educational Research, 61*(4), 505–532.

Kett, J. F. (1994). *The pursuit of knowledge under difficulties: From self-improvement to adult education in America, 1750–1990.* Stanford, CA: Stanford University Press.

Knowles, M. (1975). *Using learning contracts.* San Francisco, CA: Jossey-Bass.

Lindeman, E. (1926). *The meaning of adult education.* New York, NY: New Republic.

Lowenstein, M. (2005). If advising is teaching, what do advisors teach? [Abstract]. *NACADA Journal, 25*(2), 65–73.

Michelson, E. (2015). *Gender, experience and knowledge in adult learning: Alisoun's daughters.* New York, NY: Routledge.

Parsloe, E., & Wray, M. J. (2000). *Coaching and mentoring: Practical methods to improve learning.* Philadelphia, PA: Kogan Page.

Roberts, A., (1999). Homer's Mentor: Duties fulfilled or misconstrued? Adapted from: The origins of the term mentor. *History of Education Society Bulletin, 64*, 313–329. Retrieved from http://www.nickols.us/homers_mentor.pdf

Rogers, C. R. (1969). *Freedom to learn.* Columbus, OH: Merrill.

Schein, E. H. (2013). *Humble inquiry: The gentle art of asking instead of telling.* San Francisco, CA: Berrett-Koehler.

Schneider, C. O., Klemp, Jr., G., & Kastendiek, S. (1981). *The balancing act: Competencies of effective teachers and mentors in degree programs for adults.* Boston, MA: McBer.

Shiner, M., Young, T., Newburn, T., & Groben, S. (2004). *Mentoring disaffected young people.* York, England: Joseph Rowntree Foundation.

Tough, A. (1979). *The adult's learning projects: A fresh approach to theory and practice in adult learning* (3rd ed.). Toronto, ON: Ontario Institute for Studies in Education.

Vella, J. (2008). *On teaching and learning: Putting the principles and practices of dialogue education into action.* San Francisco, CA: Jossey Bass.

Wlodkowski, R., & Kasworm, C.E. (2003). Accelerated learning for adults: The promise and practice of intensive educational formats. *New Directions for Adult and Continuing Education, 98,* 49–57.

Zachary, L. J. (2000). *The mentor's guide: Facilitating effective learning relationships.* San Francisco, CA: Jossey-Bass.

CHAPTER 3

MULTI-DIMENSIONAL MODEL FOR MENTORING FACULTY

A College-Wide Approach

Lori E. Ciccomascolo
Anne M. Seitsinger
University of Rhode Island

The University of Rhode Island (URI), like many American universities, faced the retirements of a large group of faculty who started their careers after the post-World War II expansion of higher education. In recent years, we have seen a major turn over and hiring of faculty members. Rice, Sorcinelli, and Austin (2000) referred to this as a generational "changing of the guard" in the American professoriate. Significant differences in technology and funding between an academic career in the 1970s and that in the twenty-first century emphasize this change. Large differences in the ways retiring, senior faculty experienced their careers and quality-of-life expectations exist for newer faculty (Rice, Sorcinelli, & Austin, 2000). Along with employment conditions, the millennial generation, those born after 1980, requires a different set of retention strategies (Deloitte, 2014; Millennial Branding & Beyond.com, 2013).

Mentoring in Formal and Informal Contexts, pages 43–56
Copyright © 2016 by Information Age Publishing
All rights of reproduction in any form reserved.

Increasingly, new faculty encounter changing requirements for tenure, including increased teaching loads and service demands, a more competitive research climate, and overall earlier vulnerability (ADVANCE Resource Center, 2008; Collaborative on Academic Careers in Higher Education, 2014). These Millennial faculty have needs and desires that differ from their predecessors regarding the balance between work life and family (Kelly, 2007; Philipsen, 2008). In addition, institutions of higher education now have a more diverse faculty with a greater proportion of traditionally underrepresented faculty (e.g., faculty of color, women, nontenure track) for whom these issues manifest differently (Hall & Sandler, 1983; Philipsen, 2008). Therefore, the workplace of the academy needs to address these changes.

A review of multidisciplinary literature by Grawitch, Gottschalk, and Munz (2006) suggests that a healthy workplace takes into consideration the individual as well as the organization. Sauter, Lim, and Murphy (1996) defined a healthy workplace as any organization that "maximizes the integration of worker goals for well-being and company objectives for profitability and productivity" (p. 250). Promoting healthy workplace programs and policies are best achieved at the organizational level, rather than at a department level, and should be geared toward the needs of individual employees (DeJoy & Wilson, 2003).

MENTORING PROGRAMS

One healthy workplace practice in institutions of higher education is mentorship (Sorcinelli & Yun, 2009). Mentoring programs provide a means of personal, professional, and social support. There is considerable evidence of the benefits of mentoring in an academic career (de Janasz & Sullivan, 2004; Girves, Zepeda, & Gwathmey, 2005; Johnson, 2007; Mathews, 2003). Mentoring programs are designed to support the personal and professional development of new faculty as they develop their careers and professional identities (Hanover Research, 2014). The five broad areas in which mentors generally support new faculty are (a) getting to know the institution; (b) excelling in teaching and research; (c) understanding tenure and evaluation; (d) creating work–life balance; and (e) developing professional networks (ADVANCE Resource Center, 2008; Hanover Research, 2014). Mentoring affords the new faculty member psychosocial support, thus reducing stress and helping to make one feel welcomed and valued as a member of the university community (ADVANCE Resource Center, 2008). This type of support has a particularly significant impact on the professional development of women and minority faculty as they strive for a balance between their academic and personal lives (Philipsen, 2008; Sorcinelli & Yun, 2009).

Mentoring provides benefits not only to new faculty, but the mentor(s) and the institution of higher education as well (ADVANCE Resource Center, 2008). Mentors gain satisfaction in guiding the development of a new colleague and contributing to improved institutional climate change. Additionally, mentors benefit from opportunities for new research collaborations. Institutions of higher education benefit from an increased level of commitment, productivity, and satisfaction from new faculty, as well as encouragement, cooperation, and cohesiveness for those involved in the mentoring program. These benefits contribute to the overall stability and health of the institution (ADVANCE Resource Center, 2008).

MODELS OF FACULTY MENTORING

Different models for mentoring exist in academia and have evolved over the years, including one-on-one mentoring, reverse mentoring, multiple mentors, group or peer mentoring, mentoring networks, and e-mentoring (ADVANCE Resource Center, 2008; Hanover Research, 2014; Murphy, 2012; Sorcinelli & Yun, 2007).

One-on-One Models

Traditional models of mentoring have been defined as top-down, one-on-one relationships where a more senior faculty member is paired with a new faculty member (Sorcinelli & Yun, 2007). The senior faculty mentor is usually from the same department as the new faculty member. Departmental mentors can provide guidance relative to department policies and procedures (ADVANCE Resource Center, 2008). One drawback to this model is that it can lead to discipleship. New faculty members may find it "difficult to establish or express their own views on departmental issues and developments" (Cartwright, 2008, p. 6). Additionally, early career faculty may be reluctant to show weaknesses to colleagues within the same department, particularly to those who may be involved in their tenure and promotion decisions. This can be particularly detrimental to women and minority faculty (ADVANCE Resource Center, 2008).

Being supported by a faculty member outside one's home department is another form of one-on-one mentoring. This model can provide the new faculty member with a broader perspective of the university. It can also lead to collaborative, interdisciplinary research. The disadvantage of this model is the unfamiliarity the mentor might have with the new faculty members' department (ADVANCE Resource Center, 2008).

When a new faculty member with more expertise in a specific area is paired with a senior faculty mentor, the model is referred to as reverse mentoring (Hanover Research, 2014). This model is often used when knowledge of new technology, diversity, or cross-generational understanding is desired. Murphy (2012) defined reverse mentoring as "the pairing of a younger, junior employee acting as mentor to share expertise with an older, senior colleague as the mentee" (p. 550). Pioneered in industry by Jack Welch at General Electric in 1999 to teach top-level executives about the Internet, many businesses and institutions now recruit younger professionals to teach new technologies to senior staff members who want to learn more (DeAngelis, 2013). Reverse mentoring provides an opportunity for learning by both participants and is a creative way of engaging millennial employees in leadership development (Murphy, 2012). Changes in work culture and increased retention of millennial employees are some of the benefits of reverse mentoring. However, because new faculty have relatively little expertise in other areas of the academy, reverse mentoring works best when used in conjunction with other mentoring models (Hanover Research, 2014).

Multiple Mentors Models

Two decades ago Tierney and Bensimon (1996) argued that "the notion of a single experienced faculty member being willing and able to play the all-inclusive role of mentor to a protégé is wishful thinking" (p. 52). More recently, multiple mentors and group approaches are seen as viable alternatives to the traditional one-on-one model (ADVANCE Resource Center, 2008; Mathews, 2003; Sorcinelli & Yun, 2007). One of the goals of these newer models is to engage an array of people with different skills, knowledge, and values in mentoring the new faculty member.

Multiple mentorships engage faculty in non-hierarchical, collaborative, cross-cultural partnerships to support teaching, research, community outreach, work–life balance, and/or the tenure and promotion process (Sorcineli & Yun, 2007). This less-hierarchical and more reciprocal relationship may be more effective, especially for women and minority faculty (Chesler & Chesler, 2002; Sorcinelli & Yun, 2007). Another advantage this model affords new faculty is the opportunity to consider advice from multiple perspectives. The need to match a new faculty member with the perfect mentor is eliminated. More senior faculty may be willing to participate in mentoring when they realize they do not have to meet all the needs of a new faculty member.

Another non-traditional form of mentoring is group or peer mentoring. This highly effective, collaborative model takes place in group settings, such as a brown bag lunch, where new faculty members meet for informal information-sharing and/or problem solving. Participants are usually similar in age, rank, and experience within their institution (Angelique, Kyle, & Taylor, 2002). These meetings may be organized and facilitated by a college dean, department chair, or another leader (ADVANCE Resource Center, 2008). The advantage of peer mentoring is its informality. An agenda may or may not be set. Participants are free to share their concerns, frustrations, and doubts in a safe environment. Additionally, this mentoring model helps ease isolation and establishes professional relationships among early career faculty. The flexibility and informality of peer mentoring allow faculty to participate at their own pace. The flexibility in time and level of commitment address issues women often experience with the traditional mentorship model; that is, unpredictable family responsibilities and career interruptions (Chesler & Chesler, 2002).

Another approach to faculty mentoring being adopted by more and more institutions is mutual mentoring, also referred to as peer mentoring networks (Hanover Research, 2014). Peer communities advance teaching and scholarship, as well as provide advice on work–life balance, time management, and the tenure process (Angelique et al., 2002). Using a multicultural framework, Girves, Zepeda, and Gwathmey (2005) viewed the peer networking model of mentorship as more inclusive of women and minorities. Several universities including Northern Arizona University, the University of Massachusetts Amherst, the University of Southern Florida, and the University of Wisconsin at Oshkosh, offer a variety of on-line resources for network-based mentoring for new and minority faculty (Sorcinelli & Yun, 2007). Through peer mentoring networks "new faculty have the potential to evolve as change agents in the institution, instead of assimilating into the existing system" (Angelique et al., 2002, p. 196).

Mentoring networks are not necessarily institution-based. Several professional organizations offer early career support to its members. For example, the Earth Science Women's Network offers online international peer networking mentorship "to promote career development, build community, provide opportunities for informal mentoring and support, and facilitate professional collaborations" (Earth Science Women's Network, 2013). Additionally, the Society for Teaching of Psychology, a division of the American Psychological Association, pairs early career psychology faculty with mentors with similar interests via email, Internet, or telephone (Society for the Teaching of Psychology, n.d.).

Each model of mentoring has strengths and limitations; thus, many institutions of higher education are implementing a variety of mentoring models ranging from traditional one-on-one mentoring to peer mentoring, team mentoring, reverse mentoring, and mentoring networks in order to support and guide new faculty (Hanover Research, 2014).

BEST PRACTICES FOR FACULTY MENTORSHIP PROGRAMS

Regardless of the type of model or aims, successful faculty mentoring programs have the following characteristics:

- Administrative support at institution, college, and department levels
- Part of a more comprehensive faculty development program
- Clear purposes, goals, and strategies
- Voluntary participation
- Thoughtful mentor matching at hire
- Orientation/training for mentors and mentees
- Flexibility in mentoring style
- A welcoming and supportive climate of diverse populations
- Regular monitoring and evaluation (ADVANCE Resource Center, 2008; Hanover Research, 2014)

With these characteristics in mind, our university and college developed a mentoring program to recruit and retain a more diverse faculty.

FACULTY MENTORING AT URI

The primary goal of our university-wide mentor faculty initiative is leading new faculty toward successful promotion and tenure decision. In December 2006, URI's Provost approved a formal faculty mentoring policy stating,

> All URI colleges shall implement a mentoring policy that provides for effective mentoring for their new faculty. This mentoring shall consist of career-advancing guidance, as well as social and psychological support for the new faculty member. College policies shall include the provision of one or more mentor(s) to each new faculty member, some form of mentor training, and regular "checking in" to ensure that the needs of junior faculty are being met. (ADVANCE Resource Center, 2008, inside cover)

Nested in the work of URI's ADVANCE Institutional Transformation Project, a 5-year National Science Foundation grant (2003–2008) to improve and enrich science, technology, engineering, and mathematics faculty development through increased representation of women faculty, the university-wide mentoring policy addressed the goals of "(a) faculty recruitment and retention; (b) faculty development; (c) work–life balance; and (d) climate change" (ADVANCE Resource Center, 2008, p. i).

MENTORING MODEL IN THE URI
COLLEGE OF HUMAN SCIENCE AND SERVICES

Although the University has historically assigned a departmental mentor for new faculty members in each of the academic colleges prior to the start of the academic year, the College of Human Science and Services (HSS) established a faculty mentoring program of its own in the mid-1990s. HSS values the thoughtful mentor match at the time of hire, but recognizes the limitations of this traditional one-on-one mentoring model. The HSS Faculty Mentoring (HSSFM) program was established to help junior/pre-tenured faculty, first year to fifth year (prior to submitting a dossier for promotion and tenure), to create an effective career development plan in balancing teaching, research, and service during their untenured years. In addition, there was a psychosocial support backdrop to the program where pre-tenured faculty members could confidentially talk to each other about issues in their department and classrooms. The framework was centered on Sands and colleagues (Sands, Parson, & Duane, 1991), who suggested four categories of mentoring: (a) career guide; (b) friend; (c) information source; and (d) intellectual guide. Overall, the HSSFM program was created as a way to welcome pre-tenured faculty members to the College and to communicate that the HSS Dean's office cared about them and wanted to invest in their professional career and personal welfare.

HSSFM Program Format

Historically, at the beginning of the year, newly hired pre-tenured faculty members would complete a questionnaire designed by the Dean's office that would indicate their areas of interest (e.g., What do you feel you need mentoring on the most? How can we best serve you in terms of research, teaching, and service; work–life balance programs, workshops, networking, as you move through the University?) to be covered for the year. The Dean and Associate Dean would then create three to four meetings that would focus on these areas. One year the results of the questionnaire indicated that the new faculty wanted to oversee their own mentoring program; however, they never did meet due to a lack of structure with the meetings. They then asked the Dean's office to help them in planning the last two meetings of the year.

More recently, the Dean's office has taken a less hierarchical approach to the needs assessment of the new faculty. Instead of a questionnaire, the Deans meet with the new faculty at the beginning of the academic year to discuss and decide, in a more organic manner, what they would like their meetings to focus on throughout the year. This approach has resulted in more engagement and interest from the participants, as they wanted to be a part of that which they helped create.

Based on these collaborative discussions, the Dean's office organized three to four mentoring sessions a year around topics, including (a) best practices in pedagogy; (b) how to navigate the URI Research Office; (c) how to successfully submit grants and submit a successful IRB proposal; (d) how to manage disruptive students in the classroom; (e) how to develop a plan to balance teaching, research, and service; (f) what it means to be a twenty-first century scholar; (g) how to build a research lab that involves undergraduate and graduate students; (h) how to infuse cultural competence into one's curriculum; (i) how to work with a targeted mentor (a scholar outside of the college who has similar research interests); (j) what is required for a successful promotion and tenure decision, particularly if there were changes in senior administration; (k) how to couple one's service and outreach with his/her research agenda; and (l) best practices in writing and publishing, both collaborative and sole authored manuscripts.

This HSSFM program has utilized different models over the years, such as the traditional one-on-one, individualized model, peer mentoring, and informal mentoring (Sorcinelli & Yun, 2007) when planning meetings to discuss the aforementioned topics.

Since the composition of our newer faculty has changed with more lecturers and clinical faculty hired in addition to the tenure-track faculty, the Dean's office has had to ensure that the mentor faculty meetings met the diverse needs and concerns of the faculty. For example, one year we added an additional meeting on best practices of pedagogy because teaching was a significant responsibility for the large number of new lecturers as well as the pre-tenured faculty. It was also important for the Dean's office to send the message that although the responsibilities may differ among the tenure-track faculty, lecturers, and clinical faculty, each plays a vital role in meeting the strategic objectives of the College and University.

In addition to the different types of faculty, another matter for consideration in the HSSFM program was the number of years in rank. A first-year pre-tenured faculty member may have different needs and concerns compared to a pre-tenured faculty member who is submitting a promotion and tenure package in the next year.

Further, in an attempt to introduce new faculty in HSS to other faculty and administrators internal and external to our college, the Dean's office often invites successful and well-respected faculty and administrators from HSS and other colleges, who are at an advanced rank, to serve as guest speakers at some of the HSSFM program meetings. It was important for our faculty to gain other perspectives on the similarities and differences in teaching, research, and service and expectations across disciplines in the College as well as the institution.

Addressing Diversity

One of the transformation goals of the President of URI, Dr. David Dooley, is "to build a community that values and embraces equity and diversity," where every member of the community will feel supported, and valued, and a part of the larger campus community (Dooley, 2011, p. 2). Since higher education institutions today realize the benefits of diversity and recognize the contributions and achievements of a diverse faculty, the HSSFM program wanted to make certain that discussions on diversity were had with the pre-tenured faculty.

One diversity-centered meeting we organized focused on methods of infusing cultural competence into one's curriculum. There had been some questions during one of the discussions on best practices in pedagogy about how to handle questions sensitively and respectfully that arise during classroom discussions about race, religion, sexual orientation, and gender. Consequently, we asked one of our faculty members, who was an expert in the field of diversity and social justice and who had been a part of the HSSFM program two years prior, to lead a workshop in this area that highlighted the need for more of this type of training other than just in the HSSFM program. As a result, the Dean organized a college-wide professional development retreat on teaching twenty-first century students including a professional acting group from Massachusetts who, through live character interaction and role-play, helped our faculty at all levels to examine complex issues of diversity.

In addition to working together to build a culture where diverse students are embraced and valued, it is imperative that we build a culture where we recruit, mentor, and retain faculty and scholars of color (Guzman, Trevino, Lubuguin, & Aryan, 2010). As a result, the Dean's office also encouraged faculty to attend URI's Safe Zone training. This two-hour workshop focused on basic issues affecting the LGBTQ community and how to be an ally. By increasing awareness, knowledge, and support of the LGBTQ community, the goal is to mitigate potential micro aggressions between and among new faculty, their fellow colleagues, and their students.

Mentoring cultural competence for women is important with scholars of color and the LGBTQ community. Research suggests that a successful mentoring program for women includes a traditional model (i.e., more experienced faculty member mentoring a pre-tenured faculty member), as well as alternative models including multiple mentoring (one mentor and a team of mentees), and creating a culture that values mentorship and relationship building and devalues competitive relationships (Chesler & Chesler, 2002). Further, Kosoko-Lasaki, Sonnnino, and Voytko (2006) found that implementing a mentoring program for pre-tenured faculty women and for underrepresented minorities increased the retention rates and promotion of women faculty.

Expansion From Pre-Tenured Faculty to Mid-Career Faculty

The HSS Dean's office took the initiative to expand the HSSFM program to include informal discussions with the mid-career faculty, or associate professors, in our college (see Figure 3.1). These discussions were prompted by the literature on the gender imbalance of women associate professors, nation-wide, in earning promotion to full professor and research suggesting that associate professors are some of the most unhappy faculty on campus (Wilson, 2012). For example, it has been reported that women full professors, in four-year higher education institutions comprised only 27% of the total in 2010–2011 in that rank (Knapp, Kelly-Reid, & Ginder, 2011). Further, the average time women associate professors spend in rank prior to promotion is 8.2 years compared to 6.6 years for men.

In addition to the gender imbalance, associate professors reported overall dissatisfaction with regard to mentoring and research support (Modern Language Association, 2009). At most higher education institutions, more attention is paid to navigating the path from assistant to associate professor; yet, in many cases, promotion from associate to full professor is more

Multi-Dimensional Mentoring Model

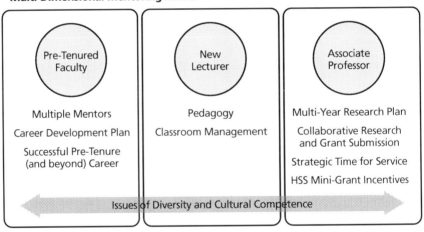

Figure 3.1 Graphic representation of the multi-dimensional model for mentoring faculty used by the College of Human Science and Services at the University of Rhode Island.

ambiguous than the tenure and promotion process. As a result, the Dean and Association Dean called a lunch meeting with all of the associate professors to discuss their progress, or lack thereof, toward promotion to full professors. We heard many of these faculty state that their careers were stagnant; they had too-high teaching loads; and that they did not have a plan, particularly in terms of research, that would lead them to a successful promotion to the next level. As a result, the Dean's office met with the associate professors who were interested in mapping a plan for promotion to full professor that included (a) developing a more collaborative approach to research and external grant submissions; (b) identifying researchers across our college and other colleges with similar interests with whom they could collaborate; (c) being more strategic in serving on less time intensive university-wide committees; and (d) developing a clear multi-year plan regarding their research production (i.e., a timeline for when they would collect and analyze data; submit a manuscript or write a book prospectus or chapter).

These discussions also prompted the Dean's office to create three internal grants for which our faculty could apply. The first was a *Midcareer Grant* made available for faculty 7 to 20 years past their first promotion to a tenured position to provide support and encouragement to faculty at this critical stage of their careers. A one-time award of $5000 was awarded based on the quality, significance, and productivity of the applicant's research project.

The second grant opportunity, *Scholarship of Teaching and Learning Grant*, demonstrated our sensitivity to our faculty's high teaching load, as well as our college's commitment to cultivating an environment for faculty to become teacher-scholars. We offered two grants, of up to $3500 each, for an individual or team of tenure-track faculty to provide support for the development, implementation, and assessment of a pedagogical approach intended to address a specific challenge to student learning. Pedagogy was defined as the art and science of teaching. Examples of pedagogical approaches included collaborative learning, problem-and project-based learning, case-based learning, game-based learning, discussion and debate, written assignments, blended/online learning, inquiry, service learning, and new uses of technology, among others. The outcome of this grant award was to take the results of the pedagogical approach, write a manuscript, and submit it to a peer-reviewed journal.

The third HSS grant, *From Presentation to Publication*, focused on the college's continued commitment to faculty research and scholarship. Whether it was due to a high teaching load and/or numerous service commitments, the data we collected on faculty scholarly productivity demonstrated that conference presentations out-numbered manuscript publications by more than 2:1. To promote more publications, the Dean's office made available four grants up to $5000 for faculty to transform a recent conference presentation into a manuscript and submit it for publication. With the awarding of these grants, the Dean's office saw an increase in faculty publications and increased collaboration between assistant and associate professors in submitting grant proposals and manuscripts.

In addition to the grants, the Dean's office continued to be sensitive to the gender imbalance of associate professors and was vigilant in asking both men and women faculty to serve on college and/or university-wide committees. The Dean would also highlight the importance and legitimacy of service-related committee work in meeting the strategic university objectives in annual review and promotion letters at the Dean's level.

The Dean and Associate Dean also played an integral role in calling attention to the inequities between men and women associate professors' promotion to full professor. During the University's inaugural Women's Leadership Initiative, a day-long conference held in fall 2015, faculty, staff, and graduate students focused on gender and leadership, exploring communication strategies, and engaging networks and mentoring.

CONCLUSION

The HSSFM program was created as a way to ensure a successful pre-tenure career (and beyond) for pre-tenured faculty. As the path to promotion and tenure becomes more competitive and challenging with increasing teaching and research demands, mentoring pre-tenured faculty should be a fundamental role and responsibility of any college's Dean's office. To attract and retain talented faculty, colleges and universities need to create an authentic mentoring program that uses various models where peers and administrators can obtain information about a pre-tenured faculty member's ambitions, needs, and capabilities. We have provided intellectual, professional, and social support in the HSSFM program by using models such as one-on-one, informal, peer, and group mentoring. Our HSSFM program provides faculty with administrative support at the university, college, and department levels. Perhaps it will be necessary to examine and implement other models in tandem, such as one-on-one mentoring and reverse mentoring, where an untenured faculty member mentors a senior faculty member in the area of their expertise (e.g., ways to use technology to be more effective in writing a manuscript). We will continue to review trends in higher education that will inform us on how we can meet the needs of our diverse, untenured faculty to help them successfully navigate their career trajectories.

REFERENCES

ADVANCE Resource Center. (2008). *Faculty mentoring handbook: A tool for ensuring faculty success.* Kingston, RI: University of Rhode Island.

Angelique, H., Kyle, K., & Taylor, E. (2002). Mentors and muses: New strategies for academic success. *Innovative Higher Education, 26*(3), 195–209.

Cartwright, D. G. (2008). *Western guide to mentorship in academia.* London, Ontario, Canada: The University of Western Ontario Teacher Support Center.

Chesler, N. C., & Chesler, M. A. (2002). Gender-informed mentoring strategies for women engineering scholars: On establishing a caring community. *Journal of Engineering Education, 91*(1), 49–55.

Collaborative on Academic Careers in Higher Education. (2014). *Benchmark best practices: Tenure & promotion.* Cambridge, MA: Harvard Graduate School of Education.

DeAngelis, K. L. (2013). *Reverse mentoring at The Hartford: Cross-generational transfer of knowledge about social media.* Chestnut Hill, MA: Sloan Center on Aging & Work, Boston College.

De Janasz, S. C., & Sullivan, S. E. (2004). Multiple mentoring in academe: Developing the professional network. *Journal of Vocational Behavior, 64*(2), 263–283.

DeJoy D. M., & Wilson, M. G. (2003). Organizational health promotion: Broadening the horizon of workplace health promotion. *American Journal of Health Promotion, 17*, 337–341.

Deloitte. (2014). *Big demands and high expectations: The Deloitte millennial survey, Executive summary.* London, England: Deloitte Touche Tohmatsu Limited.

Dooley, D. (2011). Transformational goals for the 21st century. Retrieved from http://www.uri.edu/president/TransformationalGoals.pdf

Earth Science Women's Network. (2013). Retrieved from http://eswnonline.org/

Girves, J. E., Zepeda, Y., & Gwathmey, J. K. (2005). Mentoring in a post-affirmative action world. *Journal of Social Issues, 61*(3), 449–479.

Grawitch, M. J., Gottschalk, M., & Munz, D. C. (2006). The path to a healthy workplace: A critical review linking healthy workplace practices, employee well-being, and organizational improvements. *Consulting Psychology Journal: Practice and Research, 58*(3), 129–147.

Guzman, F., Trevino, J., Lubuguin, F., & Aryan, B. (2010). Microaggressions and the pipeline for scholars of color. In D. W. Sue (Ed.), *Microaggressions and marginality: Manifestation, dynamics, and impact* (pp. 145–167). Hoboken, NJ: Wiley.

Hanover Research. (2014, January). *Faculty mentoring models and effective practices.* Washington, DC: Author.

Hall, R. M., & Sandler, B. R. (1983). *Academic mentoring for women students and faculty: A new look at the old way to get ahead.* Washington, DC: The Project on the Status and Education of Women, Association of American Colleges and Universities.

Johnson, W. B. (2007). *On being a mentor: A guide for higher education faculty.* Mahwah, NJ: Lawrence Erlbaum Associates.

Kelly, R. (2007). Now is the time to prepare for millennial faculty. *Academic Leader, 23*(2), 1, 6.

Knapp, L. G., Kelly-Reid, J. E., & Ginder, S. A. (2011). *Employees in postsecondary institutions, fall 2011, and salaries of full-time instructional staff, 2010–11* (NCES

2012-276). U.S. Department of Education. Washington, DC: National Center for Education Statistics. Retrieved from http://nces.ed.gov/pubsearch .

Kosoko-Lasaki, O., Sonnnino, R. E., & Voytko, M. L. (2006). Mentoring for women and underrepresented minority faculty and students: Experience at two institutions of higher education. *Journal of the National Medical Association, 98*(9), 1449–1459.

Mathews, P. (2003). Academic monitoring: Enhancing the use of scarce resources. *Educational Management and Administration, 31*(3), 313–334.

Millennial Branding & Beyond.com. (2013). *The cost of millennial retention.* Boston, MA: Authors.

Modern Language Association. (2009). *Standing still: The associate professor survey: Report of the Committee on the Status of Women in the Profession.* Retrieved from www.mla.org/cswp_report09

Murphy, W. M. (2012). Reverse mentoring at work: Fostering cross-generational learning and developing millennial leaders. *Human Resource Management, 51*(4), 549–573.

Philipsen, M. I. (2008). *Challenges of the faculty career of women: Success & sacrifice.* San Francisco, CA: Jossey-Bass.

Rice, R. E., Sorcinelli, M. D., & Austin, A. E. (2000). *Heeding new voices: Academic careers for a new generation.* New Pathways Inquiry #7. Washington, DC: American Association for Higher Education.

Sands, R., Parson, A., & Duane, J. (1991). Faculty mentoring faculty in a public university. *The Journal of Higher Education, 62*(2), 174–193.

Sauter, S., Lim, S., & Murphy, L. (1996). Organizational health: A new paradigm for occupational stress research at NIOSH. *Japanese Journal of Occupational Mental Health, 4,* 248–254.

Society for Teaching of Psychology. (n.d.). Retrieved from http://teachpsych.org

Sorcinelli, M. D., & Yun, J. (2007). From mentor to mentoring networks: Mentoring in the new academy. *Change Magazine, 39*(6), 58–61.

Sorcinelli, M. D., & Yun, J. (2009). *Mutual mentoring guide.* Amherst, MA: University of Massachusetts.

Tierney, W., & Bensimon, E. (1996). *Promotion and tenure: Community and socialization in academe.* Albany, NY: State University of New York Press.

Wilson, R. (2012, June 3). Why are associate professors so unhappy? *Chronicle of Higher Education.* Retrieved from http://chronicle.com/article/Why-Are -Associate-Professors/132071/

CHAPTER 4

THREE Ds ON MENTORING

Different Experiences, Different Stages, and Different Disciplines

Amy L. Sedivy-Benton
University of Arkansas at Little Rock

Nancy Feyl Chavkin
Texas State University

Carrie J. Boden-McGill
Texas State University

Mentoring on university campuses is indeed a very popular concept. Mentoring is often mentioned as the policy solution for increased standards and retention of both faculty and students (Colley, 2002). Frequently, new faculty are either assigned mentors or asked to seek out mentors. Student mentoring programs have also become major initiatives at the university level. There is a National Mentoring Summit (MENTOR, 2015), and even a National Mentoring Month toolkit (2015). A brief search reveals that the Internet is replete with many websites, blogs, conferences, and tools devot-

Mentoring in Formal and Informal Contexts, pages 57–76
Copyright © 2016 by Information Age Publishing

ed to mentoring (e.g., ProfHacker, 2014; Mentoring, 2015; Mentoring Institute, 2015). There are also a number of recent books such as W. Brad Johnson's *On Being a Mentor: A Guide for Higher Education Faculty* (2015); Susan L. Phillips and Susan T. Dennison's *Faculty Mentoring: A Practical Manual for Mentors, Mentees, Administrators, and Faculty Developers* (2015); and Dwayne Mack, Elwood D. Watson, and Michelle Madsen Camacho's edited book on *Mentoring Faculty of Color: Essays on Professional Development and Advancement in Colleges and Universities* (2012). It seems that everyone has something to say about the word mentor, whether it is a noun or a verb (Ferriss, 2014).

At first glance, it would seem that mentoring is an exciting new phenomenon; however, mentoring is not new. Barondess (1995), Schwiebert (2000), and Colley (2001, 2002) have written about the history of mentoring and report that the concept of mentoring has been around since the time of Homer's *The Odyssey* (1996), an epic poem from more than 3000 years ago. *The Odyssey* has a character named Mentor, who functions as a trusted advisor. Interestingly, some literature uses this example from *The Odyssey* to argue for the functions of a mentor as a very nurturing, supportive role model. Other literature focuses more on the relationship stating it was actually the Goddess Athene disguised as Mentor who was the real mentor representing self-sacrifice and inspiration. Still others, according to Colley (2002), use Feminist, Marxist, and anti-racist lenses to try to define mentoring by this historical myth. Colley argues that one needs to consider the context of mentoring, and that none of these approaches individually helps us understand the current context of mentoring. Other authors such as Kram (1985) and Chao (1997) suggest that mentoring has four phases (Initiation, Cultivation, Separation, and Redefinition), and that we need to consider mentoring by each phase.

Whether one agrees with the descriptions of mentoring that were developed in earlier times, this previous literature raises important questions about the need for more discussion on mentoring and clearer definitions of the types of mentoring on university campuses. Our purpose in this chapter is to expand the understanding of what mentoring means at a university level in the twentieth-first century. There has been a great deal written about mentoring of youth and children (Colley, 2002; Kram, 1985). Although mentoring at the university level has some similarities to mentoring of youth and children, it also varies by discipline and career stage. This chapter provides three personal perspectives on experiences with mentoring from mentors at three different stages in their careers in three different academic disciplines. We explore questions about the differences (our 3 D's—experiences, stages, disciplines) and the lessons learned from each.

The chapter begins with a literature review of formal and informal mentoring experiences followed by vignettes. Each vignette presents the professional's personal knowledge, background, and attitudes toward mentoring related to stage and field. Following the vignettes, the authors discuss lessons learned for their fields and for higher education.

SELECT REVIEW OF MENTORING LITERATURE

Formal Mentoring

There are a variety of discipline-specific and interdisciplinary studies of mentoring in professional fields such as education, law, and medicine, which require some type of apprenticeship (Kram & Ragins, 2007; Rockoff, 2008). Much of this literature discusses benefits of formal mentoring such as employee satisfaction and retention. Formal mentoring programs are often facilitated by a coordinator (Bell & Treleaven, 2011), and the premise of these programs is to pair one individual with a peer who is generally more experienced in the field (Ferman, 2002). Formal mentoring programs often focus on measurable outcomes and passing on information and knowledge from the mentor to the mentee. There is often little flexibility in selecting a mentor, and compatibility is not considered. Rather, the mentor and mentee are paired based upon specific criteria (Hamburg, 2013). Formal mentoring tends to be set for a fixed amount of time, which is determined by the completion of the mentoring goal or objective.

Formal mentoring programs are helpful in that they have specific outcomes and allow the mentor and mentee to move forward toward the same goal. The training and structure is well-defined with set meeting dates and goals associated with each meeting. Since mentors are assigned, mentees do not need to find a mentor, and there is a sense of knowing that help will be present if needed. Formal mentoring programs tend to fall in line with the overall goals and objectives of the organization, furthering the premise of the group working collaboratively toward the same goal as a team. The idea behind this is that, overall, there will be increased outcomes from both the mentor and the mentee (Chun, Sosik, & Yun, 2012). In many instances, such as in a study of teachers by Glazerman et al. (2010), formal mentoring programs did indeed contribute to professional development and were beneficial.

In other instances, formal mentoring is less helpful. A downfall of formalized mentoring structures is that close and supportive interpersonal relationships may not form (Borders et al., 2011; Management Matters, 2013). Simply because someone is assigned or matched to a mentor does not mean that these individuals will find compatibility with one another. Incompatibilities could range from personality conflicts, to work habits, to methods for how deadlines are met. If a relationship is forced, it could be a mismatch that provides an unpleasant result for both the mentor and the mentee. Sometimes, assigned mentoring relationships simply do not meet the needs of mentees, and informal mentoring relationship may fill these gaps (Desimone et al., 2014).

Informal Mentoring

Unlike formal mentoring, informal mentoring has no pre-planned agenda. The nature of the mentoring relationship derives from the individuals involved as well as their goals and needs. There is no set structure; the mentoring organically occurs between colleagues, peers, or friends. Informal mentoring relationships are generally casual, natural, episodic, and authentic (Barrett & Brown, 2014; Desimone et al., 2014; Ragins, 2007). There is less literature on informal mentorship than on other forms of mentoring (James, Rayner, & Bruno, 2015). Generally, informal mentors perform two functions to support their mentees: assistance with career development, which assists mentees with advancement in their field or organization, and psychosocial support, which contributes to the mentee's personal and professional development (Kram, 1985; Kram & Ragins, 2007).

There are many advantages to informal mentoring. In a study of more than 600 mentees in fields such as engineering, social work, and journalism, Ragins and Cotton (1999) found that mentees of informal mentors reported that their mentors were more helpful than those who worked with formal mentors. Mentees of informal mentorships also realized greater compensation and career achievement than those who worked with formal mentors or those who were not mentored. Likewise, in regard to higher education, the literature indicates that informal mentoring can have a significant positive influence on career outcomes (Barrett & Brown, 2014; Dansky, 1996; Driscoll et al., 2009; Greene et al., 2008; McGuire & Reger, 2003). Informal mentoring is credited with improving career transitions and development of professional identity (Barrett & Brown, 2014), reducing intellectual poverty and outsider status in the academy (De Four-Babb, Pegg, & Beck, 2015), and assisting with acquiring skills for a successful academic career (Leslie, Lingard & Whyte, 2005).

Although informal mentoring can be very effective, there are several potential weaknesses. Because of the informal nature of the mentoring relationship, there may be different or lacking expectations between mentors and mentees. In a recent study, Welsh, Bhave, and Kim (2012) found that neither potential mentors nor mentees were accurate at identifying reciprocal mentoring partnerships; there was little agreement that mentoring was occurring. Another weakness of informal mentoring is that there is no formal agreement or commitment that holds the parties accountable, so informal mentoring relationships may be more difficult to maintain (Desimone et al., 2014). There is also no defined time frame for informal mentoring, which could be acute (related to a professional crisis, such as a negative review), situational (in response to an upcoming deadline or meeting a specific goal, such as completing a publication), or sporadic (on an as-needed basis); this could leave both parties confused about the nature and boundaries of the mentoring relationship. Last, informal mentoring can be a matter of happenstance. Zachary (2009) points out that those who need mentoring the most, rarely find mentors on their own, especially new employees who do not want to seem aggressive or naive. Connecting with the right mentor can be a combination of initiative and good timing.

MENTORING VIGNETTES

Vignette #1: "Paying it Forward" by Empowering Others

I (Nancy) am a female, first generation college graduate and one of seven children from a large, rural family. I am currently a Regents' Professor of Social Work at a large state university. I have been teaching at the university for the last 28 years. My family was working class and valued education. I did not set out with the goal of becoming a college professor. I did not know anyone who was a professor, and the only professional career that I could envision was that of a high school teacher. The few people I knew from my small rural community who had gone to college were teachers in the public schools. All of my mentoring, from starting the college track in high school, going to college, going to graduate school, choosing to become a professor, and rising through the ranks of assistant to full professor, has been informal in nature. I have been a mentor many times through both formal programs and informal programs, and I have received awards for mentoring. My profession is social work, and mentoring is embedded in our *National Association of Social Workers' Code of Ethics*, adopted in 1996 and revised in 2008. A recent issue of *The New Social Worker* focused on the importance of mentoring in the profession and how to seek a mentor (Meyette, 2015). My profession strongly supports mentoring and sees it as a helpful tool for empowering individuals to excel. Gutiérrez (2012) writes about the need to value the role of mentor in social work, and Pomeroy and Steiker (2011) emphasize the importance of "paying it forward." Others, such as Smith (2015) discuss the challenges of virtual mentoring with online faculty. Chadiha and colleagues (Chadiha, Aranda, Biegel, & Chang, 2014) write about the importance of mentoring faculty of color.

Although I have had no personal mentoring through formal programs, I have been a mentor to others through formal programs. I cannot recall the availability of any formal mentoring programs in my personal educational and career path. Perhaps there were some, and I did not have the opportunity to take advantage of them. It is also possible that there were different words or formats for what we call mentoring today. Over the last 40 years, I have been a formal mentor to many. I will share a few of these experiences below, beginning with my first experience as a mentor.

While I was working during the second year at my first professional job as a school social worker, I had my first mentee. It was a combination of a mentee/field instructor role. She was a student social work intern just a couple of years younger than me. The university recruited me specifically because I was a recent graduate and might relate well to students. As I look back, I think there was a push at the time to soften the traditional supervisor role to more of a mentor role. I was thrilled at the opportunity and enthusiastically went to training at the university, before she came on the job, and several times during that year. The training was a bit disappointing. It was primarily about what she needed to experience during the year and the paperwork required. There was no content on the process of mentoring, just the minimum requirement for two hours of meeting a week. We decided to meet daily at first and then moved to twice weekly as she gradually took on more responsibility and did less job shadowing. We bonded and built a strong relationship which allowed for providing two-way feedback. The best part of the experience for me was that I gained so much from her questions. We were both committed to social justice issues. She was different than me in many ways, and I enjoyed having a mentee from whom I could also learn. She was not always the rule-follower, but she was passionate and creative about her work. She challenged me to think out of the box and question some of the rules. Together, I think we created some great programs and shared our commitment to making the world a better place. Interestingly, we both later became college professors of social work committed to "paying it forward." As other authors such as McGuire & Reger (2003) report, my first experience with mentoring was almost co-mentoring since I was close in age to my mentee and new to the profession. Our experience was built on a personal relationship.

After this first experience, I was sold on mentoring and took on several more formal relationships in the next five years as a school social worker. Each experience was a bit different, but each time worked out well in its own way. Without knowing the literature, I quickly learned that my mentoring needed to pay attention to the context of mentoring and many factors such as gender, race, ethnicity, generation, and culture (McAfee & Hansman, 2012). I still have relationships (albeit long distance) with most of these mentees.

My experiences in formal mentoring at the university level fall into the two main categories of student mentoring and faculty mentoring. I have mentored students at various levels in my field and not, and have been involved in faculty mentoring relationships at various levels, both in my field and not. The students I mentored in my field have been at the Bachelor of Social Work (BSW), Master of Social Work (MSW), and PhD levels. The BSW students were excited and ready to learn everything possible. They wanted it all. The MSW students were more focused and ready to narrow down their career choices. The PhD students were clearly concerned with conducting dissertation research and getting the right job. All of these mentor/mentee relationships had a connection to a formal program. Sometimes there was training, but often there was not. My experience is that doctoral students who had strong mentoring relationships finished their dissertations and got jobs, which is well supported in the literature (Liechty, Liao, & Pegorraro Schull, 2009; Tijerina & Deepak, 2014). The only negative experience I had with mentoring through these formal programs was when two undergraduate students, not in my field, were assigned as my mentees, but never really wanted a mentor. This happened on only two occasions, so it certainly has been the minority of students who have not taken advantage of the opportunity. I probably tried more than most, but, in the end, it became clear that the scheduling was not going to happen. For my faculty mentoring relationships, all the formal relationships have been positive. In relationships with faculty mentees in my field, the meetings seemed to be more frequent and more intense than with faculty mentees not in my field.

I have been informally mentored since beginning my doctoral program. I was very fortunate to have a strong support system at home because my husband had already earned his PhD in a different field. He clearly understood the complexities of moving from doctoral student to new professor. He guided me in getting my first job and handling the tenure process. Another positive informal mentoring experience came from my relationship with my first department head. She was eager to have outstanding colleagues and build our program. She let me know about opportunities, would provide feedback on publications, and co-authored publications with me.

I have been an informal mentor to many students, faculty, and staff at the university. I believe in what Pomeroy and Steiker (2011) called, "paying it forward." Many new colleagues have sought me out and asked for regular feedback about how to succeed. Some of these relationships were frequent, and some were more sporadic (on an as-needed basis). I had the privilege of watching many students blossom into excellent social workers and many junior faculty become tenured senior faculty. These mentoring relationships transformed into strong collegial relationships. I have also had the opportunity to informally mentor staff by encouraging them to seek higher education and professional development. The only informal mentoring experience that ended on a negative note was when a colleague did not get tenure. The colleague reported that she did not get the right kind of mentoring, and although I was only one of several informal mentors and not the official mentor, I have always felt sad about this occurrence. There seemed to be a difference in expectations, and I think she and all of her mentors felt disappointed by the outcome.

I have been very fortunate that most of my mentoring relationships went extremely well, but questions remain for me. What happens if mentoring relationships do not go well? What are the boundaries between supervising and mentoring? Is it okay to mix the two? Should a supervisor be a mentor? What if there were supervision issues that could not be resolved by mentoring? How much responsibility for success of the relationship should the mentor have? What are the mentee's responsibilities?

Mentoring Vignette #2: The Invisible Thread

In George MacDonald's (1911) fairy tale, *The Princess and the Goblin*, young Princess Irene is given the gift of a ring with an invisible thread attached to it from her namesake and great-grandmother. According to the great-grandmother, the magic, invisible thread will guide Irene through challenges in life and constantly connect her to home. Irene is initially disappointed in the gift because *she cannot see the thread*, but in the end, as often happens in fairy-tales, Irene learns to appreciate the power of the thread, and this seemingly dud of a gift saves the life of Irene and others. This story provides a perfect metaphor—on many levels—for how I think of the role of mentoring in my professional life.

I (Carrie) grew up on the Great Plains of Texas, Nebraska, and Kansas in a middle-class family that touted education and hard work as the pathways to "getting ahead." I always knew that I would attend college, but was less certain of what I might study. As a traditionally-aged student, the mentoring I received both inside and outside the classroom determined the life trajectory that has followed—particularly in relation to the value placed on further education and the importance of social justice, threads that have run through my career. I was encouraged by my many mentors to pursue advanced degrees and to select fields of study that made a positive impact on others. I finished an undergraduate degree in four years and went straight into a master's and then a PhD program.

In the second semester of my master's program, I started teaching; I was just a few years older than the majority of the students in the class. Later in my career, I taught exclusively in programs designed for adult students, where it was not uncommon for the average age of students to be 10 years my senior. Throughout my career in academe thus far, I have been relatively young in relation to the roles I have performed. I have also specialized in fields, first English/creative writing and later adult education, which focus on individual development and meaning-making as an integral part of learning. Due in part to the age-role discrepancies and in part to my constructivist leanings, I have often considered myself a co-learner in the classroom and in mentoring relationships, regardless of what side of the desk I occupy at any given moment.

Currently, I find myself on both sides of the desk quite often. I am a mid-career academic who was recently promoted to Professor of Occupational, Workforce, and Leadership Studies at a large state university. I am simultaneously the senior faculty member and one of the youngest members of my department. On any given day, I mentor students and junior faculty and am mentored by administrators, colleagues, and friends. I consider mentoring faculty and students my responsibility as a professor (Commission of Professors of Adult Education, 2014), and I intentionally seek out opportunities to mentor others. For example, I founded a book series associated with the AHEA annual conference with the intent to create a space for doctoral students, junior faculty, and others to transform a conference presentation into a publishable paper. The book series established both emerging and established voices and has grown and evolved. Currently, the series uses a competitive proposal process and has become a venue for new and established editors to share their passions, hopes, and visions for the field. In ways beyond my initial conception, the series lived out its mission in providing a supportive venue for those in the field to learn the publication process. Simultaneously, I am also mentored almost daily and engage in tasks, such as in learning new course content or incorporating new technologies into my online courses, where I seek out the council of specialists and more-experienced peers. As I reflect back on my experiences, I realize that I have seen this dual-role modeled extensively—during my undergraduate studies at Bethel College, early in my career at Friends University, during my doctoral program at Kansas State University, and currently in the professional field of adult education. I have had—and continue to have—the good fortune of immersion in communities that value co-learning and co-mentoring.

The first instance of co-mentoring and learning I can recall is during my undergraduate program. While studying literature and creative writing, my role was as much to absorb information from the literary tradition as it was to continue the conversation through literary analysis and creation of new literary works. During my undergraduate and graduate studies, revered professors and mentors shared works that they loved deeply, in the sensibility of Wordsworth, "what we have loved, others will love, and we will teach them how . . ." (as cited in Schmidt, 1999), while also inviting me to discover my own literary sensibilities and individual voice as a writer. I distinctly remember one time when I asked a beloved professor, "How do I learn to think more like you?" and the reply was, "You don't. I'm not trying to create a clone but to nurture something in you that is not within me."

During my doctoral studies, the roles of co-learner and co-mentor continued. I already held a terminal degree and was working full-time as a tenure-track professor when I began a PhD program. I was also an early adopter of technology and online teaching. Because of these factors, I was often seen as both a colleague and a student to the PhD program professors. As a colleague, I had a similar work-a-day world, and I was "ahead of the curve" in terms of my facility with online tools. Yet, as a learner, I was exposed to a completely new field of study and was in need of guidance in learning the culture, context, history, and future dreams for the field. Throughout my studies, I was on firm ground both as a student and as a contributor to a learning community.

In my first tenure-track position, I was informally and extensively mentored by senior faculty, who taught me how to be a productive faculty member, colleague, and university citizen. I was schooled in the rights and responsibilities of faculty life, expectations for engaging in collaboration and lifting up one another as colleagues, and importance of the role of educating and mentoring students. This foundation has allowed me to build strong mentoring relationships with students and faculty throughout my career; I simultaneously "lifted and climbed" as I navigated the tenure-track and academic ranks while encouraging colleagues and students to reach their goals.

In retrospect, few of my mentoring relationships have been formal; all have been intentional. The individuals in this mosaic who mentored me decided, at some point, that it was important to assist me along the way, teach a life lesson, help me navigate a system, lead by example, take responsibility for shaping another, or create a path where a path did not previously exist. Likewise, as I have committed to investing in others, it has been a decision to be vulnerable (Brown, 2010), to trust, to be my authentic human self, and to do the best I could with any situation presented to me. The point of these mentoring exchanges were, as Freire so elegantly noted, "to make it possible for the [others] to become themselves" (as cited in Bell, Gaventa, & Peters, 1990)—their best possible selves.

The intention to help someone become their best possible self though mentoring does not always produce the desired results. It takes a certain kind of courage to invest in people, who are human and will inevitably fail, stumble, or disappoint, but who also have the ability to dazzle, amaze, and transcend. When the investment is made up-front, it is a gamble—no guarantee of a return. There is only a hope for the future, for the person, or something much larger than oneself. As mentee and mentor, I have had my share of both successes and flops—both provided learning and growth opportunities and ultimately were gifts. These gifts are the reason I recommit to mentoring and to being mentored on a continual basis.

At a fairly recent women professor's retreat, the attendees discussed the story of *The Princess and the Goblin* and participated in an exercise to make the invisible threads of connection among us visible—each person told a story of connection and then tossed a ball of yarn to the other person in the story. The end result was a web of beautiful connections unfolding in authentic and unanticipated ways. When I use this as a starting point to make the invisible threads of mentorship visible in my life, the mental map of connections stretches from this circle on Yukon Island, Alaska, to Washington State, across the northwest to Chicago, on to the East Coast, and through the South to Florida. There are multiple threads in Kansas, Arkansas, and Texas. There are threads that span the globe. Like the magic thread in the story of *The Princess and the Goblin*, these connections lead me "home" to my field and to relationships that have defined and will define my career—who I am and who I will become. The strands unfurl to reach people I know as well as ones I do not know—these are my teachers and my students, my colleagues and my friends, friends and students of my colleagues and students. I came into the academy because I wanted to work with both people and ideas. The invisible thread of mentoring—made visible through this reflection—demonstrates the ways that I am deeply connected with both.

Mentoring Vignette #3: The Mentee

I (Amy) am currently an Assistant Professor in Teacher Education in a mid-sized university in an urban setting. Coming from a working class family in rural Colorado, I was one of two children. Education was something that was always stressed, but there was not a clear path on how this might be achieved. Other than knowing that education was important, it was up to me to navigate the college experience. While there were guidance counselors placed within my school, there was no direction regarding what areas of study might be available or how to go about the application process. This lack of mentorship and guidance may help explain why only four students from my graduating class went on to college right after high school. As I tried to navigate this path to college independently, there were a few mistakes along the way. For example, I applied to too many schools because I did not know which ones I could afford to attend. I needed mentoring to figure out where I should go and how I might pay for my education. There were many facets of college, such as the involvement in various student activities, which I was unable to experience because I worked many hours per week in order to pay for my college tuition. The best advantage that I had was the emotional support from my family. These are all characteristics that are commonly found in first generation college students (Johnson, Richeson, & Finkel, 2011). Looking back on this experience, there was a void of any type of mentor in my life to help lead and support me through this process. While I successfully navigated this process, it was done primarily by trial and error.

I became the first and only person in my family to obtain a bachelor's degree. As time went by, I pursued and received advanced degrees, and this was enhanced by the college experiences in which I was able to participate (Astin, 1984). Upon completion of my master's degree, I knew that I would like to go on to earn my doctorate. It was during my doctoral experience that I learned what it meant to have a mentor/mentee relationship.

The doctoral program that I attended had several faculty members who were well known in their fields. These faculty members were open to sharing their knowledge and experiences. One of the most valuable things that they provided to current students was connections to alumni of the program. I took advantage of this opportunity, and this is how my first mentor and I found one another. Shortly after we were connected, we discovered that we both worked for the same not-for-profit organization and shared a passion for education and assessment. As a new professional in the field, this was an ideal match; we were able to share ideas and learn from one another (Ragins & Cotton, 1999). My mentor's door was always open; he challenged me, acted as a sounding board for my ideas, and allowed me to fail. I learned from failure because he also supported me when I had to correct my course of action. Our working relationship was very fluid. His approach to problems was always broad and at times a bit vague. Based on our interactions, I was able to take those broad issues and turn them into workable projects. My mentor always encouraged me and challenged me at the same time. It was as if he recognized that I needed to grow both professionally as well as personally. He put forth the effort to make sure that I was present when our collaborative work was being shared; he also made sure that I was part of the decision-making process. While I did not realize it at the time, this informal mentoring experience was invaluable to my professional and personal growth. To this day, we are still friends, and even though he has since retired, we remain in contact. I recently exchanged a call with him pertaining to an evaluation project, and he commented on how much I had grown since the inception of our relationship. I look back fondly on that experience and still smile as I reflect on how much I learned from him.

As I moved on through my profession, I had a desire to recreate the relationship that I had with my first mentor. This desire exposed me to a side of mentoring for which I was not prepared. As I moved from the not-for-profit sector into academia, I sought to establish a mentor/mentee relationship based upon my prior experience. After a few months in my new position, I felt that I potentially had found a mentor. The characteristics were similar to my first experience, and there were commonalities between both the faculty member and me. We were both open to working and supporting one another. However, as time progressed, I discovered that the more I shared with my mentor, the more obstructions were placed in my path. These entailed potential research projects being dismissed or deemed unworthy of publication or collaborative research projects not moving forward because there was no movement on my mentor's side. Over time, this became frustrating for me. I wanted a relationship that was built on implicit trust; I desired a mentor who had my best interest at heart. I began to feel that this relationship was a hindrance to my ability to move forward and accomplish my goals. This type of mentor/mentee experience closely aligns with the literature in which the mentor tries to impose their beliefs, and when the mentee does not comply, the mentor tends to feel threatened (Sánchez & Colon, 2005).

Based upon this frustration, I elected to end that relationship once I felt that I no longer had the mentor's support. Still struggling to adapt to the academic world, a colleague simply opened her door to me and stated that she would be willing to help me navigate the world of academia from publication to advising. This new informal mentorship was the exact opposite from my initial experience at the university; my new mentor helped me to successfully publish my first article and has continued to assist me as I go into the promotion and tenure process. Much like my first experience with a mentor, my latest experience has proven to evolve once again into not just a mentoring relationship, but one that has crossed over into friendship as well. While my personal experiences have not been vast, I have yet to fully experience a formal mentoring relationship. I am able to appreciate how positive informal mentoring can be.

LESSONS LEARNED

While we cannot possibly presume to discuss mentoring comprehensively, we would like to share some key lessons learned in our experiences with mentoring. These lessons span the 3Ds—different disciplines, career stages, and experiences. The following lessons learned include the importance of setting expectations, the positive effect of compatibility between mentors and mentees, the value of focusing on the individual needs of the mentee, the benefits of co-learning and co-mentoring opportunities, the necessity of multiple mentors, and the imperative not to take mentoring failures—or successes—personally.

Setting Expectations is Important

With both formal and informal mentoring, one of the most significant lessons we have learned is that it is crucial to discuss and clarify the expectations for mentoring. As Wilson, Pereira, and Valentine (2002) report, mentors and mentees often have different views of what the process should look like and what the outcomes should be. Programs for formal and informal mentoring are becoming more prevalent in higher education, and some mentees believe that having a mentor will fix everything. In actuality, mentoring is a very vague term. It means different things to different people (Ellison & Raskin, 2014; Rowan, 2009; Sands, Parson, & Duane, 1991; Strand & Bosco-Ruggiero, 2010). Clarity at the beginning, middle, and end of the process is needed to facilitate successful mentoring. It is important to understand what mentoring is and what mentors and mentees want to give and get from the process. Another important lesson that flows from getting clarity about the definition of mentoring is that there is a difference between supervision and mentoring. These boundaries may be obtuse in field settings; defining boundaries around summative evaluations and formative comments is essential. Both mentor and mentee need to understand the boundaries.

Mentoring Is About Relationships— Compatibility Is a Must

The mentoring experiences we have had that were most positive were always built on strong, open relationships. While the relationship part of the mentoring definition is hard to put into words, it cannot be dismissed. In the words of Titus, "It is the relationship that teaches" (as cited in Henschke, 2009). It does begin with open, clear communication and then continues with the development of trust. The mentoring relationship needs to be organic and rooted in compatibility. Just as other kinds of relationships need to evolve on their own, so do mentoring relationships. In our experiences, informal mentoring relationships were strengthened by development of mutual goals and outcomes that evolved over time.

Mentoring Is About the Mentee

Another lesson learned from our formal and informal experiences, as well as from the literature, is that the best mentoring is individualized to the needs of the mentee. A one size fits all approach to mentoring—especially those approaches focused on transmission of information—can be hit or miss in terms of effectiveness. Weimer (2015) shares the wisdom of her colleague and long-time teacher, Linda Shadiow, who notes, "Mentoring isn't about answering questions.... It's about asking questions ... those questions they [the mentees] are on the cusp of asking themselves" (para.

2). By asking the right questions, mentors can find answers to deeply rooted questions, concerns, and motivations of mentees. For mentoring students, answers to questions such as: Who are you? What do you hope to accomplish? Who do you admire? What are your goals? and What is most important to you?, can set a course for the mentoring to follow. In faculty-to-faculty mentoring, answers to the previous questions, as well as others such as: Why do you teach? What research questions interest you? What content do you love? Why is it important? What are your beliefs about teachings and learning? can also set the stage for effective mentoring.

Mentoring Is a Two-Way Street

In our experiences, as well as in the literature, there is a trend of mutual growth and enjoyment through mentoring. As mentees, we have gained much from those who came before us. As mentors, we have learned and grown from relationships with our mentees in tangible and intangible ways. When relationships are reciprocal and based on mutual respect, they can be enduring. Borders et al. (2011) found that under these circumstances, the mentoring relationships "are seen by some as more effective, meaningful, comfortable, relational and enduring" (p. 173).

Multiple Mentors Are Needed

Another theme that runs through our mentoring experiences and the literature is the idea that multiple mentors are needed and that the mentoring may take different forms. Mentoring may come from individuals who have differing strengths, expertise, and dispositions; in order to access this wellspring, multiple mentoring relationships are required (Bloom, 2007; McGuire & Reger, 2003). Another key to working with multiple mentors is finding the right format, such as learning communities, mastermind groups, one-on-one mentoring, etc. Sorcinelli and Yun (2007) advocate establishing mentoring networks that are flexible and "in which no single person is expected to possess the expertise required" for every facet of success (p. 5).

Mentoring Is Personal—But Do Not Take It Personally

Personal and professional growth cannot be dictated, forced, cajoled, or divined into being. A final lesson learned from our experiences and the literature is that responsibility for mentoring is with the mentee, and the outcome of the mentoring experience should not be taken personally. It is the responsibility of the mentee to operationalize (or not) the best advice and mentoring that has been given. It is also the responsibility of the mentee to seek out more or other mentors if a particular mentoring relationship is not helpful. It is the responsibility of the mentor to attend to the change that is already at work within the individual (Dirks, 1998). At times, this works gracefully, and other times, and for a variety of reasons (e.g., once mutual-goals are no longer shared, political situations change, the mentee is unsuccessful, there is unethical behavior or professional shenanigans), the process fails. It is as imperative to deal with the disappointments as it is to relish the successes. In either case, it is also necessary not to take the outcome personally. Ongoing mentoring is a professional responsibility, as outlined in ethics of our fields, as a well as a vocational calling. While the outcomes do matter, so do the intentions and commitments to continue to mentor and to learn. Mentoring is a mindset, and without it being nurtured and modeled, mentoring will not come into being and flourish on its own.

REFERENCES

Astin, A. W. (1984). Student involvement: A developmental theory for higher education. *Journal of College Student Personnel, 25*, 297–307.

Barondess, J. A. (1995). A brief history of mentoring. *Transactions of the American Clinical and Climatological Association, 106*, 1–24.

Barrett, J., & Brown, H. (2014). From learning comes meaning: Informal co-mentorship and the second-career academic in education. *The Qualitative Report, 19*, 1–15.

Bell, A., & Treleaven, L. (2011). Looking for professor right: Mentee selection of mentors in a formal mentoring program. *Higher Education, 61*(5), 545–561.

Bell, B., Gaventa, J., & Peters, J. (Eds.). (1990). *We make the road by walking: Conversations on education and social change. Myles Horton and Paulo Freire.* Philadelphia, PA: Temple University Press.

Bloom, L. Z. (2007). Mentoring and mosaic: Life as Guerilla Theater. *Composition Studies, 35*(2), 87–99.

Borders, L. D., Young, J. S., Wester, K. L., Murray, C. E., Vilalba, J. A., Lewis, T. F., & Mobley, A. E. (2011). Mentoring promotion/tenure-seeking faculty: Principles of good practice within a counselor education program. *Counselor Education & Supervision, 50*, 171–188.

Brown, B. (2010). The power of vulnerability TED talk. Retrieved from https://www.ted.com/talks/brene_brown_on_vulnerability/transcript?language=en

Chadiha, L. A., Aranda, M. P., Biegel, D. E., & Chang, C. (2014). The importance of mentoring faculty members of color in schools of social work. *Journal of Teaching in Social Work, 34*(4), 351–362.

Chao, G. T. (1997). Mentoring phases and outcomes. *Journal of Vocational Behavior, 51*, 15–28.

Chun, J. U., Sosik, J. J., & Yun, N. Y. (2012). A longitudinal study of mentor and protégé outcomes in formal mentoring relationships. *Journal of Organizational Behavior, 33*(8), 1071–1094.

Colley H. (2001). Righting re-writings of the myth of Mentor: A critical perspective on career guidance mentoring. *British Journal of Guidance and Counselling, 29*(2), 177–198.

Colley, H. (2002). A "rough guide" to the history of mentoring from a Marxist feminist perspective. *Journal of Education for Teaching: International Research and Pedagogy, 28*(3), 257–273.

Commission of Professors of Adult Education (2014). *Standards for graduate programs in adult education.* Retrieved from https://cpae.memberclicks.net/

Dansky, K. H. (1996). The effect of mentoring on career outcomes. *Group & Organization Management, 12*(1), 5–21. doi:10.1177/1059601196211002

De Four-Babb, J., Pegg, J., & Beck, M. (2015). Reducing intellectual poverty of outsiders within academic spaces through informal peer mentorship, mentoring & tutoring. *Partnership in Learning, 23*(1), 76–93. doi: 10.1080/13611267.2015.1011038

Desimone, L. M., Hochberg, E. D., Porter, A. C., Polikoff, M. S., Schwartz, R., & Johnson, L. J. (2014). Formal and informal mentoring: Complementary, compensatory, or consistent? *Journal of Teacher Education, 65*(2), 88–110.

Dirks, J. (1998). Transformative learning theory in the practice of adult education: An overview. *PAACE Journal of Lifelong Learning, 7,* 1–14.

Driscoll, L. G., Parkes, K. A., Tilley-Lubbs, G. A., Brill, J. M., & Pitts Bannister, V. R. (2009). Navigating the lonely sea: Peer mentoring and collaboration among aspiring women scholars. *Mentoring & Tutoring: Partnership in Learning, 17,* 5–21.

Ellison, M. L., & Raskin, M. S. (2014). Mentoring field directors: A national exploratory study. *Journal of Social Work Education, 50*(1), 69–83.

Ferman, T. (2002). Academic professional development practice: What lecturers find valuable. *International Journal for Academic Development, 7*(2), 146–158. doi:10.1080/1360144032000071305

Ferriss, L. (2014). Mentor, the verb. Retrieved from http://chronicle.com/blogs/linguafranca/2014/10/08/mentor-the-verb/

Glazerman, S., Isenberg, E., Dolfin, S., Bleeker, M., Johnson, A., Grider, M., & Jacobus, M. (2010). *Impacts of comprehensive teacher induction: Final results from a randomized controlled study* (NCEE 2010-4027). Washington, DC: National Center for Education Evaluation and Regional Assistance, Institute of Education Sciences, U.S. Department of Education.

Greene, H. C., O'Connor, K. A., Good, A. J., Ledford, C. C., Peel, B. B., & Zhang, G. (2008). Building a support system toward tenure: Challenges and needs of tenure-track faculty in colleges of education. *Mentoring & Tutoring: Partnership in Learning, 16,* 429–447.

Gutiérrez, L. M. (2012). Recognizing and valuing our roles as mentors. *Journal of Social Work Education, 48*(1), 1–4. doi:10.5175/ jSWE.2012.334800001

Hamburg, I. (2013, May). Facilitating learning and knowledge transfer through mentoring. *Proceedings of the 5th International Conference of Computer Supported*

Education (pp. 219–222). Retrieved from http://dblp.uni-trier.de/db/conf/csedu/csedu2013.html

Henschke, J. (2009). Engagement in active learning with Brazilian adult educators. In G. Strohschen (Ed.), *Handbook of blended shore education: Adult program development and delivery* (pp. 121–136). New York, NY: Springer.

Homer (1996). *The Odyssey.* (Robert Fagles, trans.). New York, NY: Penguin Books.

James, J. Rayner, A, & Bruno, J. (2015). Are you my mentor? New perspectives and research on informal mentorship. *The Journal of Academic Librarianship, 41*(5), 532–539. doi: 10.1016/j.acalib.2015.07.009.

Johnson, S. E., Richeson, J. A., & Finkel, E. J. (2011). Middle class and marginal? Socioeconomic status, stigma, and self-regulation at an elite university. *Journal of Personality and Social Psychology, 100,* 838–852. doi:10.1037/a0021956

Johnson, W. B. (2015). *On being a mentor: A guide for higher education faculty* (2nd ed.). New York, NY: Erlbaum Associates.

Kram, K. E. (1985). *Mentoring at work: Developmental relationships in organizational life.* Glenview, IL: Scott Foresman.

Kram, K. E., & Ragins, B. R. (2007). The landscape of mentoring in the 21st century. In B. R. Ragins, & K. E. Kram (Eds.), *The handbook of mentoring at work: Theory, research, and practice* (pp. 427–446). Thousand Oaks, CA: Sage.

Leslie, K., Lingard, L., & Whyte, S. (2005). Junior faculty experiences with informal mentoring. *Medical Teacher, 27*(8), 693–698.

Liechty, J. M., Liao, M., & Pegorraro Schull, C. (2009). Facilitating dissertation completion and success among doctoral students in social work. *Journal of Social Work Education, 43*(3), 481–497.

MacDonald, G. (1911). *The princess and the goblin.* London, England: Blackie and Son.

Mack, D., Watson, E. D., & Camacho, M. M., Eds. (2012). *Mentoring faculty of color: Essays on professional development and advancement in colleges and universities.* Jefferson, NC: McFarland.

Management Matters. (2013). 2 things to consider when matching pairs in a mentoring program. *Business Mentoring Matters.* Retrieved from http://www.management-mentors.com/about/corporate-mentoring-matters-blog/bid/100725/2-Things-To-Consider-When-Matching-Pairs-In-A-Mentoring-Program

McAfee, K., & Hansman, C. (2012). Improving faculty development through peer coaching, learning communities, and mentoring. In C.J. Boden-McGill & K. P. King (Eds.), *Conversations about adult learning in our complex world* (pp. 223–236). Charlotte, NC: Information Age.

McGuire, G. M., & Reger, J. (2003). Mentoring: A model for academic professional development. *NWSA Journal, 15*(1), 54–72.

MENTOR. (2015). 2015 National mentoring summit. Retrieved from http://www.mentoring.org/

Mentoring: The National Mentor Partnership. (2015). Expanding the world of quality mentoring. Retrieved from http://www.mentoring.org/

Meyette, G. C. (2015). Welcome to the social work profession: Seeking a mentor in a first job. *The New Social Worker: The Social Work Careers Magazine.* Retrieved from http://www.socialworker.com/feature-articles/career-jobs/welcome-to-the-social-work-profession-seeking-a-mentor-in-a-/.

National Association of Social Workers Code of Ethics (1996). Code of ethics. Retrieved from http://www.socialworkers.org/pubs/code/code.asp

National Mentoring Month Campaign. (2015). *Toolkit and digital materials.* Retrieved from http://www.nationalmentoringmonth.org/mediacenter/toolkits

Phillips, S. L., & Dennison, S. T. (2015). *Faculty mentoring/mentee guide: Tips for mentors inside or outside the department.* Sterling, VA: Stylus Publishing.

Pomeroy, E. C., & Steiker, L. H. (2011). Paying it forward: On mentors and mentoring. *Social Work, 56*(3), 197–200.

ProfHacker. (2014). ProfHacker series on mentoring. *The Chronicle of Higher Education.* Retrieved from: http://chronicle.com/blogs/profhacker/the-profhacker-series-on-mentoring/22730

Ragins, B. R. (2007). Diversity and workplace mentoring relationships: A review and positive social capital approach. In T. Allen & L. Elby (Eds). *The Blackwell handbook of mentoring: A multiple perspectives approach* (pp. 281–300). West Sussex, England: Blackwell.

Ragins, B., & Cotton, J. (1999). Mentor functions and outcomes: A comparison and men and women in formal and informal mentoring relationships. *Journal of Applied Psychology, 84*(4), 529–550.

Rockoff, J. E. (2008). *Does mentoring reduce turnover and improve skills of new employees? Evidence from teachers in New York City* (NBER Working Paper 13868). Cambridge, MA: National Bureau of Economic Research.

Rowan, N. L. (2009, Fall). Mentorship in social work: A dialogue of powerful interplay. *Reflections,* 51–55.

Sands, R. G., Parson, L. A., & Duane, J. (1991). Faculty mentoring faculty in a public university. *Journal of Higher Education, 62*(2), 174–193.

Sánchez, B., & Colón, Y. (2005). Race, ethnicity, and culture in mentoring relationships. In D. DuBois & M. Karcher (Eds.), *Handbook of youth mentoring* (pp. 191–204). Los Angeles, CA: Sage.

Schmidt, M. (Ed.). (1999). *Lyrical ballads.* London, England: Penguin Group.

Schwiebert, V. L. (2000). *Mentoring: Creating connected, empowered relationships.* Alexandria, VA: American Counseling Association.

Smith, W. (2015). Relational dimensions of virtual social work education: Mentoring faculty in a web-based learning environment. *Clinical Social Work Journal, 43*(2), 236–245.

Sorcinelli, M. D., & Yun, J. (2007). From mentor to mentoring networks: Mentoring in the new academy. *Change, 39*(6), 58–62.

Strand, V. C., & Bosco-Ruggiero, S. (2010). Initiating and sustaining a mentoring program for child welfare staff. *Administration in Social Work, 34,* 49–67.

The Mentoring Institute. (2015). Annual mentoring conference. Retrieved from http://mentor.unm.edu/

Tijerina, M., & Deepak, A. (2014). Mexican American social workers' perceptions of doctoral education and academia. *Journal of Social Work Education. 50*(2), 365–378.

Weimer, M. (2015). Making the most of the mentoring relationship. Faculty focus: Higher ed teaching strategies from magna publications. Retrieved from http://ww1.facultyfocus.com/db/mlm4.fwd.email.prompt?data=facultyfocus/269X

Welsh, E., Bhave, D., & Kim, K. (2012). Are you my mentor? Informal mentoring mutual identification. *Career Development International, 17*(2),137–148.

Wilson, P. P., Pereira, A., & Valentine, D. (2002). Perceptions of new social work faculty about mentoring experiences. *Journal of Social Work Education, 38*(2), 317–332.

Zachary, L. (2009, May). Filling in the blanks. *T+D*. Retrieved from http://www.centerformentoringexcellence.com/upload/Filling_in_the_Blanks_Informal_Mentoring.pdf

CHAPTER 5

FACILITATING THE DOCTORAL MENTORING PROCESS IN ONLINE LEARNING ENVIRONMENTS

Kathleen P. King
University of Central Florida

In the process of mentoring 40+ doctoral students at three universities, I have realized that the process is as much *Science* as it is *Art*. Many of us had excellent mentors, but if we compared their strategies, they likely pursued that role in very different ways. Part of the richness of the mentor-mentee experience may emerge from the dynamic, open ended relationship and understanding, which develops between two adults during the doctoral training journey. Furthermore, since mentoring is facilitated through human relationships, it can be experienced in many different ways. There are cascades of varied shades of abilities, expertise, vision, dedication, and personality with which both mentor and mentee approach this dynamic dialogue. Nonetheless, customarily there are several common, foundational elements of doctoral mentoring as it is frequently understood in the field of education.

Mentoring in Formal and Informal Contexts, pages 77–96
Copyright © 2016 by Information Age Publishing
All rights of reproduction in any form reserved.

Mentors, major professors, dissertation chairs, (whatever title is ascribed to them by a particular institution), seek to guide their doctoral candidates through their dissertation planning, design, implementation, and completion. However, this journey does not only include the processes related to the dissertation, but also very likely guidance in their future career (Roberts, 2010; Rudestam & Newton, 2014). Yet, mentors engage in much less exciting duties as well. In order to successfully guide students to complete their doctoral degrees, mentors also must address their mentees' scores of other needs. No one who has completed the process will deny that it is critical to not only navigate the research process, but also institutional requirements. And at times, student and mentor alike may wonder which is more difficult to conquer.

Moreover, applying what we know about adult learners to doctoral candidates confirms that the students are most likely not only coping with these explicitly stated requirements, but also a host of other demands. Considering the complex lives adult learners have, doctoral students will encounter multiple challenges, barriers, or conflicts during their four to seven plus years of studies. Such challenges may include, but are not limited to, any assortment and severity of issues across personal, workplace, professional, time management, health, marital, social, political, governmental domains (for international students for example) (Council for Adult and Experiential Learning [CAEL], 2005; Zambrana et al., 2015). These demands and complications may range from slight disturbances to severe life altering events.

These challenges also serve as potential opportunities for online learning environments to create greater efficiencies, overcome time and travel limitations, and address internal and external demands. Since 2000, I have used online spaces to support mentoring with doctoral students. Recently, I have heard several colleagues mention they struggle with how to serve the needs of their many doctoral candidates who are not able to visit campus frequently, and yet need sustained accountability and support. Not only can effective online mentoring address these institutional needs, but also faculty who have large doctoral student assignments, like myself, may find these strategies helpful.

This chapter describes and explains how and why one may leverage online Learning Management Systems (LMS) to bridge the many gaps and overcome several hurdles synonymous with dissertation mentoring. How can mentors guide our mentees best within the scope of their circumstances, and how do mentors refrain from exhausting themselves in the process? What strategies can mentors scaffold efficiently? How can basic LMS functions be used to increase communication with all assigned mentees, cultivate self-directed learning, and foster greater accountability? In this chapter, some of the best practices of adult learning and technology opportunities available serve as a foundation. The ultimate goal of these efforts is to better address and conquer the multiple needs and constraints experienced by mentor and mentee.

FOUNDATIONAL LITERATURE

This chapter celebrates the Science and Art of mentoring. The Science of mentoring is recognized when mentors understand the processes, demands, and pitfalls, navigating each dissertation in succession. While the Art of mentoring is witnessed in the unique journey mentors craft for individual doctoral candidates based on their disposition, skills, needs, and dreams. In order to present this approach to online mentoring, the research and literature of graduate education, online learning, and adult learning provide substantial direction. The specific foundational literatures which support this discussion include three areas: doctoral mentoring, online learning, and self-directed learning.

Doctoral Mentoring

When discussing doctoral mentoring, there are several common themes which frequently emerge in the discussions: (a) Is mentoring teaching or research?; (b) Is the focus of this mentoring professional advancement, or completion of the dissertation requirement?; and (c) How do mentors describe their roles and relationship with mentees?

Teaching or Research?

With new efforts to address demands of accountability and budget constraints, it is very common for academics to be required to document their work activities. Often these requirements are in the form of annual reviews, annual reports, workload allocations, etc. In addition, faculty workloads, performance, and achievement across disciplines and departments are compared. However, the extensive responsibility of the dissertation chair spans at least two familiar categories: teaching and research. Unfortunately, many higher education evaluation or reporting systems want each activity allocated artificially into a single "slot."

In dissertation mentoring, faculty work with students not only to conceptualize and design their research projects, but also to guide them through implementation, ethical concerns, data analysis, and interpretation (Locke, Spirduso, & Silverman, 2010; Roberts, 2010; Rudestam & Newton, 2014). Certainly, faculty do not complete these activities for the students; however, the mentors sometimes need to spend extensive time and effort in explaining the theoretical and practical purposes, processes, and pitfalls of research to their mentees. In some disciplines, the dissertation might be the first major research project a student completes. Given the complex nature of research design, it is little wonder that students need guidance in bridging theory and practice.

However, given all the research activity doctoral mentors guide students through, there are issues that arise. Is this support to be considered teaching or engaging in collaborative research? In many organizations, the answer is very important in determining how one's professional activity is interpreted and valued. In order to communicate the vast scope and dual role of importance of doctoral mentoring, faculty need to persist in crafting a unique and valued space for this work. Doctoral mentoring includes extensive work in both teaching and research.

Professional Advancement or Degree Completion?

Another critical question has to do with the professional focus of our doctoral student mentoring. In conversations with colleagues, it seems that there may be two camps of thought with a small contingent embracing a "both/and" perspective regarding the role of the doctoral mentor in professional advancement or degree completion (Rudestam, & Newton, 2014).

When faculty hold professional development as the focus of mentoring, dissertation work takes on a much larger scope and purpose. In this context, rather than developing and completing a research project, mentoring becomes a commitment to developing the person's professional development vision and skills. Faculty mentors can play a critical role in guiding students through such important experiences as developing their professional identity development (Erikson, 1968; Lunsford, 2012); assimilating into academic culture; understanding higher education culture, governance, and dynamics; developing a research agenda; and coordinating effective time management practice (Carpenter, Makhadmeh, & Thornton, 2015). Dissertation completion not only creates students' unique contribution to the literature and knowledge base in their field, but also plays an important part in their development, because it cultivates independent research, writing, problem solving, and time management skills (Lunsford, 2012).

Analogies of Doctoral Mentoring

Given the expansive role and responsibility which major professors agree to when invited to chair a dissertation, there are many analogies used to describe it. Many faculty describe mentoring as walking alongside their students in their doctoral journey or climbing the massive mountain; however, they are guiding or supporting through the experience.

Traditional mentoring literature, such as Kram's theory (1985) of mentoring, identifies two major areas of mentoring which faculty may engage or combine: career or psychosocial. In Kram's theory (1985), career mentoring concentrates on research and degree completion, networking, preparation for job interviews, etc. whereas, psychosocial mentoring includes empathizing with student needs and concerns, and providing resources to address those issues. Literature further demonstrates that women tend to include more psychosocial support in their mentor roles than men (Carpenter, et al., 2015). Recent quantitative research reveals that there are in fact four areas of mentoring identified by faculty who are mentors: career, psychosocial, research, and intellectual (Carpenter, et al., 2015). This more detailed model affords greater accuracy in recognizing the work of doctoral mentors.

Online Learning

From research and experience with distance, distributed, and online learning since the early 1990s, higher education has learned that in order to serve students well via technology, several characteristics of design and implementation are non-negotiables (Lehman & Conceição, 2010). From among the scores of valuable recommendations and best practices which exist, there are at least five essential elements to apply to online doctoral mentoring. All of these characteristics reduce the "transactional distance" between faculty and student, thus increasing the learning outcomes (Moore, 2007). In essence, since we are not face to face with students in this teaching mode, we need to use several conventions to increase communication and access (Garrison, 2003). These principles apply not only to doctoral mentoring, but also across postsecondary education.

The four essential elements discussed in this chapter are (a) sustaining a consistent and clean design; (b) communicating clear expectations; (c) focusing on feedback; and (d) cultivating self-directed learning skills.

Consistent Design

Observation number one: If mentees cannot find the information they need, they cannot use it. Everyone has encountered websites, online resources, and online courses which are muddled at best and maddening at the worst extreme (Kuniavsky, 2010). Most likely, the designers did not intend to obscure their extensive work with confusing design, duplicate entries, misdirected and "dead" links, but the total result is that many users, if there is no negative consequence (aka no grade penalty), just surrender to failure and move to another site.

Therefore, thinking back to which websites and online courses appealed to us, makes us consider which ones were easy to navigate and encouraged us, or our students, to delve deeper for more information. This reflective exercise will provide direction in recognizing clear and consistent online design. At this point in time, most LMS have a standard format embedded, one or more templates or shells, which greatly assist faculty in designing clean and consistent designs.

The term *clean* is used here in the sense of meaning no (to little) clutter. "Less is more" applies absolutely to web and LMS design. Another way to articulate this principle is, "White space is our friend!" When faculty use a simple menu at the top or side of the screen and place the primary content for a page in the center, the user's eyes are drawn to the content and the choices are all clustered in one area. In this case, no time is lost searching the page for options to consider or select. Moreover, the user is not afraid of missing content that may be "hidden" in multiple screens down the page (Gagne, Wager, Golas, & Keller, 2004).

Additionally, when one has multiple pages of content, converting it to a PDF document provides several clues to the technology literate user. (a) This material is more than a small amount of content; it is likely several pages long; (b) The formatting is preserved, so when the reader views the document, it looks just like you laid it out; and (c) The user can download the content for safekeeping, future reference, mobile reading, etc. All these observations, and more, stream through the tech savvy users' subconsciousness and consciousness as they navigate online content (Dirksen, 2012; Gagne et al., 2004).

Consistent design refers to the similar characteristics which users expect or rely on web pages to have; it also can refer to inter-related design or a theme within a website, course, etc. If faculty members use bold to highlight key points, they should be featured in bold on all the pages. If instead, the key points are emphasized with highlight, then faculty need to be consistent using that formatting. Consistent design allows online users to quickly find and recognize information through the cues systematically employed by the site designer.

The use of fonts and images provide more examples of how to use consistent design. A given site or online course space should have only a few variations of design. For example, an effective online design might have three to five different layouts, which slightly vary from the home page and display detailed content in different formats. Users will become accustomed to these layout options quickly.

In contrast, reflect upon those websites which seemed to be designed by people who had just discovered new fonts. In the technology world, we describe websites and documents which lack consistency as a "ransom note" style. When there is no consistent design, letters and images seem askew, there is no apparent rhyme or reason, and while much confusion abounds, little learning occurs. Research reveals that consistent visual and navigational design creates less cognitive dissonance (aka static) and allows learners to focus on content rather than the technology. Therefore, consistent design enhances learning outcomes (Gagne et al., 2004; Wang & Hannafin, 2005).

Clear Expectations

In the world of dissertation mentoring, often students embark on an isolated, even deserted, journey in comparison to the formal, traditional course work which preceded it. While prior coursework included course goals, objectives, reading lists, and schedules, according to the literature and in my experience, few faculty mentors provide goals or expectations for their students (Roberts, 2010).

Why do we suddenly change the rules when doctoral students need mentors' support? Even though this is a space and time of transitioning into professional roles and independence, it is also a time of great stress and anxiety. It is more effective to scaffold these new experiences by developing goals and expectations with mentees and gradually shifting responsibility to them (Roberts, 2010).

Just as it is with adult learners, engaging mentees in determining and defining their goals and objectives provides a powerful learning experience (CAEL, 2005). Not only does such shared responsibility engage mentees in discovering their learning needs and preferences, but also it cultivates their skills in planning for independent and self-directed learning.

Additionally, by explicitly discussing learning goals, mentors create an opportunity to develop transparency in dissertation requirements, in general, and the mentor's expectations specifically. When mentors decide to fully engage in dialogue on such matters, there are new opportunities to cultivate mutual professional respect. In such actions, mentors may be for the first time, explicitly, inviting students into the conversation about what they want, need, and are expected to learn.

In much of the literature about doctoral mentoring, such valuable discussions illustrate core principles. These tenets allow mentors and mentees to walk alongside each other through the emergence of professional identify and independence (Palmer, Zajonc, & Scribner, 2010; Robert, 2010).

Via online learning, such discussions might be live via Voice Over Internet Protocol (VOIP), Skype, FaceTime or asynchronously (non-simultaneously) via reflective papers, recorded audio or video messages, written journal entries, a private online threaded discussion with the mentor, or phone call. The possibilities of *how* to engage in discussions of learning goals and expectations are endless; the scope and form of such dialogue are even more expansive.

A favorite strategy for broad-based transparency in online course spaces is using rubrics. Over the years, I have adopted the practice of developing rubrics for every assignment and milestone in the courses I teach. Rubrics define the levels of performance which are expected for each assignment grade (Conrad & Donaldson, 2011).

Upon asking students, they have said that rubrics provide much greater information about what is expected of them, what the assignment's purpose and scope is, and the value of different aspects of each assignment. Furthermore, they echo the findings of the literature that rubrics, which are carefully written, can create a more democratic classroom (DiMartino, Clark, & Wolk, 2002).

Students and mentees have discussed the power of rubrics in their learning process and provided advice regarding how to improve their design and use. Specifically, graduate students who I have had in my classes have indicated that the use of rubrics

- Reassure them that professors are not "hiding things" about their expectations for the assignments.
- Provide student greater choices in what they plan to achieve.
- Develop a level playing field in the classroom. (Students refer to all knowing the same insights, expectations, etc.).
- Reduce student anxiety greatly.
- Develop greater peer to peer, and mentor-mentee respect and trust.

Certainly, these outcomes and benefits are immensely valuable for all students; however, they have special meaning for those who are guiding their doctoral dissertation mentees. For instance, I have been developing rubrics, not only for comprehensive exams, but also for academic writing, in general, and for each dissertation chapter. Current and future mentors should realize many meaningful uses of rubrics with doctoral mentees.

Focus on Feedback

In all forms of our teaching, feedback is one of the vital contributions faculty offer students. However, in dissertation mentoring, perhaps it is most important of all. Without essential and frequent feedback, how can students progress to proposal defense and final defense? Simultaneously, it is this enormous burden of providing proposal and dissertation feedback which bogs mentors down with copious pages of corrections and notes as well as face to face discussions. Is there a way to use online spaces to facilitate and streamline this process?

Before some of the LMS had online document editing available, many faculty mentors were downloading student work and using word processor Track Changes features to both document and expedite corrections and comments. If the LMS does not have online editing available follow these steps (a) download the file; (b) open it in your word processor; (c) use the Track Changes or other inline editing feature; (d) save it under a new name; and (e) upload to send it back to the student. In this manner, you can email the file to the mentee and speak by phone/VOIP/etc. while you review it together.

Documenting the feedback in this manner provides another point of progress for you in guiding your mentees. When the next version of the document is uploaded or mailed, ask students to compile and include a bullet list of the changes they made with pages listed for the major areas. Faculty can then compare the changes to the file previously annotated and readily determine which recommended changes were completed and how.

Cultivate Self-Directed Learning Skills

The literature has much evidence to support the primary role of motivation in distance learning. When all other variables are compared, students' motivation to learn is the greatest influence on their success. However, one of the greatest contributions that online learning can offer our doctoral students is that it provides a strong platform to develop self-directed learning skills (Fink, 2003). These skills align with the characteristics which are needed for success in most twenty-first century careers, including the academy (Gardner, 2007; Partnership for 21st Century Skills, 2009, 2015).

Self-directed learning skills include those elements which afford the ability to determine one's learning objectives, pursue, learn, and apply the desired skills, information, etc. (Knowles, 1975). In doctoral mentoring, faculty are guiding students into many aspects of their professional careers. To accomplish this goal within the framework of self-directed learning, the students must develop responsibility for learning, identifying learning goals, setting learning goals and timelines, identifying resources for learning, overcoming barriers, and self-assessment for continuing improvement.

Responsibility for learning also includes the widely researched self-regulated learning. Dembo, Junge, and Lynch (2006) define self-regulated learning as "the ability of learners to control the factors or conditions affecting their learning" (p. 188). From graduation onward, most academics will engage in informal learning, which requires them to take responsibility for their continuing professional development. Self-regulated learning is a skill set needed in this shift from teacher-centered instruction to student-centered and needs to be an essential element of mentoring.

The next three elements (identifying learning goals, setting learning goals and timelines, identify resources for learning) enumerate the skills needed to plan and pursue learning independently. When we include such activities in our courses, we help future professionals scaffold these skills. Setting deadlines and creating timelines, when there are no grades or supervisors, is a hard discipline for some people to adopt. Therefore, gaining potential support and building accountability through peer groups might be a valuable discussion with mentees.

Since Cross's work in the 1970s, educators have understood the many barriers to participation in formal education (Chao, DeRocco, & Flynn, 2007; Cross, 1981). However, we remain less schooled in overcoming the barriers which prohibit continuing lifelong learning and self-assessment for continuing improvement. In the dissertation process, mentor and mentee have opportunities to discuss these challenges one-on-one, thus providing new strategies for recognizing and analysing barriers and revising or changing course.

Finally, mentoring relationships may serve as powerful platforms for self-assessment and resulting continuing improvement. It is a powerful experience when mentees recognize that because of the many challenges faced daily, even mentors need to continue to grow personally and professionally. When mentors share conversations about identifying resources and pursuing our own growth, students listen. When we enroll in a workshop with them at a conference or discuss our plans, mentors reveal the power of lifelong learning, which otherwise is too often hidden behind the Wizard's curtain.

DISCUSSION: THE FLEXIBLE MODEL OF ONLINE DOCTORAL MENTORING

The Flexible Model of Online Doctoral Mentoring (FMDM) is grounded in the concept and vital work of a community of learners who consist of the mentor and mentees (See Figure 5.1). The FMDM includes five elements which dynamically coordinate to provide (a) organized; (b) anytime/anywhere; (c) community; (d) expert; and (e) participatory professional and dissertation mentoring and support. This section describes each element and their respective benefits for mentor and mentee.

Organization Description

The structural and andragogical foundation of this dynamic platform is rooted in greater organization and increased efficiencies afforded by twenty-first century LMS technology applications. Examples of features which are often embedded in LMS and valuable for doctoral mentoring include, but are not limited to, messaging (integration of text, audio and video communication), one on one and group conferencing, remote communication, document storage, document reviewing/tracking, document sharing, and resource sharing. When used consistently and harmoniously, such capabilities can provide students and faculty with many benefits (Kuo, Walker, Schroder, & Belland, 2014). Coordinated planning of student learning and engagement using these features may yield greater flexibility; increase

Figure 5.1 FMDM community of learners as grounding concept.

efficiencies of distribution of resources; allow on-demand availability of resources; develop greater skills in self-directed, peer, and lifelong learning; and provide secure environments for storing, sharing, and retrieving drafts and edits of documents.

In my experience, it is beneficial to structure the LMS Modules of content as Syllabus, Institutional Policies and Procedures, Research Resources, Writing Resources, and Professional Associations. In the Discussion area, students can create special interest or concern folders, but the Discussion Space is also initially populated with these folders: Introductions, Goal Setting, Questions about Dissertation Policies and Requirements, Research Related Questions, Writing Related Questions, Publishing Related Questions, Progress Reports, etc.

Benefits to Mentor

In order to maximize the organization capabilities of the LMS, there are several specific strategies available. The following list includes several LMS design and use practices, which have been used within the FMDM framework and resulted in reducing many otherwise redundant mentoring activities.

- Document and post expectations and procedures for dissertation and proposal defenses, academic writing, final dissertation standards, etc.
- Document and post current lists of resources relevant to dissertation research, writing and procedures, graduation procedures from across the unit/department, college, university, professional associations, and when relevant, other online sources.
- Schedule and conduct online, phone, and campus consultations, both individual and group.
- Form a Discussion folder for students to ask questions about the dissertation process.
- Add common/frequent questions to the Frequently Asked Questions (FAQs) list regarding the dissertation process (Update each semester).
- Require students to upload any draft dissertation chapters they submit to the mentor as LMS Assignments. This approach provides (a) a permanent archive of student work; (b) secure storage; and (c) online editing. Note: once the proposals and dissertations are more developed and longer, mentors might request hardcopy delivery as some faculty prefer editing on paper.
- Once online edits or tracking are complete, save the file with a new name to reduce confusion. If hard copy edits were completed, scan the document in order to use the LMS storage and distribution system

- Return edits of student chapters via the LMS grading system in order to have an archive of progress and permanent storage.
- Post broadcast Announcements to all members of the online doctoring mentoring group regarding relevant conference and journal proposal submission and participation opportunities, workshops, changes in processes or policies, deadlines, etc.

By designing the LMS with the goals of doctoral mentoring communication, information distribution and feedback, and guidance in mind, mentors will discover greater efficiency, and opportunities to incorporate student feedback in next semester's dissertation hours.

Benefits to Mentee

From candidates' perspectives, leveraging an LMS to support dissertation mentoring provides a unified, organized framework with less time wasted on searching for resources/articles/handouts, which the professor has distributed previously, and increases their current and future efficiency. These factors are amplified by the common LMS space enabling doctoral students to continue their academic work in a learning community rather than experiencing sudden and prolonged isolation during dissertation (Lehman, & Conceição, 2010). Furthermore, the structured format of the FMDM provides a model which encourages the development of self-directed learning skills and self-regulation (Andrade, & Bunker, 2009). By using these structured strategies, many students will develop better organizational skills which will be invaluable as administrators and faculty members.

Anytime/Anywhere Description

The ubiquitous access, which LMS platforms provide, are invaluable for the dissertation mentor and mentee, as issues arise no matter where they are and whether it is day, evening, or weekend. With this platform, they can review the existing resources, discussions, and other material to solve issues immediately. And if not possible, they can also message their peers and mentor. Rather than access a single person or slice of time, this model affords a flexible base for support from a group of colleagues with a persistent sense of community presence and opportunities to build a network of mutual mentoring relationships (Bernier, Larose, & Soucy, 2005; Lehman, & Conceição, 2010). Certainly, the model requires a shift in our perspective regarding the true meaning of doctoral mentoring, but the benefits should outweigh the process of adjustment.

Benefits to Mentor

Added to this strong foundation are the dynamic and powerful modalities of greater efficiencies, flexibility, scope of intellectual sharing, self-directed learning, and lifelong learning. Greater efficiencies are experienced because everyone in the dissertation group, regardless of location and schedule, receives the same information. Such increased reliability of communication more fully assures that all student and faculty are accurately communicating, notified of deadlines, timelines, requirements, etc. In essence, we have a better likelihood of all "being on the same page."

Faculty also have reduced redundant communication, as they inform all students of opportunities, deadlines etc. at one time. The flexibility of communication and accountability is also vital for faculty, since the LMS allows them to provide real-time, on-demand, or asynchronous wherever they have access to the web. Reliable and effective communication with students no longer has to be *confined* to simultaneously sharing the same physical space (e.g., office hours, lunch meeting, etc.). Today, mentors have the flexibility to schedule other real-time discussions through a host of technology; smartphone, tablet, and computer applications and programs.

Benefits to Mentee

When utilizing technology, just as faculty members do not have to be on campus at the same time as the student, this is also true from the student perspective. By dissertation stage, many students have, or could have, significant barriers to traveling to campus for in-person dissertation advising sessions. For instance, not only do family and work obligations demand their presence, but some have also advanced in their careers and might live anywhere from two to 25 hours or more from campus! In many cases, it is inordinately cumbersome, and unnecessary, to require students to be in-person for *every* dissertation advising session. Technology options provide viable virtual, collaborative workspaces for mentoring to thrive when planned strategically. A most powerful approach is to complement, alternate, and strategically plan a combination of any or all of the following: conference calls, video conferencing, detailed written feedback, in person sessions, small group video conferencing (or "learning community think tank sessions"), etc.

Research demonstrates that students frequently felt very isolated during the off campus and "independent study" portion of the dissertation process (Pololi, & Evans, 2015; Roberts, 2010). Using collaborative technology tools and peer learning strategies for project support helps to challenge assumptions and consider alternate vantage points more fully than is possible when restricting feedback to only the major professor (Pololi & Evans, 2015).

Moreover, when faculty create resources and post them in the LMS for the students, students have access to on-demand resources. Today, most professionals are technology savvy users to such an extent that they expect on-demand access to specialized information (i.e., YouTube, Online library access, etc.). Furthermore, the literature reports that a dominant learning strategy for dynamic professionals is the ability to engage in "just in time learning" (Fink, 2003). Students may access the resources mentors post in the dissertation LMS when they need them: 2 a.m., 2 p.m., weekdays, weekends, and any other time.

Community Description

During their formal coursework, many doctoral students develop and depend on a community of learners. The FMDM leverages the strengths of psychosocial and academic peer support *and* learning while facilitating highly individualized work with a student's mentor (Bernier et al., 2005; Gadbois & Graham, 2012). In this context, peer support includes at least three major, different dimensions of benefits: accountability, shared knowledge, and writing support.

Benefits to Mentor

At the very foundation of these benefits is the fact that students' support is no longer formally restricted to their individual mentor; instead, faculty are part of a larger, focused learning community. Our dissertation communities are dedicated to everyone moving ahead (Pololi, 2015). In addition, everyone (including the mentor!) works to improve their own professional skills, practice, and development. These dynamics create a vibrant *culture* of professional learning.

Additionally, as many professors experience, students may often communicate or encourage their peers more effectively than we can as the instructor. This benefit can occur for many reasons ranging from shared life experiences, word choice, cohort characteristics, etc. The dissertation community scaffolds these several relationships and their individual and collective benefits in order to achieve a shared goal/purpose.

Benefits to Mentee

Another positive dynamic of learning communities in this context is that candidates are accountable to more people. Therefore, the stakes become more public and "higher" in meeting self-established deadlines, etc. Secondly, while everyone has a different topic, all the candidates progress through the *same* process. Therefore, they can share knowledge about deadlines, expectations, pitfalls, etc. with one another. Thirdly, the dissertation process includes endless writing and rewriting. As part of a community, students have an invested group of critical friends to invite to read their drafts, provide feedback, and push them to think about different audiences. Beyond basic psychosocial support, academic peer support and insight is vital when mentees' family and friends get tired of hearing about an academic pursuit with which they cannot identify (Gadbois & Graham, 2012). The learning community approach to dissertation mentoring provides a wider base of support, more lines of communication, and greater accountability for everyone involved.

Expert Description

As the expert scholar in their field of research, faculty have a different role in students' LMS experiences than either the student or their classmates. Not only do we construct and initially populate the shell with content, but we are also ready and available to provide content area and procedural insight throughout the dissertation process. During the past several years, the FMDM assisted me greatly in providing such support in a timely and efficient manner as my dissertation candidate load has ranged from five to 18 and may temporarily rise further.

Benefits to Mentor

The FMDM is scalable in allowing faculty to provide a more consistent level of mentoring. By distributing material to everyone at once, having a repository of essential content, and building a community of learners at the same point in their dissertation process, we can enjoy greater confidence of equitable treatment and opportunity. As the expert in the content area, one can be assured all students receive the professional and research related material, which is crucial (for instance, create and fill a Module Resource Folder). When mentors want to know if they are providing in-depth feedback, they may create a discussion folder or post a questionnaire for the students labelled "Assignment Feedback and Document Editing."

Moreover, when faculty encounter additional resources, research books, articles in our field, conference and journal opportunities, we want a direct and immediate communication line to our mentee/scholars. A LMS Announcement is invaluable in distributing and archiving these resources all in one step while one also incorporates persistent resources into the online community. Overall, the strategies of the FMDM provide increased flexibility and power to determine how I want to use it to much more efficiently and consistently address mentees' needs and the demands of my field.

In addition to these more universal types of resources (one size fits all as it were), the FMDM also encourages the use of two individualized, ongoing activities: Goal Setting and My Completion Plan. As the expert in the field, I provide feedback to the students on whether their initial aspirations in these areas are too weak or too rigorous (usually). These activities also are opportunities to guide mentees to realistic, but meaningful, goals and timelines, which will advance their progress steadily.

In the FMDM, to complement the virtual platform, a blended format is designed (Fink, 2003). The best practice is for mentors to invite mentees to connect face to face (virtually, if they are out of state) at least twice per semester. These sessions are essential to review the Goal Setting and Completion Plan activities, their written work, specific concerns about dissertation progress, professional advancement, and, when relevant, position searches.

Benefits to Mentee

These one-on-one sessions with the students have been invaluable for mentors, because mentors can better assess the well-being, energy level, investment, and understanding of students. Moreover this information is critical to help students progress or recommit to their plan ("get back on track"). Some mentees are skillful at hiding their anxiety or denying their needs. Without face to face sessions, more mentees will struggle and wander aimlessly into the world of ABD (All But Dissertation). The blended format will help reduce such costly fallout in terms of expended resources.

Participation Mentoring Description

The FMDM creates and sustains participatory professional and dissertation mentoring and support. This format cultivates both functional and philosophical purposes. Regarding functional goals, this chapter has described several examples in which the FMDM provides mentees with many opportunities for using peer learning, team work, collaboration, critical thinking, problem solving, and synthesis. All of these skills are directly translated to valuable current and forecasted workplace needs because each is characterized and predominate in professional work in the twenty-first century (Gardner, 2007; Partnership for 21st Century Skills, 2009, 2015).

At the same time, the FMDM has a humanistic, philosophical orientation which encourages mentees to identify and pursue their professional goals in the midst of progressively developing self-agency, self-directedness, and lifelong learning perspectives. The ultimate goal is that mentees realize that a vital professional must be a self-directed, lifelong learner.

Benefits to Mentor

From the mentor's perspective, a participatory approach to mentoring has many benefits. While it is customary to have dissertation committees, many university faculty today have adopted practices where the committee is not involved in the dissertation until the final approval of the proposal and the dissertation. Instead of working with the committee throughout the process, students interact almost solely with the major professor, up to the point of needing final approvals. Certainly, this isolated process was not the original concept of the dissertation committee (Roberts, 2010); but, due to various historical, cultural, personal, and fiscal concerns, such is the current pattern.

While other committee members still might not be available for frequent dialogue or feedback in the FMDM, the mentoring group is. One of the greatest benefits of the participatory approach to mentoring is expressed in the adage, "Many hands, make the work light." In this model, mentors have the academic community to support their work with mentees. In this case, the adage might read, "Many *minds*, make the work lighter!"

Benefits to Mentee

By design, the FMDM community coordinates supporting everyone moving ahead. Moreover, the process, community, resources, and process have incorporated valuable skills which will sustain mentees' professional lives and work beyond their formal education.

An LMS provides several strategies which are effective in cultivating participatory peer mentoring and support at the dissertation level: (a) Building discussions among mentees; (b) Overseeing the development of "accountability/study groups"; (c) Using discussion folders for questions; (d) Forming virtual writing groups, and more. Indeed, examining the literature related to democratic classrooms' social dynamics, mutual accountability, and knowledge construction in peer collaborative groups reveals some of the reasons such group learning is a powerful motivator and device for doctoral students' success.

For example, DiMartino, Clark, and Wolk (2002) found democratic classrooms include much more student engagement, dialogue, and self-efficacy. In addition, often when students are working in peer collaborative groups, they work harder than usual (more hours and attention) because they are depending on one another, and knowledge construction occurs (Lyublinskaya, & Kerekes, 2009).

Finally, Jonassen, Howland, Mooreland and Marra (2003) and others have consistently demonstrated the power of collaborative groups in building new knowledge. Strategies for constructivist learning are often used in young math and science classes to cultivate complete understanding as well as build critical thinking and problem solving skills (Biggs, 2003; Lyublinskaya, & Kerekes, 2009; McAlpine & Allen, 2007). However, faculty less frequently apply constructivist strategies through collaborative groups with dissertation students.

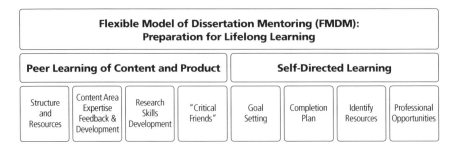

Figure 5.2 FMDM Concept Map.

SUMMARY

Based on this chapter's discussion of the FMDM, Figure 5.2 presents the FMDM Concept Map. Figure 5.2 displays a more detailed perspective of the relationship among some of the FMDM's critical elements. The concept map provides a visual representation of how peer learning and self-directed learning are core principles under which many of the activities can be identified. This visualization is an innovative proposal in comparison to the traditional higher education paradigm of mentoring. Major differences between the FMDM Concept Map and the traditional model include the mentor being (a) a facilitator; and (b) on the periphery of processes, rather than being the locus of power, knowledge, and learning activities.

The FMDM Concept Map more accurately addresses the twenty-first century learning skills needs of doctoral students and provides new opportunities for the reconceptualization of roles and relationships. The entire FMDM demonstrates how the resources available in a LMS can be used to cultivate doctoral mentees as innovative and valuable professionals and scaffold mentors' expertise as facilitator for the group and individual.

REFERENCES

Andrade, M. S., & Bunker, E. L. (2009). A model for self-regulated distance language learning. *Distance Education, 30*(1), 47–61. doi: 10.1080/01587910902845956

Bernier, A., Larose, S., & Soucy, N. (2005). Academic mentoring in college: The interactive role of student's and mentor's interpersonal dispositions. *Research in Higher Education, 46*(1), 29–51.

Biggs, J. (2003). *Teaching for quality learning at university* (2nd ed.). Maidenhead, England: Open University Press.

Carpenter, S., Makhadmeh, N., & Thornton, L. (2015, July). Mentorship on the doctoral level: An examination of communication faculty mentors' traits and functions, *Communication Education, 64*(3), 366–384. doi: 10.1080/03634523.2015.1041997

Chao, E. L., DeRocco, E., & Flynn, M. K. (2007). *Adult learners in higher education: Barriers to success and strategies to improve results.* Washington DC: US Department of Labor. Retrieved from http://www.jff.org/sites/default/files/publications/adultlearners.dol_.pdf

Conrad, R., & Donaldson, J. A. (2011). *Engaging the online learner.* San Francisco, CA: Jossey-Bass.

Council for Adult and Experiential Learning (CAEL). (2005). *Serving adult learners in higher education.* Chicago, IL.: CAEL.

Cross, K. P. (1981). *Adults as learners: Increasing participation and facilitating learning.* San Francisco, CA: Jossey-Bass.

Dembo, M. H., Junge, L. G., & Lynch, R. (2006). Becoming a self-regulated learner: Implications for web-based education. *Web-based learning: Theory, research, and practice,* 185–202.

DiMartino, J., Clark, J., & Wolk, D. (2002). *Personalized learning,* New York, NY: Rowman and Little.

Dirksen, J. (2012). *Design for how people learn.* Berkeley, CA: New Riders.

Erikson, E. H. (1968). *Identity: Youth and crisis.* New York, NY: W. W. Norton & Company.

Fink, L. D. (2003). *Creating significant learning experiences.* San Francisco, CA: Jossey-Bass.

Gadbois, S. A., & Graham, E. (2012). New faculty perceptions of supervision and mentoring: The influence of graduate school experiences. *Collected Essays on Learning and Teaching,* 5, 44–49. Retrieved from http://celt.uwindsor.ca/ojs/leddy/index.php/CELT/article/download/3416/2819

Gagne, R. M., Wager, W. W., Golas, K., & Keller, J. M. (2004). *Principles of instructional design* (5th ed.). Belmont, CA: Wadsworth.

Gardner, H. (2007). *Five minds for the future.* Cambridge, MA: Harvard Business School Press.

Garrison, R. D. (2003). Self-directed learning and distance education. In M. G. Moore & W. G. Anderson (Eds.), *Handbook of distance education* (pp. 161–168). Mahwah, NJ: Erlbaum.

Jonassen, D. H., Howland, J., Moore, J., & Marra, R. M. (2003). *Learning to solve problems with technology* (2nd ed.). Upper Saddle River, NJ: Merrill Prentice Hall.

Knowles, M. S. (1975). *Self-directed learning. A guide for learners and teachers.* Englewood Cliffs, NJ: Prentice Hall/Cambridge.

Kuo, Y. C., Walker, A. E., Schroder, K. E., & Belland, B. R. (2014). Interaction, internet self-efficacy, and self-regulated learning as predictors of student satisfaction in online education courses. *The Internet and Higher Education,* 20, 35–50.

Kram, K. E. (1985). *Mentoring at work: Developmental relationships in organizational life.* Glenview, IL: Scott Foresman.

Kuniavsky, M. (2010). *Smart things: Ubiquitous computing user experience design: Ubiquitous computing user experience design.* Atlanta, GA: Elsevier.

Lehman, R. M., & Conceição, S. C. O. (2010). *Creating a sense of presence in online teaching.* San Francisco, CA: Jossey Bass.

Locke, L., Spirduso W. W., & Silverman, S. (2010). *Proposals that work.* (6th ed.). Thousand Oaks, CA: Sage.

Lyublinskaya, I., & Kerekes, J. (2009). *Integrating Mathematics, Science and technology in the elementary classroom* (2nd ed.). Oceanside, NY: Whittier.

Lunsford, L. (2012). Doctoral advising or mentoring? Effects on student outcomes. *Mentoring & Tutoring: Partnership in Learning, 20*(2), 251–270. doi: 10.1080/13611267.2012.678974

McAlpine, I., & Allen, B. (2007, December). Designing for active learning online with learning design templates. In Atkinson, R. J., McBeath, C., Soong, S. K. A., & Cheers, C. (Eds.). ICT: Providing choices for learners and learning. *Proceedings Ascilite Singapore 2007.* (pp. 639–651). Singapore: Centre for Educational Development, Nanyang Technological University. December, 2–5, 2007. http://www.ascilite.org.au/conferences/singapore07/procs/

Moore, M. G. (2007). The theory of transactional distance. In M. G. Moore (Ed.), *Handbook of distance education* (2nd ed., pp. 89–105). Mahwah, NJ: Erlbaum.

Palmer, P. J., Zajonc, A., & Scribner, M. (2010). *The heart of higher education: A call to renewal.* New York, NY: John Wiley and Sons.

Partnership for 21st Century Skills. (2009). *Partnership for 21st Century Skills framework definitions.* Retrieved from http://p21.org/storage/documents/P21_Framework_Definitions.pdf

Partnership for 21st Century Skills. (2015). *Partnership for 21st Century Skills framework.* Retrieved from http://www.p21.org/storage/documents/docs/P21_Framework_Definitions _New_Logo_2015.pdf

Pololi, L. H., & Evans, A. T. (2015). Group peer mentoring. *Journal of Continuing Education in the Health Professions, 35,* 192–200. doi: 10.1002/chp.21296

Roberts, C. M. (2010). *The dissertation journey* (2nd ed.). Thousand Oaks, CA: Corwin Sage.

Rudestam, K. E., & Newton, R. R. (2014). *Surviving your dissertation* (4th ed.). Thousand Oaks, CA: Sage.

Wang, F., & Hannafin, M. J. (2005, Dec). Design-based research and technology-enhanced learning environments. *Educational Technology Research and Development 53*(4), 5–23.

Zambrana, R. E., Ray, R., Espino, M. M., Castro, C., Cohen, B. D., & Eliason, J. (2015). "Don't leave us behind" The importance of mentoring for underrepresented minority faculty. *American Educational Research Journal, 52*(1), 40–72.

CHAPTER 6

DEVELOPING SUPPORTIVE MENTORING MODELS FOR GRADUATE EDUCATION

Catherine A. Hansman
Cleveland State University

I begin this chapter with two stories that represent many of the students with whom I work in graduate and doctoral programs. The first is Mary, who was accepted and enrolled in graduate school in an urban education doctoral program at a state university only ten miles from her home. In her mid-forties, she is a full time employee in a non-profit organization as well as a single mother of two children. Mary knew that becoming a student would be challenging, yet the doctoral degree would give her the credentials she needed to achieve her dream of becoming a faculty member at a university. As Mary began and progressed in her program of study, she struggled to keep up with her course work and attend to her career and family, yet she persevered in her academic work. However, the conflicting "pulls" of family, career, and academic work on her time and energies meant that she only came to campus when she had face-to-face classes, and when on campus, she had little time to spend cultivating relationships with faculty members and students in her classes. When Mary was finally able

Mentoring in Formal and Informal Contexts, pages 97–117
Copyright © 2016 by Information Age Publishing
97

to begin work on her dissertation, she chose as her dissertation chair a faculty member who had been her instructor in two doctoral classes and who seemed moderately interested in her dissertation topic. Mary planned on finishing her dissertation within a year of beginning the research and writing process, but without the structure of coursework to keep her motivated and the limited support from peers and faculty members, her dissertation developed very slowly. During this time, her dissertation chair left and took a job at a different university, and one other dissertation committee member retired, requiring Mary to find other faculty members willing to serve on her committee, even if she did not know them very well and they had only marginal interest in her research. Finally, ten years after she began her program, Mary successfully defended her dissertation and graduated. She submitted an article written from her dissertation research to a regional peer reviewed journal, and after several revisions, her article was published. However, although she has sent out numerous curriculum vitas for assistant professor positions, five years after graduating with her PhD, Mary is still working at the same non-profit organization in which she was employed when she began her doctoral work. Mary rarely sees her peer students with whom she attended graduate school or the faculty members who were on her dissertation committee, and although her hard-earned credentials has helped her advance in her career into a senior management position, she has been unsuccessful in following her dream of becoming a tenure-track faculty member at a college or university.

Sharon, in contrast to Mary, was only 28 when she was accepted into the same doctoral program as Mary. When she entered the PhD program, Sharon had only recently graduated with her master's degree in higher education. Because she was single, she was able to support herself as a graduate assistant in the department in which her PhD degree would be granted. Her graduate assistantship (GA) required that she be on campus at least three or four days a week, and her GA job assignment was to work with a faculty member who was researching and writing a new text in the field in which Sharon was studying, affording Sharon the opportunity to learn how to research and write for publication. She became known to other faculty members for her research diligence, so she took advantage of opportunities offered her to be second or third author on publications with faculty members in her department, resulting in her being a published author by her fourth year in the program and allowing her opportunities to present research at professional conferences in her field. Since Sharon was on campus frequently, she made friends with her peers in graduate school and was able to form study groups in which they supported each other's research interests and provided critical friendships to critique and sustain each other's writing. Sharon became familiar with many of the faculty members on campus, particularly those in her field, so when she selected her dissertation committee she was able to choose from faculty members who knew her and were interested in her research interests and capabilities. With strong support and peer and faculty mentoring, Sharon was able to successfully defend her dissertation within a year and a half of beginning her research study, in part due to the support of a student peer writing group that she helped form. Because she had published in national peer reviewed journals and attended and presented at numerous conferences in her field during her years as a doctoral student, she had many contacts at many different universities, so her job search was more successful than Mary's, and within a year of graduating with her PhD, Sharon was successful in obtaining a tenure track assistant professor position at a state university.

Although these stories are somewhat exaggerated and may seem extreme examples of what can go wrong and right while matriculating through a doctoral program, the two students in these stories and their experiences as adult learners in graduate school point to the important role that a mentoring relationship and peer support systems can have on graduate and doctoral students throughout their academic careers. Yet, as Mary's cautionary tale demonstrates, not all students are able to form and take part in these relationships, sometimes, as in her case, due to life events and challenges. However, issues such as race, class, gender, sexuality, and ability may also come into play when protégés try to participate in mentoring opportunities (Hansman, 2000, 2003, 2012).

There is much research concerning mentoring relationships in academic contexts (i.e., Creighton, Parks, & Creighton, 2007; Hansman, 2012, 2014; Kram, 1985, 1988; Mullen, 2009, 2012; Marsick & Maltbia, 2009; Mullen, Fish, & Hutinger, 2010), and most of the research generally discusses the worth of mentoring relationships or peer support mentoring groups to prepare or enhance graduate and doctoral students current and future academic careers. Like Mary and Sharon in the stories above, many graduate students enter masters and doctoral programs and hope to form mentoring relationships with faculty members to prepare them for their future roles in higher education or other professions. However, as state budgets are reduced and institutions of higher education experience significant funding cuts, universities are not replacing retiring faculty members, resulting in faculty members teaching increased course loads and at the same time, struggling to advise, mentor, and support the numerous doctoral and graduate students (Hansman, 2013). In addition, relationships between teachers/mentors and learners in the mentoring process contain acknowledged and unacknowledged power structures that may affect the relationship (Hansman, 2003). These issues of power and empowerment in mentoring relationships are not always acknowledged when discussing mentoring models, programs, or relationships (Mullen, 2012; Hansman, 2012, 2013); yet, awareness of these concepts may positively or negatively affect the quality and helpfulness of mentoring relationships between faculty members and their students as well as student peer-to-peer mentoring.

Developing formal and informal mentoring relationships requires all persons involved to understand theoretical concepts as well as practical mentoring models. But consideration concerning how mentoring relationships can best be developed and sustained given the many struggles and challenges to faculty members' and students' time, attention, and workloads are also important to address. Thus, the purpose of this chapter is to explore research, literature, and practical mentoring models, theories, and applications that frame formal and informal mentoring relationships within graduate degree programs in order to understand mentoring relationships, how these relationships allow for professional and personal growth by both mentors and their mentees, and how mentoring models can help support the goals of supportive mentoring. The major issue this chapter addresses is how mentoring models from research, literature, and practice assist both faculty members and students to successfully engage in mentoring relationships that benefit both mentors and mentees. A secondary issue that will be examined is how mentoring models that expand beyond one-to-one mentoring may allow sharing of power among mentors and protégés. Faculty members and current and prospective graduate and doctoral students may find value in this discussion as part of their personal and professional exploration and growth.

DEFINING MENTORING

Merriam (1983) discusses mentoring as involving skill building and knowledge acquisition. In business, education, and community contexts, mentoring may refer to "interactions between more-experienced mentors and less experienced protégés" (Schunk & Mullen, 2013, p. 362), where mentors may provide professional and psychological support to help protégés achieve career and personal successes in their lives. When examining mentoring relationships in higher education, Schunk and Mullen (2013) define academic mentoring as "the involvement of post-secondary faculty, advisors, or supervisors in learning relationships oriented toward career and personal development with students, graduates, or junior faculty at the same or different higher education institution" (p. 362). Research concerning mentoring in academic settings has typically focused on how best to match mentors and protégés; recruiting, preparing and rewarding mentors willing to work with students; measuring career successes as the result of participating in mentoring relationships; and evaluating formal mentoring programs (Mullen, 2008).

To add to the discussion of mentoring models and theories, Mullen (2012) further contends that "technical mentoring involves the transfer of skills within authoritative and apprenticeship contexts whereas alternative mentoring questions hierarchical learning and favors new forms of socialization" (p. 9). Alternative mentoring theories focus on models and practices that might empower all those involved in mentoring relationships. Further, this alternative mentoring perspective may examine the power dynamics in mentoring relationships, non-hierarchical mentoring models, ethical agendas of power (Hansman, 2003), and intentional mentoring that challenges the contexts in which mentoring occur (Galbraith, 2003).

In a recent article, Dawson (2014) discussed Jacobi's (1991) claim that mentoring lacked a common definition, making it difficult to conduct and evaluate the worth of research concerning mentoring relationships. Schunk and Mullen (2103) made a somewhat similar argument, contending that although academic research concerning mentoring is increasing, little attention is paid to processes of mentoring, making it difficult at times to compare research concerning mentoring models. Clearly, although many studies exist concerning mentoring, there is still much research that can be done to understand and improve mentoring relationships and the models upon which they may be built. The next section of this chapter will discuss traditional and alternative mentoring theories and the typical phases in mentoring relationships.

MENTORING THEORIES AND PHASES OF MENTORING: A BRIEF OVERVIEW

Traditional Mentoring Theories

Mullen (2012) describes traditional mentoring theory as encompassing "skills-based, goals-oriented learning passed down through generations" (p. 10), and these mentoring relationships are often carried out in one-to-one mentoring relationships with one protégé being mentored by one mentor. In her view, however, traditional mentoring theory also includes mandated or formal mentoring relationships, where mentors and protégés may be assigned to each other through a matching process and in which goals and expectations for the relationship may be clearly outlined and measured (Hansman, 2000, 2003). This can potentially lead to mechanistic outcomes rather than a process which allows mentors and protégés to build personal and professional relationships that might further their careers or result in them accomplishing their personal and professional goals. In other words, mandated mentoring programs, such as those created by school reform policy for mentoring beginning teachers, can "turn mentoring into a mere achievement measure for schools for purposes related only to school improvement, accreditations, and testing" (Mullen, 2012, p. 12).

However, formal mentoring programs are also developed by organizations and educational institutions to provide opportunities for mentoring, matching mentors with protégés (Hansman, 2000, 2003) around the potential mentors' and protégés' interests, career goals, or other criteria. Organizations many times develop formal mentoring programs for career development for employees (Galbraith & Cohen, 1995) and also to "provide opportunities for mentoring between disparate groups to occur, to achieve racial balance" (Hansman, 2003, p. 103), which may address problems that potential protégés may encounter forming mentoring relationships due to their race, class, gender, sexuality, or ability. In higher education contexts, the goals of formal mentoring programs may be to match students to other students or faculty members based on their subject area or research interests. Formal mentoring programs are likewise sometimes employed by universities to provide junior tenure-track faculty members opportunities to work with senior tenured faculty.

Alternative Mentoring Theories

Although traditional mentoring theory that addresses formal and informal mentoring relationships predominate the literature and research concerning mentoring, Mullen (2012) describes emerging alternative mentoring theories that "expands upon and even resists traditional mentoring theory..." (p. 14), further explaining that "Ideologies of alternative mentoring are value laden, promoting the values of collaboration, co-mentorship, democratic learning, humanistic mentoring, and shared leadership" (p. 15). Traditional mentoring theory assumes that all persons have equal access to mentoring opportunities; alternative mentoring theory encompasses broader worldviews and exposes the "paternalism, dependency, privilege, and exclusion" (Mullen, 2012, p.15) that can occur in traditional mentoring relationships. Alternative mentoring theorists (i.e., Antrop-Gonzalez & De Jesus, 2006; Dawson, 2000; Hansman, 2000, 2003, 2012; Johnson-Bailey, 2012; Johnson-Bailey & Cervero, 2004) are critical of the paternalistic practices that lead to exclusion and disparity in mentoring opportunities in relationships. Alternative mentoring theories and theorists promote democratic concepts of collaboration and shared decisions concerning activities and outcomes within mentoring relationships. However, although alternative mentoring theories critique the ideological constructs of traditional mentoring theory in structure and practice, actual mentoring relationships within the two broad theoretical lens of traditional and alternative may be similar in structure. Nevertheless, the mentoring models related to each theoretical lens epistemologically reflect the beliefs under-pinning them.

Humanistic mentoring is included in alternative mentoring theory and describes a more personal mentoring relationship which includes nurtur-ing the protégé (Mullen, 2012; Varney, 2009). Humanistic mentoring in-cludes psychosocial mentoring, usually considered as an integral part of informal mentoring relationships and that assists development of the proté-gé's self-esteem through interpersonal dynamics between mentors and pro-tégés (Hansman, 2000, 2012, 2013). One example in the academic world of informal mentoring relationships is when faculty members and students en-ter into mentoring dyad arrangements for thesis or dissertation advisement. Other types of informal mentoring in the academic world may include peer mentoring groups, which may be formed through friendships among stu-dent colleagues who provide mentoring to each other while supporting and providing psychosocial as well as career learning and development.

Critical reflection plays a key role in humanistic psychosocial mentoring relationships. Brookfield (2009) describes critical reflection as:

> A social learning process involving a great deal of peer learning...people come to a better understanding of their own assumptions and develop the ability to judge their accuracy and validity only if they involve peers as criti-cally reflective mirrors who provide them with images of how their practice looks to others. (p. 133)

Cranton (2009) contends that the critical reflection process exposes "in-dividuals to alternative perspectives" (p. 185) through reading, discourse, and additional activities that are designed to encourage self-reflection as well as reflection within the group. Peer mentoring groups may provide the means for individuals to be critically self-reflective concerning both their personal and professional identities while supporting each other through graduate school.

Typical Phases of Mentoring

In reviewing the rich literature concerning mentoring programs, it is clear that prescriptions for phases in mentoring that may be useful for plan-ning and implementing formal mentoring programs are common. Cohen (1995) and Galbraith and Cohen (1995) describe mentoring relationships as interactive processes that evolve through set phases: the early phase, where foundations of trust between mentors and protégés are established; the middle phase, where mentors help their protégés define and establish goals; the third phase in which mentors and protégés engage in interac-tions that explore interests, beliefs, and decisions; and finally, the final phase when mentors function as models who spur their protégés to reflect upon their goals and pursue challenges.

Mullen and Schunk (2012) and Schunk and Mullen (2013) describe the mentoring process as unfolding over time, developing a phase process adapted from Kram (1985/1988). They describe a four phase mentoring process from the protégés' perspective. In the first phase, initiation, protégés engage in self-reflection to determine their strengths and weaknesses, learning goals, and the skills, expertise, and psychosocial and/or career support they hope their mentor or mentors might provide in the mentoring relationship. This phase requires intense self-reflection on the part of the protégé concerning their goals and active work in finding and identifying potential persons who might serve as mentors.

The next phase is the cultivation phase (Mullen and Schunk, 2012). Kram (1985/1988) and Mullen and Schunk (2012) estimate that this phase can last two to five years because much is accomplished or attempted during it, and Zachary (2000) contends that it is the most challenging phase for protégés and mentors. The cultivation phase may overlap the initiation phase as goals are further defined and revised and mentors and protégés agree upon how to structure their relationship and the issues, content, and learning goals that might be addressed in the mentoring relationship. Mentors and protégés may engage in "open conversations, affirming cultural differences, asking probing questions, and receiving feedback perceived as thoughtful, timely, and constructive" (Mullen & Schunk, 2012, p. 95). Protégés may develop their skills and knowledge further through considering new and possibly different learning strategies and may monitor their progress through receiving constructive feedback from mentors. Mentors and protégés communicate habitually and engage in close communication that leads to productivity. Crow (2012) asserts that successful mentoring relationships move beyond providing career or psychosocial support, and that mentors and protégés need to be ardently committed to a shared purpose; the cultivation phase is where the work to forge the relationship between mentor and protégé is accomplished.

The separation phase of mentoring follows cultivation and is the natural "beginning of the end" for mentoring relationships. Protégés begin to seek more autonomy and independence and may not need as much of their mentors' support as they had during the cultivation phase. The path this phase progresses along depends in large part on how the goals of the relationship were defined and developed, as "in mentoring theory and practice, separation is an inventible outcome that follows from an intense learning experience, even one of mutual benefit" (Mullen & Schunk, 2012, p. 99). Whether protégés experience this phase positively or negatively depends in large part on how mentors and protégés have defined and revised their relationship during the previous cultivation phase. The experience is also more positive when protégés feel self-confident about their abilities and mentors are supportive of their protégés growing independence (Ragins & Kram, 2007). Mentors can work with their protégés to make this phase successful, lessening the intensity of the learning process while evaluating their work together and celebrating their protégés' achievements. The goals of this phase are for protégés to "separate themselves from their mentors and redefine themselves by continuing to develop their identity" (Mullen & Schunk, 2012, p. 100). Mentors may continue to provide support through promoting their protégés' careers in professional networks, writing letters of recommendation or support, and continuing to provide support as needed and as comfortable to both protégés and mentors. As the separation phase continues, the protégés' need for support has lessened, meaning that there will be less contact between protégés and mentors. However, so that misinterpretation of actions does not occur during this phase, mentors and protégés should engage in clear communication and pay attention to the dynamics of the relationship.

The final phase discussed by Mullen and Schunk (2012) and Schunk and Mullen (2013) is redefinition, where mentors and protégés may become more like peers rather than the empowered all-knowing mentor working with developing protégés; in short, they must "redefine" their relationship. Former mentors and protégés may stay in contact, and in some cases, the mentoring relationship after redefinition becomes more like friendship, where mutual support and respect undergird the relationship. In the academic world, former mentors and protégés may engage in research projects together, write for publication, and present at conferences as peers rather than mentor/protégé.

The typical phases of mentoring relationships presented in this section appear in some variation in many models for mentoring relationships (i.e., Hansman, 2012, 2014; Henrich & Attebury, 2010, Mullen, 2003; Mullen, Fish, & Hutinger, 2010; Mullen & Hutinger, 2008; O'Neil & Marsick, 2009). These phases are also frequently present in traditional and alternative mentoring theory models. Concepts from alternative mentoring theories will ground the discussion of the mentoring models in the next section of this paper. These models encompass ideals of non-authoritative dynamics allowing for holistic development of individuals as well as group learning and development through their engagement in mentoring.

FROM RESEARCH AND LITERATURE: MODELS FOR MENTORING GRADUATE STUDENTS

Finch and Fernandez (2014) assert that "research has shown the important role of faculty mentors in shaping graduate students to become future scholars" (p. 69). In graduate school masters and doctoral programs, there are various forms of mentoring, such as traditional individual mentoring dyads with one-on-one mentoring relationships, mentoring mosaics, formally organized cohort mentoring programs, informal mentoring critical friends, informal mentoring between faculty members and students, peer mentoring groups formed among graduate students, and e-mentoring (Hansman, 2012; Mullen, 2009, 2012).

Peer mentoring dyads or groups may develop through friendships among student colleagues who provide mentoring to each other while supporting and providing psychosocial as well as career learning and development (Hansman, 2014). Additionally, peer or co-mentoring is an approach to mentoring that is grounded in adult learning theory in that it involves individuals participating in the mentoring relationship to "proactively teach each other in ways that are completely respectful while being critically supportive" (Mullen, Fish, & Hutinger, 2010, p. 182). All types of mentoring relationships usually allow for psychosocial and/or career growth for both mentors and protégés (Kram, 1985/1988); however, an area of research that needs more attention from researchers and practitioners is the outcomes of mentoring relationships for mentors (Hansman, 2012).

Many mentoring models have phases that inform and structure the work of mentors, peer mentors, and protégés. Mentoring using these models may foster change and transformative learning (Mezirow, 2009) through drawing on andragogy (Knowles, 1980), constructivism (Phillips, 1995), cognitive apprenticeship (Collins, Brown, & Newman, 1989), and Community of Practice (CoPs) (Wenger, 1998) frameworks, as well as paying attention to issues of power in and outside the relationships. The next section presents mentoring models which reflect these theoretical concepts.

The FCCIC Model for Mentoring Graduate Students Into Teaching

Many mentoring models concerning graduate students focus on developing their research and writing skills to support their future careers in academe, but Finch and Fernandez (2014) point out that learning to teach is often overlooked in doctoral program curriculum. Their model "From Conception to Co-instructor to Completion" (FCCIC) seeks to fill this void by providing a way to integrate faculty and graduate student mentorship in teaching. The model "takes a graduate student (under the supervision of an experienced faculty member) through the entire teaching process: course conceptualization, preparing a syllabus, developing assignments and exams, applying to have the course approved, co-instructing the course, grading, dealing with student issues, and finally, evaluation of the course" (Finch & Fernandez, 2014, p. 70). Through working closely with a faculty mentor, the graduate student or junior faculty member learns the intricacies of developing, teaching, and evaluating a class from start to finish, including navigating the administrative and bureaucratic challenges that must be addressed.

The phases of the model begin with Conception, where the graduate student protégé and her or his faculty mentor choose a topic for course development in which they are both very interested, but one that is not necessarily a specialty area for either. Through Collaboration, the second phase, the protégé and mentor begin developing the course (or possibly revising a pre-existing course), with the faculty mentor guiding the student through the various skills needed to develop a course, such as reviewing and selecting appropriate literature and summarizing goals to develop and produce a syllabus. Finch and Fernandez (2014) maintain that this step is "set apart from the TA model because the student has direct input into the development of the course before execution . . . the graduate mentee has sufficient understanding of the substantive area to be a full co-instructor of the course" (p. 71), including sharing with his or her mentor the development of evaluation and assessment assignments and other instruments to measure student learning.

The third step, Course Approval, requires the protégé and faculty mentor to collaborate through all the steps to achieve approval of the course from the university. This includes completing all necessary forms and paperwork, monitoring the course review process as the course approval works its way through the university system, and being present for relevant committee meetings to answer questions and concerns about the new course. Exposing student protégés and allowing them to participate in the bureaucratic process helps them gain understandings of how they might navigate academic systems in their future careers. The fourth step, Co-Instructorship, allows protégés to be immersed as much as possible in actually teaching the course they co-designed with their mentors. Protégé instructors play an equal role with their mentors in teaching the course; faculty mentors should "feel free to ask for equal participation from the mentee, who in return should feel secure enough to ask for assistance whenever needed" (Finch & Fernandez, 2014, p. 72). This co-instructorship requires faculty members and their protégés to address the inherent power relationship in the professor-student relationship, including putting significant factors about the arrangement into a written agreement so they know what is expected of their collaborative teaching and work. Continual conversations about jointly teaching the course can include discussions and decisions made about course housekeeping, grading assignments, leading in-class activities, and course evaluations. In the final step of the FCCIC model, Completion, protégés and mentors discuss their experiences, evaluate their actions, and discuss the future of the course after the semester ends. Mentors and protégés actively reflect upon the successes and issues they experienced while teaching together and look to the future and discuss future collaborations.

Although the FCCIC model may bear some similarity to the Teaching Assistant (TA) experience utilized by many universities as the only source to prepare graduate students to teach in higher education classrooms, the FCCIC model is different because it provides a "teaching specific mentoring approach expressly for those faculty and graduate students who desire to assure teacher training beyond what the traditional TA model provides" (Finch & Fernandez, 2014, p. 70). Furthermore, since graduate student protégés are more or less equal partners from the conception of the class until its conclusion, the model allows, through both mentors and protégés engaging in active critical reflection, for growth and development of faculty mentors and their protégés as teachers. What is unique about this model is the shared power among mentors and protégés; protégés make decisions along with their mentors on the direction the course and mentoring takes.

The WIT Program: Peer Mentoring

Other mentoring models for graduate students focus on developing the writing and research skills of graduate students. For example, Mullen (2003) developed the Writers in Training Program (WIT) with a cohort of 25 doctoral students who were all at different stages of their programs. The WIT model is a "collaborative faculty-student support group that brings together doctoral students and their academic mentors" (p. 412) to engage in discussions and to rehearse the skills necessary for them to advance as researchers, scholars, and teachers in academe. Through engaging in research projects with her own doctoral advisees, Mullen and her student protégés established goals of building relationships within the peer mentoring cohort that would also afford a safe place for cohort members to review and critique each other's dissertation research and writing. Engaging within the WIT framework encouraged cohort peer group members to develop deeper connections beyond that of one-to-one student/faculty mentoring relationships, allowing faculty member Mullen and the doctoral student cohort peer members to experience mutual support of their shared and individual goals.

As a mentor, Mullen met with the peer student cohort group for five hours biweekly to instruct and help them practice academic writing while modeling, coaching, and giving feedback and encouragement. From these meetings, the cohort peer group learned strategies to mutually critique each other's research and writing while reflecting about their scholarly development. Participation in the WIT cohort encouraged students to practice their research and writing skills outside of the group meetings, and cohort peer students viewed the WIT program as a strong and supportive mentoring network that enabled them to complete their dissertations while moving forward in their academic career paths.

Longitudinal research concerning the WIT cohort group (Mullen & Tuten, 2010) showed that helpful mentoring behaviors, such as modeling and demonstrating academic writing skills, resulted in raised self-confidence among cohort peer students concerning their disciplinary knowledge. Cohort members also reported better understandings of collaboration in learning, more motivation, and gains in academic productivity, such as finishing their dissertations, presenting at conferences, and submitting publications to journals. Overall, through sustained participation in the WIT program, students learned how to successfully pursue careers in academe.

Cognitive Apprenticeship Model

Rogoff (1995) contends that learning involves development in personal, interpersonal, and community processes, although these phases are not necessarily sequential and may be somewhat fluid as members may move between phases. These processes/phases may be considered cognitive apprenticeships (Hansman, 2001), which in the academic world may focus on teaching metacognitive processes such as reading and writing (Collins et al., 1989). Farmer, Buckmaster and LeGrand (1992) describe cognitive apprenticeship in education as occurring in five sequential phases: modeling, approximating, fading, self-directed learning, and generalizing. Modeling occurs in two parts: behavioral modeling allows learners to observe performance of an activity by experienced members of a community, while cognitive modeling allows experienced members to a community to share "tricks of the trade" with newer members.

Using the concepts of cognitive apprenticeships, Austin (2009) developed her cognitive apprenticeship mentoring model to assist first year doctoral students. Her model focuses on assisting students to develop academic/professional skills such as critical scholarly reading, research, and writing, along with psychosocial skills that allow students to learn to socialize in higher education, practicing interpersonal skills within the cohort to prepare them for their future careers. Schunk and Mullen (2013) describe the phases of her model: for proposal writing, "the instructor provides examples of strong proposals (models) and coaching and scaffolding (e.g., feedback from the instructor and peers) as students wrote proposal drafts" (p. 369). Students could then engage in critical reflection on what they had learned and their successes and failures while practicing these skills with the support of their peers and others. The cognitive apprenticeships model allowed students to learn and practice valuable skills for their future careers in academe.

Community of Peer Mentors Model

Wenger's (1998) concept of Communities of Practice (CoPs) incorporates some of the key concepts from cognitive apprenticeships and provides the framework for the design for Community of Peer Mentors (Hansman, 2013) as a model for doctoral student peer mentoring. CoPs are formed by people "around common interests, ideas, passions and goals—in other words, the things that matter to people" (Hansman, 2008, p. 299). Communities of practice are "self-organized and selected groups of people who share a common sense of purpose and a desire to learn and know what each other know. They are self-organized by the members themselves and may exist within larger organizational structures" (Hansman, 2001, p. 48). Wenger (1998) contends that in CoPs, group members, not people or conditions external to the CoP, set the goals and the "practice" in which the group engages. Members of CoPs share a repertoire of communal resources and common activities to build their knowledge. Group leadership is decided within the group through negotiations concerning the purpose for the group (Hansman, 2008) to avoid hierarchical power relationships.

The overall purpose of Community of Peer Mentors Model is to provide the opportunities for peer community members, graduate/doctoral students, to engage in learning and development to prepare for their future careers in academe. The Communities of Peer Mentors Model is similar to, yet different from, Wenger's Community of Practice and the mentoring models (Kram, 1985/1988; Mullen & Schunk, 2012) described earlier in this chapter. Student and faculty peer community members (Peer Mentors) share power in decision making, participate in individual and group critical reflection and discourse, as well as sustain peer relationships among themselves that can support them as they transition from student roles to faculty members or other roles in academe.

The Community of Peer Mentors Model consists of five critical phases or points that lead to new phases: Forming, Connecting, Engaging, Concluding and New Beginnings, and Enduring Networks (Hansman, 2013). During Forming, graduate and doctoral students at any point in the progression of their programs are invited to an organizing meeting by sponsoring faculty members who are not in positions of power, but rather serve as unifying coaches to assist participants in the program. In this critical point of Forming, students learn about the overall purpose for the Community of Peer Mentors and make decisions as to whether to join the group. The second critical point of Connecting begins with engaged dialogue among Peer Mentors to promote self and group critical reflection in the form of questioning activities and discourse aimed at furthering knowledge and understandings of each other, the individual stages in their graduate or doctoral programs, and the types of support they would like and may be able to provide to other members of the group. Faculty member coaches, as part of the community, may also provide support at this phase.

In the third critical point, Engaging, mutually defined goals are collaboratively decided through problematizing questions and issues concerning the nature of academe and the skills and knowledge perceived as needed by Peer Mentors to further their careers in higher education. Peer Mentors develop further knowledge and insights concerning the issues raised by the group, advance their understandings of changing perceptions and actions related to these issues, and further, cultivate the knowledge and skills required to address them. Through discourse about these issues, Peer Mentors collaboratively make decisions regarding in which activities to engage. As an example, Peer Mentors may decide that presenting their research projects and then receiving supportive critical feedback from community members may help them individually improve their writing and presentation skills while furthering research collaborations among the members of the community. The Engaging point may be the lengthiest phase in the Community of Peer Mentors Model, as it is a continual phase or reiterative process; as more experienced graduate and doctoral students move onto the fourth and next critical point, Concluding and New Beginnings, less experienced doctoral students will move into Engaging, allowing for new collaboratively defined problems, issues, and goals to be addressed by Peer Members.

As more senior Peer Members enter the fourth critical point, Concluding and New Beginnings, they may distance themselves somewhat from the "younger" Peer Members as they successfully complete and defend their theses or dissertations and graduate from their programs. Peer Members at the Concluding and New Beginnings point may continue the work of the Engaging critical point; however, they may design new activities such as mock interviews and role play with other group members to learn essential skills and gain support as they apply for academic or other types of positions. These Peer Members are now senior members of the Community of Peer Mentors and may take on and share more responsibility with faculty Peer Mentor coaches for recruiting newer doctoral students to the Community of Peer Mentors.

The fifth and final critical point, Enduring Networks, allows the continuation of the peer mentoring process. Peer Mentors maintain connections with each other in face-to-face meetings or through email or social media sites to provide support and critical friendships to Peer Mentors throughout their careers. In this way, community Peer Mentors may continue to provide their support and critical friendships to doctoral students in earlier points of the Community of Peer Mentoring as well as the Peer Mentors with whom they interacted throughout their own experiences in the community.

DISCUSSION

The models presented in this chapter may provide graduate and doctoral students with some much needed peer mentoring throughout their doctoral programs. Each model presented here, the FCCIC, WIT, Cognitive Apprenticeship, and Community of Peer Mentor models, embrace some facet of alternative mentoring theory proposed by Mullen (2012). Many of these models loosely follow the phases discussed by Mullen and Schunk (2012) and Kram (1985/1988) earlier in this chapter. Each model illustrates, through their critical points and phases, methods to empower graduate and doctoral students to pursue careers as future faculty members or higher education administrators. Through building in support and empowerment into these mentoring models, protégés who participate in these or similar mentoring models or programs may in their future careers become supportive mentors to others through assessing needs, engaging in collaboratively dynamic dialogue, designing active learning activities, sharing power while co-constructing mutual goals and outcomes, measuring the outcomes in terms of successful thesis or dissertation defenses or other means, and planning continuing personal and professional development and interactions throughout their careers. All these models also provide the means for mentors and protégés to question the culture of academe, allowing them the "safe space" that is essential to question the power structures and status quo in higher education, which in turn may foster the development of transparent and equitable practices for understanding knowledge construction, learning, and development through mentoring relationships. Finally, these models may aid the development of a new generation of mentors; in other words, those who experience supportive and empowering mentoring while they are students may be more likely to become gifted mentors to others in their future careers.

CONCLUSION

Remember Mary and Sharon, the doctoral students whose stories were featured at the beginning of this chapter? Mary, who due to her work responsibilities could not spend quality time with mentors while a student in her doctoral program, would probably have benefited from participating in mentoring programs that adapt some of the phases of the programs discussed in this chapter. For example, if Mary's university had a mentoring program that incorporated some of the principles of Finch and Fernandez's (2014) FCCIC model, she may have been able to gain valuable experience planning and teaching courses, which would have given her knowledge and skills that might be valuable to her as she searched for faculty positions in higher education. Even if she could not teach during the day due to her work conflicts, perhaps her university could foster a program that encouraged collaboration with mentors who were willing to work with her to teach an evening course that would not conflict with her daily work obligations. Another way the FCCIC model might be implemented is to incorporate online teaching so that students like Mary who cannot be on campus would still have opportunities to learn to work with students in a "real-world" context. Sharon also would benefit and gain teaching experience through a program like the FCCIC model, and participating in a program like this would help prepare both students for the realities of teaching in higher education.

Other models discussed in this chapter, like the WIT mentoring program (Mullen, 2003), the cognitive apprenticeship models (Farmer, Buckmaster & LeGrand, 1992; Austin, 2009), and the Community of Peer Mentors Model (Hansman, 2013) could also prove helpful to students like Mary and Sharon. All of these models feature not only mentoring opportunities with faculty members but also activities and ways to engage with other students in peer mentoring. Peer mentoring is an increasingly important way for students to learn and practice research, conference presentation, and writing skills. Doctoral students and new faculty members need to have opportunities to gain competence in these abilities, and peer mentors can provide support and feedback concerning their research, writing and presentation accomplishments that will serve them well in their future academic careers. In this way, peer mentors not only learn more about the research, publication and conference presentation expectations they will face as faculty members, but they also have opportunities to practice mentoring others and support their own and others' learning. The experience they gain as peer mentors might assist them in the future as they serve as mentors to their own students when they become faculty members. Opportunities for on-line peer mentoring might also be an exciting option in the FCCIC, WIT, cognitive apprenticeship, and Community of Peer Mentors models, as each of these models could be easily adapted for on-line interactions using course shells such as Blackboard. Other electronic means for peer mentoring might be peers engaging in two-way video conferencing (Skype, FaceTime, etc.), sending emails, or posting and participating in discussions on social media sites dedicated to the peer mentor groups. These kinds of innovative practices would benefit students such as Mary and Sharon as they matriculate through doctoral programs.

The stories of Mary and Sharon are important to me, as they represent a composite of the many doctoral students with whom I work. But on a more personal note, they also depict my own journey as a doctoral student. I commuted almost four hours twice a week to attend classes during my doctoral program, so for the first two years of my program I was "Mary"—I only showed up for classes and left as soon after class as I could to begin my long journey home. However, during my final two years of study, my experience became more like Sharon's story. Although I still had a long commute, I began working as a Graduate Assistant on the campus, arranging my work and family schedule to allow me the time to do this. It was only through working on campus, getting to know faculty members, and engaging in peer mentoring with other students that I began to understand what I needed to do to succeed in my goal of becoming a faculty member. But without the supportive mentoring of a key faculty member and engaging in peer cohort mentoring, I would not have gained the research, presentation, and writing experiences I needed to establish my academic credentials to become a faculty member. In the 20 years since I graduated with my doctoral degree, I still reflect upon and feel grateful for the support and mentoring I was fortunate enough to receive, and also the peer networks that empowered me to mentor others.

Paulo Freire (1997) said that mentors should "transcend their merely instructive task and assume the ethical posture of a mentor who truly believes in the total autonomy, freedom, and development of those he or she mentors" (p. 324). Faculty members, as mentors and coaches to their graduate students, must provide mentoring opportunities and creatively design mentoring models that will enhance the personal and professional development of their students. Through modeling behaviors and attitudes and sharing power within mentoring relationships and programs, mentors can assist and empower their students to achieve their career goals while creating networks of support that will sustain their own and their students' future goals and careers.

REFERENCES

Antrop-Gonzalez, R., & DeJesus, A. (2006). Toward a theory of *critical care* in urban small school reform: Examining structures and pedagogies of caring in two Latino community based schools. *International Journal of Qualitative Studies in Education, 19*(4), 409–433.

Austin, A. E. (2009). Cognitive apprenticeship theory and its implications for doctoral education: A case example from a doctoral program in higher and adult education. *International Journal for Academic Development, 14*, 173–183.

Brookfield. S. (2009). Engaging critical reflection in corporate America. In J. Mezirow & E. Taylor & Associates (Eds.), *Transformative learning in practice: Insights from community, workplace and higher education* (pp. 125–135). San Francisco, CA: Jossey-Bass.

Cohen, N, (1995). *Mentoring adult learners: A guide for educators and trainers.* Malabar, FL: Kreiger.

Collins, A., Brown, J. S., & Newman, S. E. (1989). Cognitive apprenticeship: Teaching the crafts of reading, writing, and mathematics. In L. B. Resnick (Ed.),

Knowing learning and instruction: Essays in honor of Robert Glaser (pp. 453–492). Hillsdale, NJ: Erlbaum.

Cranton, P. (2009). From tradesperson to teacher: A transformative transition. In J. Mezirow & E. Taylor & Associates (Eds.), *Transformative learning in practice: Insights from community, workplace and higher education* (pp. 182–192). San Francisco, CA: Jossey-Bass.

Creighton, T., Parks, D., & Creighton, L. (2007). Mentoring doctoral students: The need for a pedagogy. *The NCPEA Handbook of Doctoral Programs in Educational Leadership: Issues and Challenges*, 1–10.

Crow, G. M. (2012). A critical–constructivist perspetive on mentoring and coaching for leadership. In C. Mullen & S. Fletcher (Eds.), *Handbook of mentoring and coaching in education* (pp. 228–242). London, England: Sage.

Dawson, P. (2014). Beyond a definition: Toward a framework for designing and specifying mentoring models. *Educational Research, 43*(3), 137–145. doi: 10.3102/001389X14528751

Dawson, R. (2000) Knowledge capabilities as the focus of organisational development and strategy. *Journal of Knowledge Management, 4*(4), 320–327.

Farmer, J. A., Buckmaster, A., & LeGrand B. (1992). Cognitive apprenticeship: Implications for continuing professional education. In H. K. Baskett & V. Marsick (Eds.), *New directions for adult and continuing education: No. 33. Professionals' ways of knowing: Findings on how to improve professional education* (pp. 41–50). San Francisco, CA: Jossey-Bass.

Finch, J. K., & Fernandez, C. (2014). Mentoring graduate students in teaching: The FC-CIC model. *Teaching Sociology, 42*(1), 69–75. doi: 10:11777/0092055X13507781

Freire, P. (1997). A response. In P. Freire, (Ed.), *Mentoring the mentor: A critical dialogue with Paulo Freire* (pp. 303–330). New York, NY: Peter Lang.

Galbraith, M. W. (2003). The adult education professor as mentor: A means to enhance teaching and learning. *Perspectives: The New York Journal of Adult Learning, 1*(1), 9–20.

Galbraith, M. W., & Cohen, N. H. (Eds.). (1995). *New directions in adult and continuing education: No. 66. Mentoring: New strategies and challenges*. San Francisco, CA: Jossey-Bass.

Hansman, C. A. (2000) Formal mentoring programs. In A. Wilson & E. Hayes (Eds.), *Handbook of Adult and Continuing Education* (pp. 493–507). San Francisco, CA: Jossey-Bass.

Hansman, C. A. (2001). Context based adult learning. In S. B. Merriam (Ed.), *New directions for adult and continuing education: No. 89. An update on adult learning theory.* (pp. 43–51). San Francisco, CA: Jossey-Bass.

Hansman, C. A. (2003). Power and learning in mentoring relationships. In R. Cervero, B. Courtenay, & M. Hixson (Eds.) *Global perspectives: Volume III* (pp. 101–121). Athens, GA: University of Georgia.

Hansman, C. A. (2008). Adult learning in communities of practice: Situating theory in practice. In C. Kimble, P. Hildreth, & I. Bourdon (Eds.), *Communities of practice: Creating learning environments for educators, Vol. 1* (pp. 279–292). Charlotte, NC: Information Age.

Hansman, C. A. (2012). Empowerment in the faculty-student mentoring relationship. In C. Mullen & S. Fletcher (Eds.), *Handbook of mentoring and coaching in education* (pp. 368–382). London, England; Sage.

Hansman, C. A. (2013). Mentoring doctoral students: Challenges and models for success. In C. J. Boden-McGill & K. P. King (Eds.), *Conversations about adult learning in our complex world* (pp. 195–207). Charlotte, NC: Information Age.

Hansman, C. A. (2014). Mentoring in graduate education: Curriculum for transformative learning. In V. Wang & V. Bryan (Eds.), *Andragogical and pedagogical methods for curriculum development* (pp. 101–117). Charlotte, NC: Information Age.

Henrich, K. J., & Attebury, R. (2010). Communities of practice at an academic library: A new approach to mentoring at the University of Idaho. *The Journal of Academic Librarianship, 36*(2), 158–165.

Jacobi, M. (1991). Mentoring and undergraduate academic success: A literature review. *Review of Educational Research, 61*, 505–532.

Johnson-Bailey, J. (2012). Effects of race and racial dynamics on mentoring. In C. Mullen & S. Fletcher (Eds.), *Handbook of mentoring and coaching in education* (pp. 155–168). London, England: Sage.

Johnson-Bailey, J., & Cervero, R. (2004). Mentoring in Black and White: The intricacies of cross-cultural mentoring. *Mentoring & Tutoring: Partnership in Learning, 12*(1), 7–21.

Knowles, M. (1980). Th*e modern practice of adult education: From pedagogy to andragogy* (2nd ed.). New York, NY: Cambridge Books.

Kram, K. E. (1985/1988). *Mentoring at work: Developmental relationships in organizational life.* Glenview, IL: Scott, Foresman & Company.

Marsick, V. J., & Maltbia, T. E. (2009). The transformative potential of action learning conversations: Developing critically reflective practice skills. In J. Mezirow, E. W. Taylor, & Associates (Eds.), *Transformative learning in practice: Insights from community, workplace and higher education* (pp. 160–181). San Francisco, CA: Jossey-Bass.

Merriam, S. B. (1983). Mentors and protégés: A critical review of the literature. *Adult Education Quarterly, 33*, 161–173.

Mezirow, J. (2009). Transformative learning theory. In J. Mezirow & E. Taylor & Associates (Eds.), *Transformative learning in practice: Insights from community, workplace and higher education* (pp. 18–31). San Francisco, CA: Jossey-Bass.

Mullen, C. A. (2003). The WIT cohort: A case study of informal doctoral mentoring. *Journal of Further and Higher Education, 27*, 411–426.

Mullen, C. A. (Ed). (2008). *The handbook of formal mentoring in higher education: A case study approach.* Norwood, MA: Christopher-Gordon.

Mullen, C. A. (2009). Re-imagining the human dimension of mentoring: A framework for research administration and the academy. *The Journal of Research Administration* (*40*)1, 10–31.

Mullen, C. A. (2012). Mentoring: An overview. In C. Mullen & S. Fletcher (Eds.), *Handbook of mentoring and coaching in education* (pp. 7–23). London, England: Sage.

Mullen, C. A., & Hutinger, J. L. (2008). At the tipping point? Role of formal faculty mentoring in changing university research cultures. *Journal of In-Service Education, 34*(2), 181–204. doi: 10.1080/13674580801951012.

Mullen, C. A., Fish, V. L., & Hutinger, J. L. (2010). Mentoring doctoral students through scholastic engagement: Adult learning principles in action. *Journal of Further and Higher Education, 34*(2), 179–197.

Mullen, C. A., & Tuten, E. M. (2010). Doctoral cohort mentoring: Interdependence, collaborative learning, and cultural change. *Scholar-Practitioner Quarterly, 4,* 11–32.

Mullen, C. A., & Schunk, D. H. (2012). Operationalizing phases of mentoring relationships. In C. Mullen & S. Fletcher (Eds.), *Handbook of mentoring and coaching in education* (pp. 89–104). London, England: Sage.

O'Neil, J., & Marsick, V. (2009). Peer mentoring and action learning. *Adult Learning, 20*(1–2), 19–24.

Phillips, D. C. (1995). The good, the bad, and the ugly: The many faces of constructivism. *Educational Researcher, 24*(7), 5–12.

Ragins, B. R., & Kram, K. E. (Eds.). (2007). *Handbook of mentoring at work: Theory, research, and practice.* Los Angeles, CA: Sage.

Rogoff, B. (1995). Observing sociocultural activity in three planes: Participatory appropriation, guided participation, and apprenticeship. In J. Wertsch, P. del Rio, & A. Alvarez (Eds.), *Sociocultural studies of the mind.* Cambridge, England: Cambridge University Press.

Schunk, D. H., & Mullen, C. A. (2013). Toward a conceptual model of mentoring research: Integration with self-regulated learning. *Educational Psychology Review, 25,* 361–389. doi: 10.1007/s10648-013-9233-3.

Varney, J. (2009). Humanistic mentoring: Nurturing the person within. *Kappa Delta Pi Record, 45*(3), 127–131.

Wenger, E. (1998). *Communities of practice.* Cambridge, England: Cambridge University Press.

Zachary, L. J. (2000). *The mentor's guide: Facilitating effective learning relationships.* Thousand Oaks, CA: Jossey-Bass.

CHAPTER 7

LEADERSHIP THAT LASTS A LIFETIME

Collegiate Advising as Mentoring in a Black Greek Letter Organization

Sean Dickerson
University of South Florida, Tampa

Vonzell Agosto
University of South Florida, Tampa

Maniphone Dickerson
University of South Florida, Tampa

Michael Dove
University of South Florida, Tampa

During the nineteenth century, African American Collegiate Fraternities and Sororities, also known as Black Greek Letter Organizations (BGLOs), resulted in part from the exclusion and marginalization of Black people in society—and college more specifically. As a reminder of racial segregation

Mentoring in Formal and Informal Contexts, pages 119–136
Copyright © 2016 by Information Age Publishing
All rights of reproduction in any form reserved.

within the Greek system, past and present, a predominantly White fraternity on a college campus in Oklahoma was closed in 2015 when some of its members made racist chants depicting exclusionist ideology directed at Black people. Since their inception, the main aims of BGLOs have been to support the development of its members and participation of the larger community in activities associated with social/emotional, economic, and academic success (Baker, 2008). Linked by African American cultural traditions and aims, BGLOs have contributed to African American culture and college culture through their leadership on campuses and in communities (Goss, Harris, Spencer, & Hughey, 2014). Such contributions and aims continue a century later; however, the intended outcomes and unintended consequences of membership do not always converge into an unequivocally positive narrative about BGLOs.

Historically, BGLOs have been accused of being elitist, only catering to the Black bourgeoisie, and for profit rather than for service (free of charge) (Frazier, 1957). More recently, BGLOs have been referred to as 'educated gangs' after rituals involving violence led to the deaths of fraternity members (Hughey & Hernandez, 2013). Hughey (2008) has argued that this moniker, when directed towards BGLOs rather than the Greek system overall, has racist underpinnings. He further argues that the overall discourse about BGLOs rests on a binary of goodness/badness rather than more complex renderings of their organizational structures (Hughey, 2008). Despite these negative perceptions generated by media or academic communities, the aims of BGLOs and their socialization process stem from more altruistic intentions (Kimbrough, 1995).

This chapter focuses on the formal and informal processes of preparing certified collegiate advisors to mentor members of one BGLO, Phi Beta Sigma. More specifically, the following question guided us in writing this chapter: How is mentoring in Phi Beta Sigma being institutionalized in the advising program, informally and formally? We examine how the position of *collegiate advisor* is conceived of as a leadership role involving mentoring that is framed within the broader principles of the organization and responsive to socio-political drivers external to the organization. In addition to analyzing organizational documents (such as the Collegiate Advisor University Certification manual and Anti-hazing facilitator's guide), we drew on first-hand knowledge of a high-level administrator, Michael Dove, who had been instrumental in designing and implementing the advising program. The perspectives of top-level administrative roles in BGLOs are seldom featured as an authorial voice in the scholarship (e.g., Parks, 2008; Ray, 2012). As one of the authors of this chapter, Dove helps us provide a scholar-practitioner perspective to the study of BGLOs, namely the mentoring support provided within a chapter of Phi Beta Sigma that is located in the southeastern region of the United States.

LITERATURE ON MEMBERSHIP
AND MENTORSHIP OF AFFILIATES

According to Molasso (2005) the majority of research on fraternity and sorority membership focuses on problems related to alcohol and other drug abuse. Molasso (2005) cautioned that other issues relevant to fraternity/ sorority membership such as psychosocial, cognitive, and identity development should not be precluded. In response to the limited focus of the research on membership have come studies exploring the role of Greek letter affiliation in college outcomes. Martin, Hevel, Asel, and Pascarella (2011) studied first year affiliated students' college outcomes related to (a) moral reasoning; (b) cognitive development; (c) intercultural effectiveness; (d) inclination to inquire and lifelong learning; and (d) psychological well-being. Although their study was broader in scope than much of the research on Greek letter affiliation, the particularities of BGLOs were not considered. More specifically, the authors noted that it was likely that most participants were affiliated with a sorority in the National Panhellenic Conference or a fraternity in the North American Interfraternity Conference, which primarily includes traditionally White sororities and fraternities.

Harris and Harper (2014) situated the recurring negative themes about BGLOs—sexism, racism, and homophobia—in the broader education and social science literature, and encouraged researchers to move beyond the narrative of 'brothers behaving badly' to consider how young men in fraternities perform masculinity in more productive ways. However, only one Black male was interviewed and they noted that the racial/ethnic composition of the study's sample was not diverse, although it was representative of the membership of the fraternity they were studying and of most fraternities in the Interfraternity Conference (IFC). Dancy and Hotchkins (2015) also studied the construction of manhood by members of a BGLO and found positive constructions associated with a sense of 'brotherhood.' For instance, members' expectations around persistence and leadership were reinforced and their worldviews were expanded.

Despite the broadened focus of inquiry and positive outcomes depicted by these studies of fraternities by Harris and Harper (2014) and Dancy and Hotchkins (2015), neither considered the role of mentoring or advising. Given the limited research on mentoring in fraternities, especially in BGLOs, we turn to literature on mentoring models used in higher education to consider how mentoring development occurs within a social network of various actors and influences.

Developmental Mentoring Network Model

Although there are various approaches to formal and informal mentoring (e.g., peer to peer, dyads), we found the developmental mentoring network to be an approach that is expansive and amenable to an organizational structure with various roles (Dobrow, Chandler, Murphy, & Kram, 2011). There are four fundamental attributes of engagement among mentors/developers within developmental mentoring networks:

1. Those involved as developers take an active interest in, and actions toward, advancing the protégé's (or peer mentor's) career.
2. They involve multiple developers (usually four to five).
3. They are characterized by their inclusion of a broad range of social spheres—people from inside and outside the organization, people from different hierarchical levels (superiors, peers, and subordinates), and people from a wide range of domains beyond work (e.g., friends, family members, and community groups).
4. The content of exchange between parties is broader, such that developers can provide varying amounts (e.g., high vs. low) and types of developmental support (e.g., career and psychosocial). (Dobrow et al., 2011)

Developmental mentoring networks move beyond traditional mentoring dyads toward networks of actors (Chandler & Kram, 2005). Career support and psychosocial support are typically provided within developmental mentoring networks. For instance, career support can be provided through the sponsorship, exposure and visibility, coaching, protection, and challenging assignments mentors make available to others in the network, whereas psychosocial support can be provided through counseling, role modeling, acceptance and confirmation, and friendship (Kram, 1985). Both career and psychosocial support are areas of concern in the literature on how to support college students.

Phi Beta Sigma emphasizes the development of individuals and the organization through mentoring and can be understood as a developmental mentoring network. Within the network, we focus on the preparation of advisors who have mentoring responsibilities and their certification through the *Collegiate Advisor Certification Training* program, including their interactions with others who mentor within the fraternity. To illustrate the network of fraternity members and development of mentoring capacity within it, we rely on a model outlining stages of development in mentoring programs (Barrera, Braley, & Slate, 2010; Sindelar, 1992). The stages include: (a) establishing a rationale; (b) selecting mentors and mentees; (c) preparing/training mentors; (d) monitoring the mentoring process; (e) evaluating the program; and (f) revising it (Barrera et al., 2010; Sindelar, 1992). Although this model of mentoring program development is based on the preparation of teachers, we think it is useful for exploring the development of mentoring associated with adults who work as collegiate advisors to ensure success of college students/fraternity affiliates. We focus on mentoring in the fraternity in association with the *Collegiate Advisor Program,* current initiatives (*I Am My Brother's Keeper*), and the broader socio-cultural landscape concerning the role of Black men in the education and development of Black men.

"CULTURE FOR SERVICE AND SERVICE FOR HUMANITY": A MOTTO TO INSPIRE MENTORING

Phi Beta Sigma is one of the 'divine nine,' or one of nine historically BGLOs under the coordinating body of the National Pan-Hellenic Council, Incorporated (NPHC). According to its website, Phi Beta Sigma was organized by three students at Howard University in 1914 who wanted a "Greek letter fraternity that would truly exemplify the ideals of brotherhood, scholarship, and service" (History section, ¶1). The ideal of service was directed toward the general community and codified in Phi Beta Sigma's motto: "Culture for Service and Service for Humanity" (Mission Statement section, ¶1).

Michael Dove, now Director of the Sigma Beta Club—a program supporting young Black males ages 10–18—was recruited into the graduate or alumni chapter of Phi Beta Sigma in 2011 as a result of his work in the community with another mentoring program for Black males. After gaining the attention of members from local fraternity chapters, he was invited to an 'informational' event focused on recruiting new members. Although the presidents of each of the BGLO fraternities were present, only the president of Phi Beta Sigma spoke with Dove, which left him feeling "a sense of brotherhood," concluding the president thought enough of him to tell him about the fraternity.

Another influential factor that motivated Dove to join Phi Beta Sigma, rather than another fraternity, was its motto: Culture for Service, Service for Humanity. Dove's belief in Karma helps explain why the motto is important to him: "I think that the good that you put out you'll receive back even twofold" (personal communication, May 4, 2015). He claimed to have always believed that if you strengthen those around you, "you'll be strengthened as well" (personal communication, May 4, 2015). Although Dove is a certified collegiate advisor for the undergraduate chapter, he currently meets the expectation given to advisors by mentoring the Sigma Beta Club. For him, working with the younger males engaged with the fraternity affords him the opportunity to impact multiple generations as the younger participants are on a pathway toward undergraduate chapter membership, potentially.

COLLEGIATE ADVISOR PREPARATION
AND CERTIFICATION TRAINING

The organizational structure of Phi Beta Sigma has four distinct layers with a fifth that is not as common across the organization. First is the international body of the fraternity with officers representing chapters across the globe. Second is the regional level organization, similarly consisting of members from the specified regions in positions of organizational leadership. The third organizational level is described as the state level. The fourth organizational level, which is typically familiar to those inside and outside of Greek-life culture, is the local or collegiate level. Included at this level are both the graduate and undergraduate chapters of Phi Beta Sigma, which are directly associated with a college or university campus. Finally, the fifth level of Phi Beta Sigma is the Sigma Beta Club. Our focus is on the fourth level, which is where the collegiate advisor is positioned.

The role, characteristics, and responsibilities of the collegiate advisor are detailed in the *Collegiate Advisor University Certification Training* (CAUCT) manual (2011). The training manual details how collegiate advisors are to handle themselves as representatives of the fraternal chapter who engage with affiliates of both the graduate and undergraduate chapters. A collegiate advisor is expected to be a guide for the other members of the fraternity.

The expectation of mentoring by those undertaking the collegiate advisor's role is clearly stated in the CAUCT (2011) manual. First, the introduction begins with a citation from Dunkel and Schuh (1998) and the essential roles for advisors of student groups they have outlined to include mentor, supervisor, teacher, leader, and follower. Dunkel and Schuh caution that the role of mentor cannot be pressed upon someone, but is a relationship resulting from one's willingness to mentor and be mentored. This statement suggests that not all collegiate advisors will have the opportunity to mentor, for instance, when there is no one willing to be mentored. However, the collegiate advisor training manual deviates from the cited research to list mentoring as an expectation of the advisor. It states, "As a collegiate advisor, you are expected to mentor, monitor, and counsel your collegiate brothers" (CAUCT, 2011, p. 13). The stated expectation in the CAUCT manual is that advisors will "build strong mentoring/coaching relationships" (p. 45) and, through the coaching and development process of the program, become a "mentor rather than merely an advisor" (p. 49). Mentoring is institutionalized through the manual with its explicit statements about the prominence of mentoring and the intentional role that advisors are encouraged to take in building mentoring relationships. Although collegiate advisors are assigned to a specific collegiate chapter, together they provide a network of support for one another. The following sections follow the outline for developing mentoring programs: (re)establishing a rationale, selecting mentors/mentees, preparing/training mentors, monitoring the mentoring process, evaluating the program, and revising it (Barrera et al., 2010; Sindelar, 1992).

Re-Establishing a Rationale

In the case where the establishment of a mentoring network is ongoing, as was the case with Phi Beta Sigma, re-establishing a rationale can occur as needed rather than just at the inception of a program as indicated by stage models of how mentoring networks develop (e.g., Barrera et al., 2010; Dobrow et al., 2011; Kegan, 1982; Sindelar, 1992). Rationales guiding how mentoring should proceed also can be informed by the broader socio-political context. Two recent developments, internal and external to Phi Beta Sigma, have been instrumental in shaping its expectations and opportunities for mentoring. The first development was a national initiative to mentor Black youth (males) and the second was the development of the collegiate advisor certification process.

Mentoring has taken a stronger foothold in Phi Beta Sigma Fraternity, Inc. since it publicly announced its commitment to President Obama's My Brother's Keeper Initiative (Phi Beta Sigma, n.d.). As part of this initiative, the Fraternity adopted the program, *I Am My Brother's Keeper*, which included a 10-point agenda to address issues impacting men of color. One of these agenda points was to "educate 10,000 African-American males on the essentials of being engaging and effective mentors to African-American youth, while successfully establishing relationships that will increase community awareness of the potential of our youth and the power of diversity" (Phi Beta Sigma, "10 Point Agenda section," n.d., ¶1). The adoption of the program provided Phi Beta Sigma the opportunity to re-establish its rationale for developing mentoring capacity among its members.

> The brothers of the chapter [non-certified collegiate advisors] can engage the collegiate, it's just that you have to have an officially trained [collegiate] advisor as part of the process. So it can be one on one but it may not be the actual [collegiate] advisor that is working one on one with the [collegiate]. [It] may be, you know what, this brother had the similar experience as you, [but] he's not the advisor ... Remember, these are university [chapters], they can be from same state [or] city ... so the college advisor could leverage the entire chapter to assist." (personal communication, May 4, 2015)

Not only was the role of mentoring of young African American men in colleges and communities an expectation of all affiliates of the fraternity, it was an expectation that was supported within the collegiate advisor role.

(Self) Selecting Mentors

The training manual guiding the certification process provides a set of personal characteristics against which prospective advisors can assess their potential to do well in this role (CAUCT, 2011). The personal characteristics identified in the manual are *genuine interest, street savvy,* and *patience.*

- Genuine Interest: He must possess a genuine and lasting interest in young people—their problems, their objectives and their limitations. He must deal with a group of particularly sensitive young men who respond to genuine interest and are very perceptive in identifying perfunctory and apathetic performance.
- Street Savvy: He must have a thorough knowledge and understanding of the sociological and psychological changes, which are taking place on campuses throughout the country.
- Patience: He must possess an infinite amount of patience to understand young people, and even more patience to forgive the many errors, which are a consequence of their dynamic learning experiences. As a chapter advisor, you must guide and direct this total learning process as it relates to the management and operation of the fraternity. (CAUCT, 2011, p. 6)

While the culture of the fraternity provides the norms, traditions, tools, and values that contribute to how one is socialized within the organization, those who pursue the role of collegiate advisor self-select to enter the certification training program. As described below, the personal characteristics were accompanied by a shift in perspective (toward safety) as Phi Beta Sigma responded to broader social concerns over how affiliates at the collegiate level demonstrate and encourage brotherhood, scholarship, and service.

Safety First

According to Dove, the purpose of the collegiate advisor is multifaceted yet one of its major purposes is safety. He commented that it was "unfortunate" that safety became one of focus areas, if not the major focus, alongside the related purpose of "working well with the college" (personal communication, May 6, 2015). His comment is situated within a longer historical context, which colleges and universities eventually phased out, known as hazing, as part of the higher education experience by 1950; however, both White and Black Greek Letter Organization's kept the practice going as part of the final week of initiation into their fraternities (Kimbrough, 1997). As Dove recounted,

Ten to fifteen years ago ... there was work to do, it wasn't just signing a paper and learning some things. There were other things you had to do. They tested

your loyalty, they tested your trust, and they tested your beliefs and values—
before you could join—a little more stringently than they do today. (personal
communication, May 4, 2015).

According to Kimbrough (1997), the hazing process became "part of the
American college experience beginning in the 1850s" (p. 231). At that
time, the physical and psychological initiation rituals were used on first-
year freshmen by upperclassmen. However, hazing has fallen out of favor as
a result of several deaths related to hazing activities, so it is now associated
with risk to the health or safety of 'pledges' or non-members and is discour-
aged. The following is Dove's recount of the historical context that shaped
how the role of the collegiate advisor and the certification process were re-
imagined at the onset of the twenty-first century.

> The collegiate have historically had issues with things happening on campus
> whether it be drinking, or you know, parties and things going wrong. One of
> the key [purposes] of the training is to help us identify those risks—to mitigate
> or prevent them from occurring. If they do occur, we need to do the work with
> the college to remediate the issue. (personal communication, May 4, 2015)

The section of the CAUCT manual (2011) on legal responsibilities notes,
"hazing still occurs and has resulted in numerous deaths and injuries"
(p. 67). It also lists death-related incidents alongside the names of the fraternities with which the deceased were affiliated. In an effort to move away
from the traditions associated with the hazing of potential and new members at both the collegiate and alumni induction levels of the organization,
Phi Beta Sigma partnered with the National Action Network in 2012 and
pushed for federal anti-hazing legislation.

To underscore the importance of breaking away from the culture of hazing, Dove spoke about the separate certification program involved in what
is now referred to as the membership intake process (MIP). Chapter alumni, who have completed certification to serve as Membership Intake Chair-
men, guide the process for new members to join the fraternity. Having this
step in place provides additional assurance that the new member intake
process adheres to the guidelines surrounding the anti-hazing policies of
Phi Beta Sigma. Although the process of applying is one of self-selection,
there is an additional component in which chapter alumni serve as membership chairs who ensure that the anti-hazing policies are communicated
within the process of becoming certified to serve as a collegiate advisor
(personal communication, May 6, 2015)

The testing of loyalty today has shifted from rituals like pledging (given
the cases where the practice involved extreme and/or harmful tests), to
classroom activities and symbolic acts of commitment (signing a form).
Now safety is a prominent value attached to the role of collegiate advisor

and how he mentors collegiates into the culture of the organization. Prior to the new training protocol of the fraternity, any member could initiate a potential new member of the fraternity with little oversight or guidance. However, the formal nature of the certification process establishes additional parameters for those who self-select as a future collegiate advisor; they do so with the intentions of accepting the responsibilities that come along with the role.

Training Mentors

The certification training program is offered as a series of modules, as outlined in the CAUCT (2011) manual (hereon referred to as "the manual"), and conducted during a one-day workshop. According to Dove, those who deliver the certification training "must be a member of the graduate [alumni] chapter, in good financial standing, and [have] no disciplinary actions" (personal communication, May 4, 2015). In order for chapters to be in compliance, these requirements must be in place. Although becoming a collegiate advisor has become a more formalized process and an entry-level leadership role, the preparation (i.e., training) is ongoing through acculturation into the organization and socialization into the role.

Pre-Certification Mentoring Training

Changing from the role of mentee to mentor is developmental and transitional (McLean, 2004; Moore, 2008). Certification marks the transition from collegiate to collegiate advisor and, within that role, mentee to mentor. Most collegiates of Phi Beta Sigma are mentored (as mentees) before transitioning into leadership roles through which they serve (to mentor) others. This structure mirrors what has been called in teacher education, "growing your own" (Skinner, Garreton, & Schultz, 2011; Swanson, 2011). In other words, mentoring middle and high school students (Sigma Beta Club) and selecting and recruiting collegiates begins the socialization process comprised of formal and informal mentoring. The expectation is that mentoring provided today will be recouped by the organization as incoming affiliates take on leadership roles and fulfill the mentoring expectation. Since collegiates are directly engaged by a certified collegiate advisor who is their mentor, they are able to witness the network of support that an advisor provides (CAUCT, 2011).

Not all collegiate advisors become affiliated at the undergraduate level. Dove is such a case in that he did not follow the traditional path most affiliates take; he did not enter the fraternity as a brother while in college. He joined the chapter as an alumni chapter member and, within a few years, became president of an alumni chapter, certified collegiate advisor, and director of the Sigma Beta Club program. Therefore, he did not experience being mentored by a collegiate advisor during his undergraduate or graduate studies. Instead, his experience came from mentoring young Black men as part of an international mentoring organization and while participating in the fraternal organization called the Freemasons (Masons). Involvement in these organizations suggests he valued a sense of brotherhood, was committed to serving communities and organizations, and was willing to apply his background in adult learning to support Black males at the inter-organizational nexus between community and educational organizations. Dove's leadership trajectory reflects the historical aim of Phi Beta Sigma to "select leaders who are committed and have demonstrated their ability to lead" (History section, ¶1), and its contemporary focus on leading and mentoring within an organizational culture where brotherhood and service are key values.

Post-Certification Mentoring Training

Once a member completes the training workshop and is certified as a collegiate advisor, support is provided to the advisor and chapter overall. According to Dove, "the manual itself is a great guideline"; however, he cautioned, it also is necessary "to get out there in the field to see what you're dealing with." While he asserted that college students have a lot of resources, he added that most collegiate chapters need some sort of guidance; "[the] coaching and the mentoring piece" (personal communication, May 4, 2015). In other words, not all of the fraternity members make good use of the resources so they, along with their advisors, are provided support in the form of coaching and mentoring. Dove indicated that the collegiate advisors needed coaching with understanding the policies of the Phi Beta Sigma organization and the required mentoring on how to professionally communicate with university administrators when situations occur on campus. However, coaching and mentoring of certified collegiate advisors is needed less when the chapter has "a strong president and officers" (personal communication, May 4, 2015).

Developmental mentoring networks typically include multiple developers (Dobrow et al., 2011). Depending on the chapter's needs, the mentoring network extends beyond the role of the certified collegiate advisor to include access to brothers within the local alumni chapter who are not necessarily certified as collegiate advisors but who have access to resources that support the collegiate chapter. These resources may include knowledge about internships and job opportunities to support the needs of the collegiate members. Additional support is available from more experienced collegiate advisors across the chapters who comprise a network of experienced advisors who can be tapped for support as needed.

Monitoring the (Mentoring) Process

Monitoring of the mentoring process primarily occurs in a formal context at the local level as part of the experienced collegiate advisor's responsibilities in working with the collegiate chapter but also in an informal context—indirectly monitoring social media sites of the chapter and collegiate members. In the formal context, advisors are tasked with ensuring the collegiate chapter operates within the guidelines and structure of the Phi Beta Sigma fraternal organization. Thus, the inter-organizational nexus, between the BGLO and the college/university, is taken into consideration in the training program to promote success of its collegiate advisors in supporting the chapter.

The monitoring process involves experienced collegiate advisors who monitor and guide the chapters (collegiate advisors) on what they can or cannot do. Experienced collegiate advisors help less experienced collegiate advisors and members of the collegiate chapter understand the conditions for growth in judgment, decision-making skills, and personal responsibility. In the CAUCT (2011) Coaching and Development of Phi Beta Sigma Collegiate Chapters section are strategies that the fraternity views as the foundation to becoming an effective advisor: To (a) listen with empathy; (b) build personal value; (c) focus on performance; (d) recognize the efforts of others; and (e) influence, not control. At the core of this foundation is the element of trust between the collegiate advisor and the collegiate chapter. Using this strategy, the collegiate advisors are expected to "assess a chapter's performance and apply the necessary action for the most positive outcome" (CAUCT, 2011, p. 49).

Although it is not directly stated within the CAUCT manual, Dove emphasizes the expanded role of advisors in monitoring the chapter in this era of increased social media presence. According to Dove, "[W]e're [the experienced advisors] the ones [who] go to their Facebook page checking [it] out to say hey, hey, get that off of there. We're the ones who monitor. The [experienced collegiate] advisors do all of that stuff" (personal communication, May 6, 2015).

With the foundation of trust built up between the collegiate advisor and members of the collegiate chapter, the collegiate advisor is able to monitor activities that are not necessarily part of the explicit responsibilities outlined in the manual. While not specified in the CAUCT manual (2011), given Dove's description of social media monitoring, the process seems responsive to changes in society and shifts in how students experience life on campus and amid changes in the socio-cultural context of campus and beyond.

Evaluating and Revising the Program

To address the question of how mentoring aides in the development of Phi Beta Sigma's undergraduate members, Dove indicated that brothers who graduate from the collegiate level come back to support the next generation of college members. It is not uncommon for graduates not only to be part of the developmental network, but also to take on leadership roles within the alumni chapter, including becoming a collegiate advisor who mentors. The creation of a pipeline signifies the successful development of collegiate members "not only in general [life situations], but in the fraternity, to maintain the life blood of the fraternity" (personal communication, May 6, 2015).

Mentoring programs have experienced increased attention regarding measurement of their effectiveness (Deutsch & Spencer, 2009). Evaluation, as described in the CAUCT manual (2011), "the first step in the Coaching and Development Process" (p. 50), is meant to help the collegiate advisor ascertain how well the collegiate chapter is performing or behaving. The manual further states, "The advisor observes and compares all aspects of the chapter's performance, provides feedback, and provides the opportunity for the chapter to do the same" (p. 50). However, there is no detailed explanation of how mentoring is being monitored. Instead, the focus on monitoring is directed toward the performance of the chapter rather than of the collegiate advisor's expression of mentoring capacity or development of mentoring capacity in others.

However, the opportunity to evaluate and revise the collegiate advisor training program is available during off-site retreats scheduled by alumni. During such retreats, alumni are able to hear from the leadership of the collegiate chapter. The retreat is an opportunity for the collegiate chapter to express issues and concerns as the alumni chapter is, "there to listen to, to anything that we are not doing to assist them" (personal communication, May 6, 2015). In a particular meeting attended by Dove, the collegiate chapter voiced concerns over seeing the same members at the collegiate events. Specifically, the request from the chapter was to have more variety in who was showing up to interact with the collegiate chapter. As president of the alumni chapter during this time, Dove believed the alumni chapter was doing an excellent job by having a consistent number of alumni present for collegiate events. During such meetings, fraternity members from both levels were able to assess what was happening and get feedback on what was expected of them. As a result of the meeting, the alumni chapter revised its approach and encouraged a more diverse representation at the varying events of the collegiate chapter.

DISCUSSION

Overall, strengthening the pipeline of service leadership is a key theme that was observed through written documentation of Phi Beta Sigma and personal communication with Michael Dove as a current leader within the organization. Alumni chapter members, such as Dove, set a standard for what is expected from collegiate advisors who mentor and potential mentees.

> We help them develop their community involvement and activities and help support them through that or bring them to our activities so they can see how to engage in the community and represent the fraternity well and complete the mission of the fraternity which is a call to service, service to humanity. (personal communication, May 4, 2015)

Dove was drawn to Phi Beta Sigma's established commitment to service and investment in promoting brotherhood and fellowship, which aligned with his personal values. The structure of Phi Beta Sigma, and its aims to promote a sense of 'brotherhood' among its affiliates, illustrates the attributes of developmental mentoring networks (CAUCT, 2011).

First, the development of mentoring capacity within Phi Beta Sigma involves multiple actors (e.g., collegiate advisors, graduate/alumni chapter members) who offer contacts and networking for collegiate members. Second, much of the mentoring activity revolves around the role of the certified collegiate advisor who is situated inter-organizationally between the BGLO and the college/university. Third, there is a network of collegiate advisors from across the chapters who can serve as mentors to collegiates on an as-needed basis or when having similar experiences that would provide a stronger base for relating to the advisees/mentees (CAUCT, 2011).

We have come to understand mentoring as a fraternity-wide expectation. However, as Dove noted, not all members have been prepared for or committed to mentoring according to the values of the organization. Previous to the inception of the certification process, any member who wanted to volunteer their time could serve as collegiate advisor. Having no formal method in place to acclimate the collegiate advisor into the role, his mentoring expectations were often communicated implicitly. The CAUCT manual (2011) outlined the "necessary operational training" that would help "Collegiate Advisors to perform their job in an exemplary fashion" (p. 3). Completion of the training not only offers guidance and support, but also establishes a commitment from the collegiate advisor to mentor.

As Dove often emphasized in discussions with us (his co-authors), Phi Beta Sigma's commitment to the concept of service leadership builds the pipeline to realize the fraternity's motto—"culture for service and service for humanity." The Sigma Beta Club, collegiate undergraduate chapter, and alumni chapter form an interorganizational and interindividual

mentoring relationship whereby mentoring occurs formally in a hierarchical fashion (i.e., collegiate advisor to collegiate members) and informally
in peer-to-peer relationships between and among undergraduate collegiate
members. This pipeline highlights the characteristics of the developmental
mentoring network's point of a broad range of social spheres that support
the overall network (Kram, 1985). The programs, initiatives, and insights
offered by Dove suggest a narrative of brotherhood that includes mentoring in response to broader issues, such as committing to mentoring Black
youth in its chapters and communities.

RECOMMENDATIONS

The Phi Beta Sigma fraternity has put forth a substantial effort to emphasize the process to be undertaken in developing future leaders. Thus, our
recommendations are for evaluating the advising program for the influence of mentoring on advisee/mentees development in accordance with
the expectations of membership, and for future research on mentoring
development as a relational process between individuals situated in organizational cultures.

Attention to how mentoring and the coaching modules of the program are evaluated regarding how they add to collegiate advisors' capacity
to mentor is not addressed in the CAUCT manual (2011). According to
Deutsch and Spencer (2009), to fully understand mentoring, one must consider both the mentoring relationship and the mentoring program within
which the relationship operates. In the case of Phi Beta Sigma, brotherhood is a sense of belonging around which mentoring relationships are
developed and, thus, the program evaluation should be responsive to the
cultural context of the mentoring network of the BGLO as well as the institutional context in which the chapters operate the advising program.

Although the fraternal chapters across the organizational structure of
Phi Beta Sigma may vary in their structure and access to resources, outlining methods for collecting information to evaluate the progress of the
mentoring relationship between current students and alumni is a vital
step. Deutsch and Spencer (2009) provide a list of measurement approaches with details on who is best targeted through each approach, which can
serve to guide alumni chapters in evaluating all aspects of the mentoring
approach—programmatically and interpersonally. As such, an incorporation of evaluation approaches into the advising program could benefit all
parties engaged in the mentoring process (CAUCT, 2011).

Considering the recently developed initiative, *I Am My Brother's Keeper*,
there are specific goals in place that can be used to assess how well a chapter has attained and progressed toward them (Phi Beta Sigma, n.d.). The

specific goals reflected in the agenda can allow the fraternity to "begin to narrow" its scope, according to Dove, who stated, "I think we will actually achieve some measurable results" (personal communication, May 6, 2015). This is especially so, given the specific goals outlined in a 10-point agenda listed on the fraternity's website "to address issues impacting men of color in our communities" (Phi Beta Sigma, I Am My Brother's Keeper section, n.d., ¶1). Some of the goals listed in the agenda are: recruit and develop of 10,000 mentors by Phi Beta Sigma nationally, increase membership participation in the Sigma Beta Club by 20%, sponsor two job fairs for men of color, and adopt 100 schools throughout the United States.

Evaluation associated with mentoring generally focuses "on evaluating the effectiveness of mentoring programs by assessing specific youth outcomes, typically at a single point in time" (Deutsch & Spencer, 2009, p. 47). However, since collegiates can range in age and, therefore, fall outside the range associated with youth and young adults and the collegiate advisors are adults, evaluations used with youth mentoring programs may not be adequate to address the mentoring received by advisors.

Evaluation approaches targeting adults situated intra-organizationally are recommended. For instance, the model offered by Chandler and Kram (2005) draws on adult development theory and considers that the development of individuals may vary and, therefore, some network structures may be more conducive for mentoring depending on individuals' stages of development. Such a framework can be useful for program development and evaluation since it takes into account the development of the individual within a program who serves multiple mentees and organizations. Future research into mentoring provided by BGLOs might benefit from engaging a theoretical model of interrelationships among developmental stages, developmental networks, and individual outcomes. Given the emphasis on service with a sense of purpose and brotherhood with Phi Beta Sigma, frameworks and evaluation procedures that acknowledge the cultural dimensions of the developmental network and program are recommended.

REFERENCES

Baker, C. N. (2008). Underrepresented college students and extracurricular involvement: The effects of various student organizations on academic performance. *Social Psychology of Education, 11*(3), 273–298.

Barrera, A., Braley, R. T., & Slate, J. R. (2010). Beginning teacher success: An investigation into the feedback from mentors of formal mentoring programs. *Mentoring & Tutoring: Partnership in Learning, 18*(1), 61–74.

Chandler, D. E., & Kram, K. E. (2005). Applying an adult development perspective to developmental networks. *Career Development International, 10*(6/7), 548–566.

Collegiate Advisor University Certification Training Manual. (2011). *PHI BETA SIG-MA collegiate advisor work group. Revised edition of the training manual.* Retrieved from http://www.phibetasigma1914.org/forms/

Dancy, T. E., & Hotchkins, B. K. (2015). Schools for the better making of men? Undergraduate Black males, fraternity membership, and manhood. *Culture, Society and Masculinities, 7*(1), 7–21.

Deutsch, N. L., & Spencer, R. (2009). Capturing the magic: Assessing the quality of youth mentoring relationships. *New Directions for Youth Development, 121,* 47–70.

Dobrow, S. R., Chandler, D. E., Murphy, W. M., & Kram, K. E. (2011). A review of developmental networks: Incorporating a mutuality perspective. *Journal of Management, 38*(1), 210–242.

Dunkel, N. W., & Schuh, J. H. (1998). *Advising student groups and organizations. The Jossey-Bass higher and adult education series.* San Francisco, CA: Jossey-Bass.

Frazier, E. F. (1957). *Black bourgeoisie.* New York, NY: The Free Press.

Goss, D. R., Harris, D., Spencer, D., & Hughey, M. W. (2014). Teaching and learning guide for Black Greek letter organizations. *Sociology Compass, 8*(5), 571–587.

Harris III, F., & Harper, S. R. (2014). Beyond bad behaving brothers: Productive performances of masculinities among college fraternity men. *International Journal of Qualitative Studies in Education, 27*(6), 703–723.

Hughey, M. W. (2008). Brotherhood or brothers in the 'hood'? Debunking the 'educated gang' thesis as Black fraternity and sorority slander. *Race, Ethnicity and Education, 11*(4), 443–463.

Hughey, M. W., & Hernandez, M. (2013). Black, Greek, and read all over: Newspaper coverage of African-American fraternities and sororities, 1980–2009. *Ethnic and Racial Studies, 36*(2), 298–319.

Kegan, R. (1982). *The evolving self: Problem and process in human adult development.* Cambridge, MA: Harvard University Press,

Kimbrough, W. M. (1995). Self-assessment, participation, and value of leadership skills, activities, and experiences for Black students relative to their membership in historically Black fraternities and sororities. *The Journal of Negro Education, 64*(1), 63–74.

Kimbrough, W. M. (1997). The membership intake movements of historically Black Greek-letter organizations. *Journal of Student Affairs Research and Practice, 34*(3), 229–243. doi: 10.2202/1949-6605.1024

Kram, K. E. (1985). *Mentoring at work: Developmental relationships in organizational life.* Glenview, IL: Scott Foresman.

Martin, G. L., Hevel, M. S., Asel, A. M., & Pascarella, E. T. (2011). New evidence on the effects of fraternity and sorority affiliation during the first year of college. *Journal of College Student Development 52*(5), 543–559. doi: 10.1353/csd.2011.0062

McLean, M. (2004). Does the curriculum matter in peer mentoring? From mentee to mentor in problem-based learning: A unique case study. *Mentoring & Tutoring: Partnership in Learning, 12*(2), 173–186. doi: 10.1080/1361126042000239929

Molasso, W. R. (2005). A content analysis of a decade of fraternity/sorority scholarship in student affairs research journals. *Oracle: The Research Journal of the Association of Fraternity and Sorority Advisors, 1,* 1–9.

Moore, A. A., Miller, M. J., Pitchford, V. J., & Jeng, L. H. (2008). Mentoring in the millennium: New views, climate and actions. *New Library World, Vol. 109*(1/2), 75–86. doi.org/10.1108/03074800810846029

Parks, G. S. (2008). *Black Greek-letter organizations in the twenty-first century: Our fight has just begun.* Lexington, KY: The University Press of Kentucky.

Phi Beta Sigma. (n.d.a). *Phi Beta Sigma Fraternity, Inc.* Retrieved from http://www.phibetasigma1914.org

Phi Beta Sigma. (n.d.b). *I am my brother's keeper.* Retrieved from http://www.phibetasigma1914.org

Ray, R. (2012). Sophisticated practitioners: Black fraternity men's treatment of women. *Journal of African American Studies, 16*(4), 638–657.

Sindelar, N. (1992). Development of a teacher mentorship program: High professionalism and low cost. *ERS Spectrum, 10*(2), 13–17.

Skinner, E. A., Garreton, M. T., & Schultz, B. D. (2011). *Grow your own teachers: Grassroots change for teacher education.* New York, NY: Teachers College Press.

Swanson, P. B. (2011). Georgia's grow-your-own teacher programs attract the right stuff. *The High School Journal, 94*(3), 119–133.

CHAPTER 8

SHE'S YOUNGER THAN ME

A New Look at Age and Mentoring in Doctoral Education

Geleana Drew Alston
North Carolina A&T State University

Doctoral programs in the United States frequently equate a doctoral faculty mentor with the dissertation supervisor/advisor. Functionally, there are areas in which the former terms overlap; however, these terms, often used interchangeably, can be seen to have differences in meaning. This notion may be due in part to the traditional perspective of the roles of faculty members with regard to doctoral advising. Nettles and Millett (2006) define doctoral supervisor/advisor as "a faculty or research advisor assigned by the department or program to act in an official capacity in such ways as discussion and approving course work or signing registration forms" (p. 265). For example, the doctoral supervisor/advisor assists students in planning a course of study, helps them register for classes, conducts formative assessments of students' progress, and guides them through the program of study toward a degree. Doctoral students are usually assigned to a doctoral supervisor/advisor who typically serves as the Chair of his/her committee, and the appointment is based on a mutual commitment between the faculty member and student.

Mentoring in Formal and Informal Contexts, pages 137–154
Copyright © 2016 by Information Age Publishing

Contrary to the doctoral or dissertation supervisor/advisor role, doctoral faculty mentorship involves a more holistic or spiritual approach to the student-faculty relationships. According to Johnson and Huwe (2003), the term *mentoring* signifies a commitment to a relationship of knowing the mentee, where the focus of the relationship is the development of the mentee. Various faculty members may know students on a surface level demographically —name, research interest, professional goals—but mentors really know their students on a deeper level. Clark and Garza (1994) suggest,

> Faculty mentorship involves professors acting as close, trusted and experienced colleagues and guides... It is recognized that part of what is learned in graduate school is not cognitive; it is socialization to the values, norms, practices, and attitudes of a discipline and university; it transforms the student into a colleague. (p. 308)

This notion of mentoring was used to contextualize this study. Although it is possible that a faculty member assigned as doctoral supervisor/advisor may also serve as mentor, the unit of analysis remained the faculty mentor-doctoral student mentee pair for this study.

Much of the research to date has focused on a traditional conception of mentoring in higher education, wherein age is highlighted solely by describing the mentor as being older and wiser than the mentee. Scholars have recently explored age and mentoring in the areas of communication studies (Kalbfleisch & Anderson, 2013), legal education (Schneider & Hanna, 2012), and occupational therapy (Wilson, Cordier, & Whatley, 2013) and have often studied adults and youth. With regard to faculty in higher education, Finkelstein (2012) published the findings of a study completed in 2007 that compared the career characteristics of faculty in 13 developed countries. The results of this study indicated that three-fifths of full-time faculty within institutions of higher education in the United States are younger than age 55 (Finkelstein, 2012). If we consider the findings of Finkelstein regarding gender and age, perhaps younger female faculty mentors at the doctoral level are not so uncommon after all, but they are understudied.

All things considered, there is paucity in the literature that explores age within student-faculty mentoring relationships in higher education. Specifically, there is little to no literature on cross-age mentoring dyads within the context of higher education. Therefore, the aim of this research was to capture the essence of the relationship between younger female faculty mentors and their older female doctoral student mentees.

WOMEN MENTORING WOMEN IN DOCTORAL EDUCATION

We need to acknowledge the multiple identities, including gender and professional identities, and the identity politics that women bring into relationships,

and the unconscious and hidden biases that individuals in mentoring relationships have about particular groups and individuals. (Mejiuni, 2009, p. 277)

Within the past 30 years, research focusing on mentoring relationships has
increased, and scholars have concluded that the student-faculty mentoring
relationship is a crucial factor in doctoral education (Castro, Caldewell, &
Salazar, 2005; Chandler, 1996; Gilbert & Rossman, 1992; Gillon & Place,
2011; Hansman, 2002; Heinrich, 1995; Mullen, Fish, & Hutinger, 2010). Although women are graduating from doctoral programs in increasing rates,
little is known about women doctoral students' experiences, and even less is
understood about doctoral student-faculty mentoring relationships between
women (Heinrich, 1995). Women faculty members of the academy remain
disproportionately gendered: "Women frequently lack access to within-
profession (and more frequently within-department) mentors to help them
clarify and maneuver within the unwritten rules of their profession's culture" (Castro et al., 2005, p. 331). To that end, with regard to power and
influence, some doctoral student mentees (both women and men) may perceive women mentors as less desirable than men mentors (Hansman, 2002).

THEORETICAL FRAMEWORK

The incorporation of feminist theory offers a framework that challenges the
dominant discourse, conceptualizing mentoring in the context of higher education, since this particular context is influenced by patriarchy (Cochran-
Smith & Paris, 1995; DeMarco, 1993; Standing, 1999). Keeping in mind the
gendered disproportionality within higher education, female doctoral students often lack access to a female faculty mentor to assist them with the
socialization into the professional culture (Castro et al., 2005). As a female
researcher, I chose to use a feminist lens to explore the multiple experiences and realities of the study participants as they occupied academic spaces,
which often perpetuate hegemony and male domination to a degree.

In the seminal work of Hartmann (1984), patriarchy is defined as the
"systemic dominance of men over women," derived from a "set of social relations between men, which have a material base, and among men that enable them to dominate women" (p. 197). Not only are men united as they
share this relationship of dominance, they are dependent on each other to
maintain that domination within this systemic structure. Hartmann further
suggests, ". . . patriarchy is not simply hierarchical organization by hierarchy
in which particular people fill particular places" (p. 199). One could argue
that that the academy is considered one of these particular places. Onto-
logically and epistemologically, feminist standpoint theory acknowledges
this system of dominance and refutes it by uncovering the power relations

within which men's lives and interests circumscribe, or attempt to circumscribe, those of women. "Feminism has been instrumental in exposing the gendered nature of social life..." in that, feminist standpoints are an integral part of the individual and collective female epistemologies (Ford, 2011, p. 447).

In offering an alternative, yet unique perspective of feminism, Gilligan (2011) views feminism purposefully through the lens of social change. Specifically, she shared, "I say that I see feminism as one of the great liberation movements in human history. It is the movement to free democracy from patriarchy" (p. 176). Therefore, feminist epistemologies offer a framework to renounce voicelessness within the dominant discourse of the female faculty mentor and the female doctoral student mentee in the efforts of gaining a better understanding of the phenomenon.

METHODOLOGY

To develop an understanding of the ways in which women make meaning of their dyadic mentoring relationships, a feminist grounded theory (Wuest, 1995) approach was used in this study. Using qualitative techniques (Merriam, 2015), this study specifically sought to understand the individual and collective experiences of female faculty mentors and their female doctoral student mentees. This chapter will present findings associated with the following research question: *What is the nature of the mentoring experiences between younger female faculty and their older female doctoral student mentees?*

I ascribed to a constructivist approach to grounded theory methodology in an effort to prioritize the phenomenon of the study (Charmaz, 2005). Additionally, it was important to recognize that the data and analyses were created from the shared experiences of the participants (Charmaz, 2005). Therefore, a feminist grounded theory approach was deemed most appropriate.

Participant Sample

In an effort to identify participants for my study, the sample was maximized as I sought certain dimensions of variation including (a) age; (b) faculty rank; (c) enrollment status; (d) doctoral candidacy status; (e) field of study (restricted to social sciences—education, psychology, sociology); (f) institutional affiliation; and (g) geographic location in the United States. Initially, using the Internet, I searched various university websites to obtain email addresses of female doctoral level faculty teaching in the social sciences and sent them an invitational email for them to consider becoming a study participant. In addition, the faculty members were asked to provide the contact information of their female doctoral student mentees. Next, preliminary surveys inviting participation were sent to the faculty members and their mentees to ensure they met the inclusion criteria based on the previously mentioned distinguishing characteristics in an effort to achieve maximum variation within the sample. The survey included a short description of the research study, demographic information necessary for achieving maximum variation, and two open-ended questions: (a) In your own words, define faculty mentor; and (b) In your own words, define doctoral student mentee. The purpose of these questions was to understand the participants' perspectives of a faculty mentor and a doctoral student mentee and compare their perspectives to the definitions identified within this study. From those who agreed to participate, two dyads who met the variation criteria (two complete cross-age, faculty-student mentoring pairs) from the fields of adult and higher education were selected. The pseudonyms and demographics of the participants are shown in Table 8.1.

In this section, I provide a brief profile for each participant and specifically highlight how the women came to participate in their mentoring relationships.

Shelia

The mentoring relationship with Shelia and her mentee, Ivy, began when Shelia taught several classes that Ivy took as she pursued her master's degree. In addition, Shelia served as the supervisor for Ivy's assistantship. When Ivy graduated and decided to continue in her studies toward a doctorate, Shelia continued to serve as her mentor. Shelia and Ivy have collaborated on various research projects and they identify each other as peer mentors.

Ivy

Ivy was enrolled full-time during her doctoral studies. In addition, she worked as a graduate assistant in the same department wherein her doctoral program resided. As mentioned above, she became acquainted with

TABLE 8.1 Research Study Participants' Demographics

Pseudonym	Mentor/ Mentee	Academic Rank	Age Group	Field of Study	Geographic Location in US
Shelia	Mentor	Assistant Professor	40–49	Adult/Higher Education	Southeast
Ivy	Mentee	Graduated 2012	60–69	Adult/Higher Education	Midwest
Ella	Mentor	Associate Professor	30–39	Higher Education	Southeast
Rose	Mentee	Graduated 2013	40–49	Higher Education	Southeast

Shelia when she took some of her classes during her master's program and subsequently became her mentee.

Ella

The mentoring relationship with Ella and her mentee, Rose, began when Ella taught several classes that Rose took during her doctoral studies. Rose asked Ella to mentor her, as she believed they had similar personalities. Ella also served as the chair for Rose's dissertation committee.

Rose

While pursing her doctoral degree, Rose worked as an administrator at the same institution where she was enrolled as a part-time doctoral student.

Data Collection

Birks and Mills (2011) tell us, "The value of interviewing in grounded theory research is evidenced by the extensive number of studies that rely on it as the principal mechanism for the generation of data" (p. 74). I conducted one audio-taped interview with each participant and each interview lasted approximately one-hour. Paired dyads (mentor and mentee) were interviewed separately and the interviews were guided by semi-structured interview protocols (Patton, 2005). Since I used a constructivist grounded theory approach (Charmaz, 2005), I adjusted my probing questions accordingly as each interview was informed by the previous data collection sessions.

After conducting the interviews, I developed and electronically administered a critical incident questionnaire (Butterfield, Borgen, Maglio, & Amundson, 2009) in an effort to elicit participants' reflections on significant events that occurred while participating in their mentoring relationship. In the efforts to collect additional data, I administered the critical incident questionnaire to the participants that asked the following:

> Describe a time or times while participating in a mentoring relationship, that you felt was critical to your current participation in mentoring relationships.
>
> Describe in your own words why you are defining these incidents as critical and describe the factors surrounding each situation.

As the nature of the cross-age mentoring experience between female faculty and their female doctoral student mentees is currently understudied, the information collected via the critical incident questionnaire assisted me in identifying significant areas that otherwise might have been missed. According to Butterfield, Borgen, Maglio, and Amundson (2009), critical incident questionnaires are advantageous in the attempt to elicit participants' reflections on significant events. Therefore, data from the critical incident questionnaire highlighted or elaborated on some areas previously mentioned by the participants during the interviews, and ultimately this assisted with the triangulation of data (Merriam, 2015).

Data Analysis

Ascribing to constructivist grounded theory methodology (Charmaz, 2005) I used a systematic inductive approach to analyzing the data. Particularly, within this approach, "coding is the pivotal link between collecting data and developing an emergent theory to explain those data" (Charmaz, 2006, p. 46). Interview transcripts and responses from the critical incident questionnaires were coded using a combination of the following analytic techniques: (a) Initial & Process coding; (b) Values coding; (c) Versus coding; (d) Open coding; and (e) Focused coding (See Alston, 2014, for details regarding a multi-step coding process). Specifically, I used Values coding to capture the values, attitudes, and beliefs (Saldaña, 2009) of mentoring relationships from the perspectives of the participants. "Values coding is appropriate for virtually all qualitative studies, but particularly for those that explore cultural values and intrapersonal and interpersonal participant experiences and actions . . . " (p. 90). Therefore, I believed it was important to use Value coding in order to gain an understanding of:

- the way the participants think and feel about themselves, their reciprocal mentor or mentee, and mentoring in general; and,
- the combination of the participants' values, attitudes, and personal interpretations of the social context of mentoring relationships.

Feminist critiques of mentoring aim to disrupt the dominant discourse that conceptualizes mentoring as hierarchical and/or directive, even in all-female dyads (Cochran-Smith and Paris, 1995; DeMarco, 1993; Standing, 1999). For this reason, Versus coding was used because it "looks for patterns of social domination, hierarchy, and social privilege" and "examines the power that holds patterns in place, how people accept or struggle against them" (Agar, 1996, p. 27). Thus, while analyzing data within the interview transcripts, I identified binary terms that appeared to be in direct conflict with each other (Saldaña, 2009). For example, the following sentences were coded YOUNG vs OLD: "I don't call you by your first name. I don't criticize you! You are the elder and so I have that respect for you . . . "

This coding technique was beneficial considering how moiety may exist in many facets of mentoring relationships and there is generally an asymmetrical power balance between the mentor and mentee (Hansman, 2002, 2005; Ragins, 1997).

Limitations

In an effort to achieve trustworthiness (Merriam, 2015) and minimize threats to credibility, transferability, dependability, and confirmability, the strategies of reflexivity, maximum variation, triangulation, member checking, and peer review were incorporated to ensure that this research was carried out with integrity and represented my ethical stance as a researcher (Merriam, 2015).

FINDINGS

In this section, I present the findings associated with the ways that participants described their experiences in their mentoring dyads. The themes of (a) Age and Respect; (b) Power; and (c) Role Reversal emerged from the data analysis.

Age and Respect

As one participant described it as an "upside-down mentoring relationship," all participants mentioned the significance of participating in a cross-age mentoring relationship. In addition, the women expressed how critical respect was to their participation in cross-age mentoring dyads.

Rose and Ella

When I asked Rose to tell me about some of the key similarities and differences that stood out between her and her mentor, Ella, she immediately spoke about their age difference. She mentioned,

> Um, she is younger than me, I know that and so, um, you know, and I actually, when I came on, she started at the university the same time I did and we were actually in, um, the new faculty orientation together and she's a brilliant individual but, um, she's younger and so I think some of the, um—I think it's more of an age issue, um, because she has young children so, you know, there's an understanding.

It appears their age difference was something that Rose struggled with. Further, she tried to make sense of it by reminding herself of how brilliant Ella was despite her age and that they had a connection because they shared the culture of motherhood. Rose continued to paint a picture verbally that vividly portrayed her internal dissonance because of the age difference between her and her mentor. For example, Rose described their relationship as "a unique relationship that I don't think necessarily occurs, usually, you know, you've had these professors that have been here a long time and they're older, wisdom, all of those things." In another instance, Rose commented,

> I think she's amazing in terms of what she's done and to be very young, um, but that was very different and I was ok but I think that sometimes, again, it wasn't about me, it's about this was the process and going through.

Once I probed a little more to gain more insight about the age differences, Rose shared, "I mean I think, uh, you know I very much respect her being as young as she is and having had the experiences that she has…" It is obvious that Rose struggled as she negotiated the tension of her experience participating in a mentoring relationship where her mentor was younger than she. This appeared to be unchartered territory for her.

Ivy and Shelia

Like Rose, Shelia also mentioned age as one of the key differences between her and her mentee. Sheila, as the mentor of an older mentee, admitted her initial struggle with, as she puts it, their "non-traditional" mentoring dyad, and confessed:

> For us, our biggest issue was in terms of the age difference and the roles that our ages dictated. So a person who is in my mother's age group, actually she is only a couple years younger than my mother…you know the "yes ma'am, no ma'am"…you know "Miss"…I don't call you by your first name, I don't criticize you! You are the elder and so I have that respect for you…so I had that there. And I think on her end, I am the same age as her son. So she really viewed me as a kid…not in a negative way, but in a nurturing way.

For this reason, it was awkward, initially, for Shelia to critique her mentee as she was an elder. Within many cultures, elders are to be highly respected, obeyed, and considered a source of wisdom (Chen, Kim, Moon, & Merriam, 2008; Kim & Merriam, 2010; Merriam & Kee, 2014; Merriam & Mohamad, 2000).

Like Shelia, respect was important to Ivy. When Ivy shared with me what she perceived as key similarities and differences between her and her mentor, she also mentioned the age difference. However, she was very surprised when I asked her if her perception of the age difference was culturally based. After pausing momentarily, Ivy answered:

> I think culturally it probably helped us that the culture that we were from and the generational thing because I think she—her generation was taught to respect older people, you know, in her culture much more than in my culture they are it seems and so my kind of maybe you'd think of as my old fashion approach to things, uh, was comfortable to her because of her culture and I think she would have been, had a different feeling about me if she was from my culture and had been younger and I think—I don't think we had a lot of cultural conflict.

It is clear Ivy understood her mentor's position on the importance of respect and age because Ivy also taught her children to respect older people. The significance of respect was salient in both Ivy's and Shelia's mentoring relationships and appeared as intertwined with age.

Power

Power dynamics could not go overlooked as power is definitely integral within a faculty-student mentoring relationship. In this section, I will share the findings relative to the women's perspective on power while participating in the cross-age mentoring relationship.

Rose and Ella

Notably, as Rose continued to loop the conversation back to her feelings about the age difference between her and her mentor, she would incorporate her tension with the power dynamics within their mentoring relationship. Rose shared:

> I think the age is a little different in terms of my journey. I've been to a lot of different places and in a lot of different political environments. I think she's very much a faculty member and I'm very much an administrator. So, I think there were those kinds of nuances.

She elaborated further:

> Given my current role as an administrator and my mentor's role as a faculty member, I felt there was disconnect at times with an understanding of my situation in trying to balance work, school, family. I think this is the nature of faculty in higher education. She brought me some information and shared some things with me that she'd [Ella] like me to do, but it's very much faculty-type of prospect. I did not go to school to be teaching faculty and my perspective is very different. So, that kind of changes that power that the faculty have. Administrators, we're the bean counters, the spreadsheet people.

As previously mentioned, Rose was negotiating power with the fact that her mentor was younger than she. However, it appears this negotiation was coupled with their difference of academic roles as well. Rose, the mentee was an administrator and, Ella, the mentor, a faculty member; thus, the issue of power is inherent in those roles.

Ivy and Shelia

It appears that Ivy had certain expectations with regard to the power dynamics within their mentoring relationship. To be specific, she expected her mentor, Shelia, to have more power within their mentoring relationship. When Ivy was asked to describe the ideal mentor, she replied:

> I think the mentor creates time for the mentee but also understands that the mentor is sort of the driver of the relationship and so I think there needs to be some boundaries and I think that's the responsibility of the mentor to establish boundaries and establish a, you know, sort of—oh what's the right word? A plan for the relationship.

In another instance, Shelia was initially uncomfortable with mentoring someone older than herself because her perception of the roles and functions of a mentor conflicted with her perspective of respect for elders. During the beginning of their relationship, Ivy and Shelia both suppressed their feelings about their age difference. To further explain this, Ivy confessed:

> We didn't tell each other the truth in some cases that things were bothering us and I—that was a mistake and once we broke the ground and started talking about, you know "I didn't understand how you felt when you said that, it bothered me" and now with that sort of conversation, we were able to move into a closer relationship and I would suggest that, that people need to even if they feel they have respect for their, you know, mentor but you need to say it because if not it could become such a problem for me, you know, getting it out there. Usually you understand where the other one is coming from but you might not have thought about, previously and that helps. So I guess communicate, communicate, communicate.

Even though the lack of communication briefly stunted the growth of their mentoring relationship, Ivy and Shelia eventually negotiated the tension of power and age difference, addressed communication flaws, and gained a better understanding of the power dynamics within their mentoring relationship.

Role Reversal

The participants often shared examples of when role reversal occurred as the women participated in cross-age mentoring relationships. Specifically, the following findings will draw attention to how, sometimes, the roles of the mentee and mentor would temporarily reverse.

Rose and Ella

Rose and her mentor exhibited role reversal with regard to the culture of motherhood. During our conversation, Rose mentioned:

> Because she has young children so, you know, there's an understanding. My child's a little older so I think some of the conversations, um, you know, in terms of her coping with having three children, and babies and all that, you know, I had kind of been through all of that . . .

Rose's age and wisdom allowed her to be of assistance and support to Ella in ways that a 30-something-year-old possibly could not, due to limited life experiences.

Ivy and Shelia

The role reversal came about in this dyad when Ivy began taking on a mentoring role when her mentor Shelia was contemplating pursuing a faculty position at another institution. When I asked Ivy if she believed she had a specific impact on the professional development of her mentor, she replied:

> I think I did have an impact on her and on her development professionally and that was during a time when she was trying to decide whether she should stay at the institution or move on. We talked about it a lot and my advice to her was one of the most important aspects of the career is she should be happy and I didn't think she was where we were and I thought maybe changing to a different university was a good idea for her and she eventually did that and is much happier (laughs) so I think that probably my support through that time helped her make that decision.

Shelia expressed her gratitude for the role reversal that occasionally occurred between her and her mentor. As previously mentioned, Shelia is younger than her mentee, Ivy, and she was candid as she remarked:

> So she really viewed me as a kid . . . not in a negative way but in a nurturing way. So if I were having issues, she would step out of student role and try to help me on an interpersonal level to navigate my life as a 30-something [year old person] at that time. Her *motherness* made her attuned to the struggles of juggling the professional with the personal. She was mentoring me in life stuff while I was mentoring her in school stuff.

This quote illuminates how participating in a cross-age or intergenerational mentoring relationship can be mutualistic because the mentor can also learn from, and be mentored by, the mentee.

DISCUSSION

Ella, Ivy, Rose, and Shelia were expressive about their experiences with age and respect, power, and role reversal while participating in a mentoring relationship. In this study, age, intertwined with the notion of respect, emerged as a major theme in the participants' conception of their mentoring relationship. Power dynamics is a *hot topic* in mentoring and it is rare for it not to be discussed within literature focusing on mentoring practices. Essentially, power dynamics are constant due to the hierarchal nature of the mentoring and have been portrayed in the literature as a relationship involving a "mentor being more powerful and having more knowledge than the mentee" (Woodd, 1997, p. 334). With regard to power dynamics, the responses of the women in this study reveal an issue that has yet to be addressed within the literature on mentoring in adult and higher education—the issue of *non-traditional* ages of the mentors and mentees in current day contexts of doctoral education, such as the case with this study. I place emphasis on the adjective *non-traditional* as the literature frequently discusses age with regard to traditional mentoring in one way; the mentor is older than the mentee (Mott, 2002). Nonetheless, the findings in this study trouble the aforementioned conceptualization of age and mentoring because the mentors were younger than their mentees.

Arguably, mentoring is relational and cannot be discussed without considering respect as a representation of power (Hansman, 2002). Additionally, as Hansman so eloquently states,

> The power mentors have and exercise within a mentoring relationship can be helpful or hurtful. Indeed the biggest paradox surrounding mentoring relationships is that although mentors seek to "empower" their protégés, the relationships themselves are entrenched with power issues. Thus mentoring relationships involved the negotiation of power and interests of all involved, including mentors, protégés, and sponsoring organizations or institutions. (pp. 45–46)

This power dynamic is typical as the traditional model of mentoring consists of a patriarchially influenced hierarchical structure grounded in superiority and inferiority with regard to the mentor and mentee, respectively. Ella, Ivy, Rose, and Shelia each placed emphasis on the importance of respect while participating in their cross-age mentoring relationships. To respect an individual is to be considerate of her or his personhood in such a manner that it is reflected by one's action toward the individual. While mentoring involves power that is socially constructed and sustained (Johnson-Bailey & Cervero, 2004), it appeared the women who participated in this study experienced tension while negotiating power and age as they participated in their mentoring relationships. Yet, the element of respect remained a significant component of their approach to mentoring.

A point to bring to bear is that these women shared the culture of academia while participating in their cross-age mentoring relationships. As Rose highlighted, the culture of academia consists of subcultures—of students, faculty, administrators, support personnel, and alumni—and within this culture, power is ever circulating. As Cook (2006), commented:

> Power and politics are part of every conversation on campus. Despite talk of community, an "us–them" mentality pervades higher education: faculty vs. administration, students vs. faculty, and so forth. It happens because "power over" is built into the structure (para. 2).

To that end, the question remains: How does age, respect, and power influence the mentoring relationship between a faculty member and a doctoral student who is also an administrator within the same university? While this was the case with only one of the pairs in the study, this dimension of Rose's and Ella's mentoring relationship was striking.

It is critical to address my decision to utilize the term, *role reversal*, purposefully and how this differs from what the literature defines as *reverse mentoring*. In various fields of study, scholars have deemed reverse mentoring as the pairing of a younger employee to serve as a mentor in the efforts to share knowledge and expertise with an older, more seasoned colleague as the mentee (Cotugna & Vickery, 1998; Leh, 2005; Meister & Willyerd, 2010). I have deliberately elected to reject the use of the term reverse mentoring for two specific reasons. First, the term reverse means opposite or contrary in position, and it is a derivative of revert. Therefore, reverse mentoring appears grounded in a patriarchal definition of mentoring, wherein the mentor and mentee are situated in top-down positions with regard to power relations. On the contrary, the women in this study shared examples of when the roles of the mentee and mentor would temporarily reverse because of their difference in age. For Ella, Ivy, Rose, and Shelia, sometimes this role reversal appeared to be prompted by an experience in a personal context, while at other times, by an experience in a professional context. Specifically, their approach to mentoring counters the dominant patriarchal conceptualization of mentoring as the findings exemplify Cochran-Smith's and Paris's (1995) notion of "women's ways of collaborating" as an alternative approach for women mentoring women (p. 182).

CONCLUSION

Age influenced the power dynamics within their mentoring relationships as the dyads involved a mentor who was younger than the mentee. In one particular instance, Rose, a mentee, struggled as she negotiated the tension of age, power, and the binary of faculty role versus administrator role in higher education. Ultimately, the differing ages and academic roles often appeared to be connected to the women exercising role reversal with regard to the personal and professional well-being of each other.

The mentors and mentees understood the consequence of not communicating as they negotiated their tensions with the power dynamics of the mentoring relationship. Miscommunication can often be associated with the lack of expressing initially the expectations of self and others when participating in a mentoring relationship. This is especially essential in a cross-age mentoring relationship as miscommunication may prevent learning about generational differences and similarities. Once the mentees and mentors engaged in conversations, they began to learn about and from each other.

Absent from the current literature on mentoring is the discussion of the power dynamics and age (i.e., respect for elders). Exclusive to adult higher education contexts, it is possible for the difference of age to influence student-faculty mentoring in graduate education in a less than *traditional* conceptualization as the academy continues to welcome younger aged faculty members. It is necessary to express the understandings of mentoring in relation to age differences that may exist within the mentor-doctoral student relationship as this may impact the communicative behaviors of the mentee and the mentor. Ultimately, this could hinder or prevent the fruition of an authentic connection between the participants of the mentoring relationship.

While findings from this small, non-random, context-specific sample cannot be applied to all female mentoring relationships, they may provide insight in continuing to explore and understand student-faculty mentoring interactions at the doctoral level. Although the findings presented here originated from a study of female faculty mentors and the experiences of their female doctoral student mentees, they may certainly have transferability to other pairings. Other groups within various settings may find the study findings to be useful as they attempt to explore alternative practices for mentoring, inside and outside of the context of graduate education. Moreover, the data presented offer a unique perspective on the experiences of a cross-age mentoring dyad when both individuals are women with different values and ideas because of their age group.

REFERENCES

Agar, M. (1986). *Speaking of ethnography.* Beverly Hills, CA: Sage.

Alston, G. D. (2014). *Cross-cultural mentoring relationships in higher education: A feminist grounded theory study* (Doctoral dissertation). Retrieved from Texas State University Digital Collections, https://digital.library.txstate.edu/handle/10877/4953

Birks, M., & Mills, J. (2011). *Grounded theory: A practical guide.* Thousand Oaks, CA: Sage.

Butterfield, L. D., Borgen, W. A., Maglio, A. T., & Amundson, N. E. (2009). Using the enhanced critical incident technique in counselling psychology research. *Canadian Journal of Counselling, 43*(4), 265–282.

Castro, C., Caldwell, C., & Salazar, C. F. (2005). Creating mentoring relationships between female faculty and students in counselor education: Guidelines for potential mentees and mentors. *Journal of Counseling & Development, 83*, 331–336.

Chandler, C. (1996). Mentoring and women in academia: Reevaluating the traditional model. *NWSA Journal, 8*, 79–100.

Charmaz, K. (2005). Grounded theory in the 21st century: Applications for advancing social justice studies. In N. Denzin & Y. Lincoln (Eds.), *The Sage handbook of qualitative research,* (pp. 507–535). Thousand Oaks, CA: Sage.

Charmaz, K. (2006). *Constructing grounded theory: A practical guide through qualitative analysis.* Thousand Oaks, CA: Sage.

Chen, L., Kim, Y. S., Moon, P., & Merriam, S. B. (2008). A review and critique of the portrayal of older adult learners in adult education journals, 1980–2006. *Adult Education Quarterly, 59*, 3–21.

Clark, M., & Garza, H. (1994). Minorities in graduate education: A need to regain lost momentum. In M. J. Justiz, R. Wilson, & L. G. Bjork (Eds.), *Minorities in higher education.* (pp. 297–313). Phoeniz, AZ: Oryx Press.

Cochran-Smith, M., & Paris, C. (1995). Mentor and mentoring: Did Homer have it right? In J. Smyth (Ed.), *Critical discourses on teacher development* (pp. 181–202). London, England: Cassell.

Cook, S. G. (2006). How to play nicely with colleagues on campus. *Women in Higher Education, 15*(5), 24. Retrieved from http://www.wihe.com/displayNews.jsp?id=406

Cotugna, N., & Vickery, C. E. (1998). Reverse mentoring: A twist to teaching technology. *Journal of the American Dietetic Association, 98*(10), 1166–1168.

DeMarco, R. (1993). Mentorship: A feminist critique of current research. *Journal of Advanced Nursing, 18*(8), 1242–1250.

Finkelstein, M. (2012). American faculty and their institutions: A multinational comparison. *The NEA 2012 almanac of higher education.* Washington, DC: National Education Association. Available from http://www.nea.org/assets/docs/_2012_Almanac_Fiinkelstein_final.pdf

Ford, K. A. (2011). Race, gender, and bodily (mis)recognitions: Women of color faculty experiences with White students in the college classroom. *The Journal of Higher Education, 82*(4), 444–478. doi: 10.1353/jhe.2011.0026

Gilbert, L. A., & Rossman, K. M. (1992). Gender and the mentoring process for women: Implications for professional development. *Professional Psychology: Research and Practice, 23*, 233–238.

Gilligan, C. (2011). *Joining the resistance.* Cambridge, England: Polity Press.

Gillon, K. E., & Place, L. (2012). *Critical race feminism: Black faculty mentoring White students.* Paper presented at the 2012 American Educational Research Association Annual Research Conference, Vancouver, Canada.

Hansman, C. A. (2002). Diversity and power in mentoring relationships. In C. Hansman (Ed.), *Critical perspectives on mentoring: Trends and issues* (pp. 39–48). Eric Info Series No. 388. Columbus, OH: ERIC Clearinghouse on Adult, Career, and Vocational Education, Ohio State University. (ED99CO0013)

Hansman, C. A. (2005). Reluctant mentors and resistant protégés. *Adult Learning, 14,* 14–16.

Hartmann, H. (1984). The unhappy marriage of Marxism and feminism: Towards a more progressive union. In R. Dale, G. Esland, R. Ferguson, & M. McDonald (Eds.), *Education and the state: Politics, patriarchy, and practice* (Vol. 2, pp. 191–210). Sussex, England: The Open University Press.

Heinrich, K. T. (1995). Doctoral advisement relationships between women: On friendship and betrayal. *The Journal of Higher Education, 66,* 447–469.

Johnson, W. B., & Huwe, J. M. (2003). *Getting mentored in graduate school.* Washington, DC: American Psychological Association.

Johnson-Bailey, J., & Cervero, R. (2004). Mentoring in Black and White: The intricacies of cross-cultural mentoring. *Mentoring & Tutoring: Partnership in Learning, 12*(1), 7–21.

Kalbfleisch, P. J., & Anderson, A. (2013). Mentoring across generations: Culture, family, and mentoring relationships. In H. S. Noor Al-Deen (Ed.), *Cross-cultural communication & aging in the United States* (pp. 97–120). Mahwah, NJ: Lawrence Erlbaum Associates, Inc., Publishers.

Kim, Y. S., & Merriam, S. B. (2010). Situated learning and identity development in a Korean older adults' computer classroom. *Adult Education Quarterly, 60*(5), 438–455.

Leh, A. S. C. (2005). Lessons learned from service learning and reverse mentoring in faculty development: A case study in technology training. *Journal of Technology and Teacher Education, 13*(1), 25–41.

Meister, J. C., & Willyerd, K. (2010). Mentoring millennials. *Harvard Business Review, 88*(5), 68–72.

Mejiuni, O. (2009). Potential for transformative mentoring relationships among women in academia in Nigeria. *Proceedings of the Eighth International Transformative Learning Conference,* College of Bermuda. Available at http://meridianuniversity.edu/images/tlc/proceedings/TLC2009%20Proceedings.pdf

Merriam, S. B. (2015). *Qualitative research: A guide to design and implementation* (4th ed). San Francisco, CA: Jossey-Bass.

Merriam, S. B., & Kee, Y. (2014). Promoting community wellbeing: The case for lifelong learning for older adults. *Adult Education Quarterly, 64*(2), 128–144.

Merriam, S. B., & Mohamad, M. (2000). How cultural ways shape learning in older adulthood: The case of Malaysia. *Adult Education Quarterly, 51,* 45–63.

Mott, V. W. (2002). Emerging perspectives on mentoring: Fostering adult learning and development. In C. Hansman (Ed.), *Critical perspectives on mentoring: Trends and issues* (pp. 5–14). Eric Info Series No. 388. Columbus, OH: ERIC Clearinghouse on Adult, Career, and Vocational Education, Ohio State University. (ED99CO0013)

Mullen, C. A., Fish, V. L., & Hutinger, J. L. (2010). Mentoring doctoral students through scholastic engagement: Adult learning principles in action. *Journal of Further and Higher Education, 24,* 179–197.

Nettles, M. T., & Millett, C. M. (2006). *Three magic letters: Getting to the PhD.* Baltimore, MD: John Hopkins University Press.

Patton, M. Q. (2005). *Qualitative research.* New York, NY: Wiley.

Ragins, B. R. (1997). Diversified mentoring relationships in organization: A power perspective. *Academy of Management Review, 22,* 482–521.

Saldaña, J. (2009). *An introduction to codes and coding. The coding manual for qualitative researchers.* (2nd ed.). Thousands Oaks, CA: Sage.

Schneider, E. M., & Hanna, C. (2012). The development of domestic violence as a legal field: Honoring Clare Dalton. *Journal of Law & Policy, 20*(2), 343–359.

Standing, M. (1999). Developing a supportive/challenging and reflective/competency education (SCARCE) mentoring model and discussing its relevance to nurse education. *Mentoring & Tutoring: Partnerships in Learning, 6*(3), 3–17.

Wuest, J. (1995). Feminist grounded theory: An exploration of the congruency and tensions between two traditions in knowledge discovery. *Qualitative Health Research 5*(1), 125–137.

Wilson, N. J., Cordier, R, & Whatley, L. W. (2013). Older male mentors' perceptions of a Men's Shed intergenerational mentoring program. *Australian Occupational Therapy Journal, 60*(6), 416–426. Doi:10.1111/1440-1630.12090.

Woodd, M. (1997). Mentoring in further and higher education: Learning from the literature. *Education and Training, 39*(8/9), 333–344.

PART II

MENTORING IN K–12 TEACHER EDUCATION

CHAPTER 9

PERSPECTIVES FROM FIELD-BASED AND UNIVERSITY CLINICAL EDUCATORS' IMPLEMENTATION OF INDUCTION MENTORING STRATEGIES WITH PRE-SERVICE TEACHERS

Elaine M. Silva Mangiante
Elizabeth McAuliffe
Salve Regina University

The quality of a child's learning experience depends, in part, on the expertise of a teacher and the effectiveness of the instruction (Darling-Hammond, 2000). Research has documented differences between the practice and skills of novice and expert teachers (Allen & Casbergue, 1997; Berliner, 2001, 2004). From their limited experience, novice teachers have more difficulty focusing on the context of the students and noting individual student needs

Mentoring in Formal and Informal Contexts, pages 157–177
Copyright © 2016 by Information Age Publishing

than expert teachers. To address this gap in experience, some districts provide induction coaches to guide and mentor beginning teachers and veteran teachers who need additional support in promoting student learning (Ingersoll & Strong, 2011). Pre-service teachers (PSTs) in their pre-employment education would also benefit from this type of mentorship prior to entering the workforce. Since PSTs typically focus more on lesson delivery than on student learning (Allen & Casbergue, 1997; Borko & Livingston, 1989), efforts to assist PSTs in broadening their view and practice could help them enter the teaching profession as "well-started" beginning teachers.

The New Teacher Center (NTC, 2014) is a national, non-profit organization dedicated to providing professional development in mentoring for potential induction coaches. The term, induction, refers to programs developed to orient new teachers to the teaching profession and the school district with the support and guidance of a mentor/coach (Ingersoll & Strong, 2011). The NTC focus is on "improving student learning by supporting the development of an inspired, dedicated, and highly qualified teaching force" (NTC, 2014, p. 3). Recognizing that teacher education programs prepare beginning teachers to enter the workforce, NTC recently broadened its mission by inviting teacher education faculty and their partners in school districts (teachers who offer school placements to pre-service teachers) to participate in the mentoring professional development.

As part of a pilot project, the teacher education faculty (termed university clinical educators—UCEs) from a small private university in the Northeast and teachers from a local school district who supervise PSTs in their student teaching placement in the field (termed clinical educators—CEs) agreed to participate in the NTC Professional Learning Series to develop skills in mentoring over the course of two years. The purpose of this study is to examine the perspectives of the UCEs and CEs after implementing their newly acquired mentoring strategies and tools when supervising PSTs during their student teaching experience. The following questions guided this study:

- How do school-based clinical educators and university clinical educators describe the influence of and challenges from implementing the mentoring strategies and tools when supervising their pre-service teachers during student teaching?
- How do school-based clinical educators and university clinical educators perceive the use of mentoring strategies and tools in the future for the teacher education program?

LITERATURE REVIEW

The process of mentoring, particularly in the field of education is a poorly defined concept (Aspfors, & Fransson, 2015; Colley, 2003) depicted in a variety of forms including support for an individual's professional development, collaborative professional development with peers, and supervision combined with assessment of a new teacher's performance (Kemmis, Heikkinen, Fransson, Aspfors, & Edwards-Groves, 2014). For the purpose of this study, we address mentoring as the process whereby more experienced teachers support new or prospective teachers in developing their professional practices (Kemmis et al., 2014). In this case, the mentoring process involves a long-term relationship "primarily designed to support the [newly qualified teacher's] . . . learning, professional development and well-being and to facilitate their induction into the culture of teaching and the local school context" (Aspfors & Fransson, p. 76). For this type of mentoring, Orland-Barack (2014) describes the role of mentors as mediators between the mentees and the content for professional learning within a given context. Mentors, as "gatekeepers to the work and norms of teaching," are important in guiding beginning teachers or PSTs to develop the awareness, knowledge, and responses required for the demands of teaching (Butler & Cuenca, 2012, p. 297).

The art of teaching is complex requiring years of experience to develop skill and an intuitive practice (Berliner, 2001, 2004; Feiman-Nemser, 2001). Strong induction and mentoring support for novice teachers can lay the groundwork for the intellectual work and growth needed for teaching (Feiman-Nemser, 2001). Socio-constructivist learning theory provides the conceptual foundation for understanding the value of mentoring. Vygotsky (1978) explains that through socially constructed learning, a person can mature and problem solve in areas that require guidance or collaboration for attainment with the help of a more capable adult or peer. In this way, teacher mentees can advance their learning with the support of mentors who have developed independent performance in these areas. The experience of student teaching apprenticeship provides PSTs with the opportunity to situate their learning in the actual setting of practice with the help of a mentor (Lave & Wenger, 1991). Based on Lave and Wenger's argument (1991), this situated learning or in this case, student teaching placement, offers a "transitory . . . bridge" (p. 34) for PSTs' "generative social practice" as a teacher (p. 35). During this time, mentors can guide PSTs to make sense of their socially constructed and growing practice (Butler & Cuenca, 2012).

As aids in mentoring, Helgevold, Næsheim-Bjørkvik, and Østrem (2015) argue that university teacher education and field-based mentors need to employ mediating tools as a means for PSTs to inquire about their practice and discuss essential issues in teaching. An example of one mediating tool is a lesson study cycle through which teachers can collaborate as colleagues to plan, conduct, observe each other, discuss, and refine lesson development (Dudley, 2013). Results from Helgevold et al.'s study (2015) indicated that the use of curriculum handbooks without the mediating process of collaborative lesson study for sense-making did not enhance PSTs' teaching practices. Yendol-Hoppy (2007) suggested that mentoring also can involve providing PSTs with "spaces" as pedagogical tools to grow and reflect on the increasing complex roles experienced during student teaching. These mentor-provided spaces offer opportunities for PSTs to explore, raise questions, improve, and celebrate within the student teaching experience.

New Teacher Center Mentoring Model and Conceptual Framework

The NTC provides a professional development program to prepare mentors in assisting beginning teachers and PSTs to grow their teaching practice for student learning. The original focus of the program was on developing effective induction coaches to mentor beginning teachers and veteran teachers who needed additional support. However, NTC has expanded its reach to include professional development for university teacher educators and school-based clinical educators who directly impact the preparation of PSTs. For example, through the Volusia Center for Excellence in Education Project (VCEE, 2014), NTC is working with three partners in Florida: Stetson University, a private liberal arts university; Bethune-Cookman University, a historically Black college; and Volusia County Schools, the state's 13th largest school district with high student learning needs. The goal of the VCEE project is to improve educator preparation by providing PSTs with the same instructional mentoring and coaching support that VCEE has offered new teachers.

During the 2013–2014 and the 2014–2015 academic years, NTC also has offered this professional development to the education department faculty from a small liberal arts university in the Northeast and their teaching partners in a local school district. For this research study, we chose to examine the perceptions of these UCEs and CEs who are in the early stages of adopting the NTC mentoring program. To gain a sense of the essential components of this mentoring program, we describe NTC's conceptual framework, professional learning series, and mentoring tools.

Conceptual Framework

According to the NTC's philosophy of mentoring for effective instruction, a mentor contributes to the professional development of beginner or PSTs by focusing on student learning (NTC, 2014). In this capacity, the mentor has a wide variety of roles to assume including teacher, reflective listener, assessor, learner, collaborator, advocate, coach, facilitator, problem-solver, and resource depending on the needs of the mentee. The NTC conceptual framework undergirding possible mentor actions, adapted from Glickman's framework for developmental supervision (1981), can be summarized through three differentiated mentoring strategies: instructive, facilitative, and collaborative.

When implementing the *instructive* approach, a mentor can model instructional strategies, share ideas and processes for promoting student learning, suggest solutions for challenges, and provide or suggest sources of information. Using a *facilitative* strategy, a mentor can assist a mentee in analyzing observation data, posing clarifying questions, and facilitating a mentee's thinking and problem-solving. Through *collaborative* strategies, mentors and mentees can co-develop lesson plans, problem-solve issues, analyze student work, co-observe other teachers, and reflectively debrief their observations or experiences. This framework of strategies serves as a guide for mentoring choices.

Professional Learning Series

The NTC prepares mentors through a two-year Professional Learning Series addressing mentoring for effective instruction in the first year and how to reach all learners in the second year. Mentors-in-training participate in eight full-day professional development sessions each year. Tables 9.1 and 9.2 depict the topics and outcomes for each year (NTC, 2014, p. 4).

TABLE 9.1 Year 1: Mentoring for Effective Instruction

Session	Outcomes
Instructional Mentoring	To support mentors in responding to each new teacher's developmental and contextual needs and promote the ongoing examination of instructional practice.
Observing and Conferencing	To provide mentors with tools and processes for collecting and analyzing observation data in alignment with professional teaching standards to improve teaching practice.
Using Data to Inform Instruction	To deepen mentor understanding of the process of analyzing student work in order to strategically plan and adjust standards-based instruction.
Designing Effective Instruction	To develop mentor expertise in supporting beginning teachers to plan standards-based, differentiated instruction that reaches all learners.

TABLE 9.2   Year 2: Reaching All Learners

Session	Outcomes
Creating Conditions for Equitable Instruction	To advance mentoring, teaching, and learning practices that support equity and develop social and emotional learning competencies.
Advancing Instruction to Support Language Development	To deepen and extend mentoring practices that improve teachers' abilities to meet their students' language and literacy needs.
Differentiating Instruction to Support Diverse Learners	To refine mentors' knowledge, skills, and abilities to use tools and strategies that improve teaching and learning for students with learning differences.
Mentoring as Leadership	To support and challenge mentors to consider their roles as leaders and change agents in education.

Mentoring Tools

NTC (2014) provides tools to assist mentors in supporting their mentee's development. For the purpose of this chapter, we will describe selected tools introduced to mentors in Year 1: (a) collaborative assessment log; (b) selective scripting tool; (c) seating chart tool; (d) analyzing student work tool; and (e) lesson planning tool.

The *Collaborative Assessment Log* (CAL) is used by mentors when debriefing a lesson observation with their mentee. This tool prompts conversations about what worked well in the lesson requesting evidence of instructional decisions and student learning. It also provides space to list challenges and concerns. Subsequently, using collaborative strategies, the mentor and mentee make specific decisions concerning the mentee's next steps for a particular focus area and the mentor's next steps that will support the beginning or PST's chosen goal.

The *Selective Scripting Tool* is designed for mentors to record data during a mentee's lesson observation. The recorded data depends on the goal established by the mentee or co-determined in collaborative conversations. For example, a beginning teacher or PST may be interested in teacher–student talk, teacher questioning, student responses, teacher interventions, teacher directions, participation strategies (i.e., frequency, which students, how many students), and teacher decision in reaction to student responses. Mentors are encouraged to use symbols, codes, and the first five or six words of each dialog unit for ease in recording data.

The *Seating Chart Tool* provides a means for mentors to document and graphically display students' on- or off-task behavior or talk, participation frequency, students to whom the teacher directs questions, student-to-student interactions, teacher and student movement in the room, and student engagement. Again, the focus of the data collection is determined by the mentee or through a joint decision with the mentor. The seating arrangement can be drawn including the students' names, gender, special needs, language, or other relevant categories.

The *Analyzing Student Work Tool* (ASW) provides a process for determining each student's learning needs in a class in order to plan next steps for differentiated instruction. This tool involves six steps: identifying standards for student learning, determining attributes of student work to meet the standards, recording each student's performance level (far below standard, approaching standard, meeting standard, exceeding standard), describing the performance of one focus student from each category, identifying student misconceptions in each category, and planning next steps of differentiated instruction for students.

The *Lesson Planning Tool* is designed to guide teachers in planning backwards to ensure that the students' learning matches the lesson objective. The tool provides a format for identifying the key concepts of a lesson in addition to the learning outcomes and evidence of student learning. This document also specifies elements of instructional design such as: making connections for students, modeling, shared practice, guided practice, collaborative practice, closure, and extension activities, with a separate section to note ways to differentiate instruction within a given class.

To facilitate the debriefing discourse with mentees when using these mentoring tools, the NTC professional development provided opportunities for the mentors to practice mentoring language that was less directive and instructive. The language approaches for mentoring included paraphrasing, clarifying, meditational questioning, and non-judgmental responses. These mentoring strategies allowed mentors to prompt their mentees to reflect, analyze, and identify their strengths and areas in need of improvement as well as determine next steps for their growing teaching practice.

METHODOLOGY

This exploratory study employed qualitative research methods to understand the meaning that CEs and UCEs ascribed to their experience implementing mentoring strategies and tools with their PSTs during student teaching. Qualitative research is a form of inquiry that allows individual's perceptions from a social setting to emerge, building general themes from inductive analysis of the data (Creswell, 2009). For this study, using emergent design strategies from analyzing interviews, we sought to capture the participants' perspectives and personal experiences in this pilot mentoring project.

Participants and Setting

Over the course of two years, four CEs and seven UCEs participated in one or both years of mentoring professional development with NTC. Of these individuals, four CEs and five UCEs agreed to participate in the study. Three of the four CEs taught at the elementary level in the same school and one CE taught at the secondary level; all CEs were teachers in the same urban school district in the Northeast. Each of the participants had more than five years of experience as a CE or UCE. Table 9.3 documents the characteristics of each of the participants as well as the number of PSTs each mentored using the NTC mentoring strategies and tools. All names used in this chapter are pseudonyms.

Data Collection

The data sources for this study were the CEs' and UCEs' responses to interview questions. The second author conducted all the interviews and used a structured interview guide to ensure that each participant answered the same questions (Patton, 2002).

1. How has your participation in the Mentoring Professional Learning Series influenced your work with teacher candidates and university clinical educators or LEA clinical educators?
2. What, if any, challenges have you experienced in adapting the mentoring model and its tools to your work with teacher candidates?
3. What do you see as possible next steps to integrate the model into a pre-service teacher education program?

TABLE 9.3   Characteristics of Participants

Mentor's Pseudonym	CE or UCE	Attended Year 1	Attended Year 2	General or Special Education	Grade Level	Number of PSTs
Sharon	CE	√	√	General Ed.	Elementary, Grade 4	4
Cara	CE	√	√	General Ed.	Elementary, Grade 3	4
Denise	CE	√	√	General Ed.	Elementary, Grade K	2
Jim	CE	√	√	General Ed.	Secondary History	2
Miriam	UCE	√		General Ed.	Elementary	14
Linda	UCE	√		General Ed.	Pre-school	12
Kelly	UCE	√	√	General Ed.	Secondary	12
Ann	UCE	√	√	Special Ed.	Elementary	8
Jane	UCE	√	√	General Ed.	Elementary	5

4. What stories can you share from your experience using the mentoring model?

Prior to the interview, participants received the questions to provide time for individual reflection on the professional development and mentoring experience with their PSTs. Due to scheduling conflicts, the CEs participated in a 60 minute focus group interview. A focus group interview was appropriate for this study since the participants had similar backgrounds from the shared experience with the mentoring professional development (Patton, 2002). Four UCEs were interviewed individually, while one UCE responded to the interview questions in writing.

Data Analysis

To analyze the data, first the researchers read through the interview data repeatedly to code each idea based on the three mentoring components in the NTC conceptual framework: instructing, facilitating, and collaborating with the mentee. After this initial deductive analysis, we re-examined the data systematically to identify patterns for each category inductively using Miles' and Huberman's constant comparative method (1994) in order to answer the first research question: How do CEs and UCEs describe the influence of and challenges from implementing mentoring strategies and tools when supervising PSTs during student teaching?

This process also revealed the CEs' and UCEs' recommendations for follow-up to this mentoring program in answer to the second research question: How do CEs and UCEs perceive the use of mentoring strategies and tools in the future for the teacher education program? To increase the trustworthiness of the results, the first author presented the emergent themes to the participants for final member-checking (Merriam, 1998). Though the results from this limited sample of CEs and UCEs cannot be generalized to the larger population of faculty from teacher education programs or schools working with PSTs, the findings may provide insights to readers as to its applicability to their own contexts (Erlandson, Harris, Skipper, & Allen, 1993).

RESULTS

The results of the data analysis revealed common themes from both the CEs and UCEs for the instructive, facilitative, and collaborative mentoring components of the NTC conceptual framework. In addition, the findings indicated the challenges experienced by CEs and UCEs as well as their recommendations for future use of the mentoring strategies and tools when working with PSTs. These findings are described using the participants' reflective comments and stories from their experiences using the mentoring strategies and tools.

Instructive Mentoring

Prospective teachers, by the nature of their "in-training" position, require guidance, support, and instruction in the art of teaching from both CEs and UCEs. For UCEs in particular, as they implemented the mentoring strategies and tools, the UCEs experienced a need to balance their evaluative, instructional role with this newly adopted mentoring role. UCE-Miriam explained that the mentoring tools were developed for use with in-service beginning or struggling teachers: "As a teacher education program, our main focus is instructional as our candidates are not in the same place as beginning teachers for whom the tools were developed." Yet, Miriam saw how the use of the tools was "empowering to teacher candidates to identify what he/she wants and needs to work on moving forward." The following themes emerged indicating how the UCEs transformed their supervisory practice to include instructive mentoring.

Pre-Service Teachers Encouraged to Identify Own Instructional Needs
Both the CEs and UCEs noted that previously they assessed their PSTs' teaching by identifying the PSTs' strengths and weaknesses. From this assessment, CEs and UCEs would provide the PST with specific suggestions for improvement in areas that needed further development. UCE-Ann described this approach as "giving the answer" to PSTs rather than waiting for them to process their own interpretation of the teaching. Yet, by using the *Collaborative Assessment Log* (CAL) after a PST taught a lesson, the mentors found a different dynamic developing. The tool provided a structure for the mentor to invite the PST to identify the strengths and challenges of a lesson as well as request specific next steps of support from the mentor. This support could take the form of modeling, sharing strategies, or resources. From using this tool, the CEs noted a "shift in the CE's approach" from "directing the conversation" to a non-judgmental facilitation" of their interaction with the PST. They saw that the PSTs were "taking more ownership" of their developing practice.

The UCEs also experienced this change in discourse dynamics with their PSTs when debriefing lesson observations. A veteran UCE, Ann, expressed that she had "a real ah-ha moment" when using the CAL. From asking the prompting questions, "What can I do? How can I support you?" Ann described that she was "surprised and amazed" at the PST reflection; the

PST was "taking responsibility for her own growth." UCE-Miriam also noted that "the CAL was a way to document our conversation and have all parties commit to next steps." Thus, based on the PST's request for instructional support, a mentor was able to target the area for instructional mentoring.

Development of effective questions was one area that PSTs requested support from both CEs and UCEs. One CE noted that the PST wished to work on questioning strategies. The CE provided some suggestions of "question starters" and together they brainstormed for potential questions for the next lesson. While the PST conducted the lesson, the CE noticed that the PST was struggling to engage the students. The CE gave instructional support by giving the PST "the look" as a signal, meaning "Remember the question starters!" As a result, the PST incorporated the questions into the lesson and the students' engagement improved. Likewise, UCE-Jane's PST requested support in formulating questions. Having a toolkit of instructional supports available for each PST debriefing session, Jane addressed her PST's need by providing a list of question stems arranged according to Bloom's taxonomy of learning (remembering, understanding, applying, analyzing, evaluating, creating) (Anderson et al., 2001). From access to this resource, the PST was able to revise her questions prompting her students to engage in more critical thinking.

Instructional Mentoring Within Methods Courses

An outcome of the UCEs' participation in the NTC mentoring professional development was their incorporation of instructional mentoring strategies and tools in the education methods courses. As UCEs used the tools when mentoring PSTs, they recognized that prospective teachers who were beginning to learn about educational pedagogy would benefit from instructional support before they began student teaching. UCE-Kelly explained that she chose to embed the *Analyzing Student Work Tool* (ASW) into her expectations for lesson plan development and reflection. Kelly noted that the use of the ASW allowed her to transform the work in the methods course from "a portfolio system to a performance assessment." The PSTs in her methods course would plan a lesson to teach in their practicum placement with a focus on what they wanted the students to learn and how they were going to assess that learning. After instruction, the PSTs would examine the student work samples, sort the samples into four categories of student achievement, identify students' misconceptions in each category, and then determine follow-up steps and instructional modifications to address these misconceptions. The use of the tool facilitated a shift in her education course expectations with a focus on student outcomes. The ASW tool became a vehicle for Kelly to provide instructional mentoring to her methods students in how to plan, assess, and determine next steps with student learning in mind.

Facilitative Mentoring

The mentoring strategies and tools are designed for the mentor to generate observational data during a PST's teaching. Through facilitative questioning, the mentor can promote the PST's thinking, self-analysis, and problem-solving. The following themes emerged depicting the CEs' and UCEs' experiences with facilitative mentoring.

Data Provides Objective Means for Facilitative Questioning

The *Selective Scripting Tool, Seating Chart Tool*, and *Analyzing Student Work Tool* all require the CE or UCE to collect data while a PST teaches a lesson. This observation data provides an unbiased documentation of the PST's instructional choices and language used in the lesson. Both CEs and UCEs emphasized the value of this data as an entry point for conversation. For example, UCE-Jane provided an example of how the *Seating Chart Tool* generated data that she would not have noticed without using the tool. Jane remarked that by focusing solely on the student engagement while a PST taught a lesson, she was able to identify unengaged students, students who were overlooked, students with whom the PST focused attention, students who raised their hands without being called on, and students who were called on without raising their hands. This rich data source provided a seedbed for analysis and conversation when facilitating discussion with the PST. UCE-Miriam recalled that her PST requested that she document the students' on-task behavior as she was teaching. She explained that when she debriefed with the PST and the CE, "the CE and I had similar notes and it was such an ah-ha moment for the PST." From their facilitated conversation regarding the data, the PST realized "how her positioning blocked off students" from the lesson and resulted in off-task behavior.

Facilitative Approach Emphasizes Mentee Ownership

The mentors also found that facilitative mentoring resulted in PSTs taking ownership of their reflection and development. The CEs noted that by using the *Selective Scripting Tool* to record teacher–student interactions or teacher questioning during a lesson, they were able to ask questions and facilitate the PST in examining the data specifically. The CEs explained that this approach resulted in "greater depth of discussion and more PST involvement." For example, from examining the data generated from UCE-Ann's use of the *Seating Chart Tool*, her PST discovered that "her language used during the lesson did not move her students forward." The PST came to her own realization that she needed to provide clearer language describing her expectations of students. Likewise, UCE-Linda experienced that her PST was able to take it upon herself to adopt more intentional use of language as a result of reviewing data generated from the mentoring tools.

It is noteworthy that prior to participating in the mentoring professional development, UCE-Jane had observed PSTs teaching lessons during their student teaching without engaging in pre-lesson planning with the PST. Jane assumed that the field-based CE would fill that role. However, the NTC *Lesson Planning Tool* provided her with the means to assist a PST who requested help in designing a math lesson for students who struggled with fractions. Jane was able to facilitate the PST's creation of questions to engage students during the lesson. During the lesson observation, Jane used the *Seating Chart Tool* and documented the students that the PST called on during the mathematics discussion. From the facilitated debriefing conversation, the PST realized that he had focused on students who typically struggled with math, but avoided calling on students that he viewed as strong in math. Following the lesson, the PST took the initiative to complete the *ASW* on his own and discovered that the students with whom he gave the most attention performed best on the formative assessment, while those that he thought understood the concept did not perform well. Jane reported that the mentoring process resulted in the PST recognizing for himself the need to "make sure you engage all students."

Collaborative Mentoring

Inherent in the term, collaboration, is the expectation that the individuals are equal partners, co-constructing their understanding and next steps. In the case of CEs and UCEs working with PSTs, they experienced a new collaborative role with their supervision. A common theme emerging from the interview data was that both the CEs and UCEs experienced a more collaborative partnership with the PST by using the mentoring strategies and tools.

Partners in Reflection and Analysis
During the CE focus group interview, the CEs remarked that their interactions with their respective PSTs were more collaborative than in the past. They found that the PSTs were "not intimidated" as a result of the mentoring approaches used. The UCEs had similar experiences. UCE-Jane emphasized that by using the mentoring tools whereby she and her PSTs examined data together, they were able to approach this analysis task as team members seeking to discover areas of strength and areas needing improvement. Jane provided an example exemplifying the partnership that emerged from collaborative mentoring. In keeping with the NTC mentoring approach, PSTs typically identify focus areas for a UCE before the UCE observes a PST teaching a lesson. Early in her student teaching experience, one of Jane's PSTs could not identify a focus area, so Jane offered to use the *Selective Scripting Tool* to document the PST's words during the lesson.

During the post-observation conference, the PST read the script and placed a check mark next to each section that she felt indicated a strong teaching practice and a delta next to each area needing improvement. As a result of this data processing, the PST identified that she wanted to work on her questioning skills. Together, the UCE and the PST collaborated in brainstorming options for reshaping the questions she identified as in need of improvement. For Jane, this team approach differed from her previous interaction with PSTs in which she provided directive feedback, identifying that the PST would need to work on her questioning skills. However, from using collaborative mentoring, Jane reported the PST was enthusiastic about the analysis process and felt empowered in identifying areas for her own personal growth.

Challenges

Both CEs and UCEs indicated that they felt that their mentoring was challenged by the limited time they had available for discourse with PSTs. The mentors recognized the level of discussion needed to process the data obtained from the tools used during the lesson observations. Two of the UCEs, Linda and Ann, noted that since they observe the PSTs four times during a semester, they did not have regular opportunities for weekly interactions to use the tools fully and enact the follow-up plans. The UCEs had to rely on the CEs for more consistent use of the tools to help PSTs process their daily planning.

Another limiting factor was that not all PSTs were assigned to CEs who participated in the mentoring professional development. UCE-Kelly noted that the education program was "caught in between the old and the new" system and could not fully implement the mentoring program without a "partnering team" of CEs. The ideal situation would be to match CEs and UCEs who had both participated in the mentoring professional development. With the limited number of CEs who participated in the mentoring program, UCEs found that they had to introduce the mentoring tools not only to the PST, but also to untrained CEs.

The UCEs faced their own set of challenges when attempting to integrate the mentoring tools into their supervisory and evaluative role given the different nature of these two systems. For example, some UCEs explained that since UCEs needed to provide both mentoring and evaluation of PSTs when using the NTC program, the mentoring tools did not address the evaluative function that the UCEs had to complete. UCE-Miriam explained, "It was challenging to think outside the instructional realm to mediating and encouraging teacher candidates to reflect on *their* determination of strengths and needs." Other UCEs noted that the current lesson plan format and observation assessment form developed by the university education department did not reflect the goals of the mentoring project and became a challenging "misfit" when debriefing a lesson. Another factor impacting this challenge was the situation that not all UCEs in the university education department chose to participate in the mentoring professional development. The non-participating UCEs did not experience the misalignment between the previous supervisory format and the mentoring approach and, thus, they did not recognize the need to revise the education department formats.

Future Directions for Mentoring Pre-service Teachers

To address these challenges, the CEs and UCEs provided recommendations for possible next steps to integrate the mentoring model into a pre-service teacher education program. From an examination of the data, three categories of recommendations emerged regarding next steps for CEs, UCEs, and the university education program as a whole.

Recommendations for Field-Based Clinical Educators

The CEs generated their own recommendations for their next steps in implementing the mentoring strategies when working with their PSTs. First, they noted that it would be useful for the PST to use the mentoring tools when observing the CE—a reversal of roles. In this way, the PST could become familiar with the tools and have a professional lens through which to observe an experienced teacher. Like the UCEs, the CEs suggested that the required university education department evaluation forms needed revision to align with the mentoring approaches that they were using. Given the limited number of CEs who participated in the mentoring professional development, UCEs recommended that the university education department develop a mentoring workshop for all CEs so that they could become familiar with mentoring approaches when supervising a PST. However, given the proprietary nature of NTC materials requiring teachers to fully commit to the professional development in order to use the mentoring tools, this workshop would need to provide a general overview of the mentoring process and provide the education department's own version of mentoring tools so that all CEs could use these strategies and tools more consistently with PSTs.

Next Steps for University Clinical Educators

The CEs provided recommendations for UCEs that would prepare PSTs for this mentoring approach during student teaching. In alignment with the vision of UCEs, the CEs noted the benefit of introducing the mentoring observation tools to PSTs early in the teacher education program for use when teacher candidates visit and observe teachers and students in the classroom setting. This approach would ensure more focused observation time and provide the potential for rich conversations in the university classroom. Teacher education faculty members could use mentoring language as these observations are debriefed in order to acclimate PSTs to the mentoring discourse approach. In addition, teacher educators could use the mentoring tools when PSTs analyze videos of classroom instruction to build their ability to view teaching situations with a professional lens.

The CEs also recommended that the mentoring tools, particularly the ASW, be used during the PSTs' methods courses. By using the ASW tool when teaching in practicum experiences, the PST could begin to assimilate the expectation of setting clear measurable goals, assessing student learning, analyzing student work, and determining next steps to address student misconceptions. The CEs also suggested that the PSTs could observe each other during practicum teaching and learn to use the tools. The UCEs, themselves, also recommended that the ASW be used in all methods courses. Since the UCEs noted that there was variability among PSTs in their ability to reflect upon their practice during the mentoring, incorporating the mentoring tools in coursework early in PSTs' educational studies may promote the growth of their professional vision.

Suggestions for the University Teacher Education Program

Several UCEs emphasized the need for the university teacher education faculty to review their lesson plan and PST evaluation forms to reflect not only the goals from the NTC mentoring, but also the focus areas of the state-wide teacher evaluation system developed to assess the effectiveness of each in-service teacher. The PST forms had been developed prior to the new teacher evaluation program. In order to prepare PSTs for the expectations they will experience upon employment, both CEs and UCEs stressed the necessity for the PST evaluation forms to align with the format used to assess in-service teacher performance. Concomitantly, the UCEs also suggested that the mentoring tools needed to be adapted to meet the dual role played by UCEs in terms of both mentoring and supervision. UCE-Miriam noted that the mentoring tools needed to "be tweaked . . . to reflect the balance of roles." Upon revision, UCE-Kelly expressed that the education department needed to train all UCEs, whether or not they participated in the NTC mentoring professional development, in order to establish a common language and protocol for the department when working with PSTs.

Finally, UCE-Kelly recommended two large-scale efforts. First, the university education department faculty could seek grant funding to increase the number of CEs participating in this mentoring program and to include other school districts in this project. Next, by conducting research with employed graduates from the teacher education program who received mentoring during their student teaching, the department could examine the effectiveness of the PST mentoring in preparing new teachers for their first year of teaching.

DISCUSSION

The results of this study provided insight into the possible outcomes of implementing NTC induction mentoring strategies and tools when supervising PSTs in their student teaching placement. Consistent with Vygotsky's sociocultural learning theory (1978), the CEs and UCEs, as more experienced and knowledgeable veteran teachers, provided a means for PSTs to reflect upon, analyze, and construct understanding of how to grow their teaching practice. The findings showed that the CEs and UCEs' collection of specific data during lesson observations gave PSTs access to information they may not have been aware of when engaged in teaching. By using a range of mentoring tools, the CEs and UCEs, serving as neutral observers, were able to offer the PSTs a window into the reality of the learning experience and outcomes for each student. In alignment with research reports from Helgevold et al. (2015) on the use of mentoring tools, the results of this study suggested that the PSTs' learning was dependent, in large part, on the opportunity they were given to analyze the observation data generated from the mentoring tools. Based on the interview reports from CEs and UCEs comparing the reactions of PSTs in previous years with those who participated in the mentoring program, we argue that the use of the mentoring strategies and tools resulted in greater PST ownership of their practice to make sense of the complexities of teaching. By replacing the directive stance of "giving" PSTs advice/critiques with a facilitative or collaborative approach to process observation data, the CEs and UCEs were providing PSTs with "spaces" to explore and question their student teaching experience for themselves (Yendol-Hoppy, 2007).

However, to establish a teacher education program that is consistent in its practices of preparing PSTs for the teaching profession and coherent with its field-based partners requires communication and joint decision-making by the involved parties (Butler & Cuenca, 2012). The results of this study pointed to challenges in creating this level of coherence both within the university program and between the university and field-based professionals who support the preparation of future teachers. First, the UCEs noted a need to review not only the existing protocols for student teaching supervision in order to emphasize mentoring strategies, but also to adapt the NTC mentoring tools, originally designed for induction coaching, in order to incorporate the evaluative function required of UCEs when working with PSTs. The CEs also recognized the need for revision of the required university education department evaluation forms to reflect the current state teacher evaluation formats and to address the goals of the mentoring program.

Next, the effectiveness of adopting the mentoring program, in terms of the PST supervision in the education program as a whole, was impacted by the extent of participation at both the university and field-based level. Not all university education department faculty members participated in the mentoring professional development. In addition, only four field-based CEs out of 54 CEs received the training. Therefore, most PSTs in the teacher education program did not have an opportunity to experience the NTC mentoring strategies and tools during their student teaching supervision. A consistent program would need full participation by all parties. However, such an endeavor would require additional funding and the time commitment of all UCEs and CEs, factors that pose realistic obstacles.

Finally, since researchers have indicated that the student teaching experience has a profound impact on the developing practice of PSTs (Hammerness & Darling-Hammond, 2005), the coordination of university and field-based supervision is essential to ensure the coherence of educational philosophy and teaching practices (Hammerness, 2006). Given that PSTs are serving as apprentices situated in a field-based placement (Lave & Wenger, 1991), the consistency among the student teaching placements will depend on the preparation that each CE receives regarding mentoring approaches and expectations from the university education program. As noted by Yendol-Hoppy (2007), university teacher education programs can help their field-based partners embrace the mentoring role when working with PSTs. Given the benefits that the mentoring strategies and tools appeared to offer PSTs, the results of this study suggest that teacher education programs can support their field-based partners by providing an adapted form of mentoring professional development to their cadre of CEs who supervise PSTs. By taking an active role in promoting mentoring practices, university education department faculty who are training in mentoring can support CEs and promote a means to build PSTs' capacity to reflect and take the initiative to analyze and improve their beginning teaching practices.

CONCLUSION AND IMPLICATIONS

The adoption by the faculty of a university education program and their field-based partners in a school district of the NTC mentoring program designed for induction coaches provides an encouraging approach to ready pre-employment teachers as well-started beginners in their first years of teaching. Despite the hopeful findings from this study indicating that PSTs take more ownership of their growing teaching practice when receiving mentoring from their CE and/or UCE, the results also indicate that there are challenges when attempting to implement the mentoring strategies for induction with a different population—teacher candidates who are beginning to learn about and practice teaching. This chapter identifies additional steps needed to adapt the NTC mentoring tools and strategies for application with pre-service teacher training.

Overall, from analysis of empirical studies examining the impact of induction programs on beginning teachers' commitment and retention, classroom instructional practices, and student achievement, the evidence suggests a positive outcome (Ingersoll & Strong, 2011). However, research efforts to investigate the impact of using induction strategies at the pre-service level are limited (VCEE, 2014). The results from this study suggest a need for additional research to examine the impact of applying the induction mentoring model to support PST development during their university training and student teaching. Questions remain for which the answers are unclear: What types of mentoring tools are most effective for use at the pre-service level? Do mentoring approaches that are effective with secondary PSTs differ from those used with elementary PSTs? Does mentoring at the pre-service level impact a first year teacher's teaching performance? As more teacher education programs embrace the mentoring tools and strategies for use with their PSTs, continued research can provide insight into these issues.

REFERENCES

Allen, R. M., & Casbergue, R. M. (1997). Evolution of novice through expert teacher recall: Implications for effective reflection on practice. *Teaching and Teacher Education, 13,* 741–755.

Anderson, L. W., Krathwohl, D. R., Airasian, P. W., Cruikshank, K. A., Mayer, R. E., Pintrich, P. R., Raths, J., & Wittrock, M. C. (2001). *A taxonomy for learning, teaching, and assessing: A revision of Bloom's taxonomy of educational objectives.* New York, NY: Longman.

Aspfors, J., & Fransson, G. (2015). Research on mentor education for mentors of newly qualified teachers: A qualitative meta-synthesis. *Teaching and Teacher Education, 48,* 75–86.

Berliner, D. C. (2001). Learning about learning from expert teachers. *International Journal of Educational Research, 35,* 463–482.

Berliner, D. C. (2004). Describing the behavior and documenting the accomplishments of expert teachers. *Bulletin of Science, Technology & Society, 24,* 200–212.

Borko, H., & Livingston, C. (1989). Cognition and improvisation: Differences in mathematics instruction by expert and novice teachers. *American Educational Research Journal, 26,* 473–498.

Butler, B. M., & Cuenca, A. (2012). Conceptualizing the roles of mentor teachers during student teaching. *Action in Teacher Education, 34,* 296–308.

Colley, H. (2003). *Mentoring for social inclusion: A critical approach to nurturing mentoring relationships.* London, England: Routledge Falmer.

Creswell, J. W. (2009). *Research design: Qualitative, quantitative, and mixed methods approaches.* Los Angeles, CA: Sage.

Darling-Hammond, L. (2000). Teacher quality and student achievement: A review of state policy evidence. *Education Policy Analysis Archives, 8*(1), 1–44.

Dudley, P. (2013). Teacher learning in lesson study: What interaction-level discourse analysis revealed about how teachers utilized imagination, tacit knowledge of teaching and fresh evidence of pupils learning, to develop practice knowledge and so enhance their pupils' learning. *Teaching and Teacher Education, 34,* 107–121.

Erlandson, D. A., Harris, E. L., Skipper, B. L., & Allen, S. D. (1993). *Doing naturalistic inquiry: A guide to methods.* London, England: Sage.

Feiman-Nemser, S. (2001). From preparation to practice: Designing a continuum to strengthen and sustain teaching. *Teachers College Record, 103*(6), 1013–1055.

Glickman, C. (1981). *Developmental supervision: Alternative practices for helping teachers improve instruction.* Alexandria, VA: Association for Supervision and Curriculum Development.

Hammerness, K. (2006). From coherence in theory to coherence in practice. *Teachers College Record, 108*(1), 1241–1265.

Hammemess, K., & Darling-Hammond, L. (2005). The design of teacher education programs. In L. Darling-Hammond & J. Bransford (Eds.), *Preparing teachers for a changing world: What teachers should learn and be able to do* (pp. 390–441). San Francisco, CA: Jossey-Bass.

Helgevold, N., Næsheim-Bjørkvik, G., & Østrem, S. (2015). Key focus areas and use of tools in mentoring conversations during internship in initial teacher education. *Teaching and Teacher Education, 49,* 128–137.

Ingersoll, R. M., & Strong, M. (2011). The impact of induction and mentoring programs for beginning teachers: A critical review of the research. *Review of Educational Research, 81*(2), 201–233.

Kemmis, S., Heikkinen, H. L. T., Fransson, G., Aspfors, J., & Edwards-Groves, C. (2014). Mentoring of new teachers as a contested practice: Supervision, support and collaborative self-development. *Teaching and Teacher Education, 43,* 154–164.

Lave, J., & Wenger, E. (1991). *Situated learning: Legitimate peripheral participation.* Cambridge, England: Cambridge University Press.

Merriam, S. B. (1998). *Qualitative research and case study applications in education.* San Francisco, CA: Jossey-Bass.

Miles, M. B., & Huberman, A.M. (1994). *Qualitative data analysis: An expanded sourcebook.* Beverly Hills, CA: Sage.

New Teacher Center (NTC). (2014). *Mentoring for effective instruction field guide.* Santa Cruz, CA: New Teacher Center.

Orland-Barak, L. (2014). Mediation in mentoring: A synthesis of studies in teaching and teacher education. *Teaching and Teacher Education, 44,* 180–188.

Patton, M. Q. (2002). *Qualitative research & evaluation methods* (3rd ed.). Thousand Oaks, CA: Sage Publications.

Volusia Center for Excellence in Education (VCEE). (2014). *About the Volusia Center for Excellence in Education*. Retrieved from www2.stetson.edu/vcee

Vygotsky, L. S. (1978). *Mind in society: The development of higher psychological processes*. London, England: Harvard University Press.

Yendol-Hoppy, D. (2007). Mentor teachers' work with prospective teachers in a newly formed professional development school: Two illustrations. *Teachers College Record, 109*(3), 669–698.

CHAPTER 10

IMPROVING SPECIAL EDUCATION TEACHER CANDIDATE COLLABORATION WITH FAMILIES THROUGH MENTORSHIP

Adam Moore
Catherine Semnoski
The University of Rhode Island

The provision of formal and informal mentorship for novice teachers has been an important topic in teacher preparation for the last two decades (Ingersoll & Strong, 2011). Particularly in the field of special education, high teacher attrition rates have prompted an even closer look at the factors contributing to struggles that novice special educators encounter (Billingsley, 2010; Griffin, 2010; Israel, Kamman, McCray, & Sindelar, 2014).

While new teacher induction programs are designed to support newly hired teachers in school districts and have become increasingly present in schools (Ingersoll, 2012), mentorship often begins in teacher preparation

Mentoring in Formal and Informal Contexts, pages 179–196
Copyright © 2016 by Information Age Publishing

programs from university supervisors and cooperating teachers during student teaching (Patte, 2011). Also known as an apprenticeship or internship, student teaching requires pre-service teacher candidates (PSTCs) to work with at least one in-service teacher to learn alongside an experienced professional (Ronfeldt & Reininger, 2012). Though teacher preparation programs may differ in the length of time that PSTCs work in a student teaching placement, commonalities include each PSTC taking over daily teaching responsibilities, classroom management duties, and communication with families during the placement. During student teaching, which typically occurs during the last semester of their university education, PSTCs receive mentoring from cooperating teachers and university supervisors (Ronfeldt & Reininger, 2012). The student teaching experience is a vital part of teacher preparation programs, yet PSTCs typically spend three years in a university classroom learning theoretical pedagogy that is often disconnected from the day-to-day work that effective in-service teachers employ (Korthagen, 2010; Patte, 2011).

A particularly important skill for special education teachers is to be able to successfully collaborate with families of children with disabilities (Friend & Cook, 2010); yet, opportunities in a university classroom are scarce for PSTCs to interact with families of children with disabilities (Patte, 2011). Using the tenets of Vygotsky's Zone of Proximal Development (ZPD) (1978) and Lave and Wenger's situated learning theory (1991), this chapter highlights authentic ways teacher educators can mentor PSTCs prior to student teaching so they have more opportunities to see, experience, and practice essential skills necessary for collaborating with families.

RESEARCH ON FAMILY ENGAGEMENT WITHIN SPECIAL EDUCATION

All educators must have the skills necessary to work with families; however, the Individuals with Disabilities Education Improvement Act (IDEIA) of 2004 sets legal mandates for special educators to involve families in their child's education and gives families legal rights, specifically because of their child's disability (Friend & Cook, 2010; Valle, 2011; Zirkel, 2013). This law places a greater focus on ensuring that special education teachers, regardless of their number of years of teaching experience, are well-versed in working with families and incorporate their ideas into the child's Individualized Education Program (IEP).

The university setting is at a disadvantage in providing PSTCs with authentic opportunities to acquire skills in creating teacher-family partnerships since it does not provide a contextually relevant setting for teacher candidates to practice these skills (Patte, 2011). As a result, teacher preparation programs have used an apprenticeship, or student teaching placement, to serve as a setting in which teacher candidates learn important skills from a more experienced professional (Ronfeldt & Reininger, 2012). Many traditional teacher preparation programs require PSTCs to reflect on their level of family participation during their student teaching placement. However, across various student teaching settings, these opportunities vary greatly (Patte, 2011; Ronfeldt & Reininger, 2012). For instance, in one setting a PSTC may be mentored by a teacher who actively works with families, organizes family-engagement nights, or requires their student teacher to communicate with families. A different setting may not be as rich with opportunities, and the PSTC will lack guided training in working with families.

Additionally, practice in interacting with families of children with disabilities is crucial for novice special education teachers (Walker & Dotger, 2015). Waiting until the last semester of a PSTC's training does not guarantee the PSTC will be equipped to demonstrate these skills nor does it ensure they will receive mentorship from a more experienced professional (Patte, 2011). Examining the impact that teacher collaboration skills have on families and their children provides insight into why teacher educators should strive to create authentic opportunities for their candidates to learn from families. The subsequent section briefly describes current research regarding teacher-family engagement.

Research About Families

Literature has shown that families are: (a) often left out of the IEP planning process (National Council on Disability, 1995; Valle & Aponte, 2002); (b) ill-informed about the meaning of various educational jargon (Fish, 2008; Goldstein, 1993); (c) strategically placed in a passive role in the IEP meeting (Darch, Miao, & Shippen, 2004; Vaughn, Bos, Harrell, & Lasky, 1988); and (d) marginalized because of perceived differences of culture, race, and ethnicity (Valle, 2011; Yull, Blitz, Thompson, & Murray, 2014).

Educator Attitudes

Research conducted with teachers has shown that educators' attitudes and beliefs about families play a critical role in collaborating with families of children with disabilities. Researchers have attributed unsuccessful teacher-family collaboration experiences to educators who perceive families as indifferent about working with their child's educators (Luckner & Hanks, 2003), have an incongruence between their beliefs as an educator and their family-centered actions (Bezdek, Summers, & Turnbull, 2010; Hilton & Henderson, 1993), highlight too much or too little family involvement as a barrier for collaboration (Bezdek et al., 2010; Campbell & Halbert, 2002), and blame families for lack of collaboration (Bezdek et al., 2010).

Partnerships with families are essential in meeting the needs of children both in and out of school. When families feel included in their child's education, their children have better educational outcomes (Flouri, 2006; Henderson, 1987; Howard & Reynolds, 2008; Sui-Chu & Willms, 1996). These factors highlight the imperative role that teacher educators can play in preparing future teachers for being effective in collaborating with families.

THEORETICAL UNDERPINNINGS

Given the breadth of research highlighting the importance of preparing PSTCs for collaboration with families, we propose mentorship that has theoretical ties to Vygotsky (1978) and Lave and Wenger (1991). Vygotsky (1978) asserts that learning occurs in a social and cultural context, is often co-constructed, and can be mediated in the Zone of Proximal Development (ZPD). The ZPD is defined as, "the distance between the actual developmental level as determined by independent problem solving and the level of potential development as determined through problem solving under adult guidance or in collaboration with more capable peers" (Vygotsky, 1978, p. 86). Furthermore, the ZPD allows for more experienced persons to mentor novices at acquiring new knowledge and skills. The "more knowledgeable other" can mentor the novice through modeling and questioning. Successful mentorship in the field of education is often accomplished by the mentor scaffolding information, questioning the mentee with a specific goal in mind, and providing the mentee with direct, constructive feedback (Peno & Silva Mangiante, 2012). Scaffolding each learning experience supports mentees in acquiring skills and becoming more independent in their practice. Thus, Vygotsky's (1978) social development theory is vital for teacher educators to understand and apply in supporting PSTCs to acquire skills for collaborating with families of children with disabilities.

One challenge that all educators encounter is getting their students to transfer information to other contexts (Kirshner & Whitson, 1997). In this vein, teacher educators worry that PSTCs will not be able to generalize the collaboration skills they are taught in the university classroom to their future role as an educator in working with families.

Korthagen (2010) states that teacher preparation programs should rethink the divide between theory and practice. Moreover, Korthagen asserts that preparing future teachers does not occur by teacher educators "transmitting" information to them, rather, situated learning theory emphasizes learning through sociocultural experiences and actions (2010, p. 99). Lave and Wenger (1991) suggest that abstract knowledge is "meaningless unless [it] can be made specific to the situation at hand" (p. 33). This notion reinforces that PSTCs must be given opportunities that are contextually most like those they will encounter while teaching in order for the experience to be meaningful. "From an anthropological perspective, as proposed by Lave, we should view student teacher learning as being part of the process of participation in social practice, especially the social practice in the schools" (Korthagen, 2010, p. 99).

Korthagen (2010) provides a framework, using situated learning theory, for teacher educators to move toward creating practical learning opportunities for PSTCs that build background knowledge through their active learning, while asking PSTCs to reflect on their authentic learning experiences. This is in direct contrast to teacher preparation programs that often use lecture-based instruction to teach PSTCs about learning theories in the hope that they apply these in their future classrooms, concepts often too abstract and disconnected to daily teaching experience (Korthagen, 2010).

Using a sociocultural learning theoretical perspective, we describe five pedagogical approaches that teacher educators can utilize to provide better mentorship to PSTCs in collaborating with families of children with disabilities. We use the notion described by Lieberman and Friedrich (2010) that:

> [Sociocultural theories] focus on how interactions with others, both those who are peers and those with more experience and technical knowledge, deepen individuals' knowledge, and facilitate collective problem solving. They also show how individuals actually create new knowledge and shape the work of a community of practice. (p. 75)

The approaches include: (a) case-based pedagogy regarding enacting family partnerships; (b) inviting families of children with disabilities into the university classroom; (c) simulations with real families; (d) mock interviews regarding family–school philosophies by special education administrators; and (e) using mentorship to support new teachers in collaborating with families. Table 10.1 provides an overview of how mentors can promote situated learning opportunities for PSTCs in each of the pedagogical approaches.

MENTORING APPROACHES

Case Based Pedagogy

Mentorship around how teacher candidates can support families of children with disabilities should begin early on in a special education teacher preparation program (Patte, 2011). One effective way teacher educators can

TABLE 10.1 Situated Learning Experiences in Teacher Educator Mentorship

Experience	Mentor Actions
Case Studies	• Create real-world cases involving families of children with disabilities. • Facilitate groups of teacher candidates working collaboratively on case study. • Ask teacher candidates questions to probe for deeper connections to case studies.
Parent as Faculty	• Invite parents of children with disabilities to speak in class. • Ask teacher candidates to develop questions to ask parents. • Ask teacher candidates to write a reflection paper on parent experiences.
Interviewing parent(s) of child with a disability	• Require teacher candidates to develop questions for the parent(s) prior to interview, but emphasize fluidity in interview, including asking "in the moment" questions of the parent. • Ask teacher candidates to reflect on the interview, draw explicit connections to literature and personal experiences for supporting families as future special educators.
Parent Simulations	• Provide an authentic context for meeting the parent, promoting flexible thinking. • Video parent-teacher candidate interaction. • Ask parent to share teacher candidate positives and areas to improve. • Ask teacher candidates to watch video, write a reflection paper on the interaction, including the feedback that the parent gave them. • Give one-on-one feedback to the teacher candidate while viewing videoed interaction together. • Facilitate in-class discussion about the simulation experiences of the group.
Mock Interviews	• Invite special education administrators to interview teacher candidates. • Include questions central to philosophy of family collaboration. • Ask administrators to provide feedback about the performance, attitude and dispositions of the teacher candidates they interview. • Ask teacher candidates to reflect on the experience in class in small and large groups, and individually with a written reflection.
Post-Graduation Experiences	• Invite alumni to share experiences with teacher candidates; ask each teacher candidate to formulate questions of the alumni who is currently teaching; facilitate discussion with group centered on family experiences. • Invite teachers to professional association meetings and workshops. • Stay connected with alumni offering formal and informal mentoring opportunities. • Invite alumni to co-present at association meetings.

mentor PSTCs is through use of case-based pedagogy in course assignments. Case-based pedagogy refers to the use of short scenarios that are situated in a context that most reflects the learner's future professional setting (Sudzina, 1997). Within the special education field, case-based pedagogy that focuses on how teachers can collaborate with families of children with disabilities, is useful in teaching PSTCs because of the complexities involved in navigating federal regulations, advocating for the rights of families, and working on a collaborative team (Lengyel & Vernon-Dotson, 2010).

As noted earlier, families of children with disabilities often feel left out, ignored, and misunderstood by special education teachers (i.e., Valle, 2011). To help remedy this issue, teacher educators utilizing case-based pedagogy can create probing questions that prompt the small groups of PSTCs to empathize with the challenges families of children with disabilities face. The example below is a case study that aims to prepare teacher candidates to be empathetic to the needs of families they will serve.

> Felicia and John Ramirez are worried about their son, Steve, a fifth grade student who has a non-verbal learning disability that impacts his ability to read social cues, understand abstract language, and make friends. Mrs. Ramirez reports to you that Steve is being "picked-on" during his bus ride home. The Ramirez family is upset and has scheduled a meeting with you (the special education teacher) to discuss their frustrations. In your small group, discuss how you would respond to the Ramirez family. What specific supports would you employ? How would you want the families to feel at this meeting? What will you need to do to convey this tone or feeling at the meeting? What do you think it feels like for Mr. and Mrs. Ramirez about this situation?

Creating a situation that requires small groups of PSTCs to discuss the case-based scenario requires the social and cultural aspect of situated learning. PSTCs are encouraged to construct their responses by interacting with peers and any personal background knowledge from their own lives, connecting disciplinary knowledge while using higher-level thinking skills to apply, analyze, evaluate, and create possible solutions to complex problems (Lengyel & Vernon-Dotson, 2010; Sudzina, 1997). As the small groups of PSTCs discuss the situation, the teacher educator is able to walk around the room, listen to each of the groups' interactions, ask pertinent questions, and steer discussions to generate solutions. This approach allows for the more knowledgeable person (instructor and/or peers) to support learning in the ZPD (Vygotsky, 1978). While the teacher educator can certainly help facilitate the discussion among the groups, using this type of pedagogy should not require PSTCs to have one "correct" solution, as case-based scenarios should encourage multiple perspectives (Sudzina, 1997).

The goal in using case-based pedagogy in teacher education is to promote PSTCs' development and practice using problem-solving skills around collaborating with families of children with disabilities. It is through this problem-solving process that PSTCs can negotiate the situations with peers, sharing how they might approach the situations in practice. In the example mentioned above, the hope would be for the PSTCs to generalize the techniques described in their small peer group when confronted with a similar situation as an in-service special education teacher. Mentoring students through these scenarios allows PSTCs to become more familiar and comfortable with various issues that teachers come upon when collaborating with families and; therefore, better prepare them for their careers as special educators.

Families as the More Knowledgeable Other

Guest Speakers

Research shows that including the perspectives of families of children with disabilities in course work to share their experiences collaborating with educators has positively impacted teacher candidates' knowledge and understanding of family involvement (Curran & Murray, 2008; Kim & Vail, 2011). Guest speakers provide an enriching experience that helps facilitate a more meaningful and authentic perspective of what it is like to care for a child with a disability (Handyside, Murray, & Mereoiu, 2012). This unique and candid viewpoint offers wisdom that is hard to replicate through any other resource, thus providing an opportunity to foster growth, understanding, and positive interactions between families and future special education teachers. To maximize the effectiveness of each guest speaker, the teacher educator should align each discourse to curriculum goals. Additionally, he or she should prepare PSTCs beforehand by building relevant background, facilitating meaningful discussions, and providing an opportunity for the PSTCs to reflect and write down questions prior to the guest speaker's arrival (Handyside et al., 2012).

Inviting families to be guest speakers in the college classroom allows for PSTCs to hear the unfiltered experiences of real families who have considerable knowledge. This can provide novice teachers with an opportunity to hear from those who are more knowledgeable from lived experiences (Vygotsky, 1978). As Valle (2011) suggests,

> If we ask mothers to tell their stories, we learn about the consequences of our practices within their lives. They have much to teach us about the impact of disability on their identities as mothers and about the profound experience of parents of a child with a learning disability... it is within those archetypal narratives of "the reluctant hero" that we find points of resistance that tell us what is not working within our system of practice. (p. 188)

Course Participants

Murray, Handyside, Straka and Arton-Titus (2013) included parents in a 16-week special education course with university PSTCs. The parents participated in group work, course discussions, and daily activities. In addition, the authors required the university PSTCs to partner with one parent, spending 20 cumulative hours at their home, community, or school settings to learn directly from a family of a child with a disability. PSTCs wrote weekly reflections, a formal paper, and created a presentation that was shared with peers, the family, and the wider community. Murray et al. (2013) determined that the experience impacted the parents in a positive manner, viewing the PSTCs as more communicative, empathetic, and trusting toward collaborating with their family over the course of the semester. Similarly, parents reported that they felt the PSTCs' "perceptions of [them] had been altered as a result of [the] field experiences and personalization of the parent-professional partnership" (p. 164).

Including family members of children with disabilities in teacher preparation courses is a novel and exciting way to provide PSTCs with a situated learning experience—both by learning from families in the university classroom and in their required fieldwork in their homes and communities. Though the researchers acknowledged that they were able to compensate the parents for their willingness to take part in the project and this could pose as a limitation for others who wish to implement a similar idea, the impact that this experience had on both families and PSTCs is noteworthy (Murray et al., 2013).

One-on-One Interviews

To complement family members coming into the university classroom, PSTCs can interview a family member of a child with a disability. This pedagogical approach requires PSTCs to develop a set of culturally responsive questions prior to interviewing a family member individually (Kroeger & Lash, 2011). Providing guidance through modeling the interview process with the PSTCs is important. For instance, teacher educators can model effective interviewing strategies to PSTCs in helping them develop questions that are sensitive, open-ended, and convey verbal and non-verbal cues that are welcoming to the family member—all important skills for collaborating with families (Friend & Cook, 2010). Modeling is an important part of supporting learning in the ZPD and provides "a powerful means of assisting performance, one that continues its effectiveness into adult years and into the highest reaches of behavioral complexity" (Gallimore & Tharp, 1990, p. 179).

Teacher educators can situate the interview experience so PSTCs have a goal of seeking information about how family members: (a) reacted to the disability diagnosis; (b) related any cultural and/or religious impact of the diagnosis; (c) were changed by the diagnosis; (d) describe siblings' reactions; (e) describe their biggest challenges along the way (both in school and at home); (f) describe how educators best supported their child; and (g) describe the supports a teacher could provide to the family. These domains give PSTCs meaningful information when reflecting on the interview experience. Understanding a first-hand personal perspective from a family member allows teacher candidates to make connections, understand at a deeper level, and share commonalities with their peers, allowing for rapid and meaningful growth (Handyside et al., 2012).

Asking families to share their experiences affords PSTCs access to an invaluable resource and rich learning experience (Curran & Murray, 2008; Handyside et al., 2012; Kim & Vail, 2011; Kroeger & Lash, 2011; Murray et al., 2013). Perhaps the most impactful result of instructors' practice of including guest speakers who are family members of children with disabilities is that they are themselves modeling the collaboration that will be essential to their students' success as special educators (Handyside et al., 2012). Ultimately, instructors should provide guidance along with mentorship, for this interaction between guest speaker and PSTC offers true potential for professional growth (Handyside et al., 2012). Hearing from many authentic sources helps special education teacher candidates understand different perspectives and emotions, while encouraging a sense of empathy with each of the parents.

Simulations

Medical education programs across the country use simulations to allow physicians in training to interact with a healthy person, known as a standardized patient, who is portraying a person with a medical ailment (Association of American Medical Colleges, 1998; Barrows, 1987). Dotger (2009) and Dotger and Ashby (2010) have used a similar concept within the educational context to allow for teacher candidates to practice essential collaboration and problem solving skills. Standardized simulations provide an authentic experience in learning how to collaborate, problem solve, and apply critical thinking skills (Dotger, 2015; Epstein, 2005; Ferrara & Ferrara, 2005; MacLure & Walker, 2000). "The term 'standardized' references the training of multiple actors to embody a specific individual" (Dotger, 2015, p. 216). In the case of developing skills to collaborate with families, this individual can be known as a standardized parent, guardian, or caregiver. We use the term parent in the following section to describe how simulation pedagogy can be utilized by teacher educators.

Similar to the standardized parent model, asking actual parents of children with disabilities (versus standardized parents, who are typically actors) to interact with PSTCs has been a worthwhile way to mentor teacher candidates (Dotger, 2015). Asking a parent of a child with a disability to take part in a simulation offers PSTCs a chance to interact with a genuine parent in a professional situation.

Developing an authentic situation that PSTCs will likely face on a regular basis as a special education teacher is important. For instance, meeting a parent of a new child in their classroom for the first time, discussing a child's IEP, or presenting standardized testing information to a parent are all examples of common interactions special educators have with families that can be used in a parent simulation. PSTCs should be flexible in their thinking, as they do not know the exact questions that parents may pose in various interactions. This situated experience aims to promote the PSTC to use intuitive and flexible thinking in the moment, a process they will encounter regularly in their profession as they become more skilled in collaborating with families (Friend & Cook, 2010).

Families offer a unique perspective for PSTCs. While the interaction itself provides them with an opportunity to meet with a family member before getting their first teaching job, allowing the parent to share their perspective on how the teacher candidate demonstrated family-centered practices in the interaction is key. Immediately following the interaction, parents can provide feedback, stimulating authentic dialogue between a future educator and a parent. Parents provide the PSTC with positive aspects of the interaction and areas to improve upon. For instance, parents can share how the PSTC made them feel; some PSTCs may validate their concerns while others may be dismissive. This opportunity allows future teachers to be mentored by a parent in an individualized, validating manner that can meet their individual needs.

In addition to setting up an authentic situation for creating a family-teacher simulation, it is equally important to video the interaction. Video modeling provides valuable opportunities for reflection (Kotsopoulos, 2008; Tripp & Rich, 2012). By videoing the simulation, PSTCs are able to watch and reflect upon how the interaction transpired, their verbal and nonverbal communication styles, and the response from the family member.

This situated learning experience can also be designed to encourage the PSTC to navigate conflict. Experiencing conflict in a safe environment has helped professionals learn how to internalize cooperation skills and make changes as a professional (Deutsch, Coleman, & Marcus, 2006). In fact, in an environment where disagreement occurs, it is "the novice's incorrect usage that provides a crucial opportunity for the novice to reconfigure his or her understanding; alternatively, the culture may acquire new meanings and methods from the individual's variations" (Kirshner & Whitson, 1997, p. 5). Deutsch, Coleman, and Marcus (2006) suggest that successful professionals can manage conflict through building rapport, engaging in conflict resolution, and creating positive group processes. Simulations can provide an opportunity for PSTCs to experience conflict and practice how they would respond in a similar situation as a special educator (Dotger, 2015).

After the PSTCs reflect on the parent meeting, teacher educators provide feedback about their use of family-centered practices. The teacher educator can scaffold the PSTC to employ more adept skills to support families. Teacher educators can do this by asking PSTCs to think about the aspects of the simulation that went well, what could have been done differently, and how the parent was impacted by the simulation (Peno & Silva Mangiante, 2012). This is an important aspect of mentoring, as it allows for future educators to be validated for using approaches that are effective in supporting families.

Link to Employment

Demonstrating family-centered dispositional knowledge is important for special education teachers when seeking employment (LePage, Nielsen, & Fearn, 2008). Additionally, participating in a job interview is a skill that many young professionals find stressful (Jackson, Hall, Rowe, & Daniels, 2009). Since interviewing involves flexible, on the spot thinking that has high-stake consequences, teacher educators can provide a situated learning experience that supports PSTCs in practicing for a job interview. To ensure that PSTCs are able to convey their philosophy effectively during the interview process about collaborating with families, teacher educators can mentor teacher candidates in developing resumes and cover letters that highlight their approach to family engagement, model responses to interview questions related to how they will work with families in the role as a special educator, and share common strategies to develop a coherent portfolio useful for displaying tangible evidence of their skills and abilities in regard to family collaboration. Additionally, mock interviewing with special education administrators can provide PSTCs with an authentic experience that closely mirrors a real interview experience (Rohn & Lee, 2001).

To provide this level of mentorship, teams of administrators can interview each PSTC, then provide immediate feedback on how they answer questions (Rohn & Lee, 2001). Each administrator asks the PSTCs questions about family partnerships: how would they involve families of their future students; what is their philosophy toward working with families; and how would they utilize families to support learning in their classrooms? This authentic opportunity allows for teacher candidates to: (a) be mentored by administrators in a low-stakes environment prior to their first real interview; (b) receive feedback on their interview performance; and (c) reflect on the direct feedback given by the administrators.

Continuing Mentorship

On-going and continuous mentorship is essential for professional growth after PSTCs graduate from teacher preparation programs (Israel et al., 2014; Mastropieri, 2001; Peno & Silva Mangiante, 2012; Whitaker, 2003;

White & Mason, 2006). Although first year teacher induction programs can provide beginning teachers with support in their states and districts, they often need additional emotional and professional support (Billingsley, Carlson, & Klein, 2004; Whitaker, 2003). Teacher educators can play an integral role in this type of informal mentoring (White & Mason, 2006). Staying in contact with graduates through social media, informal networking sessions, and professional organization meetings, allows for the mentorship process to continue.

One way to ensure new special educators are supported is by creating purposeful opportunities for beginning teachers to share their experiences as a new teacher with current college students enrolled in teacher preparation programs (Whitaker, 2003). This method of peer-to-peer mentoring allows current teacher candidates to hear how new teachers partner with families of children with disabilities, build positive rapport with families, and face challenges along the way. The benefit of this type of mentorship is two-fold. New teachers benefit from being able to reflect on their experiences of teaching and working with families, an important part of scaffolding in the mentorship process. Similarly the PSTCs benefit from hearing first-hand experiences of new professionals working with families. Teacher educators can create a situated learning experience where PSTCs are learning alongside more knowledgeable novice in-service special educators.

Furthermore, teacher educators can encourage new teachers to join professional organizations at local, state, and national levels to further support their skill development in collaborating with families. Professional associations offer a wealth of information to new special education teachers, often publishing practitioner journals designed to help teachers in practice (Benedict, Brownell, Park, Bettini, & Lauterbach, 2014; Mastropieri, 2001). However, many young teachers lack mentors in higher education to help guide them in the process of joining and becoming an active member in an organization after they graduate. Teacher educators can encourage new teachers to join associations, attend workshops and trainings, and become an active member.

FINAL THOUGHTS

Mentoring special education PSTCs to work with families, using family-centered practices, priorHto their first teaching job poses real challenges for many teacher educators (Patte, 2011). The confines of a traditional college classroom do not naturally provide opportunities for future educators to interact with families of children with disabilities. However, being thoughtful about how to create authentic experiences with families in teacher preparation programs can help support teacher candidates. Using situated learning theory to design pedagogy in teacher education, teacher educators can simulate the experiences and challenges faced by in-service teachers (Korthagen, 2010; Lave & Wenger, 1991). When teacher educators understand the role that Vygotsky's ZPD plays in how PSTCs learn and develop skills, they can support PSTCs with authentic opportunities that help them reflect on their skills and practices. Teacher educators can scaffold learning opportunities that move the PSTC toward independently interacting with a family member. For example, by first introducing students to case based pedagogy followed by providing opportunities to learn from parent speakers during course meetings, teacher educators can tailor the support a particular PSTC needs by asking specific questions of the student, providing additional readings, and allowing for reflective practice before taking part in a parent simulation. Thus teacher educators can mentor PSTCs by scaffolding the types of family-centered learning opportunities that promote future teachers to be more successful in their professional careers.

While it is unlikely that teacher educators can provide PSTCs with the exact situations they will face in their first years of teaching (Ingersoll, 2012), they have the ability to create opportunities for PSTCs to practice collaborating with families through situated learning experiences. By inviting families into university settings and providing opportunities for educators to "hear directly from families their stories about how various actions or inactions have impacted their family and about how well intentioned actions or comments did or did not have their intended effect," teacher educators help bridge the theory to practice gap that new teachers experience (Blue-Banning, Summers, Frankland, Nelson, & Beegle, 2004, p. 181).

REFERENCES

Association of American Medical Colleges. (1998). Emerging trends in the use of standardized patients. *Contemporary Issues in Medical Education, 1,* 1–2.

Barrows, H. S. (1987). *Simulated (standardized) patients and other human simulations: A comprehensive guide to their training and use in teaching and evaluation.* Chapel Hill, NC: Health Consortium.

Benedict, A. E., Brownell, M. T., Park, Y., Bettini, E. A., & Lauterbach, A. A. (2014). Taking charge of your professional learning: Tips for cultivating special educator expertise. *Teaching Exceptional Children, 46*(6), 147–157.

Bezdek, J., Summers, J. A., & Turnbull, A. (2010). Professionals' attitudes on partnering with families of children and youth with disabilities. *Education and Training in Autism and Developmental Disabilities, 45*(3), 356–365.

Billingsley, B. S. (2010). Work contexts matter: Practical considerations for improving new special educators' experiences in school. *Journal of Special Education Leadership, 23,* 41–49.

Billingsley, B. S., Carlson, E., & Klein, S. (2004). The working conditions and induction support of early career special educators. *Exceptional Children, 70*(3), 333–347.

Blue-Banning, M., Summers, J. A., Frankland, H. C., Nelson, L. L., & Beegle, G. (2004). Dimensions of family and professional partnerships: Constructive guidelines for collaboration. *Exceptional Children, 70*(2), 167–184.

Campbell, P. H., & Halbert, J. (2002). Between research and practice: Provider perspectives on early intervention. *Topics in Early Childhood Special Education, 22,* 213–226.

Curran, E., & Murray, M. (2008). Transformative learning in teacher education: Building competencies and changing dispositions. *Journal of Scholarship of Teaching and Learning, 8,* 103–118.

Darch, C., Miao, Y., & Shippen, P. (2004). A model for involving parents of children with learning and behavioral problems in the schools. *Preventing School Failure, 48*(3), 24–24.

Deutsch, M., Coleman, P. T., & Marcus, E. C. (Eds.). (2006). *Handbook of conflict resolution: Theory and practice* (2nd ed.). San Francisco, CA: Jossey-Bass.

Dotger, B. (2009). From a medicinal to education context: Implementing a signature pedagogy for enhanced parent-teacher communication. *Journal of Education for Teaching, 35,* 93–94.

Dotger, B., & Ashby, C. (2010). Exposing conditional inclusive ideologies through simulated interactions. *Teacher Education and Special Education, 33*(2), 114–130.

Dotger, B. H. (2015). Core pedagogy: Individual uncertainty, shared practice, formative ethos. *Journal of Teacher Education, 66*(3), 215–226.

Epstein, J. L. (2005). Links in a professional develop chain: Preservice and inservice education for effective programs of school, family, and community partnerships. *New Educator, 1,* 125–141.

Ferrara, M. M., & Ferrara, P. J. (2005). Parents as partners: Raising awareness as a teacher preparation program. *The Clearing House, 99,* 78–82.

Fish, W. W. (2008). The IEP meeting: Perspectives of students who receive special education services. *Preventing School Failure, 53*(1), 8–14.

Flouri, E. (2006). Parental interest in children's education, children's self-esteem, locus of control and later educational attainment: Twenty-six year follow-up of the 1970 British birth cohort. *British Journal of Educational Psychology, 76,* 41–55.

Friend, M., & Cook, L. (2010). *Interactions: Collaboration skills for school professionals.* Boston, MA: Allyn & Bacon.

Gallimore, R., & Tharp, R. (1990). Teaching mind in society: Teaching, schooling, and literate discourse. In L. C. Moll (Ed.), *Vygotsky and education: Instructional implications and applications of sociohistorical psychology.* Cambridge, England: Cambridge University Press.

Griffin, C. C. (2010). A summary of research of education leaders on the induction of beginning special educators. *Journal of Special Education Leadership, 23,* 14–20.

Goldstein, S. (1993). The IEP conference: Little things mean a lot. *Teaching Exceptional Children, 26*(1), 60–61.

Handyside, L., Murray, M., & Mereoiu, M., (2012). Learning together: Teachers and families as learning communities. *Journal of Emerging Trends in Educational Research and Policy Studies, 3*(4), 438–443.

Henderson, A. (Ed.). (1987). *The evidence continues to grow: Parent involvement improves student achievement.* Columbia, MD: National Committee for Citizens in Education.

Hilton A., & Henderson, C. J. (1993). Parent involvement: A best practice or forgotten practice? *Education and Training in Mental Retardation, 28,* 199–211.

Howard, T. C., & Reynolds, R. (2008). Examining parent involvement in reversing the underachieving of African American students in middle-class school. *Educational Foundations, 22*(1/2), 79–98.

Ingersoll, R. M., & Strong, M. (2011). The impact of induction and mentoring programs for beginning teachers: A critical review of research. *Review of Educational Research, 81,* 201–233.

Ingersoll, R. M. (2012). Beginning teacher induction: What the data tells us. *Phi Delta Kappan, 93*(8), 47–51.

Israel, M., Kamman, M. L., McCray, E. D., & Sindelar, P. T. (2014). Mentoring in action: The interplay among professional assistance, emotional support, and evaluation. *Exceptional Children, 81*(1), 45–63.

Jackson, S. E., Hall, N. C., Rowe, P. M., & Daniels, L. M. (2009). Getting the job: Attributional retraining and the employment interview. *Journal of Applied Social Psychology, 39*(4), 973–998.

Kim, E-J., & Vail, C. (2011). Improving preservice teachers' perspectives on family involvement in teaching children with special needs: Guest speaker versus video. *Teacher Education and Special Education, 34*(4), 320–338.

Kirshner, D., & Whitson, J. A. (1997). *Situated cognition: Social, semiotic, and psychology perspectives.* New Jersey: Lawrence Erlbaum Associates, Inc.

Korthagen, F. A. J. (2010). Situated learning theory and the pedagogy of teacher education: Towards an integrative view of teacher behavior and teacher learning. *Teaching and Teacher Education, 26,* 98–106.

Kotsopoulos, D. (2008). Beyond teachers' sight lines: Using video modeling to examine peer discourse. *Mathematics Teacher, 101*(6), 468–472.

Kroeger, J., & Lash, M. (2011). Asking, listening and learning: Toward a more thorough method of inquiry in home-school relations. *Teacher and Teacher Education, 27,* 268–277.

Lave, J., & Wenger, E. (1991). *Situated learning: Legitimate peripheral participation.* New York, NY: Cambridge University Press.

Lengyel, L., & Vernon-Dotson, L. J. (2010). Case-based pedagogy in teacher preparation programs: Examples from practice. *Teacher Education and Special Education, 33*(3), 248–256.

LePage, P., Nielsen, S., & Fearn, E. J. (2008). Charting the dispositional knowledge of beginning teachers in special education. *Teacher Education and Special Education, 31*(2), 77–92.

Lieberman, A., & Friedrich, L. D. (2010). *How teachers become leaders: Learning from practice and research.* New York, NY: Teachers College Press.

Luckner, J. L., & Hanks, J. A. (2003). Job satisfaction: Perceptions of a national sample of teachers of students who are deaf or hard of hearing. *American Annals of the Deaf, 148*(1), 5–17.

MacLure, M., & Walker, B. (2000). Disenchanted evenings: The social organization of talk in parent-consultations in UK secondary schools. *British Journal of Sociology of Education, 21*(1), 5–24.

Mastropieri, M. A. (2001). Is the glass half full or half empty? Challenges encountered by first-year special education teachers. *The Journal of Special Education, 35*(2), 66–74.

Murray, M. M., Handyside, L. M., Straka, L. S., & Arton-Titus, T. V. (2013). Parent empowerment: Connecting with preservice special education teachers, *School Community Journal, 23*(1), 145–168.

National Council on Disability. (1995). *Improving implementation of the Individuals with Disabilities Education Act: Making schools work for all America's children.* Washington, DC: Author.

Patte, M. M. (2011). Examining preservice teacher knowledge and competencies in establishing family–school partnerships. *The School Community Journal, 21*(2), 143–159.

Peno, K., & Silva Mangiante, E. (2012). The journey from novice to expert: Toward a purposeful on-going mentoring model. In C. J. Boden-McGill & K.P. Kings (Eds.), *Conversations about adult learning in a complex world* (pp. 211–221). Charlotte, NC: Information Age Publishing.

Rohn, C. A., & Lee, D. (2001). A collaborative effort to provide authentic experience in interviewing for pre-service teachers and administrative interns. *Education, 121*(3), 549–553.

Ronfeldt, M., & Reininger, M. (2012). More or better student teaching? *Teaching and Teacher Education, 28*, 1091–1106.

Sudzina, M. R. (1997). Case study as a constructivist pedagogy for teaching educational psychology. *Educational Psychology Review, 9*(2), 199–218.

Sui-Chu, E. H., & Willms, J. D. (1996). Effects of parental involvement on eighth-grade achievement. *Sociology of Education, 69*, 126–141.

Tripp, T., & Rich, P. (2012). Using video to analyze one's own teaching. *British Journal of Educational Technology, 43*(4), 678–704.

Valle, J. W. (2011). Down the rabbit hole: A commentary about research on parents and special education. *Learning Disability Quarterly, 34*(3), 183–190.

Valle, J. W., & Aponte, E. (2002). IDEA and collaboration: A Bakhtinian perspective on parent and professional discourse. *Journal of Learning Disabilities, 35*, 469–479.

Vaughn, S., Bos, C. A., Harrell, J. E., & Lasky, B. A. (1988). Parent participation in the initial placement IEP conference ten years after mandated involvement. *Journal of Learning Disabilities, 21*, 82–87.

Vygotsky, L. S. (1978). *Mind in society: The development of higher psychological processes.* Cambridge, MA: Harvard University Press.

Walker, J. M. T., & Dotger, B. H. (2015). Because wisdom can't be told: Using comparison of simulated parent-teacher conferences to assess teacher candidates' readiness for family–school partnership. *Journal of Teacher Education, 63*(1), 62–75.

Whitaker, S. D. (2003). Needs of beginning special education teachers: Implications for teacher education. *Teacher Education and Special Education, 26*(2), 106–117.

White, M., & Mason, C. Y. (2006). Components of successful mentoring programs for beginning special education teachers: Perspectives from new teachers and mentors. *Teacher Education and Special Education,* 29(3), 191–201.

Yull, D., Blitz, L. V., Thompson, T., & Murray, C. (2014). Can we talk? Using community-based participatory action research to build family and school partnerships with families of color. *School Community Journal, 24*(2), 9–31.

Zirkel, P. A. (2013). Is it time for elevating the standard for FAPE under IDEA? *Exceptional Children, 79*(4), 497–508.

CHAPTER 11

CLINICAL EDUCATORS' IMPLEMENTATION OF A MENTORING MODEL

Coaching Elementary Pre-Service Teachers for Reform-Based Science

Elaine M. Silva Mangiante
Salve Regina University

Kathy Peno
University of Rhode Island

Access to mentoring in teacher education programs is essential for the development of pre-service teachers' pedagogical decision-making and professional readiness (Abed & Abd-El-Khalick, 2015). Quality mentoring is needed, particularly in the area of science education given that teachers at the elementary level generally have limited science content knowledge and low self-efficacy in teaching science (Harlen, 1997; Kennedy, 1998; Luera, Moyer, & Everett, 2005). A natural reaction for some beginning elementary

Mentoring in Formal and Informal Contexts, pages 197–223
Copyright © 2016 by Information Age Publishing

teachers is to avoid science teaching, provide 'correct answers,' or adopt fun activities without a focus on meaningful science learning (Appleton, 2003; Haefner & Zembal-Saul, 2004; Zembal-Saul, 2009). These tendencies can pose obstacles for pre-service teachers' adoption of National Research Council (NRC) reforms in science education involving more student constructivist learning (NRC, 2007).

The intent for science education reform envisioned by the developers of Next Generation Science Standards (NGSS) involves students' collaborative engagement in scientific practices and inquiry into scientific questions to construct, evaluate, and communicate evidence-based explanations of core ideas in science (NRC, 2012). For pre-service teachers to develop effective science education pedagogy, they need practicum experiences with mentors who can promote their understanding of science reforms as well as guide their awareness of how students think and what they are able to do (Davis & Smithey, 2009; Hudson, 2003; NRC, 2012).

Given that in-service teachers serve as clinical educators (CE) mentoring pre-service teachers (PST) during their student teaching, the extent of a CE's science subject knowledge and pedagogical content knowledge aligned with current reforms can impact the quality of the science education mentoring that a PST receives (NRC, 2007; Shulman, 1986). Researchers have noted a disparity between the science education approaches learned in university training and the teaching practices enacted in practicum placements, posing an ideological conflict for the PST (Yerrick, Ambrose, & Schiller, 2008; Zembal-Saul, Krajcik, & Blumenfeld, 2002). Studies have indicated that the nature of a CE's science instructional approach (i.e., student-centered and constructivist versus traditional and didactic) can influence the science pedagogical approaches adopted by the PST (Gaffey, Woodward, & Lowe, 1995; Yerrick et al., 2008).

To address this issue, CEs need purposeful professional development (PD) to improve their mentoring capabilities and understanding of science education reforms (Zembal-Saul et al., 2002). The research suggests that content-specific versus generic mentoring opportunities are necessary for elementary PSTs to develop their science teaching practice (Abed & Abd-El-Khalick, 2015; Hudson, 2004, 2005). Thus, for this study, we provided PD for CEs in their use of a science mentoring strategies tool as a guide during their meetings and observations of PSTs' lessons in science. The mentoring topics focused on two areas: the disciplinary core idea for the lesson and scientific practices to promote student thinking. The purpose of the study was to examine the CEs' experiences and feedback when using these mentoring strategies, along with the perspectives of the PST in reaction to these experiences. This research also sought to explore how CEs helped PSTs navigate the current science standards and scientific practices.

LITERATURE REVIEW AND CONCEPTUAL FRAMEWORK

Science Education Standards

The framework underlying NGSS outlined three major dimensions for science education in grades K–12: scientific practices, crosscutting concepts, and disciplinary core ideas (NRC, 2012). The scientific practices intended for students to develop include:

1. Asking questions
2. Developing and using models
3. Planning and carrying out investigations
4. Analyzing and interpreting data
5. Using mathematics and computational thinking
6. Constructing explanations
7. Engaging in argument from evidence
8. Obtaining, evaluating, and communicating information
   (NRC, 2012, p. 49)

Elementary teachers who have adopted an inquiry approach to students' science learning tend to be more familiar with the first five practices based on their efforts to engage students in generating testable scientific questions and developing fair tests to collect and analyze data. However, the last three practices are often underemphasized in the science classroom (Forbes, Biggers, & Zangori, 2013). The implementation of these practices necessitates that teachers have an understanding of scientific discourse strategies as well as ways of scaffolding students' explanation construction (Herrenkohl & Guerra, 1998; Mercer, Dawes, Wegerif, & Sams, 2003; Palinscar, Anderson, & David, 1993). Zembal-Saul (2009) found that PSTs tend to adopt fun, activity-based or investigation-based approaches to science teaching more readily than those that engage students in argumentation to evaluate evidence and claims. However, Zembal-Saul's research also showed that PSTs were able to shift their pedagogical thinking through a guided analysis approach to science teaching. This finding suggests that mentoring could aid PSTs in adopting and promoting reform-based practices in teaching science.

The extent of a teacher's science content knowledge also can impact the degree to which a teacher engages with students in scientific meaning making (Newton & Newton, 2001). The intent of NGSS (NGSS Lead States, 2013) is that students in grades K–12 develop understanding of disciplinary core ideas in four domains: physical; life; earth and space; and engineering, technology, and applications sciences as well as crosscutting concepts that apply across all science domains such as patterns, cause/effect, structure/

function, and stability/change. However, for elementary PSTs who have limited content knowledge, research has shown that they are not as successful in planning for reform-based science lessons (Luera et al., 2005) and they employ few strategies to cope with their lack of science knowledge (e.g., hesitating to use available resources or seeking out additional resources) (Symington & Hayes, 1989). Therefore, given the central role a CE plays in the development of a PST's reform-based science pedagogy, providing CEs with PD in mentoring practices is vital.

Mentoring for Novice to Expert Skill Development

In order to fully understand the power and impact of mentoring for skill development, we examined the work of Vygotsky (1978) and Schön (1983, 1987) who informed us of important components embedded in mentoring practice. Vygotsky's (1978) Zone of Proximal Development (ZPD) provides a frame for thinking about how mentors can best enact the skill development of their mentees. According to Vygotsky (1978), the ZPD is "the distance between the actual development level as determined by independent problem solving and the level of potential development as determined through problem solving under adult guidance or in collaboration with a more capable peer" (p. 86). In teaching practice, mentors scaffold their mentee's learning by modeling and demonstrating effective reform strategies while providing space for mentee rehearsal and offering effective coaching and/or feedback on their performance.

Sometimes referred to as educative mentoring (Feiman-Nemser, 2001), the mentor must balance challenging the mentee while providing the right amount of support for growth and development to occur (Tang, 2003). Through educative mentoring, "Mentors...attend to beginning teachers' present concerns, questions, and purposes without losing sight of long-term goals for teacher development. They interact with novices in ways that foster an inquiring stance" (Feiman-Nemser, 2001, p. 16). Bradbury (2010) extends this work to mentoring in science teaching by elaborating on specific processes that engage mentors and their mentees in collaborative meaning making. To support novices in learning to teach science, Bradbury (2010) suggests that rather than using traditional generic mentoring in which the mentor provides lesson plans, science activities, practical solutions, and advice to the PST, CEs could employ educative mentoring to foster "a disposition of sustained inquiry into teaching practice...and long-term orientation toward reform-based science teaching" (p. 1052). As part of the inquiry process, the mentor could assist the mentee in reflection on what occurred during the mentee's experience. The importance of reflection after action was promoted by Dewey (1910) and, later, Schön (1983, 1987) as a means for learning and professional growth. Working with the more capable person or mentor, a mentee can examine their actions and consider alternatives when necessary (Schön, 1983). Through educative mentoring, CEs not only could provide PSTs with content assistance and perspectives on teaching situations, but also encourage PSTs to engage in situated inquiry by using student work and student thinking to inform their teaching practice (Bradbury, 2010).

When designing mentoring programs to assist adults in advancing their skills, it is essential to consider the developmental stage of the adult in acquiring new competencies (Dreyfus & Dreyfus, 1980, 1988; Vygotsky, 1978). Dreyfus and Dreyfus (1986) identified a five stage model of adult skill acquisition: "novice, advanced beginner, competent, proficient, and expert" (p. 21). Berliner (1994, 2004) applied this model to the field of education to describe characteristics of teachers in different stages of their professional advancement.

Since this study focused on PSTs learning to become teachers, we examined the first two stages of novice and advanced beginner. A *novice* teacher cannot always make sense of situations that arise in the classroom given their limited experience with teaching. As a result, a novice tends to follow instructional procedures learned in pre-service training with inflexibility using an analytical and detached approach to decision-making without regard for the context of the students and their needs (Berliner, 2004; Dreyfus & Dreyfus, 1988). PSTs, as novices, typically may follow a science kit teacher's guide in a step-by step fashion without focus on student understanding. Whereas, with more experience, an *advanced beginner* teacher begins to note patterns in classroom events and among students; thus, formulating guiding maxims to employ when similar situations occur (S. Dreyfus, 2004). However, the advanced beginner still has difficulty handling challenges and continues to use an analytical approach to solve problems.

To operationalize the Dreyfus and Dreyfus adult skill acquisition model (1986) for use in mentoring adult learners for their professional growth, the authors created the Purposeful On-Going Mentoring Model (P.O.M.M.) (Peno & Silva Mangiante, 2012). The P.O.M.M. outlined specific goals and actions that a mentor could implement to assist a mentee in advancing from one stage to another. The purpose of this study was to further identify and refine the strategies that a mentor could use to promote a PST's development from novice to advanced beginner with science standards that present new expectations for teachers.

Purposeful On-going Mentoring Model:
A Science Mentoring Strategies Tool

To design a robust mentoring model to assist PSTs in acquiring knowledge and skill in reform-based science teaching (NGSS Lead States, 2013), the authors designed a conceptual framework based on the P.O.M.M. (Peno & Silva Mangiante, 2012) and Roth et al.'s (2011) work with elementary teachers in science education. Roth and colleagues (2011) developed a PD program to increase teachers' science content knowledge and their pedagogical content knowledge of how to make science content ideas understandable for students (Shulman, 1986). They focused on two areas: "creating a coherent science content storyline" and "eliciting, supporting, and challenging students' thinking about specific science content" (Roth et al., 2011, p. 120). A coherent science content storyline involves sequencing and linking science ideas in a lesson or unit so students can understand the science story. This approach counters the view held by many elementary teachers that inquiry-based science learning involves doing fun, hands-on activities in contrast to emphasis on students' scientific understanding (Zembal-Saul, 2009). The focus on student thinking addressed the need to help teachers plan for the students' role in expressing their ideas and the teacher's attention to student thinking.

Building upon the PD model designed by Roth et al., (2011), the authors created a conceptual framework with a mentoring focus aligned with two of the NGSS dimensions (2013): the disciplinary core idea context and the student thinking practices context. The disciplinary core idea context was adopted to help teachers attend to the core ideas organized in NGSS for students' scientific knowledge development. For this study, the disciplinary core idea context was referred to as the *science learning goal* in the tool provided to CEs. The student thinking practices context was included to address the scientific practices often underemphasized by elementary teachers in inquiry science—constructing explanations; engaging in argument from evidence; and obtaining, evaluating, and communicating information (Forbes et al., 2013). Table 11.1 outlines the key actions a teacher could consider when planning for each context.

Based on this conceptual framework, the authors developed a tool for the CEs to use in mentoring their PSTs in science teaching that included pre-observation and post observation discussion questions for both contexts. The CEs could reference this bank of potential questions and select those that they felt were most appropriate for the development of their novice PST. In addition, the tool provided possible focus areas in both contexts during the CE's observation of a PST's science lesson. A listing of the questions and areas of observation focus for each context at all three points in the mentoring process is provided later in Tables 11.4 and 11.5.

TABLE 11.1   Conceptual Framework for P.O.M.M.—Science Mentoring Strategies Tool

Disciplinary Core Idea Context (referred to as the science learning goal)	Student Thinking/Practices Context
• Identify science learning goal for the lesson based on NGSS disciplinary core idea standards	• Question to ascertain student background knowledge on the main learning goal
• Establish teacher or student generated focus question for the science learning goal	• Elicit student ideas and questions related to the learning goal
• Ensure that the investigation of the focus question is matched to the learning goal	• Ask probing and challenging questions to guide students in planning and carrying out an investigation
• Provide opportunities for students to document evidence that addresses the science learning goal	• Engage students in documenting, analyzing, and interpreting the data collected from an investigation
• Encourage students to link the science learning goal with previous learning	• Engage students in constructing an explanation by communicating with peers to argue the rationale for their interpretation and reasoning about data and observations
• Ensure that students summarize the key ideas	• Engage students in making sense of their learning by representing their thinking graphically and in writing based on evidence they collected and their discourse with peers.

Source: Adapted from STeLLA Conceptual Framework (Roth et al., 2011)

RESEARCH QUESTIONS

1. How do clinical educators help pre-service teachers navigate the current science standards and scientific practices?
2. What are the perspectives of clinical educators and pre-service teachers regarding the use of the science mentoring strategies tool to facilitate pre-service teachers' focus on the science learning goal?
3. What are the perspectives of clinical educators and pre-service teachers regarding the use of the science mentoring strategies tool to facilitate pre-service teachers' focus on promoting student thinking?

Research Design and Methodology

Setting and Participants

This investigation was conducted at a public elementary school in an urban Northeast district that serves a diverse student population. This school

TABLE 11.2   Characteristics of Clinical Educators

Name of CE (Name of PST)	Grade Level	Years Teaching	Number of PSTs	Previous PD in Mentoring	Previous PD in NGSS
Donna (Cathy)	2	19	11	Yes	No, but perused them
Ruth (Jean)	3	24	7	Yes	No
Joan (Ann)	3	14	3	No	No
Aaron (Ellen)	3	17	10	Yes	No, but perused them
Barbara (Corinne)	4	20	2	No	No
Sharon (Eileen)	4	22	30	Yes	One workshop
Carrie (Sue)	4	34	28	Yes	No, but perused them

Note: All names are pseudonyms.

provides student teaching clinical placements for PSTs majoring in elementary education from a local university. During the 2015 spring semester, seven elementary education PSTs were assigned to CEs at the school. All seven CEs and their PSTs consented to participate in the study. The purposeful selection of all the CE-PST pairs in one school allowed us to provide PD to the CEs as a group ensuring that they received the same training while also providing all PSTs in the school with a common science mentoring experience (Patton, 2002). The CEs were veteran teachers with teaching experience ranging from 14 to 34 years. While some CEs had years of experience supervising PSTs, others had only worked with one or two PSTs. See Table 11.2 for information about each CE. Regarding PD in mentoring, Sharon and Carrie had received extensive two-year training in general mentoring. Donna, Ruth, Carrie, and Aaron had attended a workshop seven years prior sponsored by the university teacher education program to prepare them for serving as CEs. However, no CE had received mentoring PD specific to science education. Sharon, as the lead teacher for science in the school, often provided informal mentoring to the teachers.

Professional Development Session

The first author provided CEs with PD for the P.O.M.M. science mentoring strategies tool. The CEs were introduced to the characteristics of novice teachers and their tendency to follow instructional procedures inflexibly without awareness of students' learning (Berliner, 2004; Dreyfus & Dreyfus, 1988). The goal for this project was for CEs to assist PSTs to move from novice to advanced beginner for science teaching by helping them (a) examine their pedagogical approaches chosen to achieve the lesson's science learning goal; and (b) consider ways to promote students' adoption of scientific practices to express their thinking (NRC, 2012).

To aid the CEs in visualizing how to use the P.O.M.M. science mentoring strategies tool, they examined two sample second grade lesson plans focused on identifying properties of liquids and their differences from solids. The first sample lesson was not aligned with the standards and did not allow students to explain their thinking or construct their understanding of different states of matter. For this lesson, a mentor could assist a PST in a pre-observation meeting by asking targeted questions such as, "What is the science learning goal for this lesson?" and "Explain how your teaching strategies will support your students' explaining their thinking? In contrast, the second lesson, which was aligned to the standards, provided students with the opportunity to construct explanations from evidence. In this case, a mentor could extend a PST's practice by asking questions such as, "What instructional decisions posed challenges for you?" or by brainstorming ideas for "What strategies can you use to support students who may struggle with expressing their thinking?" From these examples, the CEs viewed how a mentor could select questions or use brainstorming strategies from the P.O.M.M. science mentoring strategies tool during the pre- or post-observation meetings that met the specific needs of a PST. CEs also examined the new NGSS expectations for their respective units in terms of disciplinary core ideas and scientific practices. CEs were asked to use the tool for at least three PST science lessons and were given packets of recording sheets to note their chosen questions/strategies.

Data Collection

Data for this study included transcripts from interviews, the P.O.M.M. science mentoring strategies tool recording sheets from the CEs, and lesson documents.

Interviews

Data were collected from end-of semester interviews with the CEs and PSTs. Since the first author provided training in the use of the P.O.M.M. science mentoring strategies tool, the second author, an expert in adult education, interviewed and audio-recorded each of the CEs for 45 minutes to avoid the possibility that the trainer's presence could bias the CEs' responses (Creswell, 2009). The first author conducted individual 30 minute audio-recorded interviews with PSTs to obtain their perspective on the science mentoring experience.

Recording Sheets

Recording sheets were used for each of the three cycles of pre-observation meeting, observation, and post-observation meeting. To capture the aspects of the P.O.M.M. science mentoring strategies tool preferred by each teacher, each CE used the recording sheets to circle questions used during the pre- and post-observation meetings and observation points as the student teacher taught the science lesson.

Documents

Data also included documents such as the PST's lesson plans, graphic organizers, or student work with identifiers removed (e.g., science notebook entries, diagrams, or worksheets). We collected work samples to ascertain the nature of the thinking that students were expected to express in writing and to triangulate reports from PST interviews of how they sought to identify their students' thinking from their written communication (Denzin, 1978).

Data Analysis

To answer the research questions regarding the participants' perspectives on the mentoring strategies used to promote PST's focus on science learning goals and student thinking practices, the data were analyzed using a constant comparative method to identify emerging patterns (Miles & Huberman, 1994). First, each researcher independently conducted open inductive coding of the CE and PST interview data to generate preliminary coding categories. The results of this analysis were discussed by the researchers seeking consensus on codes. Next, the interview data were reexamined between CE-PST paired transcriptions and across all CE transcriptions as well as all PST transcriptions for confirming and disconfirming evidence. From a repeated and systematic review of the data using the agreed upon codes, the researchers identified key categories and their associated properties.

Next, two additional data sources, (a) a frequency distribution table generated from tallying CE's preferred questions or observation foci for mentoring (Gravetter & Wallnau, 2008); and (b) notes from document examination, were analyzed by researchers to provide triangulation as a means to strengthen the trustworthiness of the study design (Denzin, 1978).

RESULTS AND DISCUSSION

From analysis of the data, the following themes emerged to describe the CEs' and PSTs' perspectives on the use of the P.O.M.M. science mentoring strategies tool (hereinafter referred to as the 'tool') with regard to the science learning goal and promotion of student thinking aligned with NGSS. To report the findings, we used an analytic interpretive approach in conjunction with quotations as evidence of individual CE's or PST's perspectives to illuminate their experience with this mentoring endeavor (Miles & Huberman, 1994; Patton, 2002).

Mentoring for NGSS

The developers of the NGSS envisioned that implementation of the standards would involve states, districts, and schools providing mechanisms for "curriculum, instruction, teacher preparation, and professional development, and student assessment" (NRC, 2012, p. 241). However, they also recognized that the locus of control for educational systems resides among a complex set of stakeholders from the micro-level of the classroom to the macro-level of the state and nation. Ultimately, the decisions made by teachers are influenced by policies and institutional structures existing at higher levels of the system.

In answer to the question of how CEs helped PSTs navigate current science standards and scientific practices, the evidence was clear that NGSS were not included in the mentoring conversations since the CEs had limited knowledge of the expectations. The district had not yet provided PD on NGSS. CE-Sharon, the lead teacher for the school in science, explained that the state used a standardized science assessment based on the previous science standards. The science kits used by all the CEs were aligned to these older standards. Though the CEs had been introduced to the specific NGSS standards for their grade level and the scientific practices during the mentoring PD for this project, they did not address the standards with their PSTs because, as CE-Sharon noted, "it doesn't apply right now." The CEs needed to stay focused with the assessment and curriculum expectations that were still in place at the district and state level.

Given that the PSTs had worked with NGSS during their university science methods course, some PSTs expressed surprise that NGSS standards were not considered when planning for science lessons. PST-Ann, described her planning using the science kit teacher's guide,

> We get these units...None of this is related to NGSS, which I thought that was really weird. Inside it will show you the investigations and what they want you to do. Then the learning goal always came from the summary at the beginning. But it's funny because whenever I write my plans, I always have a content standard, and we're going through this, and I'm looking through the book. Where are the standards that go along with these lessons? It was strange. So I don't know if these lessons are even aligned with what the students need to learn in third grade.

Other PSTs confirmed this tendency that they did not discuss NGSS during their mentoring conversations except for PST-Ellen whose CE encouraged her to locate NGSS standards that coordinated with the topics they were covering in science. However, Ellen discovered that the science topics assigned for her grade did not match with NGSS. Thus, in general, the CEs were not able to assist their PSTs, at this point, in navigating the standards and scientific practices.

Mentoring for Science Learning Goal

Four themes emerged from the data (see Tables 11.3 and 11.4) regarding mentoring for the science learning goal: CEs viewed the tool as an explicit mentoring guide, emphasized content knowledge and the science learning goal, encouraged PSTs to attend to student misconceptions, and prompted PSTs to plan beyond the teacher's guide.

View of Tool as Explicit Mentoring Guide

From interviews with both CEs and PSTs, the data indicated that five of the seven CEs, who used the tool regularly, valued it as a useful guide that specified focus areas, strategies, and questions to mentor their PSTs in science lesson planning and reflection. Joan, as a relatively new CE who had not received previous PD in mentoring, particularly valued the questions and strategies noting,

> It gets the student teacher to really think about the goal and the outcome of learning and having students explain their thinking. I think that's very important.... I never had the student teacher training, so this was very helpful—short and sweet.

Her PST, Ann, indicated that, as a result of the mentoring, she considered alternative ways to have students provide evidence of their learning,

> It really helps me improve my science lessons a lot because I know exactly what students needed to learn and have some kind of concrete evidence that shows me that my students met the goal. I use different approaches to reach all my students.... Those questions were really in depth so it made me think about exactly what I did and maybe how I could have improved it and what I could do the next time to make my lessons better.

The CEs made note of the explicit nature of the tool. CE-Carrie remarked that "it keeps us on our toes. We always need to be observing and giving feedback. I think providing us with more structure and some tools just keeps us more focused." CE-Aaron commented on the specific mentoring language.

> When you ask, 'What's the goal?' that's an easy enough question to answer. But some of the other questions where you had to dig a little bit deeper to see how they were going to have their students show what they learned, I found it very helpful because I never really could put words to what I was looking for and now I've got those words.

In addition to the questioning, the CEs noted that they used the brainstorming and modeling strategies, particularly, in the early stages of the mentoring (see Table 11.3). When describing her CE's mentoring, PST-Cathy confirmed that "in the beginning, it was more suggestions" and "me being able to watch her model"; however, over time, CE-Donna used more questioning to prompt Cathy's own pedagogical decision-making. This approach is consistent with Bradbury's (2010) framework of educative mentoring behaviors, which notes that mentees need to view models of standards-based teaching rather than merely talking about pedagogical options.

The data indicated that all five CEs implemented the tool as a mentoring guide not only with science, but also in other subject areas such as math and literacy. However, two CEs did not use the tool as consistently. For example, CE-Ruth, who made limited use of the tool, felt her PST needed to focus on classroom management since many of her students had learning or behavioral challenges. This finding parallels reports that PSTs felt more successful in teaching science when their mentors provided them with ideas for classroom management (Hudson, 2003). Ruth also noted, however, that the tool helped her "refocus" her thinking and update her "mindset"

TABLE 11.3   Sample Alternative Strategies For Brainstorming or Modeling

Alternative Strategies of Brainstorming/Modeling	
Disciplinary Core Idea Context	Student Thinking/Practices Context
1. Brainstorm with the student teacher for possible alternative instructional approaches for the science learning goal. (i.e., "Perhaps _____ or _____ might work for…"	1. Brainstorm with the student teacher for possible alternative instructional approaches to use with this group of students or individual students. (i.e., "It's sometimes helpful to…" "How might that work with your student(s)?"
2. Model examples of alternative instructional approaches that could achieve the science learning goal of the lesson. (i.e., "There are a number of approaches that might work for you…"	2. Model some alternative approaches to use with different students. (i.e., What do you think might happen if you tried this with your student(s)?")

based on the pedagogy taught in university teacher education courses. As a mentor who practiced non-reform based teaching (Wang & Odell, 2007), she felt the tool promoted the growth of her own practice and helped her look at "the whole picture" with her PST. Another CE, Barbara, noted, "I thought the questions were good, but... there should have been a question about content." Consistent with research indicating that subject matter as well as process needs to be considered for effective teacher mentoring (Wang & Odell, 2002), Barbara chose to encourage her PST first to be knowledgeable with subject content before preparing for a lesson.

Emphasis on Content Knowledge and Science Learning Goal

The PSTs indicated that CEs used the tool to "push" PSTs to acquire adequate content knowledge in order to plan for the science learning goal. Research has shown that elementary teachers require knowledge of science content to implement reform-based pedagogy effectively for student learning (Kennedy, 1998; Luera et al., 2005; Roth et al., 2011). To facilitate scientific discourse among students, teachers need content knowledge to know which "ideas in a subject are interrelated and which ideas are relatively more important than others" (Kennedy, 1998, p. 260). This knowledge is needed for PSTs to assist students in making sense of the science learning goal.

For this study, each CE emphasized in their mentoring that PSTs identify and plan for a science learning goal; however, since they recognized that their PSTs had limited science content knowledge, they advised them first to research the subject matter. For example, CE-Carrie explained, "if you know and are comfortable with the content, that's the biggest part right there because then you can focus on how you're going to implement it." The PSTs reported that their CEs provided them with information from the science kit teacher's guide or suggested reference sources to increase their content knowledge. In addition, CEs would suggest PSTs work with the investigation materials first before presenting the lesson to the children. In PST-Erin's case, her CE-Aaron scaffolded her thinking about teaching a lesson on sound by suggesting she explore and learn about how tuning forks work since she was having difficulty hearing the differences in the sounds. Erin realized, "I can't teach it to someone else if I don't understand it myself."

The evidence from both the interviews and the frequency distribution chart of questions posed for the science learning goal showed that the CEs consistently asked the following questions to ensure that PSTs planned for a science learning goal (see Table 11.4):

- What is the science learning goal for this lesson?
- What strategies will you use to achieve your science learning goal?
- How will you know if your students have achieved the science learning goal?

TABLE 11.4   CEs' Recordings of Questions Asked for the Science Learning Goal at Each Mentoring Point

Mentoring Point	Questions asked at each mentoring point	
	Ratio[a]	Percentage
Pre-Observation Questions—Science Learning Goal Context		
1. What is the science learning goal for this lesson?	(11/37)	29.7%
2. Explain how this science learning goal aligns with your chosen NGSS disciplinary core idea standard?	(1/37)	2.7%
3. Tell me more about the teaching strategies you will use to achieve your science learning goal?	(13/37)	35.1%
4. How have you adapted any teacher guide directions to help your students achieve the science learning goal?	(3/37)	8.1%
5. How will you know if your students have achieved the science learning goal?	(3/37)	24.3%
Observation Areas for Science Learning Goal Context		
1. Observe the extent to which the student teacher designed a lesson to meet the science learning goal.	(9/27)	33.3%
2. Observe the extent to which the student teacher planned to meet the science learning goal with creativity and flexibility.	(10/27)	37.0%
3. What evidence shows either the student teacher's flexible thinking to address the disciplinary core idea standard of NGSS or inflexible adherence to training or curriculum guide directions?	(4/27)	14.8%
4. Identify which areas of the science learning goal the student teacher covers in the lesson and note teacher/student actions and verbalizations.	(4/27)	14.8%
Post-Observation Questions—Science Learning Goal Context		
1. In what ways did the lesson work to achieve your science learning goals?	(6/29)	20.6%
2. What instructional decisions made the lesson successful?	(8/29)	27.5%
3. What instructional decisions posed challenges for you in achieving the science learning goal?	(7/29)	24.1%
4. What is another way you might plan for addressing the science learning goal?	(2/29)	6.8%
5. How could this lesson inform your future lessons?	(6/29)	20.6%

[a] Values in parentheses indicate the ratio of the number of questions asked for a particular question out of the total questions asked in the same category.

To extend the pre-observation mentoring discussions, CEs generated their own post-observation questions to promote PSTs' reflection on student understanding of the science learning goal:

- What worked to help you achieve your science learning goal?

- What could you do differently next time?
- How did you know that they reached that goal? What is some evidence?

The data indicated that the CEs repeatedly used these questions in their mentoring of PSTs. In some cases, the CE felt that a PST tended to struggle with keeping the learning goal in mind while planning lessons. PST-Ann explained that the mentoring helped her planning since she had "the habit of straying away from my goals sometimes." The use of these questions during the post-observation meeting served to help PSTs reflect on their practice (Schön, 1983, 1987) and make adjustments to their next lesson in collaboration with their mentor. This is a clear example of educative mentoring (Bradbury, 2010; Feiman-Nemser, 2001) where the mentor scaffolds the mentee's thinking via questioning and reflection on action. With repetition, some PSTs internalized these questions and applied this thinking process as they planned. CE-Aaron noted that PST-Ellen began to answer the questions for herself. She would examine student work purposefully to ascertain each student's understanding (Sabel, Forbes, & Zangori, 2015).

The frequency distribution chart also provided insight into the types of questions that CEs tended not to ask during the mentoring. Question #2 (Explain how this science learning goal aligns with your chosen NGSS disciplinary core idea standard?) was not used by most CEs not only since CEs felt they had insufficient knowledge of NGSS, but also because the new standards did not apply to the materials and state assessment being used. In addition, only CE-Donna used question #3 (How have you adapted any teacher guide directions to help your students achieve the science learning goal?) to prompt her PST to think beyond the science kit teacher's guide and adapt the directions when planning for student learning. CE-Donna's pedagogical content knowledge in science teaching positioned her to promote her PSTs' pedagogical design capacity for reform-based science (Forbes & Davis, 2010).

Attention to Student Misconceptions

CEs and PSTs felt the mentoring questions prompted discussion during the post-observation meetings about whether students had misconceptions. CEs recognized PSTs, as novices, needed guidance in identifying each student's level of understanding and in determining how to help students who struggled with the learning goal. CE-Barbara pointed out that PSTs tend to be unaware of students' understanding. She explained, "You need to be really listening to what they're saying and being able to say back, 'Is this what you meant?'" She noted that PSTs often view student engagement in conversation as "they all really got it. But actually did they really get it?" Regarding PSTs' attention to students' understanding, CE-Carrie also reported that "Sometimes they're teaching a lesson and they don't even know who understood it, who had the big idea or not. They just assume because they taught it they all have the big idea." This tendency for PSTs to focus on the science task and not attend to students' conceptual understanding suggests a need for mentoring PSTs in their assessment of students' ideas (Talanquer, Tomanek, & Novodvorsky, 2013).

To increase PST awareness of students' understanding, each CE made a point to pose questions to the PSTs not only about which students needed additional support, but also how the PST planned to address student misconceptions in the next lesson: "So what are you going to do to know which students understood the concept and which students did not? What are you going to do about it? How are you going to clarify the misconceptions?" (CE-Carrie). PST interview data indicated that they were becoming more purposeful in identifying students' understandings by this consistent questioning. Over time, PSTs noted that they increased their focus on student thinking, their ability to pinpoint student misconceptions, and their awareness of different strategies to address them (Feiman-Nemser, 2001). Through this mentoring routine of asking questions prior to the lesson, the CE scaffolded the PST to think critically about their practice, provided the PST with opportunities to see multiple contexts, and, consequently, assisted the PST to practice more like an advanced beginner than a novice (Dreyfus & Dreyfus, 1988).

Prompt for Planning Beyond Teacher's Guide

Three CEs, (Joan, Carrie, and Donna) used the pre-observation mentoring question #4 (How have you adapted any teacher guide directions to help your students achieve the science learning goal?) to guide PSTs in considering approaches beyond the science kit teacher's guide to help students. These CEs recognized that they needed to build the PSTs capacity to evaluate curriculum materials and adapt them to be more reform-based (Forbes & Davis, 2010). To do so, the CEs focused their observation on how the PSTs planned to meet the science learning goal with creativity and flexibility as an advanced beginner rather than with strict adherence to the teacher's guide directions typical of a novice (pre-observation questions 2 and 3). CE-Carrie explained her rationale for encouraging PST-Sue to plan beyond the teacher's guide. She wanted Sue to first "read the lesson, feel comfortable with the concept that you're teaching, what is your learning goal" and then design her own lesson to meet the needs of her students. In that way, Carrie felt that Sue could enact the lesson more naturally without being afraid to say something wrong. CE-Donna felt that the tool provided "really good questions to get my student teacher to think a little bit outside the box past the guide that we are given." The mentoring questions helped her PST-Cathy "think about other strategies she could use besides what's given." These CE mentoring actions were consistent with research that suggests PSTs can adapt curriculum materials to be more aligned with reform-based science with guidance from methods courses and field placements (Forbes & Davis, 2010).

Mentoring to Promote Student Expression of Scientific Thinking

The intent of NGSS is that students develop scientific practices of constructing their understanding of core ideas in science through dialogic interactions and argumentation to evaluate evidence collected from investigations (Christodoulou & Osborne, 2014; NRC, 2012). Four themes emerged regarding the CE mentoring to promote student expression of scientific thinking: focus on oral expression, questions for critical thinking, under-emphasis of students' written explanations, and absence of student assessment criteria.

Focus on Oral Expression

In terms of promoting students' expression of their thinking, there was a tendency for the CEs to recommend that PSTs engage students in oral discourse, more so than written expression. Some CEs, such as Ruth and Barbara, felt that students could express their ideas more easily by explaining them orally rather than in writing. Therefore, CEs prompted PST to listen carefully to students' expression of their thinking. CE-Sharon explained,

> The student teachers want to get through the lesson. They're going to march on through, so they don't always listen to what the kids tell them. The kids tell you everything you need to know about whether you're meeting your goal or not.

These findings were also reflected in the frequency distribution chart that showed post-observation question #2 as the most commonly used by the CEs: How did your decisions promote your students' explaining their thinking? (see Table 11.5).

To promote scientific discourse, the CEs encouraged PSTs to emphasize students' oral expression of ideas and "support claims with evidence." CE-Carrie noted that early in the semester, PST-Sue would provide the claims and evidence from an investigation rather than have students generate ideas on their own. PSTs tend to pay insufficient attention to promoting student discourse for interpreting and evaluating investigation results (Talanquer et al., 2012). By using question #1 for the pre-observation mentoring, "How will you discover about students' conceptions of the science learning

TABLE 11.5   CEs' Recordings of Questions Asked for Student Expression of Scientific Thinking at Each Mentoring Point

Mentoring Point	Questions asked at each mentoring point	
	Ratio[a]	Percentage
Pre-Observation Questions—Student Thinking Context		
1. How will you discover about students conceptions of the science learning goal?	(7/31)	22.5%
2. Explain how your teaching strategies will support your students' explaining their ideas and thinking?	(4/31)	12.9%
3. Explain how your teaching strategies will support your students' engaging in scientific practices?	(7/31)	22.5%
4. What student behaviors do you hope to see or hear from them as evidence that they have met the science learning goal?	(9/31)	29.0%
5. What strategies can you use to support students who may struggle with expressing their thinking about the science learning goal?	(4/31)	12.9%
Observation Areas for Student Thinking Context		
1. Observe the strategies that the student teacher uses to identify students' conceptions of the science learning goal.	(8/35)	22.8%
2. Observe how the student teacher provides opportunities for all students (or individual students) to explain their ideas and thinking.	(10/35)	28.5%
3. Identify evidence that shows how the student teacher provided opportunities for all students (or individual students) to engage in any of the NGSS scientific practices.	(6/35)	17.1%
4. Identify evidence of how the student teacher supports the learning of students who may struggle with the science learning goal.	(4/35)	11.4%
5. Identify how the student teacher seeks evidence of students' meeting the learning goal (informal/formal assessment; formative/summative assessment).	(7/35)	20.0%
Post-Observation Questions—Student Thinking Context		
1. Tell me what you learned about your students' conceptions of the science learning goal?	(4/23)	17.3%
2. How did your decisions promote your students' explaining their thinking?	(8/23)	34.7%
3. For which students was it effective?	(1/23)	4.3%
4. What do you think contributed to some students' struggling with explaining their thinking?	(0/23)	0.0%
5. How do you feel students' engaged in scientific practices? I noticed when you _____, the students really _____.	(5/23)	21.7%
6. What criteria did you use to assess your students' sense making of the science learning goal?	(1/23)	4.3%
7. What did you learn from your selected assessment(s) with the students?	(3/23)	13.0%

[a] Values in parentheses indicate the ratio of the number of questions asked for a particular question out of the total questions asked in the same category.

goal?" Carrie was able to facilitate Sue's thinking about strategies such as, "turn and talk" to encourage her students to express their thinking.

Two CEs, Donna and Aaron, had knowledge of scientific discourse using evidence-based "talk moves" outlined in *Ready, Set, Science!* (Michaels, Shouse, & Schweingruber, 2007). To help students understand each other's ideas, a student could inquire, "Let me see if I've got your thinking right. Do you mean . . . ?" A student could agree or disagree with another student's ideas and then explain reasons why. CE-Aaron promoted this approach with his PST-Ellen,

> Don't ever just ask a question and have them answer and then that's it. It doesn't matter what. How do you know? Everything you say, make them verbalize how they know. Make them verbalize how they got to where they got so that eventually, their brains will start thinking that way.

There was evidence that Donna's PST had adopted these talk moves in her science lesson planning from the mentoring process. PST-Cathy explained,

> We had a conversation about that, how to make sure they're really answering with whole sentences and using details, "I agree with," and not just think, "Oh, well, I just don't think she's right." Rather, "Support your answer with what you've learned."

This explicit mentoring can help novice PSTs increase student dialogue and develop students' scientific reasoning (Mercer et al., 2004)—an expectation of NGSS.

Questions for Critical Thinking

CEs also used the tool to prompt PSTs to create higher-level questions to promote students' thinking. PST-Sue reported that after her first lesson, CE-Carrie suggested, "maybe we need to start planning questions ahead of time." Sue explained,

> I thought the most helpful questions that she asked me were what questions I was going to ask the students. . . . So then, we started writing them out ahead of time, and she gave me, a *Bloom's Taxonomy* list of question openings.

From the mentoring process, Sue was able to generate questions such as, "Why do you think that happened? How does this connect to what we've learned before on other investigations?" Sue felt that with the "higher-level questioning, the more in-depth the students' answers are going to be." Thus, she began to recognize the importance of students making meaning on their own from the investigations through their science conversations (Wallace & Brooks, 2014). Other questions that both the CEs and the PSTs reported as effective in promoting students' expressing their thinking included: "How do you know?" "What does that mean?" "Can you give me an example?" "What's the difference?" CE-Sharon described these questions as "thick questions" because they required students to explain their thinking in greater depth than "thin questions" which elicited yes/no responses or short answers. This CE mentoring focus on PST questioning prompted PSTs to consider the context of student understanding, a necessary step in their growth to the advanced beginner stage (Dreyfus & Dreyfus, 1986; Peno & Silva Mangiante, 2012).

Under-Emphasis of Students' Written Explanations

From examining the interview data and student work, the evidence indicated that most CEs did not emphasize students' independent writing of scientific explanations. Some CEs recommended that after students recorded the collected data in their science notebooks, the PST could conduct a whole group discussion to interpret the data, write conclusions on chart paper, and have students copy the conclusions in their science notebooks. For example, PST-Ann explained that her CE suggested, "They just need to know 'What was the main thing I learned today?' So they don't have to do any extra writing. That's not necessary." The students were not expected to write their ideas about the investigation on their own.

Two possible reasons emerged to explain this under-emphasis on students' explanatory writing: student's struggle with writing and limited time. CE-Ruth explained, "I have a lot of students who don't like to write, so she'd write it on the chart paper instead of them writing their own." Ruth noted, "We had to come up with a plan on how we could get all of this done because we don't have that much time to do science anymore. It is such a struggle." It is noteworthy that no CE used the post-observation question #4: "What do you think contributed to some students' struggling with explaining their thinking?" The reason for this omission is unclear from the data. Questions arise as to whether the CEs felt the PSTs were not ready to address the question or whether this question posed an ever-present challenge for the CEs themselves.

Some CEs mentored their PSTs in designing ways for students to report their thinking. These written formats included exit slips, graphic organizers, a mini-assessment, or a compare and contrast chart to show their thinking in writing. For example, PST-Ann reported that her CE-Joan would question her, "How do you know that they understood? What evidence did they show you?" Ann noted that Joan would suggest "giving each one a little post exit ticket, a slip with a question about what we learned and having evidence." These formats tended to elicit student reporting of collected data or class generated conclusions.

However, only one CE provided explicit mentoring in how to promote students' written explanations of ideas. CE-Donna had been introduced "to a book called, *Writing in Science*. I immediately thought that this is fantastic. This is how I should be teaching writing" in science. Donna modeled the shared-writing approach for her PST-Cathy. Recognizing the need to promote students' ability to acquire the NGSS practice of scientific communication, Donna noted, "I know it's outside of the investigation itself, but it's that next step." Based on her interview and students' written work, the evidence showed that PST-Cathy adopted this approach. After conducting an investigation, PST-Cathy would engage the whole class in creating a shared-writing piece from the data to answer the investigation question. The students would "use supporting examples. Then the following day, they write an independent piece answering that same question." She felt that this scaffolded approach really supported the "struggling students who have a difficult time writing" so that "eventually as the weeks go on," they are able to write their ideas from the investigation on their own (Patterson, 2010).

Absence of Assessment Criteria

It is noteworthy that only one CE, Carrie, posed the post-observation question #4 to her PST inquiring about the criteria she used to assess her students' understanding. The interview data indicated that another CE, Joan, was interested in guiding her PST to consider, "What did you learn from your selected assessments?" However, similar to the majority of the CEs, she did not prompt her PST to determine criteria for judging whether a student understood the science learning goal from a student's oral or written explanations. Research findings from Sabel et al., (2015) indicate the need for pre-service teachers to develop the ability to "diagnose perceived gaps in students' understanding" (p. 434). Thus, there is a need to place increased emphasis in the CE's mentoring PD on how to advance PSTs' skill with developing formative assessments and criteria for evaluation of student work.

RECOMMENDATIONS

From participating in this science mentoring project, the CE's provided recommendations to improve the P.O.M.M. science mentoring strategies tool. The suggestions addressed three areas: number and types of questions/strategies, format of the tool, and use of the tool. Though CE's responses varied depending on each person's preferences, the CEs felt the questions helped them focus their conversations with their PSTs. Most CEs felt that the number of questions for each point in the mentoring process allowed then to choose the area of concentration based on the needs of the

PST. CE-Aaron noted that "five questions was a very reasonable number. They weren't too specific." He appreciated questions that began with the word, "identify": "Anytime they're asked specifically to identify, it really pinpoints what they have to do. You have to show me something. I have to be able to see it. It needs to be clear." In contrast, two teachers preferred fewer questions with a more specific focus. CE-Barbara noted that "there should have been a question about content," given that one focus area was on the science learning goal. She felt that PSTs first needed to assess their science subject matter knowledge on a topic.

In terms of the format, CEs recommended that the tool include additional space for note-taking and be organized in a spiral bound book. CE-Joan noted that by writing down the PSTs decisions during the pre-observation meeting, the CE-PST pair could refer back to those pedagogical choices during the post-observation discussion and reflect on the extent of implementation in the science lesson. In addition, four of the seven CEs recommended that PSTs complete a written lesson plan for the pre-observation meeting in order to address specific areas in the lesson early such as questioning and assessment of student understanding.

To extend the use of the science mentoring strategies tool, CE-Aaron suggested that subject-specific mentoring questions be included for all content areas. He also recommended that the PSTs have access to the mentoring strategies ahead of time: "I think they need to have all of that with them ahead of time so I'm not asking them surprise questions. This is how we're going to work together." By providing the PSTs with the mentoring tool, they could plan for the science learning goal and expression of student thinking more intentionally.

CONCLUSION AND IMPLICATIONS

Developers of NGSS recognized that prospective science teachers would need a solid grounding in the dimensions of the new standards in order to engage their students in constructing understanding of cores ideas in science (NRC, 2012). Novice PSTs would need mentoring support in learning not only how to be aware of student thinking and facilitate students' scientific discourse, but also how to revise curricular materials to align with the new standards. The results of this study provide insights into CEs' use of the P.O.M.M. science mentoring strategies tool as a means to guide PSTs in their adoption of reform based science practices. Though the findings from seven CE-PST pairs' in their use of this mentoring tool cannot be generalized to the larger population of individuals who mentor prospective teachers in science education, the emerging themes suggest implications for educational stakeholders as well as considerations for operationalizing science mentoring.

The evidence indicated that CEs' mentoring decisions for science teaching were bounded by the curriculum materials they had available and the nature of the state science assessment—both of which aligned with previous science standards. These factors, in conjunction with CEs' limited awareness of NGSS, minimized PSTs' access to mentoring for NGSS implementation and resulted in PSTs' adopting their CE's science pedagogical practices. This finding is consistent with literature noting that PSTs tend to adopt CEs' approaches despite a science methods course focus on reform-based science (Bradbury, 2010; Yerrick et al., 2008).

The CEs and PSTs perceived that the questions, points for observation, and strategies listed on the science mentoring strategies tool aided CEs in mentoring and PSTs in planning and reflection. The CEs valued the structure and ease in using the tool and subsequently implemented it in other subject areas. They used the tool to promote the PST's growth from a novice to an advanced beginner (Dreyfus & Dreyfus, 1986) with increased awareness in planning for the science classroom. However, analysis of data indicated that CEs focused more on the science learning goal than on student thinking. Though CEs encouraged PSTs to use higher-order questions to promote students' science discourse, most CEs neglected to guide PSTs in how to scaffold for student writing or how to establish criteria to assess student learning.

The results of this study not only add to the extant literature recommending content-specific mentoring (Abed & Abd-El-Khalick, 2015; Hudson, 2004, 2005), but also provide insights into additional focus areas needed to promote science-specific mentoring of PSTs. First, continued mentoring training and support is warranted for CEs so they can refine their role as educative mentors who focus on collaborative, sustained, evidence-driven planning and decision-making that is formative in nature (Bradbury, 2010; Feiman-Nemser, 2001). Next, as commercially developed science kits and state science assessments are revised to align with the new standards, we recommend that CEs would benefit from in-depth district-sponsored PD in scientific practices of NGSS, science discourse strategies, and approaches to supporting students' science writing (Bradbury, 2010; Mercer et al., 2004). Finally, in order for PSTs to have consistency between science teaching field experiences and university science methods courses, these results suggest the need for a close partnership between CEs and university teacher education programs as a means to generate common understanding of pedagogical approaches aligned with science education reforms, emphasize students' oral/written explanation construction, and promote on-going science education mentoring.

REFERENCES

Abed, O. H., & Abd-El-Khalick, F. (2015). Jordanian preservice primary teachers' perceptions of mentoring in science teaching. *International Journal of Science Education, 37*(4), 703–726.

Appleton, K. (2003). How do beginning primary school teachers cope with science? Toward an understanding of science teaching practice. *Research in Science Education, 33*, 1–25.

Berliner, D. C. (1994). Expertise: The wonders of exemplary performance. In J. N. Mangieri, & C. Collins Block (Eds.), *Creating powerful thinking in teachers and students.* Fort Worth, TX: Holt, Rinehart and Winston.

Berliner, D. C. (2004). Describing the behavior and documenting the accomplishments of expert teachers. *Bulletin of Science, Technology & Society, 24*(3), 200–212.

Bradbury, L. U. (2010). Educative mentoring: Promoting reform-based science teaching through mentoring relationships. *Science Education, 94*(6), 1049–1071.

Christodoulou, A., & Osborne, J. (2014). The science classroom as a site of epistemic talk: A case study of a teacher's attempts to teach science based on argument. *Journal of Research in Science Teaching, 51*(10), 1275–1300.

Creswell, J. W. (2009). *Research design: Qualitative, quantitative, and mixed methods approaches.* Los Angeles, CA: Sage.

Davis, E. A., & Smithey, J. (2009). Beginning teachers moving toward effective elementary science teaching. *Science Education, 93*, 745–770.

Denzin, N. K. (1978). *The research act* (2nd ed.). New York, NY: McGraw-Hill.

Dewey, J. (1910). *How we think.* Lexington, MA: D.C. Heath.

Dreyfus, H. L., & Dreyfus, S. E. (1986). *Mind over machine: The power of human intuition and expertise in the era of the computer.* New York, NY: Free Press.

Dreyfus, H. L., & Dreyfus, S. E. (1988). *Mind over machine: The power of human intuition and expertise in the era of the computer.* New York, NY: Free Press.

Dreyfus, S. E. (2004). The five-stage model of adult skill acquisition. *Bulletin of Science, Technology & Society, 24*(3), 177–181.

Dreyfus, S. E., & Dreyfus, H. L. (1980). *A five-stage model of the mental activities involved in directed skill acquisition* (ORC 80-2). Berkeley: University of California, Berkeley, Operations Research Center.

Feiman-Nemser, S. (2001). Helping novices learn to teach: Lessons from an exemplary support teacher. *Journal of Teacher Education, 52*(1), 17–30.

Forbes, C. T., Biggers, M., & Zangori, L. (2013). Investigating essential characteristics of scientific practices in elementary science learning environments: The practices of science observation. *School Science and Mathematics, 113*(4), 180–190.

Forbes, C. T., & Davis, E. A. (2010). Curriculum design for inquiry: Preservice elementary teachers' mobilization and adaptation of science curriculum materials. *Journal of Research in Science Teaching, 47*(7), 820–839.

Gaffey, C. S., Woodward, H., & Lowe, K. (1995). Improving school experience: An Australian perspective. *Action in Teacher Education, 17*(2), 7–17.

Gravetter, F. J., & Wallnau, L. B. (2008). *Essentials of statistics for the behavioral sciences.* Belmont, CA: Thomson Wadsworth.

Haefner, L. A., & Zembal-Saul, C. (2004). Learning by doing? Prospective elementary teachers' developing understandings of scientific inquiry and science teaching and learning. *International Journal of Science Education, 26*(13), 1653–1674.

Harlen, W. (1997). Primary teachers' understanding in science and its impact in the classroom. *Research in Science Education, 27*(3), 323–337.

Herrenkohl, L. R., & Guerra, M. R. (1998). Participant structures, scientific discourse, and student engagement in fourth grade. *Cognition and Instruction, 16*(4), 431–473.

Hudson, P. (2003). Mentoring first-year pre-service teachers of primary science. *Action in Teacher Education, 25*(3), 91–99.

Hudson, P. (2004). Specific mentoring: A theory and model for developing primary science teaching practices. *European Journal of Teacher Education, 27,* 139–146.

Hudson, P. (2005). Identifying mentoring practices for developing effective primary science teaching. *International Journal of Science Education, 27*(14), 1723–1739.

Kennedy, M. M. (1998). Educational reform and subject matter knowledge. *Journal of Research in Science Teaching, 35*(3), 249–263.

Luera, G. R., Moyer, R. H., & Everett, S. A. (2005). What type and level of science content knowledge of elementary education students affect their ability to construct an inquiry-based science lesson? *Journal of Elementary Science Education, 17*(1), 12–25.

Mercer, N., Dawes, L., Wegerif, R., & Sams, C. (2004). Reasoning as a scientist: Ways of helping children to use language to learn science. *British Educational Research Journal, 30*(3), 359–377.

Michaels, S., Shouse, A. W., & Schweingruber, H.A. (2007). *Ready, set, science! Putting research to work in K–8 science classrooms.* Washington, DC: National Research Council.

Miles, M. B., & Huberman, A.M. (1994). *Qualitative data analysis: An expanded sourcebook.* Beverly Hills, CA: Sage.

National Research Council. (2007). *Taking science to school: Learning and teaching science in grades K–8.* Washington, DC: The National Academies Press.

National Research Council. (2012). *A framework for K–12 science education: Practices, crosscutting concepts, and core ideas.* Washington, DC: National Academies Press.

Newton, D. P., & Newton, L. D. (2001). Subject content knowledge and teacher talk in the primary science classroom. *European Journal of Teacher Education, 24*(3), 369–378.

NGSS Lead States. (2013). *Next Generation Science Standards: For states by states.* Washington, DC: Achieve Inc. on behalf of the 26 states and partners.

Palinscar, A. S., Anderson, C. W., & David, Y. (1993). Pursuing scientific literacy in the middle grades through collaborative problem solving. *Elementary School Journal, 5,* 643–658.

Patterson, E. W. (2010). Structuring the composition process in scientific writing. *International Journal of Science Education, 23*(1), 1–16.

Patton, M. Q. (2002). *Qualitative research & evaluation methods* (3rd ed.). Thousand Oaks, CA: Sage.

Peno, K., & Silva Mangiante, E. (2012). The journey from novice to expert: Toward a purposeful on-going mentoring model. In C. J. Boden-McGill & K. P.

King (Eds.), *Conversations about adult learning in a complex world* (pp. 211–221). Charlotte, NC: Information Age.

Roth, K. J., Garnier, H. E., Chen, C., Lemmens, M., Schwille, K., & Wickler, N. I. Z. (2011). Videotaped lesson analysis: Effective science PD for teacher and student learning. *Journal of Research in Science Teaching, 48*(2), 117–148.

Sabel, J. L., Forbes, C. T., & Zangori, L. (2015). Promoting prospective elementary teachers' learning to use formative assessment for life science instruction. *Journal of Science Teacher Education, 26*, 419–445.

Schön, D. J. (1983). *The reflective practitioner.* New York, NY: Basic Books.

Schön, D. J. (1987). *Educating the reflective practitioner: Toward a new design for teaching and learning in the professions.* San Francisco, CA: Jossey-Bass.

Shulman, L. S. (1986). Those who understand: Knowledge growth in teaching. *Educational Researcher, 15*(2), 4–14.

Symington, D., & Hayes, D. (1989). What do you need to know to teach science in the primary school? *Research in Science Education, 19*, 278–285.

Talanquer, V., Tomanek, D., & Novodvorsky, I. (2013). Assessing students' understanding of inquiry: What do prospective science teachers notice? *Journal of Research in Science Teaching, 50*(2), 189–208.

Tang, S. Y. F. (2003). Challenge and support: The dynamics of student teachers' professional learning in the field experience. *Teaching and Teacher Education, 19*(5), 483–498.

Vygotsky, L. S. (1978). *Mind in Society: The development of higher psychological processes.* Cambridge, MA: Harvard University Press.

Wallace, C., & Brooks, L. (2014). Learning to teach elementary science in an experiential, informal context: Culture, learning, and identity. *Science Education, 99*, 174–198.

Wang, J., & Odell, S. (2002). Mentored learning to teach according to standards-based reform: A critical review. *Review of Educational Research, 72*(3) 481–546.

Yerrick, R. K., Ambrose, R., & Schiller, J. (2008). Ascribing legitimacy: Pre-service teachers construction of science teaching expertise in multiple communities. *Electronic Journal of Science Education, 12*(2), 132–170.

Zembal-Saul, C. (2009). Learning to teach elementary school science as argument. *Science Education, 93*, 687–719.

Zembal-Saul, C., Krajcik, J., & Blumenfeld, P. (2002). Elementary student teachers' science content representations. *Journal of Research in Science Teaching, 39*(6), 443–463.

PART III

MENTORING IN HEALTHCARE

CHAPTER 12

MENTORSHIP IN ACADEMIC MEDICINE

Shadi Aminololama-Shakeri
Andreea L. Seritan
University of California, Davis School of Medicine

One of the main goals of a medical school or teaching hospital is to train competent physicians who will provide compassionate care to their patients. These professionals in training are taught to integrate a large amount of medical knowledge with information gathered from patients and their families. Frequently, working as part of an inter-professional team, they treat patients with varying levels of acuity while navigating through various institutional and idiosyncratic electronic health record systems. They learn the value of professionalism, humanism, and continual renewal of their knowledge and skills, directly or indirectly, from an expansive group of teachers (preceptors, co-residents, nurses, technologists, administrators, and patients) with a wide range of specialities (Stern & Papadakis, 2006). To successfully graduate, they must demonstrate competence through examination and evaluation (Iobst et al., 2010). Medical training also emphasizes supportive skills such as effective communication, leadership, teamwork, and thoughtful examination of scientific literature. However, a successful transition to a faculty position within an academic medical environment requires much more than the mentioned

Mentoring in Formal and Informal Contexts, pages 227–246
Copyright © 2016 by Information Age Publishing
All rights of reproduction in any form reserved.

227

tools of wisdom that are imparted to the graduating trainee (Aschenbrener, Ast, & Kirch, 2015; Carraccio, Benson, Nixon, & Derstine, 2008). Mentorship plays an immense role in the process of maturing into an independent practitioner and climbing the steps of academia. With appropriate mentorship, these lifelong adult learners can identify their core motivators for pursuing a career in academic medicine and propagate successfully through this system with those values in mind.

The prevalence of mentorship in academic health institutions has been reported to range from 19% to 93%, and its benefits have been well established (Sambunjak, Straus, & Marusic, 2006). Faculty members with mentors tend to have higher career satisfaction, higher rates of promotion and advancement, and better performance in areas of research, teaching, and patient care (Illes, Glover, Wexler, Leung, & Glazer, 2000; Palepu et al., 1998; Wingard, Garman, & Reznik, 2004; Wise et al., 2004). Having mentors has also been shown to influence career choices for trainees in medical school and beyond (Ramanan, Taylor, Davis, & Phillips, 2006). This chapter will review common models of mentoring relationships in academic medicine, with an emphasis on career paths, changing needs throughout the medical education continuum, and typically under-mentored groups (underrepresented minorities, women, and international medical graduates).

DEFINITIONS

Mentorship is a multifaceted phenomenon, with the ultimate goal of enriching the mentees' academic repertoire, expanding their horizons, and advancing their careers. In its traditional format, mentorship is a connection of two people, one who is more experienced (mentor) and the other with less experience (mentee or protégée) (Worley, Borus, & Hilty, 2006). At least initially, this relationship is formed to foster the career development of the mentee, although a successful relationship leads to mutual growth and advancement. Flourishing alliances with lasting effects are not static but rather evolve to nurture the pair. With time, dynamic mentoring may lead to power equalization of the mentor and protégée and even role reversal as the mentee's level of expertise or success rises beyond that of the mentor (Kram, 1983; Ponce, Williams, & Allen, 2005).

The overarching concept of mentorship is often used interchangeably with relationships involving supervision, teaching, coaching and/or sponsorship (Hewlett, 2013). Each of these roles may be encompassed under the mentorship umbrella; however, a mentor's role is broader than any of these singular functions. The meaning and application of mentoring may vary by professional fields. For instance, in business and education, task-specific mentoring to achieve short-term or project-oriented goals, more accurately describes coaching or advising (Stoddard & Tamasy, 2009). Coaching typically involves interactive training and instruction to hone a specific skillset (Stoddard & Tamasy, 2009). Teaming a novice with an experienced educator with the goal of improving teaching skills is an example of this. In medical education, junior and senior residents are grouped to take care of patients in teams. The overseeing senior resident supervises and teaches the more junior one how to manage a clinical service. This use of apprenticeship is ubiquitous in both business and the health sciences. While such a practice is vital for incoming trainees to develop their clinical and leadership skills, it does not necessarily equate to mentorship (Armitage & Burnard, 1991; Boudreau, Macdonald, & Steinert, 2014).

Just as mentorship is distinguishable from coaching and other such activities with singular goals, *mentors* are distinct from *sponsors* and *supervisors* (see Table 12.1). The substitution of one term for the other has become a source of role confusion in the health sciences (Armitage & Burnard, 1991; Bray & Nettleton, 2007). Mentors nurture their mentees' personal and professional development by boosting their confidence, supporting their growth, and teaching them new skills. Sponsors explicitly advocate for and help advance their protégés' careers (i.e., by strategically nominating their protégée for a key national committee or new position) (Hewlett, Peraino, Sherbin, & Sumberg, 2010; Hewlett, 2013). One important difference between sponsorship and mentorship is that mentors do not expect anything in exchange for their time and commitment to the mentees' growth. In mentoring relationships, energy flows predominantly in one direction: towards the mentee (Hewlett, 2013; Rolfe, 1990). In contradistinction, the sponsored protégée is expected to reciprocate a boost to their career by delivering nothing less than stellar performance, thereby promoting the good judgement and brand of the sponsor within the organization (Hewlett et al., 2010; Hewlett, 2013).

Supervisors are typically in higher rank positions than junior team members and direct, teach (precept), and evaluate the supervised individuals. This evaluative role sets supervisors apart from mentors (Mellon & Murdoch-Eaton, 2015). In contrast to mentors and sponsors, supervisors may not necessarily be vested in the long-term success of the supervised. Additionally, it has been shown that those who are in an evaluative role are not in an ideal position for mentorship, given an inherent conflict of interest (Leslie, Lingard, & Whyte, 2005). For example, it would be difficult for a department chair to recommend the most clinically productive faculty member for an administrative role that would leave a clinical need to be filled.

Although these roles are distinct from one another, there may be overlap. Certainly, a caring supervisor may mentor and sponsor a promising trainee. For instance, a training director who supervises the daily activities of a gifted resident may also act as a sponsor by making a recommendation for hiring the trainee. All the while, this same program director may continue to be a mentor by guiding, promoting and supporting the trainee's career for years to come.

MENTORSHIP MODELS IN ACADEMIC MEDICINE

In the extensive body of literature focused on mentoring in academic medicine, several models have been described (see Table 12.1). The best known is the traditional *dyad* model (one-to-one, senior faculty mentor with junior mentee). Included under the umbrella of the traditional dyad are the developmental and technical mentorship formats.

Developmental mentors serve as overall guides to the field, who address mentees' personal and professional goals by serving as sounding boards and offering advice based on their experience (Worley et al., 2006). In the business literature, researchers have described two types of functions that may be performed by those who facilitate an individual's professional development: career functions and psychosocial functions (Higgins & Thomas, 2001). Career functions include: exposure and visibility, coaching, protection, and providing challenging assignments; psychosocial functions involve serving as role models, validation, counselling, and support (Higgins & Thomas, 2001; Kram, 1983). Academic medicine developmental mentors may fulfil some or all of these roles. Typically, these mentors are more senior than mentees and have the ability to help their junior colleagues navigate the academic landscape and "learn the ropes." Developmental mentors are often (but not always) from the mentee's institution and are most

TABLE 12.1 Types of Relationships in Academic Medicine Career Development

Relationship type	Same department/ institution	Same specialty/area of interest	Academic rank (compared to mentee's rank)	Meet regularly
Mentor				
• Dyad				
– Developmental	Typically	Typically	Higher	Not necessarily
– Technical	Yes	Yes	Higher/Similar	Yes
• Peer	Yes	Yes/No	Similar/Lower	Yes
• Reverse	Yes	Typically	Lower	Yes
• Network	No	No	Higher/Similar	Yes
Sponsor	Typically*	Typically	Higher	Yes
Supervisor	Yes	Yes	Higher	Work together

* May be a senior faculty member from a national professional organization
Sources: DeCastro, Sambuco, Ubel, Stewart, & Jagsi, 2013; Hewlett, 2013; Worley et al., 2006)

helpful in addressing large picture questions such as work-life balance, career negotiations, deciding whether to accept additional responsibilities, leaving current institutions, or taking on new positions (DeCastro et al., 2013; Worley et al., 2006).

Technical mentors have a more clearly delineated role, namely, to help their mentees master specific skills (e.g., research, grant writing, presenting at scientific meetings, teaching, writing for publication, as well as specialty-specific skills, such as innovative surgical techniques) (Worley et al., 2006). A thorough needs assessment is recommended for all junior faculty followed by identifying those who can serve as technical mentors, depending on the areas of growth needed. Developmental mentors can also serve as technical mentors in some aspects. This also applies to supervisors (e.g., attending physicians, principal investigators), whose purpose is to teach new, specific skills to the novice team members. Technical mentors are most often at the same institution and able to meet face-to-face with mentees, although today's technological advances facilitate long-distance connections. Some mentees may continue relationships with mentors from their training programs after graduating and moving on to faculty positions. Ideally, these relationships evolve over time, allowing both mentors and mentees to benefit the most from the ongoing support.

Peer mentorship, also called horizontal mentorship, takes place between faculty of similar (or even lower) academic rank and is based on sharing and mutual learning (DeCastro et al., 2013). Peer mentoring initiatives have been effective in institutions where a group of junior faculty have similar career development goals and rely on each other for accountability (Bussey-Jones et al., 2006; Fleming et al., 2015; Johnson, Hastings, Purser, & Whitson, 2011; Seritan et al., 2007). This has also been successful across departments and in situations where few senior role models exist (e.g., female faculty in a department with no associate or full professor women). For example, junior faculty faced with similar challenges may pool their talents, forming writing groups to revise rejected manuscripts (Brandon et al., 2015). Peer mentoring has several advantages. It requires little or no effort from senior faculty who may be overwhelmed with mentoring requests already and facilitates cross-pollination through interdisciplinary and inter-professional collaborations. This results in enhanced scholarly productivity, development of new curricula and educational initiatives, as well as improved faculty interconnectedness (Brandon et al., 2015; Fleming et al., 2015; Johnson et al., 2011; Pololi, Knight, Dennis, & Frankel, 2002; Seritan et al., 2007).

Reverse mentoring has been proposed as a solution for situations where junior faculty can teach their senior colleagues new skills, such as using newer technologies for teaching (Zanni, 2009). Additionally, wherever gender and generational differences come into play, individual perspectives are likely to be different, thus both parties can learn from each other (Lee, Anzai, & Langlotz, 2006).

Mentor networks have been found to be helpful when an insufficient number of mentors or an inadequate fit exists, particularly for women and underrepresented minority (URM) mentees (Beech et al., 2013; DeCastro et al., 2013). For example, the Peer-Onsite-Distance (POD) model was developed at the University of Arkansas to enhance the career growth of URM faculty (Lewellen-Williams et al., 2006). In this multi-layered framework, each mentee was able to access several peer, on-site, and off-site mentors. Mentor networks offer comprehensive support and are more likely to help junior faculty develop a broad spectrum of skills, since mentors with diverse perspectives are involved. Ideal networks have been shown to increase retention and career satisfaction among mentees by combining mentors with varying areas of expertise, academic rank, and gender (DeCastro et al., 2013; Higgins & Thomas, 2001). *Speed mentoring* is a succession of short (ten-minute) meetings to facilitate exposure of the mentee to as many potential mentors as possible (Cook, Bahn, & Menaker, 2010). This is an emerging type of mentorship and outcomes of this approach have not yet been closely examined.

FORMAL AND INFORMAL MENTORSHIP

A systematic review of the medical mentorship literature spanning from 1966 to 2002 revealed that the informal dyad was the most frequent mentoring model used during that period (Buddeberg-Fischer & Herta, 2006). More recently, studies have shown that while informal mentoring is still commonly used, formal programs are gaining popularity, either as components of existing faculty development pathways, or as stand-alone offerings (Kashiwagi, Varkey, & Cook, 2013; Sambunjak et al., 2006). Formal mentorship programs have also grown organically from grassroots approaches, initiated by junior faculty who recognized the need for professional development and consolidated over time with departmental or institutional support (Seritan et al., 2007).

In the traditional model of informal mentoring, faculty members with common interests form supportive professional relationships. In many disciplines, the initial introduction of mentor and mentee occurs around common work tasks (Kram, 1983; Leslie et al., 2005). Often, faculty members become mentors because they are generative and find the ability to contribute to the formation of the next generation of physicians rewarding. Some "pay it forward" in order to honor their own mentors' efforts. In a survey of 24 U.S. medical school faculty mentors, 88% of respondents chose "commitment to and interest in the careers of others" as one of the three most important factors they believed contributed to their effectiveness (Palepu et al., 1998, p. 322). Informal mentorship tends to bring together individuals with a better "fit" inherent in the formation of the relationship. However, this model also has its limitations, such as time constraints, potential conflicts of interest, and fear of lack of confidentiality (Leslie et al., 2005).

Recognizing the importance of mentorship in junior faculty career satisfaction, recruitment, and retention, many academic institutions are offering formal mentorship programs. Some even give credit to mentors for their work in supporting junior faculty (Taherian & Shekarchian, 2008). Many studies describing how to construct formal mentoring programs (Kosoko-Lasaki, Sonnino, & Voytko, 2006; Lewellen-Williams et al., 2006; Morzinski, Simpson, Bower, & Diehr, 1994) can be found in the literature. In formal mentoring, protégées are assigned to potential mentors either by random selection or "matched" based on similar traits or areas of interest. Defined goals, meeting frequency requirements and expectations are pre-determined to facilitate this process (Morzinski et al., 1994; Pololi et al., 2002). Kashiwagi, Varkey and Cook (2013) performed a systematic review of academic medicine publications with the goal of identifying characteristics of successful formal mentoring programs. They analyzed 18 programs designed for the career development of physicians in practice, predominantly junior faculty in academic institutions in the United States. This study identified several factors common across institutions as key to building successful intentional mentoring infrastructures. These may be broadly categorized as mentoring team and organizational factors (Kashiwagi et al., 2013). Program components specific to the mentoring team include careful pairing of mentors and mentees, mentor preparation, and development of formal curricula for mentees. Mentor training through self-guided reading of prescribed material or participation in structured workshops was recognized as an important factor sanctioned by the institutional programs reviewed. Organizational factors leading to the success of formal mentoring programs included having a planning committee in place, securing funding, evaluating outcomes, and being aware of barriers to program development.

CAREER FOCUSED MENTORING

While the general principles of mentorship apply across disciplines, mentorship may be specialty-specific in academic medicine. For example, technical mentoring may be more applicable in the development of surgical skills or research methodologies for the physician scientist. However, young academic surgeons not only need technical but also developmental, peer, and network mentoring as optimal conditions for career success

(Staveley-O'Carroll et al., 2004). This applies to any area of academic practice in the health sciences. Regardless of specialty and academic track, most faculty members are either researchers or educators in addition to being clinicians. Faculty need mentoring to separately cultivate their success in research, teaching and clinical practice, which are the main metrics of promotion in academic medicine.

Clinician Scientist

Clinician scientists face a unique set of challenges. These include achieving a delicate balance straddling the two worlds of patient care and scientific investigation with enough knowledge and know-how to maintain the support of both clinical and research colleagues. Having foresight to clearly define research goals, maintain focus, minimize distractions, and gather technical skills such as grant writing and presenting are just a few areas that mentorship can play a major role in early career development (Steiner, Curtis, Lanphear, Vu, & Main, 2004). A good mentor will advise a mentee when to say "no" to goal deviators and when to take the opportunity to say "yes" to appropriate collaborations. This is the arena where a mentoring team may be best at directing the mentee through the complex network of issues unique to an investigator in medicine. A team approach takes advantage of advisees with different areas of expertise. It also helps in avoiding conflict of interest that may arise when a mentee that has grown in a mentor's scientific shadow has to separate and become independent. Studies have shown that mentored investigators are more productive, more likely to continue research efforts and also tend to mentor others more often (Illes et al., 2000; Ramondetta et al., 2003; Steiner et al., 2004).

Medical Educator

There is a paucity of literature on mentoring of clinical educators. Despite the many demonstrated benefits of mentoring on academic career development (Palepu et al., 1998), there is an imbalance in terms of which academic faculty groups are targets of programs and receive mentoring. A survey of junior faculty from a single institution showed that clinician-scientists were more likely to be mentored than clinician-educators (Chew, Watanabe, Buchwald, & Lessler, 2003). Moreover, having access to senior faculty did not increase the likelihood of being mentored for clinical educators. In another small study of clinical educators, only 32% reported having direct mentorship for this aspect of their careers (Marks, 1999). Lack of mentorship was perceived as being the factor with the greatest negative impact on the careers of these faculty members (Marks, 1999). Several programs within different disciplines have been designed to meet the needs of educators by providing distance or network mentorship (Farrell, Digioia, Broderick, & Coates, 2004). In part, this mentoring vacuum has been attributed to the nebulous value placed on educational contributions by promotion committees (Farrell et al., 2004).

Tangible outcomes related to research productivity of mentees, including grant funding and publications are frequently reported in the medical literature (Kashiwagi et al., 2013; Sambunjak et al., 2006). However, the benefits of mentoring for clinical educators are more difficult to measure. As academic organizations place more value on clinical educators, criteria for scholarly success and promotion of this group of faculty members will need to be better defined and further studies of mentorship models in this milieu will be necessary.

CHANGING NEEDS THROUGHOUT THE MEDICAL EDUCATION CONTINUUM

In academic medicine, mentorship is a crucial component of the successful evolution of the novice medical student to seasoned practitioner. Mentorship is hailed by medical students, residents, and junior faculty alike as an important factor for personal and career development (Aagaard & Hauer, 2003; Coleman, Power, Williams, Carpentieri, & Schulkin, 2005; Illes et al., 2000; Odom, Roberts, Johnson, & Cooper, 2007; Steele, Fisman, & Davidson, 2013; Wingard et al., 2004). Early studies by Kram (1983) have described four phases in a mentoring relationship, each with varying purpose and function (Kram, 1983). The *initiation* phase is focused on career functions. For medical students, this may involve exploration with a mentor of what it takes to apply for a position in a potential specialty choice for future training. *Cultivation* is the following phase, where both career and psychosocial functions become increasingly important. Here, the mentoring relationship has evolved from a one-way hierarchical nurturing relationship to one of mutual contribution held together with strong interpersonal ties. Junior faculty who have grown within their field of research to the point of securing independent grant funding exemplify this stage of mentorship. With increasing reciprocity of ideas, the pair takes on the role of collaborators and colleagues. The same is true for residents, as they mature in their training and prepare to join faculty ranks. This naturally leads to the *separation* phase, where the majority of trainees physically separate from mentors as they leave the institution. Other scenarios, such as growth of the mentee beyond what the mentorship provides or dysfunction of the existing relationship can lead to its termination as well. Mentoring relationships that continue to thrive beyond the separation reach the *redefinition* phase where a friendship or peer supportive relationship ensues. This may include mentor-mentee pairs that reconnect periodically at national professional society meetings and as needed. Whether mentorship relationships are formal or informal, they can dissolve spontaneously when the pair's needs are no longer met, or when the mentee advances on the academic ladder sufficiently to appear threatening to the mentor's role in the organizational hierarchy. Mentees should recognize when the relationship dynamic becomes counterproductive and take appropriate steps to separate from toxic mentors. The high emotional investment on both sides may make separation difficult and predispose both pair members to unprofessional behavior at the end. As in any meaningful human relationship, it is important to honor the gifts received and not dwell on negative aspects.

As physicians advance in their careers and become more specialized in their skillset, it is more and more difficult to identify appropriate, committed mentors. There is a paucity of mentorship programs targeting mid-career or senior faculty (Gabbe et al., 2008; Iversen, Eady, & Wessely, 2014; Lieff et al., 2013). This programmatic aspect should be addressed because this is the time when investments made by organizations pay off, when faculty members assume institutional or national leadership roles and are able to influence policies or help change institutional cultures.

UNDER-MENTORED GROUPS

Academic medicine has taken notice of the growing evidence regarding the critical role of appropriate mentorship in the recruitment and retention of URM and female faculty. Several studies have brought to light the shortage of mentorship as perceived by women and URM in training and post-graduate medicine (Yehia et al., 2014). Bickel and Rosenthal (2011) highlighted some of the difficulties faced by URMs and women in academic medicine. These include often being the token faculty member representing a gender or an entire race on committees, increasing the faculty member's burden and isolation. Compared with their non-minority counterparts, URM physicians report less career satisfaction and are mentored less (Ramanan, Phillips, Davis, Silen, & Reede, 2002).

The crucial role of mentorship for women and URM faculty has been emphasized in qualitative studies, and several programs specifically designed to support these groups have been described in the literature (Beech et al., 2013; Coleman et al., 2005; Kosoko-Lasaki et al., 2006; Lewellen-Williams et al., 2006; Odom et al., 2007; Seritan et al., 2007; Steele et al., 2013). As stated above, women and URM faculty have more difficulty finding adequate mentors and may need to be more creative in this regard, for example by relying on peer and network mentorship models (Beech et al., 2013; Brandon et al., 2015; Bussey-Jones et al., 2006; DeCastro et al., 2013; Fleming et al., 2015; Johnson et al., 2011; Lewellen-Williams et al., 2006; Pololi et al., 2002; Seritan et al., 2007). Mentors do not have to be of similar gender or racial/ethnic background as mentees; for example, men can make excellent mentors for women, and female faculty can mentor junior women, regardless of race and ethnicity (Bickel, 2014; McNiven, 1992). This type of partnership has been termed *cross-gender* and *cross-racial mentorship*, and it entails a steeper learning curve for both mentor and mentee (Koopman & Thiedke, 2005; Smith, Smith, & Markham, 2000).

Being able to recognize unconscious bias (implicitly held beliefs about others) is always important, particularly in cross-gender and cross-racial mentoring situations (Carnes et al., 2012; Johnson & Gandhi, 2014). For example, a senior male mentor might assume that a junior female mentee will not be able to meet the academic requirements for promotion because she has young children (Bickel, 2014). Gender bias is not restricted to men; studies have shown women may be equally biased against other women in hiring and promotion processes, especially if distracted by competing cognitive tasks (Moss-Racusin, Dovidio, Brescoll, Graham, & Handelsman, 2012; Sczesny & Kuhnen, 2004; Steinpreis, Anders, & Ritzke, 1999). For this reason, some academic institutions offer training in recognizing and addressing unconscious bias and have documented positive outcomes in increasing the number of women recruited and promoted through the ranks (Carnes et al., 2015; Isaac, Lee, & Carnes, 2009). Additionally, programs such as Women in Medicine and Sciences and diversity enrichment initiatives are good networking opportunities and foster mentoring relationships for women and URM faculty. Insufficient data exist regarding specific career development needs of LGBT faculty in academic medicine or mentoring programs established for this group (Mendoza et al., 2015). A strong institutional commitment is necessary, given the strategic significance of these targeted approaches.

International medical graduates (IMGs) constitute another sizeable group of physicians practicing in the United States. According to the American Medical Association, in 2008, New York had 35,000 IMGs (representing 42% of all physicians in the state), while 25,000 IMGs (23% of the state's physicians) could be found in California (American Medical Association, 2015). Among specialties, internal medicine had the highest number of IMGs (47%), followed by psychiatry (31%), exclusive of trainees. Approximately a third of applicants vying for residency positions each year are IMGs, and this number is on the rise (National Resident Matching Program, 2015). IMGs encounter specific challenges, including social isolation, language barriers, and cultural, curricular, and health system differences compared to their countries of origin (Kramer, 2006; Rao & Yager,

2012; Sockalingam, Hawa, Al-Battran, Abbey, & Zaretsky, 2012). Both IMGs and URMs may also suffer from impostor phenomenon feelings, believing that their successes are due exclusively to hard work or luck and that others overestimate their abilities (Seritan & Mehta, 2015). Specific orientation and mentorship programs have been recommended to help IMGs as well as URMs overcome these barriers in the context of a safe learning climate (Chen et al., 2011; Tan, Hawa, Sockalingam, & Abbey, 2013). Long-term follow up studies are needed to highlight the success of these programs, correlated with faculty retention data.

BARRIERS

Many barriers to forming fruitful and lasting mentoring relationships exist in academic medicine. Commonly, for the more senior participant in the relationship, the mentor, scholarly productivity is the measure of success. Time invested in developing the type of longitudinal connection necessary to nurture the more junior partner in the relationship may translate into reduced personal productivity. Additionally, mentors are not compensated for their time and effort except for gaining personal satisfaction by contributing to the development of the protégée. Mentees also face barriers in establishing meaningful connections (Bickel, 2014; Bickel & Rosenthal, 2011; Leslie et al., 2005). This begins with the search for the appropriate mentor. For junior faculty new to the academic environment, this process is remarkably difficult. Similar challenges exist at the student and resident level in finding the right mentor and forming lasting relationships (Aagaard & Hauer, 2003; Yehia et al., 2014). Some institutions have attempted to overcome these limitations by establishing formal mentorship programs where a trainee or incoming junior faculty member is "matched" with one who is more senior. While this overcomes the immediate issue of identifying a mentor in an unfamiliar environment, it is far from perfect. At its core, successful mentorship arises from mentor-mentee interactions that have the right chemistry (Jackson et al., 2003). More often found in informal mentoring models, this chemistry seems to be the critical element leading to successful mentorship.

INGREDIENTS OF SUCCESSFUL MENTORING

Ponce and colleagues (2005) suggest three interventions to cultivate a milieu in which mentoring is valued. First, based on experiential learning theory, Ponce recommends that the mentor seek continual renewal by maintaining their own ongoing mentorship and share these experiences of expert as learner. This models the value of mentorship. The second intervention is to share the importance of multi-generational mentorship with the protégée to reinforce the importance of the obligation for the mentee to become a mentor in turn. Lastly, Ponce suggests that mentors share, introduce and encourage their mentees to seek other resources. This type of cascading mentorship model was utilized at Creighton University Health Sciences Schools and Wake Forest University School of Medicine (Kosoko-Lasaki et al., 2006) where faculty and staff mentored health professions students, who in turn mentored post-baccalaureate and undergraduate students, who then did the same for high school students. This multi-layered model is an innovative one, which may help support the pipeline of talented students to enter and stay in the health professions. Although outcome measurements were not reported, both participating mentors and mentees reported a positive mentoring atmosphere.

Successful mentorship is as much a result of good mentoring as it is related to being an ideal mentee (Sambunjak, Straus, & Marusic, 2010; Straus, Johnson, Marquez, & Feldman, 2013; Worley et al., 2006; Zerzan, Hess, Schur, Phillips, & Rigotti, 2009) (see Table 12.2). While the protégée has to overcome many of the barriers already discussed to identify the ideal mentor, there are many responsibilities to take on and a code of conduct to follow once a mentorship connection is established. To be mentored well, a protégée has to be proactive in seeking opportunities rather than waiting to be helped. Preparedness always pays off if one is looking to seize opportunities. Examples of this include being ready to pitch a research idea to a potential collaborator, giving an impromptu presentation when called upon, or stepping in to help with clinical duties if a senior colleague is in

TABLE 12.2 Ingredients of Successful Mentorship in Academic Medicine

Mentee qualities	Mentor qualities
Emotional intelligence	Emotional intelligence
• Self-awareness	• Self-awareness
• Self-monitoring	• Self-monitoring
• Self-management	• Self-management
Available, flexible	Available, flexible
Prepares agenda for each meeting	Helps mentee clarify goals
Seeks and accepts feedback	Offers honest feedback
Efficient, respectful of mentor's time	Does not compete with mentee
Gives appropriate credit to mentor	Gives appropriate credit to mentee
Maintains professional boundaries and confidentiality	Maintains professional boundaries and confidentiality

Sources: Straus et al., 2013; Worley et al., 2006; Zerzan et al., 2009

a bind. The mentee who is respectful of the mentor's time, who is grateful for the investment in their career by others, and in turn who reciprocates by mentoring others will likely have a more positive mentoring experience. Successful mentees learn to "manage up" by identifying their needs and making those clear to mentors, organizing the information in the format preferred by the mentor, being available and flexible should schedules change, asking directly how their success will be judged, and being responsive to mentors' suggestions and feedback (Zerzan et al., 2009).

Good mentors are sincere in their conversations with mentees, listen actively and understand their mentees' needs, and are fair about authorship and work performed together. The ideal mentor does not compete with mentees, is friendly while maintaining professional boundaries, observes confidentiality, and monitors mentees' progress while providing constructive feedback as appropriate (Sambunjak et al., 2010; Worley et al., 2006). As Table 12.2 illustrates, qualities of good mentors and mentees mirror each other to a certain degree.

CONCLUSION

Multiple models of formal and informal mentoring with variable institutional support exist in academic medicine. Strong evidence supports the benefits and impact of mentorship approaches in the recruitment and retention of faculty, particularly URMs and women. Close attention to unconscious bias as well as facilitation of cross-gender and cross-race mentorship ensures the success of programs for the under-mentored groups. Faculty members who are mentored report higher career satisfaction, superior scholarly productivity, and a stronger degree of institutional alignment compared to their colleagues without mentors. Multiple mentorship models exist, including traditional dyad (technical or developmental), peer, network, reverse, and even speed mentoring.

Clinician educators are still in need of structured mentorship approaches, whereas clinician scientists fare better in this area. Similarly, while solid efforts are dedicated to recruiting and supporting junior faculty, there are a limited number of programs targeting mid-career or senior faculty. Barriers to fruitful mentoring relationships may be related to intrapersonal, interpersonal, and environmental (institutional) factors. Good chemistry between the mentor-mentee pair requires certain qualities of each individual which when present promotes this constantly evolving relationship. Studies are still needed to document the long-term outcome and effectiveness of these mentorship programs.

REFERENCES

Aagaard, E. M., & Hauer, K. E. (2003). A cross-sectional descriptive study of mentoring relationships formed by medical students. *Journal of General Internal Medicine, 18*(4), 298–302.

American Medical Association. *IMGs in United States.* Retrieved from http://www.ama-assn.org/ama/pub/about-ama/our-people/member-groups-sections/international-medical-graduates/imgs-in-united-states/

Armitage, P., & Burnard, P. (1991). Mentors or preceptors? Narrowing the theory-practice gap. *Nurse Education Today, 11*(3), 225–229.

Aschenbrener, C. A., Ast, C., & Kirch, D. G. (2015). Graduate medical education: Its role in achieving a true medical education continuum. *Academic Medicine, 90*(9), 1203–1209. doi: 10.1097/ACM.0000000000000829

Beech, B. M., Calles-Escandon, J., Hairston, K. G., Langdon, S. E., Latham-Sadler, B. A., & Bell, R. A. (2013). Mentoring programs for underrepresented minority faculty in academic medical centers: A systematic review of the literature. *Academic Medicine, 88*(4), 541–549. doi: 10.1097/ACM.0b013e31828589e3

Bickel, J. (2014). How men can excel as mentors of women. *Academic Medicine, 89*(8), 1100–1102. doi: 10.1097/ACM.0000000000000313

Bickel, J., & Rosenthal, S. L. (2011). Difficult issues in mentoring: Recommendations on making the "undiscussable" discussable. *Academic Medicine, 86*(10), 1229–1234. doi: 10.1097/ACM.0b013e31822c0df7

Boudreau, J. D., Macdonald, M. E., & Steinert, Y. (2014). Affirming professional identities through an apprenticeship: Insights from a four-year longitudinal case study. *Academic Medicine, 89*(7), 1038–1045. doi: 10.1097/ACM.0000000000000293

Brandon, C., Jamadar, D., Girish, G., Dong, Q., Morag, Y., & Mullan, P. (2015). Peer support of a faculty "writers' circle" increases confidence and productivity in generating scholarship. *Academic Radiology, 22*(4), 534–538. doi: 10.1016/j.acra.2014.12.006

Bray, L., & Nettleton, P. (2007). Assessor or mentor? Role confusion in professional education. *Nurse Education Today, 27*(8), 848–855. doi: 10.1016/j.nedt.2006.11.006

Buddeberg-Fischer, B., & Herta, K. (2006). Formal mentoring programmes for medical students and doctors—a review of the Medline literature. *Medical Teacher, 28*(3), 248–257. doi: 10.1080/01421590500313043

Bussey-Jones, J., Bernstein, L., Higgins, S., Malebranche, D., Paranjape, A., Genao, I., . . . Branch, W. (2006). Repaving the road to academic success: The IMeRGE approach to peer mentoring. *Academic Medicine, 81*(7), 674–679. doi: 10.1097/01.ACM.0000232425.27041.88

Carnes, M., Devine, P. G., Baier Manwell, L., Byars-Winston, A., Fine, E., Ford, C. E., . . . Sheridan, J. (2015). The effect of an intervention to break the gender bias habit for faculty at one institution: A cluster randomized, controlled trial. *Academic Medicine, 90*(2), 221–230. doi: 10.1097/ACM.0000000000000552

Carnes, M., Devine, P. G., Isaac, C., Manwell, L. B., Ford, C. E., Byars-Winston, A., . . . Sheridan, J. T. (2012). Promoting institutional change through bias literacy. *Journal of Diversity in Higher Education, 5*(2), 63–77. doi: 10.1037/a0028128

Carraccio, C. L., Benson, B. J., Nixon, L. J., & Derstine, P. L. (2008). From the educational bench to the clinical bedside: Translating the Dreyfus developmental model to the learning of clinical skills. *Academic Medicine, 83*(8), 761–767. doi: 10.1097/ACM.0b013e31817eb632

Chen, P. G., Curry, L. A., Bernheim, S. M., Berg, D., Gozu, A., & Nunez-Smith, M. (2011). Professional challenges of non-U.S.-born international medical graduates and recommendations for support during residency training. *Academic Medicine, 86*(11), 1383–1388. doi: 10.1097/ACM.0b013e31823035e1

Chew, L. D., Watanabe, J. M., Buchwald, D., & Lessler, D. S. (2003). Junior faculty's perspectives on mentoring. *Academic Medicine, 78*(6), 652.

Coleman, V. H., Power, M. L., Williams, S., Carpentieri, A., & Schulkin, J. (2005). Continuing professional development: Racial and gender differences in obstetrics and gynecology residents' perceptions of mentoring. *Journal of Continuing Education in Health Professions, 25*(4), 268–277. doi: 10.1002/chp.40

Cook, D. A., Bahn, R. S., & Menaker, R. (2010). Speed mentoring: An innovative method to facilitate mentoring relationships. *Medical Teacher, 32*(8), 692–694. doi: 10.3109/01421591003686278

DeCastro, R., Sambuco, D., Ubel, P. A., Stewart, A., & Jagsi, R. (2013). Mentor networks in academic medicine: Moving beyond a dyadic conception of mentoring for junior faculty researchers. *Academic Medicine, 88*(4), 488–496. doi: 10.1097/ACM.0b013e318285d302

Farrell, S. E., Digioia, N. M., Broderick, K. B., & Coates, W. C. (2004). Mentoring for clinician-educators. *Academic Emergency Medicine, 11*(12), 1346–1350. doi: 10.1197/j.aem.2004.07.009

Fleming, G. M., Simmons, J. H., Xu, M., Gesell, S. B., Brown, R. F., Cutrer, W. B., . . . Cooper, W. O. (2015). A facilitated peer mentoring program for junior faculty to promote professional development and peer networking. *Academic Medicine, 90*(6), 819–826. doi: 10.1097/ACM.0000000000000705

Gabbe, S. G., Webb, L. E., Moore, D. E., Jr., Mandel, L. S., Melville, J. L., & Spickard, W. A., Jr. (2008). Can mentors prevent and reduce burnout in new chairs of departments of obstetrics and gynecology: Results from a prospective, randomized pilot study. *American Journal of Obstetrics & Gynecology, 198*(6), 653. e651–657. doi: 10.1016/j.ajog.2007.11.004

Hewlett, S. A., Peraino, K., Sherbin, L., & Sumberg, K. (2010). The sponsor effect: Breaking through the last glass ceiling. *Harvard Business Review Research Report.*

Hewlett, S. A. (2013). *Forget a mentor, find a sponsor: The new way to fast-track your career.* Boston, MA: Harvard Business Review Press.

Higgins, M. C., & Thomas, D. A. (2001). Constellations and careers: Toward understanding the effects of multiple developmental relationships. *Journal of Organizational Behavior, 22*(3), 223–247. doi: 10.2307/3649595

Illes, J., Glover, G. H., Wexler, L., Leung, A. N., & Glazer, G. M. (2000). A model for faculty mentoring in academic radiology. *Academic Radiology, 7*(9), 717–724; discussion 725–716.

Iobst, W. F., Sherbino, J., Cate, O. T., Richardson, D. L., Dath, D., Swing, S. R., . . . Frank, J. R. (2010). Competency-based medical education in post-graduate

medical education. *Medical Teacher, 32*(8), 651–656. doi: 10.3109/0142159X
.2010.500709

Isaac, C., Lee, B., & Carnes, M. (2009). Interventions that affect gender bias in hiring: A systematic review. *Academic Medicine, 84*(10), 1440–1446. doi: 10.1097/ACM.0b013e3181b6ba00

Iversen, A. C., Eady, N. A., & Wessely, S. C. (2014). The role of mentoring in academic career progression: A cross-sectional survey of the Academy of Medical Sciences mentoring scheme. *Journal of the Royal Society of Medicine, 107*(8), 308–317. doi: 10.1177/0141076814530685

Jackson, V. A., Palepu, A., Szalacha, L., Caswell, C., Carr, P. L., & Inui, T. (2003). "Having the right chemistry": A qualitative study of mentoring in academic medicine. *Academic Medicine, 78*(3), 328–334.

Johnson, K. S., Hastings, S. N., Purser, J. L., & Whitson, H. E. (2011). The junior faculty laboratory: An innovative model of peer mentoring. *Academic Medicine, 86*(12), 1577–1582. doi: 10.1097/ACM.0b013e31823595e8

Johnson, M. O., & Gandhi, M. (2014). A mentor training program improves mentoring competency for researchers working with early-career investigators from underrepresented backgrounds. *Advances in Health Science Education: Theory and Practice, 20*(3), 683–689.doi: 10.1007/s10459-014-9555-z

Kashiwagi, D. T., Varkey, P., & Cook, D. A. (2013). Mentoring programs for physicians in academic medicine: A systematic review. *Academic Medicine , 88*(7), 1029–1037. doi: 10.1097/ACM.0b013e318294f368

Koopman, R. J., & Thiedke, C. C. (2005). Views of family medicine department chairs about mentoring junior faculty. *Medical Teacher, 27*(8), 734–737. doi: 10.1080/01421590500271209

Kosoko-Lasaki, O., Sonnino, R. E., & Voytko, M. L. (2006). Mentoring for women and underrepresented minority faculty and students: Experience at two institutions of higher education. *Journal of National Medical Association, 98*(9), 1449–1459.

Kram, K. E. (1983). Phases of the mentor relationship. *Academy of Management Journal, 26*(4), 608–625. doi: 10.2307/255910

Kramer, M. (2006). Educational challenges of international medical graduates in psychiatric residencies. *Journal of the American Academy of Psychoanalysis and Dynamic Psychiatry, 34*(1), 163–171. doi: 10.1521/jaap.2006.34.1.163

Lee, J. M., Anzai, Y., & Langlotz, C. P. (2006). Mentoring the mentors: Aligning mentor and mentee expectations. *Academic Radiology, 13*(5), 556–561. doi: 10.1016/j.acra.2006.01.050

Leslie, K., Lingard, L., & Whyte, S. (2005). Junior faculty experiences with informal mentoring. *Medical Teacher, 27*(8), 693–698. doi: 10.1080/01421590500271217

Lewellen-Williams, C., Johnson, V. A., Deloney, L. A., Thomas, B. R., Goyol, A., & Henry-Tillman, R. (2006). The POD: A new model for mentoring underrepresented minority faculty. *Academic Medicine, 81*(3), 275–279.

Lieff, S., Banack, J. G., Baker, L., Martimianakis, M. A., Verma, S., Whiteside, C., & Reeves, S. (2013). Understanding the needs of department chairs in academic medicine. *Academic Medicine, 88*(7), 960–966. doi: 10.1097/ACM.0b013e318294ff36

Marks, M. B. (1999). Academic careers in medical education: Perceptions of the effects of a faculty development program. *Academic Medicine, 74*(10), S72–74.

McNiven, M. D. (1992). Study of women IMGs revealing. Many have served as role models, teachers, mentors to women US grads. *Michigan Medicine, 91*(9), 43–44.

Mellon, A., & Murdoch-Eaton, D. (2015). Supervisor or mentor: Is there a difference? Implications for paediatric practice. *Archives of Disease in Children.* doi: 10.1136/archdischild-2014-306834

Mendoza, F. S., Walker, L. R., Stoll, B. J., Fuentes-Afflick, E., St Geme, J. W., 3rd, Cheng, T. L., . . . Sectish, T. C. (2015). Diversity and inclusion training in pediatric departments. *Pediatrics, 135*(4), 707–713. doi: 10.1542/peds.2014–1653

Morzinski, J. A., Simpson, D. E., Bower, D. J., & Diehr, S. (1994). Faculty development through formal mentoring. *Academic Medicine, 69*(4), 267–269.

Moss-Racusin, C. A., Dovidio, J. F., Brescoll, V. L., Graham, M. J., & Handelsman, J. (2012). Science faculty's subtle gender biases favor male students. *Proceedings of the National Academy of Sciences U S A, 109*(41), 16474–16479. doi: 10.1073/pnas.1211286109

National Resident Matching Program. *Main residency match data.* Retrieved from http://www.nrmp.org/match-data/main-residency-match-data/

Odom, K. L., Roberts, L. M., Johnson, R. L., & Cooper, L. A. (2007). Exploring obstacles to and opportunities for professional success among ethnic minority medical students. *Academic Medicine, 82*(2), 146–153. doi: 10.1097/ACM.0b013e31802d8f2c

Palepu, A., Friedman, R. H., Barnett, R. C., Carr, P. L., Ash, A. S., Szalacha, L., & Moskowitz, M. A. (1998). Junior faculty members' mentoring relationships and their professional development in U.S. medical schools. *Academic Medicine, 73*(3), 318–323.

Pololi, L. H., Knight, S. M., Dennis, K., & Frankel, R. M. (2002). Helping medical school faculty realize their dreams: An innovative, collaborative mentoring program. *Academic Medicine, 77*(5), 377–384.

Ponce, A. N., Williams, M. K., & Allen, G. J. (2005). Toward promoting generative cultures of intentional mentoring within academic settings. *Journal of Clinical Psychology, 61*(9), 1159–1163. doi: 10.1002/jclp.20157

Ramanan, R. A., Phillips, R. S., Davis, R. B., Silen, W., & Reede, J. Y. (2002). Mentoring in medicine: Keys to satisfaction. *American Journal of Medicine, 112*(4), 336–341.

Ramanan, R. A., Taylor, W. C., Davis, R. B., & Phillips, R. S. (2006). Mentoring matters. Mentoring and career preparation in internal medicine residency training. *Journal of General Internal Medicine, 21*(4), 340–345. doi: 10.1111/j.1525–1497.2006.00346.x

Ramondetta, L. M., Bodurka, D. C., Tortolero-Luna, G., Gordinier, M., Wolf, J. K., Gershenson, D. M., & Sciscione, A. C. (2003). Mentorship and productivity among gynecologic oncology fellows. *Journal of Cancer Education, 18*(1), 15–19.

Rao, N. R., & Yager, J. (2012). Acculturation, education, training, and workforce issues of IMGs: Current status and future directions. *Academic Psychiatry, 36*(4), 268–270. doi: 10.1176/appi.ap.12050095

Rolfe, G. (1990). The role of clinical supervision in the education of student psychiatric nurses: A theoretical approach. *Nurse Education Today, 10*(3), 193–197.

Sambunjak, D., Straus, S. E., & Marusic, A. (2006). Mentoring in academic medicine: A systematic review. *JAMA, 296*(9), 1103–1115. doi: 10.1001/jama.296.9.1103

Sambunjak, D., Straus, S. E., & Marusic, A. (2010). A systematic review of qualitative research on the meaning and characteristics of mentoring in academic medicine. *Journal of General Internal Medicine, 25*(1), 72–78. doi: 10.1007/s11606-009-1165-8

Sczesny, S., & Kuhnen, U. (2004). Meta-cognition about biological sex and gender-stereotypic physical appearance: Consequences for the assessment of leadership competence. *Personality & Social Psychology Bulletin, 30*(1), 13–21. doi: 10.1177/0146167203258831

Seritan, A. L., Bhangoo, R., Garma, S., Dube, J., Park, J. H., & Hales, R. (2007). Society for women in academic psychiatry: A peer mentoring approach. *Academic Psychiatry, 31*(5), 363–366. doi: 10.1176/appi.ap.31.5.363

Seritan, A. L., & Mehta, M. M. (2015). Thorny Laurels: The impostor phenomenon in academic psychiatry. *Academic Psychiatry.* doi: 10.1007/s40596-015-0392-z

Smith, J. W., Smith, W. J., & Markham, S. E. (2000). Diversity issues in mentoring academic faculty. *Journal of Career Development, 26*(4), 251–262. doi: 10.1177/089484530002600402

Sockalingam, S., Hawa, R., Al-Battran, M., Abbey, S. E., & Zaretsky, A. (2012). Preparing international medical graduates for psychiatry residency: A multi-site needs assessment. *Academic Psychiatry, 36*(4), 277–281. doi: 10.1176/appi.ap.09110219

Staveley-O'Carroll, K., Pan, M., Meier, A., Han, D., McFadden, D., & Souba, W. (2004). Developing the young academic surgeon. *Journal of Surgical Research, 118*(2), 109–113. doi: 10.1016/j.jss.2004.02.032

Steele, M. M., Fisman, S., & Davidson, B. (2013). Mentoring and role models in recruitment and retention: A study of junior medical faculty perceptions. *Medical Teacher, 35*(5), e1130–1138. doi: 10.3109/0142159X.2012.735382

Steiner, J. F., Curtis, P., Lanphear, B. P., Vu, K. O., & Main, D. S. (2004). Assessing the role of influential mentors in the research development of primary care fellows. *Academic Medicine, 79*(9), 865–872.

Steinpreis, Rhea E., Anders, Katie A., & Ritzke, Dawn. (1999). The impact of gender on the review of the curricula vitae of job applicants and tenure candidates: A national empirical study. *Sex Roles, 41*(7/8), 509–528.

Stern, D. T., & Papadakis, M.. (2006). The developing physician—Becoming a professional. *The New England Journal of Medicine, 355*(17), 1794–1799. doi: doi:10.1056/NEJMra054783

Stoddard, D. A., Tamasy, R. J. (2009). *The heart of mentoring: Ten proven principles for developing people to their fullest potential.* Colorado Springs, CO: NavPress.

Straus, S. E., Johnson, M. O., Marquez, C., & Feldman, M. D. (2013). Characteristics of successful and failed mentoring relationships: A qualitative study across two academic health centers. *Academic Medicine, 88*(1), 82–89. doi: 10.1097/ACM.0b013e31827647a0

Taherian, K., & Shekarchian, M. (2008). Mentoring for doctors. Do its benefits outweigh its disadvantages? *Medical Teacher, 30*(4), e95–99. doi: 10.1080/01421590801929968

Tan, A., Hawa, R., Sockalingam, S., & Abbey, S. E. (2013). (Dis)orientation of international medical graduates: An approach to foster teaching, learning, and collaboration (TLC). *Academic Psychiatry, 37*(2), 104–107. doi: 10.1176/appi.ap.11040074

Wingard, D. L., Garman, K. A., & Reznik, V. (2004). Facilitating faculty success: Outcomes and cost benefit of the UCSD National Center of Leadership in Academic Medicine. *Academic Medicine, 79*(10 Suppl), S9–11.

Wise, M. R., Shapiro, H., Bodley, J., Pittini, R., McKay, D., Willan, A., & Hannah, M. E. (2004). Factors affecting academic promotion in obstetrics and gynaecology in Canada. *Journal Obstetrics and Gynaecology Canada, 26*(2), 127–136.

Worley, L. L. M., Borus, J. F., & Hilty, D. M. (2006). Being a good mentor and colleague. In L. W. Roberts, D. M. Hilty (Eds.), *Handbook of career development in academic psychiatry and behavioral sciences* (1st ed.; pp. 293–298). Washington, DC: American Psychiatric.

Yehia, B. R., Cronholm, P. F., Wilson, N., Palmer, S. C., Sisson, S. D., Guilliames, C. E., ... Sanchez, J. P. (2014). Mentorship and pursuit of academic medicine careers: A mixed methods study of residents from diverse backgrounds. *BMC Medical Education, 14*, 26. doi: 10.1186/1472-6920-14-26

Zanni, G. R. (2009). Reverse mentoring: An effective strategy for career growth. *The Consultant Pharmacist, 24*(6), 465–467.

Zerzan, J. T., Hess, R., Schur, E., Phillips, R. S., & Rigotti, N. (2009). Making the most of mentors: A guide for mentees. *Academic Medicine, 84*(1), 140–144. doi: 10.1097/ACM.0b013e3181906e8f

THE INFLUENCE OF MENTORS AND ROLE MODELS ON TEACHING AND LEARNING IN ACADEMIC MEDICINE

**Teresa J Carter, Ellen L. Brock, Frank A. Fulco,
Adam M. Garber, Reena H. Hemrajani, Bennett B. Lee,
Scott C. Matherly, Emily R. Miller, and John G. Pierce, Jr.**
Virginia Commonwealth University

In academic medicine, mentoring and role modeling have been identified as crucial roles for clinician-educators (Heflin, Pinheiro, Kaminetzky, & Mc-Neill, 2009), with effective role modeling considered an essential skill to enable professional development of learners in the clinical setting (Cruess, Cruess, Boudreau, Snell, & Steinert, 2015; Goldie, 2012; Kenny, Mann, & MacLeod, 2003). A review of literature on role modeling in medical education identified three major attributes imparted by positive role models: demonstration of high standards of clinical competence, excellence in clinical teaching skills, and humanistic personal qualities (Passi et al., 2013).

However, lack of effective, positive role models has been identified as a significant issue within the hidden curriculum of medical education in

Mentoring in Formal and Informal Contexts, pages 247–262
Copyright © 2016 by Information Age Publishing

which learners observe negative behaviors that contradict the desirable professional qualities explicitly taught (Hafferty, 1998; Hafferty & Franks, 1994). For new learners entering the clinical setting as third-year medical students, the hidden curriculum poses a significant threat to the development of professional behaviors (Wear, Aultman, Zarconi, & Varley, 2009). Bandura's (1986) seminal work on social learning theory and his concept of vicarious learning provide a sound basis for examining role modeling in medical education (Jochemsen-van der Leeuw, van Diijk, van Etten-Jamaludin, & Woeromga-de Waard, 2013). In general, the study of role modeling as an important aspect of the mentoring relationship has been underdeveloped and under-researched within mentoring literature (Lankau & Scandura, 2007). One exception has been the work of Gibson (1995) and Gibson and Cordova (1999) who studied the importance of role models as exemplars in organizations.

In academic medicine, those who are mentored include medical students and residents, physicians-in-training who hone their skills and knowledge in the hospital setting where they work under the supervision of faculty members as attending physicians. Medical students, as well as junior residents, called interns, are often taught by senior residents and fellows in addition to the supervision provided by attending physicians in the hospital. The norm for licensure as a physician in most medical specialties within the United States is seven to 10 years, four years of medical school followed by three to five of residency training. However, subspecialty or advanced fellowship training can extend the time to practice independently. These years of medical training are demanding on the physical and mental stamina required of those who enter an accredited medical school through a highly competitive selection process. As Cruess et al. (2015) note, acceptance into medical school is symbolically significant in that it begins the process of socialization into the medical profession. Within this profession, mentors and role models increase the sense of belonging, since they are members of the community of practice (Lave & Wenger, 1991) that students wish to join.

During their medical school education, students focus primarily on mastering an extensive domain of content knowledge related to human health and disease before entering the clinical setting in the third and fourth years. After four years, medical students earn the M.D. degree and they become residents in a teaching hospital. This learning environment is known for an apprenticeship-like training method often described as "see one, do one, teach one," in which each level of trainee assists with the education of juniors (Kenny, Mann, Wrixon, MacLeod, & Coles, 2002). Within professional education contexts, the training required of a physician is among the most demanding of disciplines. In recent years, residents have been limited to an 80-hour work week in an effort to increase patient safety and reduce burnout and stress (Walen & Walsh, 2011). Passing on knowledge, skills, attitudes, and values is an integral part of what it means to develop the professional identity of a doctor (Cruess et al., 2015; Kenny et al., 2003). Even the word, "doctor" has its origins in the Latin *docere*, which means "to teach" (Whitman & Schwenk, 1987). Professional identity formation in medical education has been described as a transformative learning experience that fosters personal and professional development through mentoring and self-reflection, with the goal of affirming best practices, traditions, and ethics of the profession (Holden et al., 2015; Wald, 2015).

This chapter explores mentoring and role modeling in medical education through the words of eight co-authors who are physician-educators in a large, urban academic medical center in the eastern United States. They have reflected upon why they teach as part of their own continuing professional development in a course taught by the primary chapter author. Their words illuminate some of the major themes within current research on mentoring theory and place them in the context of practice within medical education. By drawing on the experience of physicians for whom teaching is a major responsibility, our chapter examines the complex phenomena of mentoring and role modeling within the specialized context of academic medicine.

DEFINING MENTORING AND ROLE MODELING IN THE LITERATURE

Kram's (1985) pioneering research on mentoring dyads discovered two major roles of developmental relationships: career-enhancing functions that included sponsorship, coaching, protection, exposure and visibility, and the ability to provide opportunities for challenging work, and psychosocial functions. The psychosocial aspects she identified enhance a mentee's sense of competence by shaping a professional identity, and include role modeling, acceptance and confirmation, counseling, and friendship. Of these psychosocial functions, role modeling appears prominently in the medical education literature, including international journals devoted to medical education (Mirhaghi, Moonaghi, Sharafi, & Zeydi, 2015). Among scholars who have studied mentoring, McCauley and Douglas (1998) adopted a framework for classifying developmental relationships according to their propensity to provide assessment, challenge, or support for the mentee. In the early research on workplace mentoring, McCauley and Douglas, as well as Fletcher (1996), Kram and Hall (1996), and Schor (1997) recognized that the traditional concept of a longstanding dyadic mentor-mentee relationship was far more likely to be replaced in today's work environment by a network constellation of relationships, with multiple individuals fulfilling different roles. Certainly, a network view of the mentoring relationship appears relevant in medical education since the physician-in-training rotates through various clinical services in the hospital with exposure to many potential mentors and role models. In recent years, the concept of a "mentoring episode" (Fletcher & Ragins, 2007; Kram & Ragins, 2007) has addressed the growth potential of short interactions with influential others to provide brief encounters associated with intense meaning. These brief mentoring encounters appear prominently in the narratives of physician-educators in this chapter.

Lankau and Scandura (2007) elaborate upon the distinct qualities of role modeling that enable personal learning within developmental relationships, building upon Kram's (1985) findings that role modeling is a process in which the mentee adopts attitudes, approaches, and values to develop a professional identity. While Kram's (1985) schema highlights role modeling as one of many psychosocial functions of the mentoring relationship, other scholars (Gibson, 1995; Gibson and Cordova, 1999) differentiate the constructs of mentor, role model, and sponsor based on the nature of identification present for the mentee, or protégé. They draw on identification theory to assert that mentoring and sponsorship activities both depend upon interaction with and active intervention by a senior person on behalf of a mentee, whereas role modeling assumes only identification on the part of the observer. Gibson and Cordova (1999) draw upon the scholarship of Bell (1970), Kelman (1961), and Kohlberg, (1963), to associate role modeling with the desire to enhance perceived similarity to another person and to assimilate aspects of the role model's attitudes, behaviors, and values into the self. In this view, the function of role modeling is to emulate by occupying the role model's life situation (Gibson & Cordova, 1999). It is this definition of role modeling that appears in the medical education literature and will be illustrated by our examples.

IDENTIFYING WITH MENTORS AND ROLE MODELS

How do physicians go about identifying with role models or finding a mentor within their specialties? Doctors-in-training seem to look to those whom they admire: the teachers who inspired them, who energetically and enthusiastically shared their love for patients as well as those who demonstrated passion for their choice of medical specialty (Wright, Kern, Kolodner, Howard, & Brancati, 1998; Passi et al., 2013). In our examples, role models appear to be discovered by the learner through specifically remembered incidents. The learner observes the teacher in action and takes notice of his or her commitment to learners and to the profession. The trainee notices that the teacher stands out from others as exceptional in some way, and this leads the learner to assimilate characteristics of the role model. Dr. Miller's narrative illustrates both the surprise of the discovery and the effect that it had on her choice to become a pediatric endocrinologist in an academic medical center:

You hear throughout medical school and internship that being a physician means you are a "life-long learner," but no one eludes that you will also be a life-long teacher or mentor. That was a stunning insight that occurred in the second year of my residency training, when it was now my responsibility to foster interns or a team of medical students. In medical school and during most of my residency training, I aspired to be an adolescent medicine physician; however, a new pediatric endocrinology faculty member joined our team and derailed my plans. *She embodied everything I wanted to be as a doctor.* She cultivated great relationships with patients and could teach them about their diagnoses in a way that matched their background and level of education. In a lecture setting, she delivered enthusiastic, comprehensive presentations that were understandable at multiple learning stages. Most dramatically, while on [hospital] service, she required residents to read about patients and come up with their own plan rather than dictate the [management] plan herself; impressively, she would let us institute a reasonable, well-thought out plan [of care], even if it was not her exact way of practicing, as long as it did not harm the patient in any way and fit within the management scope. She was relatively fresh out of fellowship and by no means the world's expert on endocrinology, yet she was a remarkable teacher. *She became a mentor and an inspiration for me.* When I became a fellow, *I knew I wanted to bring the skills she demonstrated with me and pass on the knowledge and passion she exemplifies*... It was during that year that I fell in love with teaching myself and knew it is what I want to do as a major part of my career.

The ability to be influenced by an engaging teacher to choose a similar medical specialty has been cited as one of the benefits of a role model in medical education (Wright, Wong, & Newell, 1997). Wright and his colleagues found that exposure to role models in a particular clinical field was strongly associated with medical students' choice of clinical field for residency training. As an example of this phenomenon, Dr. Matherly studied Internal Medicine with an interest in the subspecialty of Gastroenterology. However, he readily admits the influence of his teachers in other specialties whose enthusiastic approach to their work was inspirational during his years of medical education. Matherly describes how he patterned himself after an extraordinary teacher by choosing the same residency training program to develop his specialty in Hepatology. For both Drs. Miller and Matherly, the identification was so complete that their professional identities were significantly shaped by role models who were positive influences in choosing the type of medicine they would practice. Additionally, both Miller and Matherly were inspired to become better teachers as a result. Dr. Matherly explains the desire he now has to pass on to trainees what he experienced as a result of an influential mentor and role model:

A variety of teaching techniques and mentors have shaped my teaching style over the years. There was an otolaryngologist who taught me head and neck anatomy who was a huge influence on me. His enthusiasm was so infectious that it made me want to learn more about something I didn't even think I was interested in. Later in my medical school career, I was deeply influenced by one of my Internal Medicine professors. He was fairly young, but his bedside approach to the patient was phenomenal and his physical exam skill was amazing. *I patterned my approach to the patient after him even to the point of going to the same residency [program] so that I could be trained in a similar manner.* So why do I teach? *My admiration for the teachers who have guided me in the past makes me want to emulate them.* I hope to leave my mark on the world by affecting the lives and practice of a handful of physicians. I hope that in 10 years someone will tell an anecdote about the nutty hepatologist who taught portal hypertension in such a compelling way that he inspired them to want to learn more about it. I hope somewhere, someday, a physician will choose the right thing to do for a patient rather than the easy thing to do because they remember me doing it that way. I am lucky to have a job where I can take care of the patients I love while at the same time influencing the next generation of physicians.

This desire to replicate the quality of education they experienced as learners was universal with the physician-educators who contributed perspectives in this chapter. While all medical educators are well aware that expertise does not develop in a single encounter, the spirit of "see one, do one, teach one" is deeply embedded within this community of practice as the method for transferring knowledge and skills from one generation to the next (Kenny et al., 2002). Newcomers are legitimately peripheral participants (Lave & Wenger, 1991) in the provision of medical care as beginning learners, but with developing expertise, young doctors gradually progress toward full participation as they gain experience. The community of practice that exists within the medical community thus reproduces itself through time-honored traditions of teaching at bedside and in clinical encounters with patients.

In this manner, the medical community passes on the traditions, language, culture, and associated meanings of what it means to be a doctor in our society (Kenny et al., 2003). One of the major transitions from student to full participant within this medical community appears to occur during the internship year as first-year residents assimilate what it truly means to put the needs of the patient above those of the self (E. P. Marlowe, personal communication, June 10, 2015). So much of this knowledge is embedded in tacitly acquired actions and ways of being that the socialization of a physician can be considered a major outcome of a medical education (Goldie, 2012; Kenny et al., 2003).

Developing Confidence as a Teacher

Newly minted doctors, even those who have completed years of training to earn a license to practice, can still be intimidated by the heavy responsibility of teaching the generation who are just behind them in their education as doctors. Dr. Fulco, a hospitalist in Internal Medicine, describes how he learned to manage his own expectations for the teaching role, and the influence of his former teachers in helping him to shape a philosophy of practice as a teacher:

> As a young attending, I would sometimes struggle in my teaching role. I didn't feel like I had the experience or expertise to teach a talented group of residents who were not much younger than I was. But I learned I didn't have to be a content expert and that we could learn content together. It's led me to develop a more informal, collaborative teaching style when I'm teaching on inpatient ward services. I recognize that my learners all bring prior knowledge and I view my role as trying to tease out that knowledge and build on what they already know. Working with learners at differing levels of experience, I often find myself acting as a facilitator, guiding the least experienced to build knowledge by learning from those more experienced. I'm comfortable with power being diffused and truly respect my learner's thoughts. I've been incredibly fortunate to have had a number of amazing teachers who influenced not only my decision to go into academic medicine, but also to play a significant role in my philosophy of teaching and my teaching style.

Learners also provide attending physicians in an academic medical center with the motivation to continue to stay on top of their professional knowledge and skills. Fulco describes the motivation he gains from the teaching role, realizing that he has the potential to influence students and residents, as well as benefit personally from his interactions with them. The reciprocity inherent in developmental relationships first articulated by Kram (1985) has since been confirmed by other scholars as a significant reason for mentoring in organizations (Kram & Ragins, 2007; Lankau & Scandura, 2007). In this example, Fulco explains how he benefits and why he sees this as a unique aspect of his practice as a physician in academic medicine:

> While graduating from the combined Internal Medicine/Pediatrics residency, there was a time I thought I would enter community practice. Providing direct patient care is incredibly meaningful and rewarding. *But I found sharing the process with learners made me even more mindful of the importance of patient interactions.* . . . without learners you can get caught up in the chaos and pace of clinical practice . . . If I were in private practice, I fear there would be little motivation for me to keep my clinical skills as sharp as possible. I may not remain as up to date or aware of the latest literature in the rapidly changing practice of medicine. Working with students allows me to share my enthusiasm in caring for the hospitalized patient. But probably the main reason I chose to go into academic medicine is that *I truly love working with students to share my love of learning and passion for patient care.* Learners can provide such great energy in the clinical setting—they really push me to keep learning and literally make me a better clinician.

The mutuality inherent in developmental relationships is one reason for the decision to teach; the desire to give back is another. Erikson's (1959, 1980) early work on developmental stages described the generativity that occurs in midlife for those who find fulfillment in giving back in ways that benefit the younger generation and society. For those who teach in academic medicine, generativity is a strong and rewarding aspect of investing in mentoring and role modeling within the teaching role (Humphrey, 2010).

Developing the Next Generation of Doctors

Dr. Pierce describes the yearning that a physician has to pass on his expertise, and the pride and joy of being able to do so, likening it to the parenting role, a theme Kram (1985) identified in the early research on developmental relationships.

> For me, encouraging the development of students is like a father teaching his child to ride a bicycle. There are often insecurities in pedaling without training wheels and skinned knees resulting from a crash on the road. But when the child takes off riding his bike down the street for the first time, there is no greater joy than seeing the expression of pride and accomplishment. *In teaching students or residents, I have a yearning to give what I possess to the learner.* In a recent abdominal surgery, the chief resident was perplexed because the normal anatomy was distorted and a mass was firmly affixed to the left side of the belly. The resident's eyes looked bewildered as she explained her frustration contemplating her next move. "Was she inadequate and undertrained, reaching an insurmountable surgical impossibility?" I wondered. I scrubbed for the surgery and began discussing the anatomy that we could see. She understood the principles and had practiced her surgical skills, but was blocked from further progress. With a few minutes of reassurance, encouragement, and guidance, she resumed operating. She was initially tentative then gained greater confidence as she dissected the tumor from the pelvic wall. After the mass was excised and the surgery complete, I saw again the smile and countenance of a child who had ridden her bike for the first time. *"I knew I could do that. Thanks for the help!"*

Traditionally, mentoring relationships, particularly dyadic ones involving a more senior mentor and a junior learner, contain aspects of the parent-child dynamic described in Dr. Pierce's surgical encounter. Kram (1985) found that relationships were developmental when they were mutually beneficial, not a one-way giving or receiving. This mutuality has been further refined in the Stone Center's work in developing Relational-Cultural Theory of mentoring (Fletcher & Ragins, 2007). In Pierce's example, both individuals found fulfillment in their roles as teacher and learner: the trainee expressed pride and a sense of accomplishment upon successfully completing a difficult surgery, and the mentor expressed his joy at her being able to do so. Kram's (1985) research indicated that mentor and mentee would often liken their relationship to a significant familial one from earlier years in which "psychological mechanisms, shaped by earlier life experiences, give a particular importance, character, and potency to a developmental relationship" (p. 69). In this way, the generativity associated with developing the skills and knowledge of a young doctor resembles the care of the parent for the child, wanting her to develop into a fully competent surgeon. Similarly, Dr. Fulco, a hospitalist in Internal Medicine, expresses the desire to mentor the next generation of doctors as rewarding because it contributes to the development of future health care providers:

> The mentoring relationships that develop in academic medicine are so rewarding. Seeing students and residents grow over time—from medical school through residency and sometimes [becoming] faculty is an incredibly gratifying feeling. Like many teachers, *my hope is that in some way I may be making the world a better place* by teaching the next generation of health care providers.

Learning from Negative Role Models in the Hidden Curriculum

Occasionally, the influence of role models is not positive. Negative role models have been identified as nonetheless an important aspect of learning how not to act, and how not to behave in the literature on mentoring and role modeling (Gibson, 1995; Wear et al., 2009). Within medical education, this aspect of "passing on" undesirable and unprofessional behaviors is considered to be part of the hidden curriculum, an unintended consequence of observation of poor role models within the medical education environment. Some scholars claim that the hidden curriculum, that which is not explicitly taught but is learned through informal and incidental learning encounters, overshadows much of what the formal curriculum attempts to impart, particularly when it comes to learning about professional ways of engaging with patients, families, and colleagues in the health professions. As Kenny et al. (2003) note, "role modeling remains one crucial area where standards are elusive and where repeated negative learning experiences may adversely impact the development of professionalism in medical students and residents" (p. 1203).

At least two of the physician co-authors vividly recall memorable encounters with educators who provided lessons of what not to do or how not to engage with a patient. Dr. Matherly notes that observation of role models does not end with the conclusion of a formal educational experience, but is something that continues throughout one's professional career as a method for extracting valuable lessons about how to be a more effective teacher:

> As I have moved forward in my training, I find myself looking critically at different teachers' techniques. I have watched world leaders in a subject completely fail at getting a point across because they spend too much time showing off the depths of their vast knowledge without tailoring the teaching to their audience. The end result of this is that the learner feels overwhelmed and dumb or simply in awe of the speaker without gaining any tangible knowledge. I have watched enthusiastic lecturers present their material in such a scattered manner that the audience is lost. I have learned from these experiences and used them to make myself a stronger teacher.

In an incident he still vividly remembers, Dr. Garber describes what he learned about being attuned to the needs of the learner from the powerful example of a teacher who did not seem to care. This example of negative role modeling is a memory that has stayed with Garber, and he uses it to inform his own actions about how a teacher should behave. With this negative example of role modeling and personal recollection of its effects, Garber not only strives to identify with the learners' needs, but he also makes a special effort to "walk in their shoes." As a young attending physician who is relatively new to academic medicine, he uses this episode to inform a developing philosophy of practice for teaching that includes being a different kind of role model for his learners.

> While I can highlight many excellent teachers and mentors, I can also remember the teachers who were unable to connect with me as a learner and were poor teaching models. My science lab instructor made an impact on me for all the wrong reasons. While chemistry was not the most thrilling of topics to teach, he did not seem to care about us as learners. He would often explain complex topics too quickly, flashing slides faster than anyone could read or take notes, and he would not entertain questions during the lecture or at the end of class. As learners, we tried to adapt to his teaching style, a seemingly impossible task that led many of us to bring voice recorders to class in order to listen to the lecture again later at our own pace. It was extremely challenging and frustrating. I felt discouraged and as though I was set up to fail, not succeed. *I will never forget this experience, which is the antithesis of what I try to do in creating a teaching style and learning environment.* While I may be a relatively new teacher, I feel as though I have a fresh perspective on what works best in these clinical settings and what pitfalls, difficult topics, and issues my fellow medical students and residents will struggle with during their training. *I feel as though I can put myself in my learners' shoes, whether it is their first week of medical school or their last few days of residency.*

The ability to empathize with learners is significant within the psychosocial functions of a developmental relationship. Guillemin and Gillam (2015) describe the emotionally laden environment of clinical care as creating a special toll on health care providers, as well as their patients. Learning to deal with the emotional content of clinical practice is an important aspect of developing a professional identity that involves influencing trainees, and being influenced by them, as well.

Influencing and Being Influenced as a Learner

This desire to influence doctors-in-training by becoming a physician-educator did not emerge as a fully fleshed out idea for many chapter co-authors when they first began their medical careers. It was, instead, part of their own trajectory of growth as a medical professional that emerged through the influence of teachers as role models and mentors. The reasons for this early lack of identification with the teaching role were diverse: not envisioning themselves as the "expert" educator, or not wanting to relinquish the personal contact with patients by sharing the role of physician with trainees. Dr. Hemrajani, an internist, describes her initial reluctance to imagine a career as a medical educator and the influence of a role model who taught her what it truly meant to care for patients:

> On entering medical school, my major focus was to become a physician to care directly for patients each and every day; I did not envision teaching students or residents as a part of my future endeavors. At the time, I would have thought of that learner as a distancing measure between my patients and me. The medical school I attended was a brand new school . . . It was in this setting that my eyes were opened to the value of a good teacher because of the way my teachers inspired and molded me into the physician I wanted to be. They didn't just teach me history or physical exam skills; they taught me about the art of medicine. One of my Family Medicine preceptors taught me what it meant to care for patients like friends. Almost anyone can teach a simple fact that a learner will remember right after being told it, but only some teachers can create a valuable connection between what they are trying to teach and the learner's experience to create a lasting effect.

Occasionally, it is the role modeling of physician parents who influence the desire to teach in academic medicine. "Legacy" physicians are those who enter their training as the sons and daughters of physicians. Within the medical profession, following in the footsteps of mom or dad is not uncommon. Medically trained parents can have enormous influence on career decisions of their children; they can also be inspiring teachers as well as larger-than-life role models and mentors. Dr. Lee recalls the memory of his father as a teacher and the influence he had on him:

> My father was often known for using the phrase, 'I don't know, what you think?' He would use this phrase with surgical residents and students. Of course, he would already know the answer, but would use this to develop thought and reasoning skills within his learners. He would also use this with me and my sister, and we would groan and ask him to just tell us the answer. He was well known for constantly asking questions of the residents and would tell us that this was his Socratic method. To this day, his former trainees tell me how much my father's teaching influenced them and how much they appreciated his method of teaching. I think my parents' appreciation for academics and teaching stuck with me as I was considering my career, as well.

When faced with a parent who was well-known for his pioneering work as a transplant surgeon, the experiences others had under the influence of his father as a teacher contributed to Dr. Lee's sense of his father as a role model:

> One of the comments I hear about my father as a teacher that sticks with me is how he taught. When I was a [medical] student, the surgeons were famous for being hard-nosed, and, at times, downright mean and intimidating. They would 'pimp' [an aggressive form of incessant questioning] you endlessly, and would even challenge each other ruthlessly in their Death and Complications conference. One of the comments that I have often heard about my father, which has greatly influenced me, is that he was never rude or condescending toward students or residents. He was famous for keeping his cool and calmly and quietly asking questions and encouraging his learners to reason through answers. Once they had answered, he would praise what was correct and quietly encourage his learners to try again if they were incorrect. One of his former students told me that my father had a quiet confidence that commanded the respect of his students and peers. He did not need to rant or rave or use gimmicks to teach. I hope to one day achieve that same sort of quiet confidence that allows me to engage my learners and also instill in them the same quiet confidence about what they have learned.

The relationship with a father can also be a little daunting for the physician-educator who aspires to become like him. Dr. Lee expresses both awe and appreciation for the many role models in his life, including the influence of his physician parents. Significantly, what he extracts from these relationships is the desire to not ever let his learners down, but to be responsible to them as learners.

> I am often intimidated by the thought that I need to measure up to the expectations of my learners. I sometimes wonder if my teachers over the years had that same sense of intimidation or intense feeling of responsibility. *I have*

developed an increasingly strong feeling of not wanting to let my students down. I want them to have a meaningful experience that helps them transform themselves. When I look back at my most valued teachers, including my parents, I think that they had these feelings and a strong sense of responsibility towards their learners.

Appreciating Mentors and Role Models: The Sum of My Learning

These illustrations of mentoring and role modeling are descriptions from the lived experiences of physician-educators, all of whom have chosen to pursue their medical careers in a teaching hospital. They were asked to write a paper as part of a professional development course about the experiences that contributed to career decisions to teach in academic medicine. For many of them, what emerged was a description of the major, and life-changing, influence of role models and mentors on their own career choices, as well as their own desires to pass on what they had received during their medical education.

While the function of role modeling is well-documented in the medical education literature (Cruess et al., 2015; Cruess, Cruess, & Steinert, 2008; Kenny et al., 2003; Maudsley, 2001; Passi et al., 2013; Wright et al., 1998), role modeling, as a particular psychosocial element within developmental relationships, is an under-represented and under-researched concept within the extensive body of research and practice on mentoring across disciplines and areas of practice (Lankau & Scandura, 2007). For physicians, however, role modeling appears to be an essential experience that enables them to become a doctor. It involves extracting skills, knowledge, attitudes, values, and ethical beliefs through the extensive apprenticeship of clinical training. More importantly, it results in the formation of a professional identity that is transmitted from generation to generation about what it means to be a physician in our society (Goldie, 2012; Wald, 2015). For those who are exemplars and represent the noble of qualities associated with this profession, this identity embraces selfless care for patients and the mantra to do no harm. Dr. Brock describes the cumulative effect of a lifetime of influential role models and mentors, reflecting on their significance for her development as a person, as well as a teacher and a surgeon.

What if Margaret Brock hadn't instilled in me in early life the value of teaching? What if Wilma Bowie hadn't made mathematical problem solving engaging and fun? What if Gwen McCall hadn't made the words of Shakespeare and Dickens come alive for us by having us read and perform them, and discover their meaning? What if Tom Nassar (intimidating though he was) hadn't made us discover how atoms and molecules work and how they become the substance of all things? What if Steve Cohen hadn't shown me how to stop hemorrhage in a pelvis, and then made sure that I could do it independently? What if my resident hadn't put a laparoscopic instrument through a transverse colon, causing an injury that made crystal clear the moral imperative for our department that we ensure the skills mastery of our trainees prior to operating room experience? We are the sum of our experiences, and I am in no small measure the sum of what I learned from the great teachers in my life. I teach because it is so gratifying to have a similar place in the lives of my students…because it is a necessary part of carrying on the legacy of my profession.

REFERENCES

Bandura, A. (1986). *Social foundations of thought and action: A social cognitive theory.* Englewood Cliffs, NJ: Prentice Hall.

Bell, A. P. (1970). Role modelship and interaction in adolescence and young adulthood. *Developmental Psychology, 2,* 123–128.

Cruess, R. L., Cruess, S. R., Boudreau, D., Snell, L., & Steinert, Y. (2015). A schematic representation of the professional identity formation and socialization of medical students and residents: A guide for medical educators. *Academic Medicine, 90*(6), 718–724. doi: 10.1097/ACM.00000000000000719

Cruess, S. R., Cruess, R. L., & Steinert, Y. (2008). Role modelling—Making the most of a powerful teaching strategy. *British Medical Journal, 336,* 718–721. doi: 10.1136/bmj.39503.757847.BE

Erikson, E. H. (1959/1980). *Identity and the life cycle.* New York, NY: Norton.

Fletcher, J. K. (1996). A relational approach to the protean worker. In D. T. Hall & Associates (Eds.), *The career is dead—Long live the career: A relational approach to careers* (pp. 105–131). San Francisco, CA: Jossey-Bass.

Fletcher, J. K., & Ragins, B. R. (2007). Stone Center Relational Cultural Theory: A window on relational mentoring. In B. R. Ragins & K. E. Kram (Eds.), *The handbook of mentoring at work: Theory, research, and practice* (pp. 373–399). Thousand Oaks, CA: Sage.

Gibson, D. E. (1995). *Individual idols, organizational ideals: Role models in organizations.* Available from ProQuest Dissertations & Theses Global. (Order No. 9601397)

Gibson, D. E., & Cordova, D. L. (1999). Women's and men's role models: The importance of exemplars. In A. J. Murrell, F. J. Crosby, & R. J. Ely (Eds.), *Mentoring dilemmas: Developmental relationships within multicultural organizations* (pp. 121–141). Mahwah, NJ: Erlbaum.

Goldie, J. (2012). The formation of professional identity in medical students: Considerations for educators. *Medical Teacher, 34,* e641–e648. doi: 10.3109/0142159/X.2012.687476

Guillemin, M., & Gillam, L. (2015). Emotions, narratives, and ethical mindfulness. *Academic Medicine, 90*(6), 726–731. doi: 10.1097/ACM.0000000000000709

Hafferty, F. W. (1998). Beyond curriculum reform: Confronting medicine's hidden curriculum. *Academic Medicine, 73*(4), 403–407.

Hafferty, F. W., & Franks, R. (1994). The hidden curriculum, ethics teaching, and the structure of medical education. *Academic Medicine, 69*(11), 861–871.

Heflin, M. T., Pinheiro, S., Kaminetzky, C. P., & McNeill D. (2009). "So you want to be a clinician-educator...": Designing a clinician-educator curriculum for internal medicine residents. *Medical Teacher, 31*, e233–e240.

Holden, M. D., Buck, E., Luk, J., Ambriz, F., Boisaubin, E.V., Clark, M. A.,....Dalrymple, J. L. (2015, June). Professional identity formation: Creating a longitudinal framework through TIME (Transformation in Medical Education). *Academic Medicine, 90*(6), 761–767. doi: 10.1097/ACM.0000000000000719

Humphrey, H. J. (2010). Fundamentals of mentoring and professional development. In H. J. Humphrey (Ed.), *Mentoring in academic medicine* (pp. 35–50). Chicago, IL: American College of Physicians.

Jochemsen-van der Leeuw, H. G. A., van Dijk, N., van Etten-Jamaludin, F. S., & Wieringa-de Waard, M. (2013). The attributes of the clinical trainer as role model: A systemic review of the literature. *Academic Medicine, 88*, 26–34. doi: 10.1097/ACM.0b013e318276d070

Kelman, H. C. (1961). Processes of opinion change. *Public Opinion Quarterly, 25*, 57–78.

Kenny, N. P., Mann, K. V., & MacLeod, H. (2003). Role modeling in physicians' professional formation: Reconsidering an essential but untapped educational strategy. *Academic Medicine, 78*(12), 1203–1210.

Kenny, N. P., Mann, K. V., Wrixon, W., MacLeod, H., & Coles, C. (2002, August). See one, do one, teach one: Role models and the CanMEDS Competencies. Paper presented at the Association for Medical Education in Europe (AIMEE) Conference, Lisbon, Portugal.

Kohlberg, L. (1963). Moral development and identification. In H. W. Stevenson (Ed.), *Child psychology: The sixty-second yearbook of the national society for the study of education (Part I)* (pp. 277–332). Chicago, IL: University of Chicago Press.

Kram, K. E. (1985). *Mentoring at work: Developmental relationships in organizational life* (2nd ed). Landam, MD: University Press of America.

Kram, K. E., & Hall, D. T. (1996). Mentoring in the context of diversity and turbulence. In E. E. Kossek & S. A. Lobel (Eds.), *Managing diversity: Human resource strategies for transforming the workplace* (pp. 108–136). Cambridge, MA: Blackwell Business.

Kram, K. E., & Ragins, B. R. (2007). The landscape of mentoring in the 21st century. In B. R. Ragins & K. E. Kram (Eds.), *The handbook of mentoring at work: Theory, research, and practice* (pp. 659–692). Thousand Oaks, CA: Sage.

Lankau, M. J., & Scandura, T. A. (2007). Mentoring as a forum for personal learning in organizations. In B. R. Ragins & K. E. Kram (Eds.), *The handbook of mentoring at work: Theory, research, and practice* (pp. 95–122). Thousand Oaks, CA: Sage.

Lave, J., & Wenger. E. (1991). *Situated learning: Legitimate peripheral participation.* Cambridge, England: Cambridge University Press.

Maudsley, R. F. (2001). Role models and the learning environment: Essential elements in effective medical education. *Academic Medicine, 76*(5), 432–434.

McCauley, C. D., & Douglas, C. A. (1998). Developmental relationships. In D. D. McCauley, R. S. Moxley, & E. Van Velsor, E. (Eds.), *Handbook of leadership development* (pp. 160–193). Greensboro, NC: The Center for Creative Leadership.

Mirhaghi, A., Moonaghi, K., Sharafi, S., & Zeydi, A. (2015). Role modeling: A precious heritage in medical education. *Scientific Journal of the Faculty of Medicine in Nis, 32*(1), 31–42. doi:10.1515/afmnai-2015-0003

Passi, V., Johnson, S., Peile, E., Wright, S., Hafferty, F., & Johnson, N. (2013). Doctor role modelling in medical education: BEME Guide No. 27. *Medical Teacher, 35*, e1422–e1436.

Schor, S. M. (1997, September-October). Separate and unequal: The nature of women's and men's career-building relationships. *Business Horizons, 40*(5), 51–58.

Wald, H. S., (2015). Professional identity (trans)formation in medical education: Reflection, relationship, resilience. *Academic Medicine, 90*(6), 701–706. doi: 10.1097/ACM.00000000000000719

Walen, T., & Walsh, W. (2011). Going beyond duty hours: A focus on patient safety. In *The 2011 ACGME duty hour standards: Enhancing quality of care, supervision, and resident professional development* (pp. 69–74). Chicago, IL: Accreditation Council for Graduate Medical Education.

Wear, D., Aultman, J. M., Zarconi, J., & Varley, J. D. (2009). Derogatory and cynical humour directed towards patients: Views of residents and attending doctors. *Medical Education, 43*(1), 34–41. doi:10.1111/j.1365-2923.2008.03171.x

Whitman, N. A., & Schwenk, T. L. (1987). *The physician as teacher*. Salt Lake City, UT: Whitman Associates.

Wright, S., Wong, A., & Newell, C. (1997). The impact of role models on medical students. *Journal of General Internal Medicine, 12*(1), 53–56.

Wright, S. M., Kern, D. E., Kolodner, K., Howard, D. M., & Brancati, F. L. (1998). Attributes of excellent attending-physician role models. *The New England Journal of Medicine, 339*(27), 1986–1993.

CHAPTER 14

INFORMAL MENTORING IN NURSING

Theresa Criscitelli
Winthrop-University Hospital

John C. Maxwell, a great American leader and author, stated "There is no greater accomplishment for mentors than when people they develop pass them by!" In the critical state of healthcare, this altruistic belief of mentoring can be challenging and seem like an almost impossible undertaking, but mentoring has been identified as an invaluable tool. Mentoring in nursing can attract and retain nurse leaders, increase career satisfaction and development, transfer clinical skills, and provide feedback for novice nurses (Aston & Hallam, 2011; Hodgson & Scanlan, 2013; Mariani, 2012). The antecedents of mentoring in nursing dates back to the founder of modern nursing, Florence Nightingale, who described herself as a 'mentor of matrons' (Lorentzon & Brown, 2003).

The structure of a mentoring program can take on many different formats and contexts, ranging from formal to informal. Formal mentoring involves assigning a specific mentor to a mentee or protégé. This relationship, or dyad, has been successfully noted in the nursing literature. Studies with novice and expert nurse educators report an increase in open communication, guidance, support in new roles, and collegiality (Eller, Lev,

Mentoring in Formal and Informal Contexts, pages 263–277
Copyright © 2016 by Information Age Publishing

& Feurer, 2014). The context of formal mentoring has several attributes including the design to accomplish specific goals, the oversight of a coordinator, the evaluation of progress, and the finite duration of the relationship (Meier, 2013). Most often, this traditional form of mentoring provides formal mentors and is a prearranged relationship. While formal programs are very important and effective, much of the daily learning that takes place with learners at all levels occurs in a more informal context (Meier, 2013).

Due to the current state of healthcare, informal mentoring relationships are much needed at all levels of nursing. Healthcare reform, regulatory constraints, high unemployment rates, and a nursing shortage have contributed to a precarious environment. Approximately one-third of nurses in the United States are over 50 years old, with the average age of nurses increasing by almost two years for registered nurses over the past decade (HRSA, 2013). This trend can intensify as the need for health care grows due to the population of baby boomers aging.

INFORMAL MENTORING

Informal mentoring occurs every day and most often goes unidentified and unnoticed. Informal mentoring in nursing is often voluntary by nature and fostered by common interests and shared encounters. Many times, informal mentoring relationships provide information and support, guide careers, enhance skills, and increase knowledge (Meier, 2013). Informal mentoring is spontaneous and can be infinite in duration. It is quite common for nurses to create these informal mentoring relationships whether or not there is a formal mentoring program in place (Mariani, 2012). Therefore, if established, these types of informal relationships can augment the benefits of formal mentoring programs or informally provide the necessary support for nurses at any point in their careers. It is important to examine the literature to better understand the place that mentoring has had in nursing and how it can be enhanced to address changes in healthcare.

THE ROLE OF MENTORING IN NURSING

The role of mentoring in nursing has been to provide professional networking, feedback, and support (Baxley, Ibitayo, & Bond, 2014). It has also been a factor in fostering career development and job satisfaction (Mariani, 2012). This transcends clinical practice, nursing professional development and education, administration, and research. Concerns about a national nursing shortage, an aging workforce, and a global shortage of nursing professionals educated at the baccalaureate level and beyond makes it important to cultivate formal and informal mentoring programs (Grossman, 2013). Nursing leadership must identify viable options to develop and sustain present nurse leaders. Mentoring programs can provide the necessary structure to create these much-needed resources for nurse leaders (Hodgson & Scanlan, 2013).

Different types of mentoring are necessary during varying aspects of a nursing career, not only for the more traditional experiences such as career development, scholarship, and personal development, but for transition into practice, role acquisition, socialization, and support for new employees (Meier, 2013). Therefore, it is important to consider different contexts and methods of delivery that can complement the many aspects of nursing.

Barriers to effective mentoring exist in healthcare that include time constraints, lack of support from senior leadership, the culture of an organization, attributes of the job that do not lend itself to mentoring, and lack of understanding of the level of the mentee (Baxley, Ibitayo, & Bond, 2014). International nurses have found additional barriers such as cultural differences, language proficiency, and communication nuances that inhibit successful mentoring (Xu & He, 2012).

As careers in healthcare progress, the more seasoned nurse may consider other contexts for a mentoring relationship such as co-mentoring and global mentoring. Co-mentoring can be defined as "a mutual mentorship of a pair of close, collegial friends committed to facilitating each other's development" (Rymer, 2002, p. 343). This type of mentoring can transform healthcare and facilitate relationships in nursing practice, academia, and even partnerships between both entities (Mixer et al., 2012). Co-mentoring relationships exhibit qualities of shared decision making, a level hierarchy, mutual respect, and reciprocal collaboration (Diamond, 2010; Hunt, 2011; Mixer, 2011). This "trusted friend" type of relationship can strengthen the discipline of nursing in many ways and provide mutual benefits for all involved. When considering informal mentoring, it is important to use a framework that can create structure and process. Therefore, the framework can be considered a roadmap to assist in guiding the mentoring process. This will help evaluate the outcomes more accurately and potentially make them easier to attain.

INFORMAL MENTORING FRAMEWORKS

A framework of competency can be used in an informal mentoring relationship in order to assess learning accurately. Even though informal mentoring has interactions that are not well-documented, these collegial exchanges play a substantial role in learning at all levels of nursing. A framework can provide the mentor with a descriptive illustration of where the learner should be at different points in a career. For example, it is imperative not to mentor a novice nurse the same way one would mentor a seasoned nurse. The learning needs and acquisition of knowledge is quite different between the two (Benner, 2000). A mentor that can identify and quantify the different levels of a nurses' development will have greater success in the informal mentoring relationship. Two models, the Dreyfus and Dreyfus Skill Acquisition Model (1980, 1986), and the Informal Incidental Learning model (Marsick & Watkins, 1999), provide a frame for understanding and implementing informal mentoring relationships.

The Skill Acquisition Model

The Dreyfus and Dreyfus skill acquisition model (1980, 1986) identifies five levels of skill development for a learner; novice, advanced beginner, competent, proficient, and expert. Benner (2000) further utilized this model in nursing to define different levels of practice. According to the skill acquisition model (Dreyfus & Dreyfus, 1980, 1986), skills are learned by experience. A mentor can facilitate the learning by helping the mentee make sense of their experiences, by guiding them through reflection, and providing supportive feedback to challenge the learner at each stage (Peno & Silva Mangiante, 2012). Therefore, it is imperative that skills are practiced and the reflection and feedback cycle continue. An informal mentoring relationship based upon the skill acquisition model will help the mentor understand the mentee's professional development needs along the way. The mentor will be able to provide the mentee with appropriate information based upon the developmental level of the mentee.

Novice nurses rely upon discrete facts with little or no context. This learner looks for clear and cogent guidelines to follow with set expectations and expected outcomes clearly provided (Benner, 2000). Therefore, an informal mentor might provide a mentee with opportunities for goal setting, regular feedback, and suggested performance adjustments. This may involve discussing basic theories and principles that can lead to higher level decision making and skill in an actual or simulated setting (Benner, 2000). This formative feedback is necessary for the novice nurse to build confidence and move to the advanced beginner level.

Advanced beginner nurses have more practical experience than novices and are beginning to distinguish similarities of situations from prior experiences (Benner, 2000; Dreyfus & Dreyfus, 1980). Therefore, the mentor needs to focus on assisting with these connections and providing formative feedback (Peno & Silva Mangiante, 2012). Together the mentor and mentee navigate situations that still challenge the mentee.

A *Competent* nurse learns through situational experiences and will adopt a hierarchical process of decision making (Dreyfus & Dreyfus, 1986; Lyon, 2015). Since the competent nurse can make decisions based upon a vast amount of concrete experiences, more complexity and volume can be managed in a learning encounter (Benner, 2000). Therefore, the informal mentor should challenge the nurse through goal setting and creating a purposeful learning environment. A purposeful learning environment will focus on using available information to solve problems, and ramifications of practice (Benner, 2000; Peno & Silva Mangiante, 2012). While in this level, the competent nurse becomes vested in the outcomes and feels responsible for personal actions. Reflective experiences are useful, as well as high fidelity and low fidelity simulation (Decker et al., 2013; Neill & Wotton, 2011). High fidelity and low fidelity simulation is a technique to replace or enhance actual experiences with guided experiences (Gaba, 2004). This technique is used to engage the learner in clinical scenarios that construct actual clinical circumstances. Reflection upon the learners' actions during the scenario is conducted with a debriefing period where learners can reflect upon their actions and discuss alternatives or ways to improve upon their clinical decision making.

Proficient nurses are able to recognize situations, distinguish similarities or dissimilarities from prior experiences, and act upon the situation based upon prior successful outcomes (Dreyfus & Dreyfus, 1986; Lyon, 2015). Informal mentors should challenge the mentee with case-scenario learning experiences, reflective exercises, and simulation training of high risk, low volume scenarios. This will further help the nurse grow professionally and challenge them to move to the next level of skill acquisition.

Expert nurses are fully engaged with appropriate reactive responses, ownership of outcomes, and a high level of creativity to respond to any type of situation (Dreyfus & Dreyfus, 1986; Lyon, 2015). Informal mentees at this level require little guidance, but may bring more leadership and communication issues forward, as opposed to technical and situational queries. The expert nurse may benefit from advice regarding leadership, self-appraisal, and academic advancement. Since expert nurses have a high level of intuition and vast experiences, many times they know exactly what they need and will ask outright (Benner, 2000).

Informal and Incidental Learning Model

Understanding the level of the nurse is paramount, but also understanding how learning occurs in everyday work and the implications of an informal mentor on a daily basis is vital. A model that can provide insight and is easily applicable in the healthcare setting is the Informal and Incidental Learning model (Marsick & Watkins, 1999; Marsick, Watkins & O'Connor, 2011). Marsick and Watkins (1999) define informal learning as self-directed learning, networking, coaching, mentoring, and performance planning. Many times informal mentoring occurs in this type of context. This type of learning can be considered by the learner as very unstructured and incidental in nature. Therefore, the learner must see a need to learn, be motivated, and have an opportunity to learn (Marsick & Watkins, 1999). Since learning occurs from everyday events and encounters, it is important for the learner to make sense of a situation. This can bring new insight to the learner. Since everyone is unique, each person interprets context differently, which will alter a person's actions. Experience can potentially lead to a successful outcome. Also, if a new skill needs to be learned, even though the outcome may take time or be challenging, it ultimately will be accomplished. Appropriate resources (i.e., time, materials, knowledge, funding), willingness, motivation, and emotional capacity can affect solutions. The aforementioned resources can either support or constrain learning and mentoring.

It is difficult to link informal learning to performance outcomes (Werquin, 2010). Context affects choices and learning practices. Watkins, Marsick, and de Alava (2014) stated that relationships are key contributing factors to building informal learning environments. These environments of informal mentoring in healthcare can take on many different forms. Combining both the level of proficiency of the nurse and the understanding of how adults learn in an informal context can create a rich learning environment for an array of learners (Benner, 2000; Watkins et al., 2014). Therefore, nursing students, novice nurses, and experienced nurses using the Informal and Incidental Learning Model (Marsick & Watkins, 1999) can all learn from the informal mentor at a different level. The mentor can foster learning through daily experiences and help the learner associate meaning to prior knowledge and experiences. This will engage the learner and assist in developing the learner through different levels. The next sections of this chapter address informal mentoring of different levels of nurses from student through practicing nurse. The Dreyfus and Dreyfus model (1980, 1986) as well as the Marsick and Watkins model (1999) are discussed in context as well as the resources and evaluation aspects of informal mentoring for nurse development.

MENTORING NURSING STUDENTS

Nursing students can benefit from academic mentors who provide guidance and support throughout the rigor of the academic setting (Eby et al., 2013). These informal mentors provide academic support, act as a scholarly resource, support professional development, and inform regarding career-relevant support. Depending upon the relationship, these mentors may also confer emotional support and psychological assistance through the educational process.

Applying the Frameworks

It is important to consider the Dreyfus and Dreyfus (1980) skill acquisition model when working with nursing students. A nursing student would be at the novice level and require reasonable adjustment time to not only understand the basic principles, but also to be able to make sense of the context of these principles. A nursing student only has had exposure to abstract principles and lacks concrete experiences that would help create understanding of a particular context. This type of learner is very task driven and needs guidelines and rules to follow. By creating meaning, the learner better understands the purpose and becomes motivated to learn (Marsick & Watkins, 1999). The Informal and Incidental learning model supports the premise that informal mentoring is in an unstructured context (Marsick & Watkins, 1999; Marsick et al., 2011). Therefore, the learner needs to be self-motivated and personally responsible to seek out learning experiences.

Resources

Resources for the nursing student should be based upon their skill level. Resources might include checklists, procedural videos, return demonstration of basic skill acquisition (i.e., Teach back), and repetition in a safe and nurturing environment. These resources will influence academic growth and increased knowledge.

Students with a disability require additional understanding and resources. There is equality legislation that protects these students from direct and indirect discrimination (Tee & Cowen, 2012). Higher education institutions are required by law to proactively work toward ensuring the most optimum learning environment for students with disabilities. Informal mentors could foster a culture of empathetic understanding, be supportive, and tolerant to optimize learning (Tee & Cowen, 2013). It is a challenge to assure consistency within informal mentoring relationships, but the culture of the higher education institution should nurture and promote this type of relationship.

Interprofessional mentoring can be utilized with nursing students, which comprises different disciplines participating in mentoring an individual (Lait, Suter, Arthur, & Deutschlander, 2011). Interprofessional collaboration and education occurs often in healthcare settings since multiple healthcare professionals and students work together to deliver care to patients and families. These interactions can lead to informal interprofessional mentoring experiences. They are content specific and informal by nature and are most often used for clinical skill development. They can also help students identify different roles, disciplines, and health professions. Most importantly, they can teach how to provide patient-centered care in a collaborative fashion. The body of literature on interprofessional mentoring is rapidly developing and has proven to enhance clinical learning (Aston, 2011; Lait et al., 2011).

Evaluation

Evaluating the nursing student by the informal mentor requires an understanding of the level of skill acquisition coupled with the way informal learning occurs (Marsick & Watkins, 1999). Since nursing students lack the ability to discern judgment in many different situations, the evaluation of their learning is also challenging for the informal mentor. Simulation labs where an informal mentor works with a nursing student provide an opportunity to create different clinical scenarios that can be repeated and reflected upon to foster learning. Also, the mentor can question the mentee regarding sequencing of procedures and provide the mentor with verbal confirmation that the mentee clearly understands. An example of this would be asking the mentee to explain the steps in removing an intravenous tube. The mentee would have to verbalize the supplies and equipment necessary and then explain the steps sequentially that are necessary to perform this nursing skill.

MENTORING THE STAFF NURSE

The transition from a student nurse to a staff nurse in the professional nursing practice setting has a host of challenges. Research suggests that this transition is laden with anxiety, uncertainty, and a lack of confidence (Baumberger-Henry, 2012). The support of informal mentoring at this juncture can facilitate professional socialization and integration into the practice environment. This type of mentoring can be a critical element in a successful transition. It is important for a novice nurse to have strong role models and have a supportive environment in which to ask questions and learn (Benner, 2000).

Applying the Framework

The novice staff nurse is similar to a nursing student due to the lack of experience in different contexts, but the novice can move quickly to the advanced beginner level by creating meaning in different situations in concert with a mentor (Peno & Silva Mangiante, 2012). Since the staff nurse has more concrete experiences to refer back to, his/her progress can be quicker. The Dreyfus and Dreyfus model (1980) uses "aspects" as overall characteristics that require prior experience to obtain knowledge. An informal mentor can provide the verbal cues to the novice nurse and guide the recognition of these aspects (Peno & Silva Mangiante, 2012). As time goes on, learning progresses, aspect recognition improves, and priority setting can move to the forefront of the learning process.

The novice nurse will move to an advanced beginner and then to a competent nurse after approximately 2–3 years of experience (Benner, 2000). At that time, the novice nurse can begin to discuss long range goals and plans with the informal mentor and begin to understand outcomes of a situation (Benner, 2000). At this point, the acuity of a patient, a family member at the bedside, and patient/family teaching does not overwhelm the nurse, but efficiency and flexibility are still not fully developed (Benner, 2000).

Resources

The resources available for novice and advanced beginner nurses should include basic physical assessment opportunities, simulated opportunities to recognize basic heart sounds/breath sounds, and basic nursing skills. As the nurse progresses to competent, the resources can be tailored to coordinating complex patient care and the introduction of new technology. The informal mentor should scaffold the learning of the mentee by teaching how to modify and specify individual nursing care to specific patient needs.

Evaluation

Evaluation by the informal mentor can be conducted through a basic competency rubric for set nursing skills. Once basic competency is achieved, advanced clinical skills should be looked toward and in-depth priority setting and prioritization of clinical decision making should be introduced. Then the competent nurse can partake in case-based scenarios where critical thinking is utilized and assessed. Problem solving, outcome evaluation, and reflection should be used to foster learning as the nurse progresses.

MENTORING THE EXPERIENCED NURSE

The use of informal mentors for the experienced nurse can potentially center upon organizational culture, outcomes, and leadership. Not only should these nurses be mentors for new nurses, but they need to cultivate their own profession and look towards others to recognize their achievements, value them in the organization, and suggest opportunities for professional development.

Applying the Framework

The experienced nurse would be considered as proficient or expert within the Dreyfus and Dreyfus (1980, 1986) skill acquisition model. A nurse at higher levels of practice is acting on intuition and is less focused on and concerned about rules and guidelines. Their focus shifts towards situational awareness and appropriate actions. Due to the deep understanding of numerous situations and the vast experience of the nurse, aesthetic knowing takes over that is difficult to articulate. Aesthetic knowing is the ability for nurses to "perceive what is unique and significant about an experience" (Pardue, 2005, p. 334). Most often, a seasoned nurse will say that they just intuitively know what to do. The informal mentor plays a very different role with a seasoned nurse, which still is very important. The role of the informal mentor at this point is to scaffold the learner and guide the learner to be able to describe and identify clinical decisions and to assist in using alternative perspectives to further their practice (Peno & Silva Mangiante, 2012).

Resources

Resources for the experienced nurse are commonly focused on recognition, retention, and compensation. Informal mentors can often provide career counseling, a sounding board for concern, and a resource for professional growth. Reflective exercises are beneficial for the experienced nurses in order to critically appraise and examine their nursing practice. Gaining feedback from the informal mentor can enhance behavior and augment skill level.

Evaluation

Evaluation of the experienced nurse works well with the structure of a career ladder. A career ladder, also known as a clinical ladder, is a formal program created by healthcare organizations that offers opportunities for nurses to develop skills, advance practice, and in turn rewards nurses at the bedside. This provides the necessary incentive for the more experienced nurse to progress and be rewarded for longevity and progression in the nursing practice. Self-evaluation and peer evaluation at this level is very valuable and appropriate. Although the level of proficiency of the nurse and the understanding of how adults learn in an informal context are important to consider, it would be dismissive not to include the generational differences that play a role in the informal mentoring relationship.

GENERATIONAL DIFFERENCES

It is common in the healthcare environment to have multiple generations collaborating. Each generation has its own values, characteristics, and skill sets (Gursoy, Chi, & Karadag, 2013). Therefore, it is important to be cognizant of the uniqueness of each generation and the opportunities and challenges that may arise when informally mentoring an individual.

Baby Boomers

Baby boomers, born between 1946 and 1964, are the largest generation in the workplace (AARP, 2007) and most often are the more experienced nurses or managers in healthcare. This generation can be defined by their desire to work hard, to be result oriented, to be loyal, and to live to work (Gursoy et al., 2013). Most often they are goal oriented and expect the same drive by others, which can be a bone of contention with younger generations. Baby boomers most often will be a mentor, but when being mentored, they will desire informal mentoring relationships that are understanding of their point of view, are not forced, and are patient. The baby boomer likes to understand why and be given time to try the task, especially if it involves new technology. The simple verbal conversation that is reciprocal by nature is welcomed by the baby boomer and is a very productive means of communication.

Generation X

Generation X'ers, born between 1965 and 1980, have parents from the baby boomer generation who have witnessed the sacrifices of putting work first, in contrast to the desire to "have a life." They like a sense of belonging to a team and are often entrepreneurial. Generation X'ers are flexible and like feedback with short-term rewards. Due to the prominence of blended families, many Generation X nurses do not see the hierarchy as rigid and many expect the mentor to earn respect. Therefore, Generation X nurses desire informal mentoring relationships that are casual and friendly, with flexibility and freedom. At the same time, the Generation X nurse likes formative and summative feedback, while they are also comfortable with providing feedback (Gursoy et al., 2013).

Millennial

Millennials, or Generation Y'ers, born between 1980 and 2000, were raised during a time when every child was to be considered a winner and everyone received a trophy. They expect a great deal from the mentor, especially kind words of praise. The Millennial are team oriented and like a structured and supportive mentor that personalizes the relationship and is very interactive. The Millennial can be demanding and have high expectations (Gursoy et al., 2013).

On the other hand, their technology skills are exemplary and their approach to problem-solving is well-developed and acute. Millennials may be very comfortable with a form of e-mentoring, whereby the internet is used for corresponding. This type of mentoring can expand the access of mentors, minimize time restraints, eliminate geographic boundaries, and level the hierarchy (Pietsch, 2012). There are many different e-mentoring groups and internet communities that can support this type of learner.

CONCLUSIONS

Every nurse can remember at least one person that has profoundly influenced them. These experiences were very often informal in nature. Therefore, the impact of informal mentoring is far reaching. The need to challenge oneself and grow professionally is ongoing. Creating informal mentoring relationships underpins lifelong learning. The Informal and Incidental Learning model (Marsick & Watkins, 1999) is important to understand in order to better appreciate the significance and process of informal learning relationships and the deep meaning that develops within them. The Dreyfus and Dreyfus (1980, 1986) model for skill acquisition has clearly impacted nursing practice as adapted by Patricia Benner's in her Model for Clinical Competence (2000).

In nursing, lifelong learning is necessary to stay relevant and current in the clinical setting. Upon graduation from nursing school and passing the National Council Licensure Examination (NCLEX), the entry credentials are just the beginning. The NCLEX is a standardized, computerized examination that each state board of nursing within the United States uses to determine if a candidate is prepared for entry-level nursing practice. Informal mentors in nursing are vital to role promotion and the advancement of the scope of nursing practice. Nurses grow with the profession and weave a tapestry of experiences as a result of the patients they encounter and render care for, the clinical experiences they gain, and the informal mentors they meet along the way.

REFERENCES

AARP. (2007). *Leading a multigenerational workforce.* Retrieved from http://assets.aarp
.org/www.aarp.org_/articles/money/employers/leading_multigenerational
_workforce.pdf

Aston, L., & Hallam, P. (2011). *Successful mentoring in nursing.* Exeter, England: Learning Matters Ltd.

Baumberger-Henry, M. (2012). Registered nurses' perspectives on the new graduate working in the emergency department or critical care unit. *Journal of Continuing Education in Nursing, 43*(7), 299–305.

Baxley, S., Ibitayo, K., & Bond, M. L. (2014). *Mentoring today's nurses: A global perspective for success.* Indianapolis, IN: Sigma Theta Tau International.

Benner, P. D. (2000). *From novice to expert: Excellence and power in clinical nursing practice, commemorative edition.* Upper Saddle River, NJ: Prentice Hall.

Decker, S., Fey, M., Sideras, S., Caballero, S., Boese, T., Franklin, A. E., & Borum, J. C. (2013). Standards of best practice: Simulation standard VI: The debriefing process. *Clinical Simulation in Nursing, 9*(6), S26–S29.

Diamond, C. T. P. (2010). A memoir of co-mentoring: The "we" that is "me." *Mentoring & Tutoring: Partnership in Learning, 18,* 199–209.

Dreyfus, S., & Dreyfus, H. (1980). *A five-stage model of the mental activities involved in directed skill acquisition.* Berkeley: University of California ORC, 80-2, Operations Research Center.

Dreyfus, H., & Dreyfus, S. (1986). *Mind over machine: The power of human intuition and expertise in the era of the computer.* New York, NY: Blackwell Publishers.

Eller, L. S., Lev, E. L., & Feurer, A. (2014). Key components of an effective mentoring relationship: A qualitative study. *Nurse Education Today, 34*(5), 815–820. Retrieved from http://dx.doi.org/10.1016/j.nedt.2013.07.020

Eby, L. T. D. T., Allen, T. D., Hoffman, B. J., Baranik, L. E., Sauer, J. B., Baldwin, S., & Evans, S. C. (2013). An interdisciplinary meta-analysis of the potential antecedents, correlates, and consequences of protégé perceptions of mentoring. *Psychological Bulletin, 139*(2), 441–476.

Gaba, D. M. (2004). The future vision of simulation in health care. *Quality & Safety in Health Care, 13*(1), i2–10. doi: 10.1136/qshc.2004.009878

Grossman, S. (2013). *Mentoring in nursing: A dynamic and collaborative process.* New York, NY: Springer.

Gursoy, D., Chi, C. G. Q., & Karadag, E. (2013). Generational differences in work values and attitudes among frontline and service contact employees. *International Journal of Hospitality Management, 32,* 40–48.

Hodgson, A. K., & Scanlan, J. M. (2013). A concept analysis of mentoring in nursing leadership. *Open Journal of Nursing, 3*(5), 389. Retrieved from http://dx.doi.org/10.4236/ojn.2013.35052.

HRSA. (2013). *The U.S. nursing workforce: Trends in supply and education.* Retrieved from http://bhpr.hrsa.gov/healthworkforce/reports/nursingworkforce/nursing workforcefullreport.pdf

Hunt, L. (2011, February 12). *Co-mentoring: A mutually beneficial learning relationship.* Retrieved from http://lauriehunt.com/571/

Lait, J., Suter, E., Arthur, N., & Deutschlander, S. (2011). Interprofessional mentoring Enhancing students' clinical learning. *Nurse Education in Practice, 11*(3), 211–215.

Lorentzon, M., & Brown, K. (2003). Florence Nightingale as 'mentor of matrons': Correspondence with Rachel Williams at St Mary's Hospital. *Journal of Nursing Management, 11*(4), 266–274.

Lyon, L. J. (2015). Development of teaching expertise viewed through the Dreyfus model of skill acquisition. *Journal of the Scholarship of Teaching and Learning, 15*(1), 88–105.

Mariani, B. (2012). The effect of mentoring on career satisfaction of registered nurses and intent to stay in the nursing profession. *Nursing Research and Practice, 17*(10), 1–9. doi:10.1155/2012/168278.

Marsick, V. J., & Watkins, K. (1999). *Facilitating learning organizations: Making learning count.* Aldershot, England: Gower Publishers.

Marsick, V., Watkins, K., & O'Connor, B. N. (2011). Researching workplace learning in the United States. In M. Malloch, L. Cairns, K. Evans, & B. N. O'Connor (Eds.), *The SAGE handbook of workplace learning* (pp. 198–209). Thousand Oaks, CA: SAGE Publications Ltd.

Meier, S. R. (2013). Concept analysis of mentoring. *Advances in Neonatal Care, 13*(5), 341–345.

Mixer, S. (2011). Use of the culture care theory to discover nursing faculty care expressions, patterns, and practices related to teaching culture care. *Online Journal of Cultural Competence in Nursing and Healthcare, 1*, 3–14.

Mixer, S. J., Burk, R. C., Davidson, R., McArthur, P. M., Abraham, C., Silva, K., & Sharp, D. (2012). Transforming bedside nursing care through practice-academic co-mentoring relationships. *Journal of Nursing Care, 1*(3), 1–6. doi:10.4172/jnc.1000108

Neill, M. A., & Wotton, K. (2011). High-fidelity simulation debriefing in nursing education: A literature review. *Clinical Simulation in Nursing, 7*(5), e161–e168.

Pardue, K. (2005) Blending aesthetics and empirics: Teaching health assessment in an art gallery. *Journal of Nursing Education, 44*(7), 334–337.

Peno, K., & Silva Mangiante, E. M. (2012). The journey from novice to expert: Toward a purposeful on-going mentoring model. In C. J. Boden-McGill & K. P. King (Eds.), *Conversations about adult learning in a complex world* (pp. 211–221). Charlotte, NC: Information Age Publishing.

Pietsch, T. M. (2012). A transition to e-mentoring: Factors that influence nurse engagement. *Computers Informatics Nursing, 30*(12), 632–639.

Rymer, J. (2002). "Only Connect": Transforming ourselves and our discipline through co-mentoring. *Journal of Business Communication, 39,* 342–363. doi:10.1177/002194360203900304.

Tee, S., & Cowen, M. (2012). Supporting students with disabilities: Promoting understanding amongst mentors in practice. *Nurse Education in Practice, 12*(1), 6–10.

Watkins, K. E., Marsick, V. J., & de Álava, M. F. (2014). Evaluating informal learning in the workplace. In T. Halttunen, M. Koivisto, & S. Billett (Eds.), *Promoting, assessing, recognizing and certifying lifelong learning* (pp. 59–77). Dordrecht, Netherlands: Springer.

Werquin, P. (2010). *Recognising non-formal and informal learning: Outcomes, policies and practices.* Paris, France: Organisation for Economic Co-operation and Development Publications.

Xu, Y., & He, F. (2012). Transition programs for internationally educated nurses: What can the United States learn from the United Kingdom, Australia, and Canada? *Nursing Economic$, 30*(4), 215–224. Retrieved from http://www.medscape.com/viewarticle/770116.

PART IV

MENTORING IN MULTIPLE CONTEXTS

DEVELOPING FUTURE TECHNOLOGY EXECUTIVES AT COLUMBIA UNIVERSITY USING FORMAL AND INFORMAL MENTORING METHODS

Arthur M. Langer
Columbia University

The principle issue being addressed in this chapter is the mentoring of part-time professional graduate students. Mentoring has been used to initiate the process of conversation and advisement essential to the growth of learners (Daloz, 1999; Langer, 2010; Mullen, 2008). A person who mentors can help learners clarify their educational purposes, set goals, and identify learning activities (McBurney, 2015; Schlossberg, 1989). This chapter examines an actual program at Columbia University that uses professional executives from industry as mentors instead of faculty. The program uses formal and informal methods to provide succession planning for students who aspire to become future Information Technology Executives. The for-

Mentoring in Formal and Informal Contexts, pages 281–299
Copyright © 2016 by Information Age Publishing

mal part of the program allows mentors to participate in the grading of the student and also to shape the design of the student's master's project. Informal mentoring aspects of the program include monthly meetings, career advisement, and general guidance on how to become a successful executive. The program has over 170 executive mentors from industry who agree to meet with a student monthly. These meetings usually take place at the mentor's office to create a "real-world" experience—where the mentor guides the student through a complex project that would inevitably be presented to an executive team for approval. The mentor's wisdom and experience is critical. It is, in many ways, learning through apprenticeship. Mentors come from such firms as JPMorgan, Prudential, Johnson & Johnson, Colgate-Palmolive, and Hewlett-Packard. Mentors actually select a student during a formal "draft" after they review the pool of available projects and students that they are interested in mentoring. The results of the program show that industry executives are responsible and effective mentors and the mentoring program can be integrated in a degree program using formal and informal methods to help transform students. This case study shows how these executive mentors provide graduate students with practical guidance and assist them to transition into executive positions as early as one-year after graduation.

THEORETICAL CONSTRUCTS

Recognizing the value of other modes of education, a number of institutions of higher education have created mentoring programs that match faculty members with students for the purpose of enhancing student learning (Daloz, 1999; Duntley-Matos, 2014; Jacobi, 1991; Schlossberg, 1989). Langer (2010) concluded that although there are some areas of overlap in mentoring theory and practice, little consistency exists in the way mentoring is defined both within and across institutions of higher education. This lack of consistency pushes scholars to question whether there is such a thing as an ideal or optimal approach to mentoring. The questioning becomes more acute as researchers consider the increasingly diverse group of students in higher education, particularly those categorized as "working professionals" (Buckley & Zimmermann, 2003; Burke, McKean, & McKenna, 1991; Duntley-Matos, 2014; Mullen, 2006).

Mentoring has been found to be an especially helpful educational tool for nontraditional students. Traditional methods of instruction may not be the most appropriate way for institutions to address the needs of these students (Galbraith, 1991; Mullen, 2008). In particular, working students are not able to attend traditional on-campus degree programs and need alternative vehicles for faculty interaction and feedback. Mentoring has been found to be effective in improving student retention and socialization and can be extended to making nontraditional students feel comfortable in a higher educational setting. Older students returning to school may feel especially alienated by the collegiate environment. Nontraditional students who seek graduate degrees to help promote their professional growth may need mentors from non-academic faculty. Professional mentoring relationships can provide these students with the tools they need to navigate in both academic and professional environments.

While many professionals desire to attain an executive position, they typically lack the knowledge, support, and guidance to be prepared for the challenge. In order to succeed at the executive level, ongoing and focused skill development with associated support is crucial (Thompson, Wolf, & Sabatine, 2012). This is particularly critical given that the roles and responsibilities of executives are changing dramatically, mostly affected by advances in technology coupled with regulatory constraints and financial pressures of quarterly performance. Furthermore, the lack of executive succession programs has significantly impaired internal growth of middle managers. Indeed, a recent study in the healthcare industry found that 79% of the firms did not have programs to develop future leaders from within (Thompson et al., 2012).

Langer (2001) also raised the important point that the active participation of mentees in the mentoring transaction is essential to the success of the process. Indeed, much has been identified in the literature about the role of the mentee or protégé. According to Allen (2007), "the success of any mentorship is contingent on the behaviors of both the mentor and the protégé" (p. 123). A protégé should see the potential in him or herself and should possess the appropriate experience to provide adequate advice (Merlevede & Bridoux, 2003). Institutions seeking to develop mentoring programs for professional students need to provide resources from industry to be effective. Successful protégés need to have mentors that are professionally goal-oriented, understand the importance of taking responsibility, and mindful of the importance of the time constraints in business transactions (Allen, 2007; Herman & Mandell, 2004; Mullen, 2006).

Studies show that effective mentoring relationships tend to contain three key attributes:

1. A well-defined purpose
2. A collaborative learning relationship for the career path of the mentee
3. A mentor/mentee relationship that can develop over time through defined phases and more than just an informal/casual relationship.

Thompson et al. (2012) defined three essential phases to accomplish effective mentoring programs:

Phase 1: Management oversight

Phase 2: Experiential Learning

Phase 3: Advanced-level system thinking using blended instruction methods in an environment supported by a mentor

The Columbia University Program

Columbia University's Executive Masters of Science in Technology Management (EMSTM) provides "an intensive graduate level education for motivated individuals who are interested in becoming technology executives" (Columbia University, 2015). The program uses a blended on-line and face-to-face format, which includes multiple on-site residencies and a one-to-one mentoring relationship with a top-tiered IT executive (Scherer, 2010).

EMSTM is designed primarily to address the performance shortfalls that have occurred in the Chief Information Officer (CIO) and other IT executive roles. The Program, which is offered through the School of Continuing Education, requires students to have at least 10 years of experience in an IT-related position. Most students are at mid-management levels in IT and are pursuing the knowledge necessary to take the leap into an executive position. The program spans 15-months of study and requires a final Master's thesis project. Thus, the Executive Masters of Science in Technology Management is designed to help these mid-managers to become more effective executive performers. Using various organizational learning techniques and best practices, the program investigates important components of strategic thinking and learning in such areas as: relationship building, creating and managing change, leadership, management skills, and business knowledge. The most critical factor for students is to prepare for a successful executive position at the "C-Suite." The C-Suite typically represents the positions held by the most senior executives in a company who have the words "chief" and "officer" associated with their title. Example positions include Chief Executive Officer (CEO), Chief Financial Officer (CFO), and Chief Operating Officer (COO). In the technology profession there is a myriad of c-level titles that have emerged over the last 10 years including Chief Information Officer (CIO), Chief Technology Officer (CTO), Chief Digital Officer (CDO), and Chief Information Security Officer (CISO). For the purposes of this chapter, I will refer to such professionals as "IT Executives" or ITEs. Because of the complexity of education and its mission to develop IT Executive leaders, the EMSTM Program utilizes industry mentors to help students make an extremely challenging leap from being a technology senior manager to a technology executive.

EMSTM students matriculate in the program part-time, so they can continue to apply the knowledge they receive during the Program to their experiences at work. Students must develop their Master's project proposal in the first term, which will in later terms be the basis of a three chapter integrated executive proposal on a technology-related product or service. Students can select projects that relate to their professional work or propose an entrepreneurial idea that they would like to launch. The three chapters are completed by students in sequence.

How do mentors actually help their students? Mentors have an important role in the development of a student and are very much a part of the education process in EMSTM. Specifically, mentors provide a portion of their student's grade for each chapter course; that is, based on how the mentor feels the student has performed under their direction. Mentors also have the authority to modify the format of the student's thesis—in this way they can help students develop applicable business solutions.

The History and the Problem

The role of Information Technology Executives (ITEs) has continued to evolve in importance over the past 20 years. The ITE is typically responsible for all of the technology issues confronting the organization. However, with the emergence of the importance of the responsibility, the role of the ITE tends to be a challenge in many organizations. Unlike the ITE's related "C-Suite" colleagues, organizations often struggle to understand how to measure the success of the position. For example, we know that most CIOs have short tenures, the vast number only last about three years. At professional conferences, many CIOs have coined the CIO acronym as standing for "Career Is Over." But nothing should be further from the truth especially since CEO surveys have consistently rated technology as the most critical factor for attaining more competitive advantage. There is; however, a growing population of CIOs that have clearly demonstrated the success of the role by their sheer longevity in the position.

Perhaps the isolation of IT is one of the major reasons why ITE's find it difficult to gain acceptance in their organizations. Technology staff have been criticized, and in many cases rightfully so, for their inability to integrate with the rest of the organization (Langer, 2011; Milovich, 2015; Schein, 1992). Being stereotyped as "techies" continues to be relevant and the image seems to have gravitated to the level of the ITE. Even with the widespread importance of IT over the past two decades, ITEs have been challenged to bring strategic value to their companies. There is little question about the frustration that exists with CIOs at the CEO level, and satisfying the CEO is a challenge for most CIOs—it involves the complexity of explaining why IT is so expensive, understanding why projects take so long to complete, and clearly articulating how IT supports the business. Our best evidence of this communication gap between the CEO and CIO was best represented by Carr's article (2003), titled, "IT doesn't Matter" which was published in the Harvard Business Review. The article sharply criticized the IT function and attacked its overall value to organizations. It received instant popularity among CFOs and CEOs as many began to review their investments in IT and the role of the ITE in general. The question remains, why? especially since so many CEOs acknowledge that IT is the most important variable for maintaining or improving competitive advantage?

Because technology is changing at such a rapid pace, the ability for ITEs to operate in a dynamic business environment is staggering. Most ITE's fight a "two front war," keeping technology operational and secure while at the same time attempting to bring strategic advantage for the business. Certainly not an easy task, as Schein (1992) discussed in his article, "Management and Information Technology: Two Subcultures in Collision." The article disclosed much of the imbalance between the CEO and IT. This "imbalance" has continued to be the key success factor for many ITEs especially when they attempt to bring strategic value to their organizations.

The results of Langer's research suggest that the ITE's value to the business comprises the following key areas (Langer & Yorks, 2013):

- *Business Integration*: creating a culture that allows IT people and business line personnel to seamlessly work together and understand each other's needs.
- *Security*: providing a safe environment that protects employee and client information from outside threats.
- *Data Analytics*: the ability to use company data internally for the best hires and competitively for understanding consumer behavior and preferences.
- *Legal Exposure*: ensuring that IT systems and data are not violating private or public domains.
- *Cost Containment*: reducing IT costs through shared and central services to eliminate redundancies in operation.
- *New Business Ventures*: initiating "intrepreneurial" opportunities for the business to leverage technology that establish new areas of competitive advantage.

Benefits of Executive Mentoring—Previous Research Study

Empirical studies have shown that mentorship is a contributor to professional success of executives (Clutterbuck & Megginson, 1999; De Janasz & Peiperl, 2015; Fralic & Morjikian, 2006). Scherer (2010) studied Levinson's Dream Theory and its relevance in the EMSTM academic executive mentoring program. He surveyed 91 mentors ranging from 45 to 65 years of age. The results of Scherer's study showed that Levinson's theory of adult development is relevant to the mentoring philosophy used at EMSTM. Levinson's theory is based on life structures that can predict patterns of meaning making in adults at a given stage of life. The life structures, according to Levinson, is shaped by an adult's social and physical environments that primarily involve one's experiences with family and work, as well as other factors such as religion, race, and social status. Levinson's work (1978, 2011) is based on six predictable linear development stages that are delineated by age groups. In the EMSTM program, stages four and six are particularly relevant and a significant part of Scherer's conclusions. Specifically, the fourth stage depicts the age group represented by most EMSTM students (33–40) and the sixth stage is consistent with the age group represented by most of the Columbia mentor population (45–50). The fourth stage defines adults as individuals facing more demanding roles and expectations. This stage is consistent with students in the Program who are transitioning from middle-to-upper management positions to an executive role. Mentors, on the other hand, are in the stage that Levinson defined as "Middle Adulthood" in which individuals seek to focus on their personal legacy and giving back to society. Indeed, Levinson's theory established a natural way of measuring the mentoring program by comparing the patterns of need of the two constituents in the mentor/mentee relationship. Scherer's study (2010) of EMSTM mentors resulted in four major conclusions:

1. Students are able to capitalize on the strength of combining formal and informal mentoring while avoiding the use of direct supervisors. That is, a mentor who is not an official supervisor in the organizational sense, and whose compensation is not dependent on the mentee's performance, can work with the student in ways that can better facilitate their transition into an executive level manager.

2. Mentors tend to mentor in the way they have experienced mentoring. Most mentors in the Columbia programs are drawn to participate because they have themselves been mentored at some point during their own career advancement, and as such retain a similar approach to mentoring that was instrumental in helping them. The EMSTM program provides the informal freedom to practice this

with little constraints from the "formal" requirements. Another way of viewing this conclusion is that the mentors feel they have greater flexibility in how they work with their student, and that this flexibility has yielded better results.

3. While individual transformation is the ultimate goal for a mentor's student, a more significant component of the process is dealing with individual transitions that, in effect, lead to a student's transformation. It is these transitions that allow students to cope with the complexity of the leap to the so-called c-level, where the way success is measured differs drastically from lower management roles. This means that the success of the EMSTM program is rooted more in the fostering of understanding of the student's challenge in dealing with this complexity. Thus, the mentor must show confidence and believe in the student, sharing their own difficulties when they themselves completed the journey, and help them define their new self.

4. The mentors showed great motivation and enthusiasm to continue working with students. Indeed, over 20 mentors have worked with over eight different students, for over eight years of continued service in the Program.

Helping Students Make the Leap to the C-Suite

Mid-level managers have, in general, challenges when approaching positions at the executive C-Suite. While many managers succeed at senior management levels, moving to the C-Suite is a huge leap. This leap coincides with the notions of transformation as the process of changing the way one thinks how to approach decision-making and understanding methods of politicking. The changes usually require a dramatic change in the way one behaves and makes meaning of the world around them (Langer & Yorks, 2013). According to an article published by CIO Insight, "at its lowest point, the average tenure of a CIO was approximately three years" (Bonfante, 2014). Furthermore, there is a lack of new and upcoming talent that can fill new CIO positions. As discussed earlier, the role of the CIO has become even more broadly defined, that is, there are now multiple c-level positions that are emerging including the Chief Information Security Officer (CISO), the Chief Technology Officer (CTO), the Chief Digital Officer (CDO) as examples. Thus, the need for c-level technology leaders is increasing because of the extraordinary advancements in technology that are now affecting the ways organizations compete in a global economy. Indeed, the gap for well-prepared executive technology leaders is widening, and there are few academic programs that are providing the necessary skills. These skills are often referred to as "soft skills," because they do not emphasize the "technical" expertise typically recognized at more tactical management levels. Indeed, Langer and Yorks (2013) interviewed exceptional ITEs with long tenures in their positions and found 23 commonalities among them— all of which had little connection to needing technical skills to succeed at the C-Suite. Tables 15.1 and 15.2 show these commonalities broken into two groups of soft skills: Personal Attributes and Organizational Philosophy. Personal Attributes are individual traits that appear to be important leadership characteristics. Organizational Philosophy, on the other hand, represents how the IT organization needs to operate within a firm. As such, the EMSTM approach is to emphasize these components of professional development by utilizing formal and informal methods of mentoring to

TABLE 15.1 Common Personal Attributes Among Exceptional CIOs

Personal Attributes	Mentor Activity	Formal/ Informal
1. **Push yourself outside your professional comfort zone.** Successful ITEs need to keep reinventing themselves and should strive for continual excellence at their jobs. They seek more responsibilities in different places outside the normal IT functions.	Mentors review the master's proposal and coach students to expand into business areas that might not be within the current sphere of the mentee's comfort zone of knowledge and experience. Mentors need to have students meet the required sections for each chapter of the master's thesis.	Formal
2. **Communication skills are at the forefront of leadership.** Without great communication skills, ITEs cannot influence the business and develop a business integration strategy.	Mentors are responsible for approving their students' readiness to do their oral defense of each Chapter of their master's thesis project. Mentors typically have students do "trial" defenses with their senior staff members.	Informal
3. **Do not become too enamored with politics.** ITEs should not over play the power of playing politics. Successful ITEs tend to be direct with their colleagues and staff.	Chapter 1 requires students to design an organization structure for the staff involved in the project. The organization structure reflects the student's strategy for integrating IT with the business. The plan also reflects the student's leadership philosophy.	Formal
4. **Do not shy away from tough decisions.** ITEs must take the necessary actions when dealing with management dilemmas. If someone is not performing, they must address the problem timely.	Mentors challenge students on how to deal with a worst case scenario for each section of their project. This includes possible areas of exposure with the project's financial forecasts, management, and market assumptions. Students need to demonstrate the "what if" scenarios.	Formal

(continued)

TABLE 15.1   Common Personal Attributes Among Exceptional CIOs (continued)

Personal Attributes	Mentor Activity	Formal/ Informal
5. **Get used to ambiguity.** If you need to be told exactly the problem, you will likely not bring much value. The life of most executives requires an understanding of how to bring clarity to vaguely defined problems.	Mentors do not provide answers for students, rather help them formulate solutions to complex project alternatives.	Informal
6. **Take risks.** A strategic ITE cannot achieve success without engaging in projects that have risk factors—it's reality. The challenge for the ITE is to understand the extent of the challenge and the significance of the potential rewards for the business.	Chapter 2 requires students to have a section on the strategy and associated risks of their project. Mentors supervise this section.	Formal
7. **Lead without authority.** Great leaders can influence the behaviors of others without using the power of their position. Influencing the change of behavior in others is a more sustainable model of leadership.	The student's design of the organization and management philosophy completed in Chapter 1 must be operationalized in Chapter 3.	Formal
8. **The importance of technical skills diminishes as you approach the ITE position.** ITEs should not over rely on their IT technical knowledge as a substitute for good business skills.	Mentors emphasize that management style outweighs technical skills. Most mentors are no longer technical per se and represent an example of how to be successful without relying on technical skills.	Informal
9. **Have pride of ownership.** ITEs need to strive to be the best and take responsibility for their actions	Mentors dictate the quality levels needed for the student's masters project A section on Operations Quality is required in Chapter 3.	Formal
10. **Learn to listen.** ITEs must learn to listen to their seniors, peers, and staff members to better understand problems and challenges in their organizations.	Mentors share their experiences with students on how they deal with senior executives and navigate political situations.	Informal
11. **Do not accept mediocrity.** In a competitive and global world, ITE's need to expect the very best from their staff.	Chapter 1 requires a section that explains all job roles and responsibilities for the project. Students must show how they will evaluate the performance of their team.	Formal

help students adopt these patterns as part of their learning and preparation as future c-level ITEs. Tables 15.1 and 15.2 map the Personal Attributes and Organizational Philosophy skills to the specific formal and informal responsibilities of the mentor.

TABLE 15.2   Common Organizational Philosophies Among Exceptional CIOs

Organizational Philosophy	Mentor Activity	Formal/ Informal
1. **Integration of IT is a fundamental objective.** Successful ITEs understand that integration means that IT resources are truly embedded in the business.	Chapter 1 requires a section that reflects the organizational design that shows how their staff integrate with the business.	Formal
2. **ITEs must be knowledgeable about the business.** This somewhat relates to (1), but also suggests that spending time and integrating resources is not enough. IT must be intimately familiar with the challenges of the business, the way the units operate, and their culture.	In Chapter 2, students have a section on how the business mission and the project will bring value to the company.	Formal
3. **Have a roadmap.** ITEs need to develop a plan of what they want to accomplish, why it is valuable to the business, and how they will accomplish the project objectives. This includes the specifics of cost, return-on-investment (ROI), and time to completion.	Students are required to develop a three-year plan in Chapter 1 and present an implementation plan in Chapter 3.	Formal
4. **Keep your pulse on costs.** ITEs need to be fiscally responsible and must shed the reputation as big spenders. Reduction of IT costs to increase shareholder value is still very relevant at the C-Suite.	Mentors show students how to design a cost-controlled IT environment. Students see how their mentor implements fiscal controls.	Informal
5 **Having a seat at the table matters.** ITEs should report directly to the CEO and have a regular place of attendance at key Board meetings.	Mentors have philosophical discussions with their students about the pros and cons of interacting with senior executives and board members.	Informal
6. **Business comes first.** The ITE must always think about the value IT brings to the business. If that business value is not there, then the value of the IT is not relevant	Mentors provide examples to students of how to interact with the business and integrate IT resources with business initiatives.	Informal
7. **Expand the role beyond traditional IT.** Case studies show that many successful ITEs now have expanded roles outside of IT. This includes operations, infrastructure, and shared services responsibilities.	Mentors discuss the different philosophies of the ITE role and provide examples for students of the new responsibilities being undertaken by the CIO community.	Informal

(continued)

TABLE 15.2   Common Organizational Philosophies Among Exceptional CIOs (continued)

Organizational Philosophy	Mentor Activity	Formal/ Informal
8. **Have the best people.** ITEs cannot accomplish their complex roles without surrounding themselves with the appropriate staff.	Mentors work with students on developing the job description for each staff position in Chapter 1. Mentors also share how they recruit the best staff.	Formal/ Informal
9. **Pay attention to Big Data.** Data analytics have become an increasingly important conversation at the Board level. Big Data is essential for competitive advantage and also understanding a firm's legal exposures and cyber-security protection.	Students must use business data to formulate how they will develop the strategic plan portion of their project. Mentors show students how their company uses big data for competitive advantage.	Formal/ Informal
10. **Align with the business.** The ITE must be aligned with the aspirations of the business units so that there is inter-department harmony.	Mentors discuss how their IT organizations operate with business units and ensure alignment.	Informal
11. **Drive profitability.** Successful ITEs strategically support the organization to drive higher profits and as result bring more importance to their role.	Mentors provide students with examples of how IT can drive higher profits. Students may also learn how to establish stand-alone IT profit centers.	Informal
12. **Use benchmarks.** ITEs need to show they use metrics to optimize the performance of their organizations.	Students must develop statistics and industry comparisons in Chapter 1 & 2.	Formal
13. **React to the dynamics of the market.** ITEs need to be very agile to changes in the market that affect their firms.	Mentors show students how to develop strategic initiatives based on market trends and how to design risk models that are consistent with their firm's models.	Informal

THE COLUMBIA UNIVERSITY PROCESS

The Curriculum Design

As stated earlier, students admitted to EMSTM typically have at least 10 years of business experience, often in the IT profession. A bachelor's degree is required from an accredited institution of higher education. The students continue in their working environment during the program and attend five on-campus residencies over 16-months. The remaining academic interface is delivered using a technology-enhanced on-line delivery including filmed lectures, live webinars, and chat-rooms. During the first-term course, Technology in the Business Environment, students develop a proposal for their Master's Project in the form of a prospectus. The Master's Project comprises a three-chapter document on a technology-related product or service. Each of the three chapters is linked to a four-credit seminar course. Students complete each chapter seminar in succession or over three consecutive terms. During the first term, students develop their project in the form of a prospectus, which is then condensed into an Executive Summary. The Executive Summary consists of three short paragraphs that summarize the project: (a) The Problem; (b) The Solution; and (c) The Value Proposition. Once finalized, the Executive Summaries are emailed to the population of mentors along with a demographic of each student. Mentors submit their "draft" picks for students in their local area and if possible attend an "All Mentors Meeting" where student selections are finalized. Mentors who cannot attend the meeting email their picks.

Mentor Selection Procedure

Mentors who draft the same student must negotiate and ultimately decide which of them best fits the student. Mentors who have no interest in the existing pool of students are not required to select a mentee. It may be necessary to find a new mentor if there is no existing expertise to support a particular student's project. Because there are more mentors than students, mentors are not pressured or feel obligated to take on a student. In any event, there has never been a situation where a student has gone "undrafted." It is important to note that students do not select their mentor. The reason is twofold. First, students might want a mentor who they perceive has high prestige as opposed to being one that is a good fit for them. Second, it is important that the mentor be genuinely interested in the student and his/her project.

Intersection of the Curriculum and the Seminar Chapter Courses

The EMSTM program requires students to complete 36 graduate credits at the University. Eighteen of these credits are core courses that must be taken by all students. Each of the core courses contains portions of study that prepare students for specific sections of their master's project. Each of these sections is called a "Chapter," which work in concert with one another to form a fully realized project. The knowledge that is obtained by students is carefully

TABLE 15.3 Intersections of Core Course Content to Seminar Chapters

Core Course	Seminar Course Chapter	Chapter Section Covered by Mentor
Technology in the Business Environment	1	1. Requirements Analysis 2. Product Design Creation 3. Organization & Product Mgmt.
	2	1. Market Assessment 3. Go to Market Plan
Accounting & Finance for Tech	1	4. Value Proposition
	2	2. ROI Calculation
Technology and the Law	3	1. Risk Management 2. Ethics
Strategic Advocacy	2	4. Communicating the Strategy
	3	2. Operating Plan
Behavioral Challenges in Tech Management	1	3. Organization & Product Mgmt.
	3	3. Operating Plan
IT and Operations Management	3	3. Operating Plan 4. Analytics & Transition to Operations

integrated in the seminar chapter course requirements. Thus, students must "apply" the coursework to the project and develop a realistic solution with the help of their mentor. These "intersections" are shown in Table 15.3.

Formal Role of the Mentor

Mentors agree to meet with their student monthly for at least one hour, typically at the mentor's place of work, or at a location of mutual agreement with the student. Many mentors exceed the one-hour time requirement and engage additional time usually in phone and email exchanges with their mentee. Each term lasts about 13 weeks or three months, so mentors, at a minimum, meet with their student four times each term. Mentors agree to work with the student for all three terms, that is, throughout the three chapters of their master's project. Thus, mentors will spend almost one year working with their students and help them develop executive-level skills as well as supervise the completion of their master's project.

Mentors have three distinct formal responsibilities and authorities. First, they have the right to modify the master's project format, as previously stated. While each chapter course seminar has a format guideline, the mentor can override it as they see fit to meet the needs of that specific proposal. The mentor guideline does contain a suggested schedule for students and mentors to follow with respect to delivering the specific sections for each chapter. Essentially students, in coordination with the seminar chapter course, submit one section of the chapter each month and, then, they are supposed to meet with their mentor so they can review the section and receive feedback from them. Second, mentors provide one-third of the student's final grade in each seminar chapter course so their opinion has a correlation to academic performance. Third, students must orally defend each chapter at the end of the term. The mentor must approve that the mentee has completed the work on the chapter and is properly prepared to participate in the oral defense.

The Oral Defense

The oral defense consists of a panel of three judges. Two of the judges are mentors (not the student's mentor) and one faculty member from Columbia or from another university. The judges are responsible for emulating a real-world committee that is charged with evaluating the quality of the proposal. If the student's project is internal (that is, inside of an existing company), then the panel behaves as an internal executive committee. If the student proposal is external (that is, a new business venture), then the panel behaves as an outside venture firm evaluating the viability of the idea. Judges are provided with a scoring grid, which includes a weighted criterion for grading specific areas of performance on the defense. The form also allows for written comments. Students are given a "worst-case" situation; the judges have not read their proposal before the defense (something that often occurs in organizations), so they must overcome this obstacle by learning how to present to an audience that is essentially unprepared. Students may use PowerPoint slides or any other presentation materials. The oral defense is limited to 20 minutes with five minutes of verbal feedback. The 20 minutes includes presentation and answering of questions posed by the judges. Each judge fills out the grading rubric and the grades are averaged to configure the student's grade for their defense, which represents one-third of their final grade in the seminar chapter course. Copies of the graded defense forms are forwarded to the student's mentor for review, discussion, and appropriate action to improvement where needed.

Informal Role of the Mentor

While the formal process of mentoring provides an excellent structure for students and a way of "institutionalizing" the process at a university, it is limited in the context of transforming individuals to excel to a higher level of management. Informal mentoring, according to Klasen & Clutterbuck (2002), tends to provide more benefit to the mentee. As such, a major portion of the Columbia Technology Management program experience is informal so that mentors can feel comfortable providing more business-related interactions that can better prepare students for life as an executive. This is accomplished by suggesting to mentors that they should treat students as if they were subordinates and outline expectations associated with the way things get done in most firms. Indeed, the mentor's grade of the student is subjective and based more on business norms than academic performance. Furthermore, the activities that transpire between mentor and student are not dictated or restricted, so that the mentor can provide guidance and set expectations that closely mirror the requirements set forth by executives. This process does not suggest that mentors are not compassionate or nurturing to their student. Most practice what Langer defines as "Critical Love," the intersection of true caring as a teacher, but focused on properly preparing a student for the realities of life in the C-Suite (Cramm, 2013).

Mentors also play an important role in helping students develop a personal strategy on their career direction and progression. This informal role occurs in a number of ways. First, mentors typically *open* their organizations to their student. By open, we mean they introduce students to their management staff and allow them to experience first-hand the best practices of a successful technology executive. Second, mentors often have connections with other technology executives who may, in some circumstances, have specific knowledge in a particular technology or within a specific business area. As such, the mentor provides an additional network to the student by exposing them to personal and business contacts.

Student Outcomes

A recent survey of 46 alumni reported that 83% of graduates stated that their mentor relationship was a significant part of their positive experience in EMSTM. Within two-years after graduation, over 93% of the alumni were promoted or moved to a higher profile position with a different firm. Thirty percent of graduates have reached a c-level or equivalent position, and 48% have launched new business ventures.

Managing Mentor/Mentee Problems

In any established mentoring program, there needs to be an approach to dealing with problems that can occur in the relationship between the mentor and the mentee. These problems fall into two general categories at the Columbia program: (a) mentors who do not meet consistently with their students; and (b) students who fall behind in course deliverables or do not follow mentor direction.

Problems with mentor responsiveness are extremely rare but do occur. Mentor problems surface when students complain that they cannot reach their mentor or their mentor does not respond in a timely manner. When this problem occurs, it is usually associated with the mentor's travel schedule or a personal problem they may have. To monitor the mentor/mentee relationship, students must discuss their mentor progress with their seminar chapter course instructor, particularly during the Chapter 15.1 seminar, as mentor/mentee problems of this nature usually occur early in the relationship. When this occurs, the EMSTM program chair contacts the mentor and discusses the mentee's concerns, and if the problem cannot be resolved satisfactorily, the student is reassigned and, in most cases, the mentor's relationship with the Columbia program is discontinued. This has only occurred five times in 10 years, suggesting that the mentor selection and recruitment process has a high degree of success.

Problems with students, on the other hand, while actually a low percentage (less than 5%) do occur more frequently than issues with the mentor. Students who miss their monthly meetings with their mentor or consistently fall behind will be placed on probation. This means they must step out of the current seminar chapter term and likely be assigned to a different mentor. The change in mentor is usually necessary for two reasons, first, the mentor will likely want to discontinue because of frustration with the student, and second it might be best to have the student have a new relationship that is clear of any past issues—that is, a fresh start with a different mentor.

CONCLUSION

Part-time graduate students can benefit from mentoring programs that assist them in developing academic and professional capacities. Mentors need to be carefully integrated within the curriculum using formal methods of participation. Informal mentoring practices must also be used to better prepare students for professional progression. Mentoring programs that use both formal and informal approaches can be institutionalized in higher education programs when mentors have the ability to select their students and work in a one-to-one relationship that lasts over multiple terms of study. It is through the marriage of experiential learning and the 1:1 student to mentor relationship that favorable student outcomes can be achieved. Furthermore, institutions that seek to develop nontraditional, professional students must pursue mentors from the professional realm and not from the ranks of academia in order to bolster chances for success. Fostering a relationship that is business-minded is integral for working professionals to become lifelong teachers and learners.

REFERENCES

Allen, T. D. (2007). Mentoring relationships from the perspective of the mentor. In B. R. Ragins & K. E. Kram (Eds.), *The handbook of mentoring at work: Theory, research, and practice* (pp. 123–148). Thousand Oaks, CA: Sage.

Bonfante, L. (2014). Why CIO tenures aren't longer. Retrieved from: http://www.cioinsight.com/it-management/expert-voices/why-cio-tenures-arent-longer.html

Buckley, M. A., & Zimmerman, S. H. (2003). *Mentoring children and adolescents: A guide to issues.* Westport, CT: Praeger.

Burke, R. J., McKean, C. A., & McKenna, C. S. (1991). How do mentorships differ from typical supervisory relationships? *Psychological Reports, 68,* 459–466.

Carr, N. (2003, May 1). IT doesn't matter. *Harvard Business Review.*

Clutterbuck, D., & Megginson, D. (1999). *Mentoring executives and directors.* Oxford, England: Butterworth-Heinemann.

Columbia University. (2015). *Technology Management Executive Master of Science.* Retrieved from http://ce.columbia.edu/technology-management

Cramm, S. (2013). A workplace love story (about consulting). *strategy+business.*

Daloz, L.A. (1999). *Mentor.* San Francisco, CA: Jossey-Bass.

De Janasz, S., & Peiperl, M. (2015, April 1). CEOs need mentors too. *Harvard Business Review.*

Duntley-Matos, R. (2014). Transformative complicity and cultural humility: De- and re-constructing higher education mentorship for under-represented groups. *Qualitative Sociology, 37,* 443–466.

Fralic, M. F., & Morjikian, R. L. (2006). The RWJ executive nurse fellows program, Part 3: Making the business case. *Journal of Nursing Administration, 36*(2), 96–102.

Galbraith, M. W. (Ed.). (1991). *Facilitating adult learning: A transactional process.* Malabar, FL: Krieger Publishing.

Herman, L., & Mandell, A. (2004). *From teaching to mentoring. Principles and practice, dialogue and life in adult education.* London, England: RoutledgeFalmer.

Jacobi, M. (1991). Mentoring and undergraduate academic success: A literature review. *Review of Educational Research, 61,* 505–532.

Klasen, N., & Clutterbuck, D. (2002). *Implementing mentoring schemes: A practical guide to successful programs.* Oxford, England: Elsevier Butterworth-Heineman.

Langer, A. M. (2001). Confronting theory: The practice of mentoring non-traditional students at Empire State College. *International Journal of Mentoring and Tutoring, 9*(1), 49–62.

Langer, A. M. (2010). Mentoring nontraditional undergraduate students: A case study in higher education. *Mentoring & Tutoring: Partnership in Learning, 18*(1), 23–38.

Langer, A. (2011). *IT and organizational learning: Managing change through technology and education* (2nd ed.). New York, NY: Routledge.

Langer, A. M., & Yorks, L. (2013). *Strategic IT: Best practices for IT managers and executives.* Hoboken: John Wiley.

Levinson, D. J. (1978). *The seasons of a man's life.* New York, NY: Random House LLC.

Levinson, D. J. (2011). *The seasons of a woman's life.* New York, NY: Ballantine Books.

McBurney, E. (2015). Strategic mentoring: Growth for mentor and mentee. *Clinics in dermatology, 33*(2), 257–260.

Merlevede, P. E., & Bridoux, D. C. (2003). *Mastering mentoring and coaching with emotional intelligence.* Wales, UK: Crown House Publishing.

Milovich Jr., M. (2015). Moving technology leaders up the influence curve. *MIS Quarterly Executive, 14*(1), 39–49.

Mullen, C. A. (2006). *A graduate student guide: Making the most of mentoring.* Lanham, MD: Rowman & Littlefield Education.

Mullen, C. A. (Ed.). (2008). *The handbook of formal mentoring in higher education: A case study approach.* Norwood, MA: Christopher-Gordon.

Schein, E. H. (1992). *Organizational leadership and culture.* San Francisco, CA: Jossey-Bass.

Scherer, D. M. (2010). *Levinson's dream theory and its relevance in an academic executive mentoring program: An exploratory study of executive mentors practice and individuation.* Unpublished doctoral dissertation, Columbia University, Teachers College.

Schlossberg, N. K. (1989). Marginality and mattering: Key issues in building community. *New directions for student services, 1989*(48), 5–15.

Thompson, R., Wolf, D. M., & Sabatine, J. M. (2012). Mentoring and coaching: A model guiding professional nurses to executive success. *Journal of Nursing Administration, 42*(11), 536–541.

CHAPTER 16

SISTERS WITHOUT BORDERS

Collaborative Mentoring for Social and Personal Well-Being and Transformation

Rita Kenahan
DePuy Synthes Institute

Rosie Lim-Williams
Teacher's College, Columbia University

Maria Liu Wong
City Seminary of New York

Naya Mondo
Elerai Global Services LLC

Aimee Tiu-Wu
LearnLong Institute for Education and Learning Research

Connie Watson
Community College of Philadelphia

Mentoring in Formal and Informal Contexts, pages 301–320
Copyright © 2016 by Information Age Publishing

This is the story of six diverse women, *Sisters without Borders (SwB)*, who committed to continue a journey of "collaborative mentoring." Beginning as doctoral classmates in an adult learning and leadership program in 2009, reflective learning, encouragement, self and other-care enabled them to complete their dissertations. Moving forward into a season of life as scholar-practitioners, they together embraced the challenges and demands on their familial and work lives. However, they did not simply "lean in" to societal expectations of professional success. Empowered by Audre Lorde's (1988) declaration—"caring for [oneself] is not self-indulgence, it is self-preservation"—*Sisters without Borders* engaged in "collaborative mentoring" as a mutual process of encouragement and accountability with important implications for the field.

In this chapter, the group explores the evolution of their relationships from doctoral studies into post-graduate life. Their friendships evolved and shaped individual and academic pursuits, an emerging community of practice, and development of their careers. After graduation, their individual and group goals and experiences allowed for deepened learning-within-relationship and greater capacity to relate to each other—crossing borders of nationality, race and ethnicity, religious and spiritual affiliation, and marital status through correspondence in person and through technology, from North America to Kenya and Singapore.

Symbolically the group name, *Sisters without Borders* (*SwB*), came to embody the intersectionality of multiple identities and aspirations, even as they individually embarked on divergent personal, family, work, and career paths. Two distinct core values defined this "collaborative mentoring" process: self-reflection and collaborative learning through diversity. Welsh (2004) aptly describes "self-reflection [as] inherent in a mentoring relationship [which] may well inspire a changed vision of career...or self in the mentor and in the mentee, further inspiring changed behavior in support of the new vision" (p. 17). Through support, guidance, and advocacy given to one another to achieve an objective over a period of time, the mentoring relationship allowed *SwB* to identify concerns, determine effective responses to resistance, and empower each other through collaborative learning.

In retrospect, this process resonated with Shapiro, Wasserman, and Gallegos' (2012) claim that personal growth and awareness, relational empathy across differences, and critical systemic consciousness arise from group dialogue. While the group's diversity afforded them the potential for learning and transformative growth, they remained cognizant of Yorks and Kasl's (2002) supposition that the propensity for disagreement and disengagement might result from the confrontation of dissimilar perspectives in relation to increasing group diversity. Marusic (2012) also alludes to this *paradox of diversity* when she suggests that a barrier to mentoring that should not be overlooked is relational impediments caused by diversity issues. For instance, differences in race, values, gender, or ethnic backgrounds can contribute to the lack of fit between mentor and mentee (Crosby, 1999).

SwB experienced and successfully managed this paradox of diversity. They fostered a strong background of understanding that enabled each woman to appreciate others' uniqueness and various ways of being. Earlier as doctoral candidates, they had engaged in holistic learning-within-relationship embedded in a collaborative inquiry framework that facilitated individual and group learning (Diversity Divas, 2012; Yorks & Kasl, 2002). Through academic collaboration, co-inquiry, and social connectivity, they learned to consider carefully each other's viewpoints through dialogue, critical reflection, and creation of a space for other ways of knowing to occur. In doing so, they demonstrated the capacity to harness the power of their diversity in order to accomplish individual and collective goals. In the next phase of post-doctoral life, they desired to utilize this critical relational resource, their emotionally supportive connection, to underpin collaborative mentoring efforts and move forward together.

In short, *SwB* engaged in "collaborative mentoring" for three reasons: (a) to keep their friendships and supportive network alive as they undertook different life and work activities; (b) to benefit from the outcome of collaborative mentoring beyond skills attainment to include potential developmental growth; and (c) to explore and examine the dynamics of their collaborative mentoring process in order to contribute to the literature on women-to-women mentoring as it relates to diversity.

Review of Related Literature

In an increasingly complex, globally connected world, the need for mentoring relationships is indisputable. Mentoring has been historically defined as a mentee entering into a unidirectional, supportive relationship "in which the mentee is in a subservient role, molded by someone of greater age, wisdom, or position, who appears capable and complete" (Kochan & Trimble, 2000, p. 21). This perspective has evolved over time as issues of race, gender, and ethnicity have come to the forefront. Mentoring is now increasingly seen as an effective way to help people develop in their personal lives and professional careers. Mainstream literature in the field generally refers to two functions of mentoring: the first one focuses on career advancement and prepares mentees to achieve progression within an organizational hierarchy, while the second one serves a psychosocial function, building the mentee's sense of self-efficacy and "professional and personal growth identity" (Ragins & Kram, 2007, p. 5).

The literature on mentoring consistently promotes behaviors such as offering acceptance, building trust, respecting mutuality, communicating openly, and providing guidance to bring about positive outcomes for mentees, and studies over the last 30 years have consistently pointed to the benefits both women and men derive from being mentored (Crosby, 1999). However, less has been written about the outcomes for mentors. Welsh (2004) lists some benefits for the mentor:

> enhanced communication skills, improved performance, enhanced career development, additional recognition, enhanced respect, increased job satisfaction, maintenance of self-worth, rejuvenation, able to leave a legacy, increased sense of accomplishment, improved collaboration skills, enhanced leadership skills, improved network, validation and friendship. (p. 14)

While promising, Ragins and Kram (2007) pointedly state:

> we are not even clear on the functions or behaviors that protégés provide in the relationship...most research...has not examined relational outcomes that are central to effective relationships, learning and growth...the relationship has become valued for what it can do rather than for what it can be. (p. 8)

Hence, a greater understanding of the benefits for mentors must be addressed.

Kochan and Trimble (2000) and Daloz (1999) concur that the mentoring relationship should be valued beyond its instrumental means for a mentee's career advancement. The quality of the relationship can be mutually beneficial, and the developmental value can outweigh the instrumental, skill-building, work advancement goal. Welsh (2004) anticipates that "a good mentoring relationship forces both mentor and mentee into self-evaluation...[which in turn] spawns identification of current reality as well as desired reality, acting as catalyst for transformational learning...defined by two dispositions: changed vision and changed practice" (pp. 16–17).

A Developmental Perspective on Mentoring

Since Levinson and colleagues' (1978) noted work, *The Seasons of a Man's Life*, which explored specific periods of personal development that all human beings go through, mentoring as a construct has shifted away from the traditional notion of being a hierarchical, one-way relationship (Ragins, 2012) to a developmentally enriching relationship. In her seminal piece, *Mentoring at Work*, Kram (1985) systematically analyzed the concepts in the field of mentoring and introduced the notion of *developmental relationship*, one that "contributes to individual growth and career advancement" (p. 4). Furthermore, this relationship was seen to grow into a mutually developmental one where "the mentee [was] not someone waiting to be discovered but rather someone discovering herself, and the mentor, rather than serving as a font of perfect knowledge, became a co-learner in a process of discovery" (Kochan & Trimble, 2000, p. 21).

Daloz (2012) likewise elaborated on the developmental focus of mentoring in growing "fuller human beings" so that they became more critical, open-minded, and more capable of relating to people who were different from themselves (p. xxvi). In other words, the developmental outcome of mentoring might trigger movement from a "fundamentalistic, authority-bound, and tribal" mindset to a more expansive worldview that included "critical, systemic, connected, and committed ways of knowing in a radically interdependent and profoundly endangered world" (Daloz, 2012, p. xxvi).

A Relational Perspective on Mentoring

It is human nature to need to belong. The process evolves naturally as family, friends, learning communities, and professional associations give one a sense of identity and belonging over time. By combining one-on-one coaching and peer group mentoring, a robust "holding environment" for growth and transformation may be created and sustained (Drago-Severson, 2009, pp. 12–13).

Building on Ragins' (2012) relational perspective and four key principles described below, mentoring can take place in a healthy relational climate in which trust, understanding, caring, and non-judgmental listening are mutually shared (Daloz, 1999). Ragins (2012) suggests mentoring is, first, a dyadic and reciprocal relationship where inspiration and guidance is mutual, capturing and preserving each other's aspirations. Secondly, it is a relationship established by communal norms and allows a generative process to unfold. In this relationship, each person brings something to share as well as becomes open to new insights that may emerge. Thirdly, it expands the traditional range of dependent variables (e.g., advancement, compensation) used to measure "successful mentoring." Walking alongside each other, taking time to listen, encourage, and support growth, allows the organic emergence, development, and acquisition of other "relational skills and competencies that may be transportable across work roles and organizational boundaries" (Ragins, 2012, p. 522). Lastly, this holistic approach creates opportunities to influence and impact other life domains outside work.

Collaborative Mentoring: The Power of Women Mentoring Women

While scholarship and interest on mentoring started in the mid-1970s and continued to grow, it was not until the 1980s when the need to understand female mentoring was highlighted in the literature (Crosby, 1999).

Today, even with increasing numbers of educated and well-trained women in the workforce, mentoring women takes on critical significance given the dearth of women in senior leadership positions in the public and private sectors (Ncube & Washburn, 2010; Tolar, 2012). The habitual role played by women as "supporter" underscores the need to mentor women to develop leadership skills, self-authority, confidence, and the capacity to problem-solve, innovate, start businesses, and to lead change (Laff, 2009; Price-Sharps et al., 2014).

Women are generally seen to be more caring, collaborative, and appreciative of social relationships compared to their male counterparts. The perception that women are better listeners and better at sharing and self-disclosure furthers the assumption that women-to-women mentoring is naturally valuable for female mentees. Parker and Kram (1993), however, present situations in female mentor-mentee relationships where active listening and empathic connection may not be the norm, particularly when the dynamics of projective identification and transference occur. For example, mentees may project the role of mother/nurturer onto the mentor who feels apprehensive about fulfilling what she sees as the mentee's dependency needs. The mentee, who may operate from "unconscious wishes for unconditional mothering/nurturing," may feel "judged and ashamed, as a child might when scolded by her mother" (p. 44).

In contrast to female-to-male mentor relationships that can focus more on career and individual achievements, a woman-to-woman mentoring relationship may encompass nuanced identity issues around a woman's role at home and at work with choices made in that domain with which mentor and mentee may disagree. Parker and Kram (1993) suggest cultivating mutual self-awareness and unpacking unexamined assumptions to improve mentoring relationships. They also advise building a "variety of relationships (that) address different needs and offer different kinds of learning possibilities," as women can "benefit from multiple developmental relationships because each offers unique developmental opportunities" (p. 49).

SwB is an example of bringing together such "multiple developmental relationships" (Parker & Kram, 1993) in an organic, less prescriptive way. While mentoring is generally considered a formal process with prescribed rules of conduct, mentoring can take place in informal settings with significant results. In her doctoral research on pioneer women leaders in Kenya, Mondo (2014) found the ascension and success of women into formal leadership positions was highly influenced by mentoring relationships. These were both formal and informal, not always bound by age, gender, or profession. The traditional conceptualization of mentoring as "a powerful emotional interaction between an older and younger person, a relationship in which the older member is trusted, loving, and experienced in the guidance of the younger" (Merriam, 1983, p. 162) was seen, in these cases, as limiting.

Liu Wong (2015) found this also to be so in mentoring situations in a qualitative study on female professors and administrators in Christian theological higher education across Africa, Asia, and North America. Formal and informal, horizontal and vertical, as well as individual and community relationships were vital for the women to succeed and move into positions of formal leadership.

Through collaborative mentoring, *SwB* aimed to deepen the existing supportive environment by retaining its informal structure in the hope of generating spontaneity and sparking creativity while members embarked on new ventures in the post-doctoral season of life. This story has significance for women seeking emotional, psychological, and professional support in both public and private spheres. It is especially relevant for women managing multiple roles in life, for whom mentoring relationships are necessary to continue to nurture their personal, relational, and professional growth.

METHODOLOGY

The journey began in the summer of 2009 when group members were doctoral students in the Adult Education Guided Intensive Study (AEGIS) program at Teachers College, Columbia University. All members have since graduated from the program, transitioned into new roles as mothers (and for one, grandmother), and grown in their professional roles in the corporate sector, non-profit, small business, and academia. In February 2015, the group convened to share their post-AEGIS experiences. They discovered their shared experience of the AEGIS program, and the resulting bond of friendship, sustained them in their lowest points after graduation. In reflection, *SwB* decided to intentionally document and capture the nature of this collaborative mentoring relationship, a process that encouraged group members to engage in such activities as running a half-marathon for a cause (for the first time for two of the three who ran), self and group assessment, co-authoring a chapter for publication, and individual/group presentations.

Similar to Kochan and Trimble (2000), the group uses micro and macro views of mentoring to describe their relationship and process. The micro view provides an illustration of mentoring roles, how relationships developed, and reflections based on the common experience of completing a rigorous program together and, subsequently, life post-AEGIS. The macro view is offered through an analysis of the collaborative mentoring experience, capturing the themes essential to the journey together as mentors/mentees and co-researchers in this inquiry. Throughout this process, the group members kept journals, memos (Salazar, Crosby & DiClemente, 2015), and field notes (Roper & Shapira, 2000), and triangulated the data to answer the following research questions:

1. How did this mentoring group and process influence commitment to, engagement with, and confidence in individual goals?
2. What shared meaning making occurred with regard to collaborative mentoring, and what is its impact on the future direction and sustainability of the group?

In order to capture the dynamics of the collaborative mentoring project, *SwB* designed the following process (see Table 16.1) to collect and analyze data for reflection and interpretation.

TABLE 16.1 Timeline of the Collaborative Mentoring Process

Date and Agenda	Actions Taken
April 3, 2015 Determine Research Questions	Each sister wrote her conceptualization of "mentoring" and researched the topic individually. Then the sisters shared their perspectives with the group. Next, the group engaged in dialogue around the topic and came to consensus on the research questions.
April 10, 2015 Set Individual Goals	Each sister identified individual goals and described why they were important to her and how they may transform her in the future.
April 15, 2015 Self-Assessment and Professional Development	Each sister wrote a 1–2 page summary describing her goals and provided a self-assessment of strengths or internal capacities she already had that could help her succeed. She also described aptitudes, capacities, or knowledge she needed to reach her goal. These documents were sent to the entire group for review.
May 10, 2015 Dialogue with Sisters	The sisters read one another's description of the goals and the self-assessment and had one-on-one conversations with at least three other group members (and wrote a response to the other sisters) to discuss goals and developmental trajectories. They shared insights, stories, hopes, fears, and guidance that informed each sister's plan for growth and goal obtainment.
May 18, 2015 Data Collection	Four of the six sisters met in person and used the Appreciative Inquiry (AI) process (discover, dream, design, destiny) to uncover themes from the one-on-one dialogue sessions and written responses in reference to each sister's individual goals (Cooperrider & Srivastva, 1987). The AI process also led the group through a coding exercise of emergent themes. The two sisters who were not present used a modified AI process over the phone and also generated themes from the process by coding the data.
June 12, 2015 Data Analyses	Three sisters reviewed the themes generated from the two AI processes and compared them to the literature reviewed for the project. Four themes emerged, which were sent to the group for consensus. One sister wrote short narratives for each sister, utilizing the data from the AI sessions. These were reviewed and revised by the group and were also used as data when clarifying the major themes and conclusions (Cooperrider & Srivastva, 1987).
June 15, 2015– **September 28, 2015** Writing the Chapter	The sisters took turns writing the sections and making edits. Two of the sisters took the lead in making final edits and proofreading.

FINDINGS AND DISCUSSION

As mentioned earlier, the findings have been grouped into micro and macro categories. The micro category denotes each sister's individual journey through the process, addressing research question one. The macro category reviews shared themes that emerged from the Appreciative Inquiry process and data analyses. These are shared perceptions, experiences, and beliefs about the process, relating more directly to research question two.

Micro Findings

The following summary outlines each individual sister's micro-narrative, introducing goals, areas of strength, and growth while reflecting on the impact of the *SwB* group on individual commitment, engagement, and confidence through the mentoring process. To begin, Aimee's long-term vision included helping to establish the LearnLong Institute for Education, an educational think tank co-founded with Connie and another AEGIS alumni, while embracing expanded responsibilities of parenthood. She leveraged her abilities as a determined, highly motivated, and efficient planner to stay intellectually engaged through blogging, writing, and presenting at conferences, even while staying at home with three young children. Having *SwB* by her side in this post-doctoral season helped her to focus on learning to trust and develop courage and confidence during times of uncertainty and ambiguity, as she navigated the murky waters of parenting, gaining clarity on her personal and professional identities, and work-life balance. Their mutuality as professional women balancing motherhood, work, and life enabled her to see models of possibility.

After graduation, Connie broadened her career scope to include entrepreneurism. In doing, she struggled to find balance between family, work, and her health and wellbeing. Completing the half marathon in NY with two of her "sisters," and raising double their anticipated charity fund-raising goal, helped Connie recommit to running, prioritize wellness, and stay positive, engaged, and focused on her path. With the support of *SwB*, Connie was able to balance her work as a community college faculty member while starting a consulting firm, and co-founding LearnLong Institute for Education with Aimee and another AEGIS alumni. Her sisters did more than support and encourage her; they were the basis of her social and career network. Not a week would go by without an email about an upcoming conference, a request for assistance on a project, or an interesting job opportunity. *SwB* provided access to information and opportunities as well as deep friendship.

Rosie's long-term goal was to improve her leadership development facilitation skills and integrate a new program on adult growth and change in her work. Her short-term goals involved preparing for and delivering presentations at two professional society meetings and using her role as a Teaching Fellow at Harvard to cultivate deeper facilitation skills to help adult learners. During this time, Rosie experienced *SwB* as a comfortable space to share her deepest concerns, challenges, and joys. For Rosie, the group functioned as a holding environment (Drago-Severson, 2009) where she found support for her aspirations. She credited *SwB* for providing the psychological nudges to forge ahead during the times she was not sure of herself, resulting in highly satisfying outcomes for her short-term goals.

Maria, the group's most recent graduate, finished school while working full-time and raising three young children with her husband. Resilient and entrepreneurial in her leadership, she found *SwB* to be a place of transparency and trust, where group members resonated with her struggles to juggle multiple roles and responsibilities like writing, speaking, and engaging in research while raising a family. Often struggling to say "no," Maria was profoundly impacted by her sisters, who she saw as models of setting healthy limits and prioritizing self-care. As one of the half marathon runners, training with and accomplishing the run together prompted greater commitment, engagement, and confidence to follow through, try new things, and take some risks, like signing up for an additional eight races to qualify for the 2016 NYC Marathon.

Naya's long-term goal was to open a technology development center for post-college coders and developers in Kenya with plans to expand to other East African nations. She envisioned marketing her products as she developed a self-sustaining business enterprise, hiring talented youth unable to find employment in Kenya. As a mother of twins, Naya also continued to focus on supporting her daughters to their fullest potential. A creative thinker with big picture in mind, Naya admitted that she needed greater confidence in business administration skills to develop and build her company. *SwB* provided the space for her to grow and learn and kept her grounded and excited about life. Struggling to be grounded while running a new business, she needed others to cheer her on, believe in her, and encourage her no matter what; *SwB* was this 'village' of emotional, parenting, and health support.

Rita's health and fitness goals were addressed through training and completing the half marathon with *SwB* sisters. The leap to considering herself a "runner" and becoming more engaged in her own fitness was a feat, accomplished with their encouragement and support. As a single mother of three, Rita continued to nurture and inspire her adult children while working full time. Transitioning at the near conclusion of a career in the medical device industry, Rita's goal was to prepare for her "Third Chapter," described "as a time of change, growth and new learning: a time when our courage gives us hope" by Lawrence-Lightfoot (2009, p. 244). Being with her *SwB* sisters

TABLE 16.2 Beliefs about Group Process Impact on Individual Members

Beliefs	Aimee	Connie	Maria	Naya	Rita	Rosie
Commitment	High	Medium	High	High	High	High
Engagement	Medium	High	Medium	High	Medium	High
Confidence	Medium	High	High	Medium	High	Medium

strengthened her courage and sense of adventure, as she drew inspiration as well as ideas from the group for her future in post-retirement.

Comparing qualitatively the impact of the group experience on individual members, each sister identified how the collaborative mentoring processes influenced her (a) commitment to; (b) engagement with; and (c) confidence in achieving her individual goals. Table 16.2 shows how the group impacted each woman differently. There is not a single instance of complete overlap.

The narratives and reflection of beliefs noted above provide meaningful insight into research question one. All three areas were enhanced in some way by collaborative mentoring. Each sister had more commitment, engagement, and confidence in her ability to reach individual goals, though these were varied in proportion. Table 16.1 shows each sister had a different set of beliefs and internal capacities to be enhanced. The descriptors "High-Medium-Low" were not qualified and were interpreted by each sister. Therefore, there are limitations in this approach to reporting the degree of impact of these beliefs.

In order to clarify the extent to which beliefs were altered, a more developmentally focused mentoring conversation could be created and employed. In Maria's case, addressing individual goals such as running the half-marathon and preparing for speaking engagements provided a sense of camaraderie with like-minded high achieving women, raising her confidence and commitment. However, because she was faced with a number of competing commitments, the group's encouragement provided moderate support towards full engagement in all of her goals. This may have been due to her unrealistic expectations with regard to completing the range of goals listed.

Rita and Aimee also marked "medium" in the "engagement" category. In Aimee's case, time constraints limited her ability to have regular dialogues with her sister mentors, and this in turn had an impact on her level of engagement to her goals. She believed she needed stronger follow-through and consistent dialogue to help her think through her assumptions about what was blocking her (e.g., emotionally, psychologically) from fully achieving her goals. For Rita, time constraints related to her family, work, and social obligations precluded her from feeling a total commitment to the group. She would have appreciated more time in person with her sisters and preferred in-person connectivity over online meetings and phone conversations. She also felt pressure with what seemed like a restricted time frame in which to accomplish her goals.

It is somewhat surprising that confidence was not scored as "high" across the board. This may have been be due to differing individual starting points for confidence, or influenced by varying cultural and social norms for leadership roles. On the other hand, the overall lower confidence dimension, when juxtaposed with the overall high commitment and engagement dimensions, suggests that the sisters pressed on nevertheless with their goals despite feeling uncertain about themselves in the face of demanding realities.

Three sisters shared that the *SwB* mentoring process enhanced their confidence from a medium level. Rosie's confidence in achieving "successful" outcomes was moderate given there were many unknowns around some of her goals. *SwB* was appropriated as a socio-relational support structure to prompt her to try new experiences. The group's scholarly objectives to examine collaborative mentoring was a reason for high commitment and engagement in her personal goals, as she wanted to better understand and practice building developmental relationships for the benefit of self and others.

Another sister, Naya, expressed that growing confidence was a continuous journey. A few years ago when she was laid off during her studies and her twins were nearing college application time, her confidence as a productive member of society crashed. Surrounded by a group of very special friends, most of them now part of *SwB*, she was able to bounce back. *SwB* reminded Naya she could continue to grow and flourish. Now for Aimee, the mentoring journey was also a journey of self-discovery as she found confidence in her new role as a stay-home-mom. The competing demands of her home life, coupled with her desires for professional growth, had taken a hit on her confidence as a female academic. *SwB* was instrumental in helping her gain clarity, understanding, and focus of her current role and life choices. Thus, *SwB* played a critical role for all three women in the area of building confidence.

Macro Themes

The macro themes that emerged during the "collaborative mentoring" journey included: (a) fostering developmental relationships; (b) building authentic leadership; (c) emerging collaborative learning community; and (d) utilizing a dynamic and organic process. Summarized in Table 16.3, the mentorship that started from a micro (individual) to the macro (group) emerged organically. As Perrow (1970) notes, "leadership style is a dependent variable which depends on something else" (p. 6). That "something else" here was the "historic context in which they [leaders] arise, the setting

TABLE 16.3 Emergent Themes and Description

Emergent Theme	Description
Fostering developmental relationships	Valuing and cultivating a holding environment of support and challenge for transformative growth
Building authentic leadership in balance	Practicing authentic leadership behaviors by building truthful self-identities in harmony with and amidst competing demands
Emerging collaborative learning community	Reflective practice for mutual and collaborative learning
Utilizing a dynamic and organic process	Group norms of trust and respect allowing for the adoption of an organic group-work process to be possible

in which they function...in the process leaders shape and are shaped" (Gardner, 1993, p. 1). The collaborative mentoring relationships were spaces where the sisters continued to "shape" and "be shaped."

Fostering Developmental Relationships

All of the sisters felt that fostering developmental relationships—understood as transformative growth and becoming a fuller human being (Daloz, 2012)—were key to the process. Each woman came to appreciate the importance of creating a "holding environment" (Drago-Severson, 2009) earlier on as doctoral students together as well as in their subsequent participation in the collaborative mentoring project. A "holding environment" offered psychosocial support in situations of anxiety and discouragement.

Rosie and Naya were not able to attend a critical group reflection meeting they had committed to due to sudden extenuating personal circumstances. In lieu of attending, they improvised by conducting a pair-reflection activity (an adaptation of the AI process) over the telephone, and linked the data to the larger group process. Naya expressed appreciation of the sisters' support: "As much as we feel we disappointed you by not being there, we trust you all that we can share our deepest concerns...we do not have to pretend things are okay when they are not." Rosie felt that the sisters' accommodation of unintended breakdowns without quick allocation of blame was an expression of developmental relationships.

The other function of a "holding environment" is to provide challenges to expand perspective taking for transformative growth. As Rita indicated, this was a "safe space where we could practice having difficult conversations and give and get feedback. Learning to do this well with each other prepared us to do this in our work environments." Rosie noted that these and other ideas were helping the group move into more complex and integrated thinking patterns and increasing their capacity to reach individual and group goals.

One factor that may affect the quality of women-to-women mentoring is the nuanced, diverse, and even competing views of a woman's role at home and the workplace, along with the issue of balancing self- and other-care (Tolar, 2012). While the sisters converged on values around nurturing their children and families, they diverged in different seasons of family and work lives. Nevertheless, the developmental relationships they shared led Maria to comment that *SwB* operated "with an intentionality of openness and awareness that our connections as women with multiple identities and responsibilities allow us to fully embrace life lived well."

SwB provided a supportive environment for diversity. Connie stated: "It was important to pull multiple ideas together (be strategic) so we could create synergy from leveraging our expertise and networks," by drawing on the particular gifts that each sister had to offer. The findings suggest that a salient feature of the collaborative mentoring set-up, where sisters played dual roles as mentors and mentees, was the multiple developmental relationships that drove both concrete goal attainment and psychosocial growth.

Building Authentic Leadership in Balance

In pairs and as a group, the sisters discussed aspirations for becoming leaders in their fields, in business, in their communities, and within their families. The group members agreed that they were smart, capable, and achievement oriented women who wanted to be leaders who were genuine, holistic, and strategic—balancing the various elements of their lives in harmony. *How* they led was critical to them. Maria noted, "leadership is internal as well as external, and we have to be true to ourselves first." Aimee followed-up with the idea that "leadership is all about relationships," and for the mentoring group it was about how they "showed up" with each other. Taking turns leading throughout this project, she observed that each sister authentically led the project by leveraging her strengths while also being honest when things got overwhelming. This authenticity allowed each sister to step up *and* step back in leadership roles throughout the mentoring process.

The sisters agreed with Welsh's (2004) ideas that mentoring promoted self-evaluation, and Ragins' (2012) assertion that leaders both inspire and guide. The sisters led and guided each other and themselves; thus, the collaborative mentoring process was a means to build leadership skills while finding balance amongst competing commitments. Because her family supported her, Maria described including training for the half-marathon into her busy work life as a way to increase personal effectiveness, family togetherness, and create teachable opportunities for her children. Connie spoke about being purposeful as a leader, integrating different streams of formal and informal work efforts into a synergic whole. This was a way of countering the current trend of under-representation of women leaders in private and public organizations because of other demands and responsibilities (Price-Sharps et al., 2014).

Emerging Collaborative Learning Community

The sisters discussed how they became a collaborative learning community (Lorde, 1988) through this process. They built their own support structure after graduating and committed to carrying the group forward. Naya noted, "We have had conflict, we have played together, we have worked together, we have learned together, and we have grown together." Maria stated, "As mothers, we are nurturers but in this group, we nurture each other. We have had some break downs, and we will again, but how we are able to lift each other up is worth the effort."

Not only was building strong relationships essential to the emergence of a collaborative learning community, but engaging in the reflective process was critical for developmental learning (Welsh, 2004). Rosie saw this collaborative learning community metaphorically as "Wizard of Oz travelers" where the sisters helped one another "re-engineer" themselves. It helped them become aware of the strengths they may not have known they had, such as courage, passion and imagination, until they stepped into the unknown.

This suggests that the group was able to manage the paradox of diversity—potentially conflicting perspectives and experiences—in a way many of the group members had not been able to in a previous collaborative inquiry experience. The conversation surfaced diverse views on equity of contribution and moved the *SwB* sisters to a point of appreciating different ways each member "showed up" for the group. This is an example of Welsh's (2004) emphasis on reflection leading to learning.

Utilizing a Dynamic and Organic Process

Many of the group members had worked on projects with one another before. Through trial and error, it became apparent that a dynamic and organic working structure was most effective. There were still some issues with this group process, including who received credit for the work, because it was hard to determine equity in the amount of time each individual spent on the project. However, the process seemed to work best when the group applied a long-term view of their relationship and spoke openly and honestly. Aimee said, "You (all) saw me in my darkest hour and good thing I know you would objectively give me feedback I have to hear . . . when there's trust and confidence (in each other), somehow things will merge together."

Group norms of trust, respect, and appreciation made using a dynamic and organic group process successful. This is in line with Clark and Mills' (1979) idea that communal norms let a generative process unfold. Clark-Polner and Clark (2014) coined this as "communal relationships" and in this case, fostered a deep sense of security and flexibility as group members sought out growth and support from one another. On the other hand, the process may have had more structure than they realized. Besides using deadlines and ongoing communication, the group structure aligned with Drago-Severson's "Four Pillar Practices" (2009), which emphasizes creating mentoring relationships, taking turns leading projects and tasks, inquiring and conducting research together in a collegial and collaborative way, and teaming up to write and give presentations.

Summary

Reflecting on these four main themes, it is possible to gain insight into how the collaborative peer mentoring process was created and might be re-created. At its core was a common bond and friendship that inspired engagement in the process from the start. Once that was established, the *SwB* sisters were able to go deeper by constructing a "holding environment" with sufficient challenges and supports that encouraged the formation of developmental relationships (Drago-Severson, 2009). A common goal to increase authentic leadership capacities (internal and external) brought greater commitment to individual goals and the group process.

Seeing each other as co-learners and co-researchers, the *SwB* gravitated towards Lorde's (1988) conception of a "collaborative learning community." Through one-on-one and group dialogue, as well as journaling and writing memos, the sisters gained confidence in their own abilities and in the process itself. Then, by applying a dynamic and organic collaborative peer mentoring process, they were able to address breakdowns, manage disappointments, generate a learning conversation on a potentially controversial issue, and make progress toward goals.

However, it is apparent that this might not be simply a one-time achievement. With many long-term goals, and varying levels of commitment, engagement, and confidence in regard to individual goals, the *SwB* could repeat the process in order to deepen and expand their understanding of themselves and each other as collaborative mentors. The process itself might need to be more structured to move the group to an even deeper level of developmental learning, pushing the edge of reflective practice. The mentoring conversations themselves might need to be more focused, and the process could gain greater effectiveness if Drago-Severson's (2009) "Four Pillar Practices" as described earlier, were more fully integrated into the collaborative learning community structure.

CONCLUSION

In the desire to take friendship and sisterhood further, *SwB* engaged in a mutual journey of self-exploration and group identity formation. Whether juggling multiple hats at work or at home, the sisters were constantly ne-gotiating social norms and expectations. In the midst of this, they realized they must learn to care not only for themselves but also each other. Re-turning to research question one: How did the group influence commit-ment to, engagement with, and confidence in individual goals? From this inquiry, *SwB* created a "collaborative mentoring" process, which led each woman to commit further as individuals and as a group to where the jour-ney would take them. Their collective journey can be summed up in this African proverb: "If you want to walk fast, walk alone. If you want to walk far, walk together."

The sisters were faced with challenges of geographic disparity which af-fected their sense of engagement. With limited ability to convene in per-son, they were forced to connect through virtual means. While technology afforded them the opportunity to conference call, FaceTime, or utilize We-bEx, some sisters experienced varying levels of engagement related to lim-its in face-to-face experiences. In addition, the sisters found that competing priorities in their busy lives, such as family, work, and social commitments, affected their ability to feel as connected and engaged as they would have preferred. While these limitations affected their engagement, they pursued their goals through the support of this collaborative mentoring process.

Through this process, the sisters expressed increased levels of confi-dence, from medium to high, as they pursued individual goals. By sharing their goals, hopes, and insecurities with their trusted sisters, these women found enhanced confidence to approach their aspirations with determina-tion and support.

The second research question addressed: What shared meaning making occurred with regard to collaborative mentoring and what is its impact on the future direction and sustainability of the group? With individual and collective goals, from starting new businesses to running as a half-marathon team, *SwB* viewed the mentoring journey as led by relationships (Kochan, 2002). It was seen as "friendship with someone [or others] . . . a little more experienced, whom act[s] as guide in regard to a new career, profession, job, or development state" (Levinson et al., 1978, p. 100). The process was praxis-driven, experiential, and reflective in and on action (Schon, 1983).

The *SwB* model was an important catalyst for transformation as well as a way to deepen individual self-awareness and become more intimately in-volved in the learning, growth, and trajectory of others. The group nuanced the objective of creating opportunities for deeper dialogue with each other with the broader goal of becoming co-researchers in a participative action research process. The supportive relationships forged earlier, that contrib-uted to doctoral accomplishments, continued to be valued as a source of sustenance for personal and professional pursuits.

The potentially synergistic and mutually beneficial co-mentoring relationship that constitutes "collaborative mentoring" is key to developing abilities and capacities to build "collaborative work cultures." Postmodern workplaces with flatter organizational hierarchies make demands for interdependent ways of working (Kochan & Trimble, 2000). Collaborative mentoring could be a means to sustain people emotionally and socially in order to cultivate new work skills and behaviors needed for collaborative learning, trying new ventures, or instituting social change (Price-Sharps et al., 2014). As such, "collaborative mentoring" is a mentoring process focused on individual and spiritual wellbeing, relational transformation, and professional growth.

Reminiscent of "quality mentoring," this "human activity of care beyond the bounds of the family" enables one to see the other in ways not seen before (Daloz, 2012, p. 2). While comparable, this process is not simply peer coaching. *SwB* diverged to new ventures and converged in a mutual process of collaborative mentoring to strengthen each other mentally, emotionally, intellectually, and professionally. Each sister was uniquely experienced, but sought guidance in other areas of life. Each played dual and simultaneous roles of mentor and mentee, leading to individual and corporate meaning making. More importantly, each sister was grounded in her own identity and authenticity, all the while "leaning in" on others. The value of lessons learned is for the long term, embedding collaborative mentoring in relationships for time to come.

NOTE

1. "Diversity Divas" is the name of a collaborative inquiry research group adopted for the purposes of group publication. Members of the group include Maria Liu Wong, Naya Mondo, Ramona Sharpe, Aimee Tiu-Wu, Connie Watson and Rosie Williams.

REFERENCES

Clark, M. S., & Mills, J. (1979). Interpersonal attraction in exchange and communal relationships. *Journal of Personality and Social Psychology, 37*, 12–24.

Clark-Polner, E., & Clark, M. S. (2014). Understanding and accounting for relational context is critical for social neuroscience. *Frontiers in Human Neuroscience, 8*, 127. doi.org/10.3389/fnhum.2014.00127.

Cooperrider, D., & Srivastva, S. (1987). Appreciative inquiry into organizational life. In R. W. Woodman & W. A. Pasmore (Eds.), *Research in organizational change and development* (Vol. 1, pp. 129–169), Greenwich, CT: JAI Press.

Crosby, F. J. (1999). The developing literature on developmental relationships. In A. J. Murrell, F. J. Crosby, & R. J. Ely (Eds.), *Mentoring dilemmas: Developmental relationships within multicultural organizations* (pp. 11–12), Mahwah, NJ: Erlbaum.

Daloz. L. A. (1999). *Mentor: Guiding the journey of adult learners.* San Francisco, CA: Jossey-Bass.

Daloz, L. A. (2012). Foreword. In L. J. Zachary, *The mentor's guide: Facilitating effective learning relationships* (p. 2). San Francisco, CA: Jossey-Bass.

Diversity Divas. (2012). A collaborative inquiry: Raising cross-cultural consciousness. In M. Byrd & C. Scott (Eds.), *IGI handbook of research on workforce diversity* (pp. 88–108). Hershey, PA: IGI Global. (Reprinted from *Cross-Cultural Interaction: Concepts, Methodologies, Tools and Applications,* pp. 737–757, by I. Management Association, Ed., 2014, Hershey, PA: Information Science Reference.

Drago-Severson, E. (2009). *Leading adult learning: Supporting adult development in our schools.* Thousand Oaks, CA: Corwin Press.

Gardner, J. (1993). *On leadership.* New York, NY: Simon and Schuster.

Gardner, W. L., & Avolio, B. J. (1998). The charismatic relationship: A dramaturgical perspective. *Academy of Management Review, 23,* 32–58.

Kochan, F. K., & Trimble, S. B. (2000). From mentoring to co-mentoring: Establishing collaborative relationships. *Theory Into Practice, 39*(1), 20–28.

Kochan, F. K. (2002). *Perspectives in mentoring: The organizational and human dimensions of successful mentoring programs and relationships.* Greenwich, CT: Information Age.

Lawrence-Lightfoot, S. (2009). *The third chapter: Passion, risk, and adventure in the 25 years after 50.* New York, NY: Sarah Crichton Books.

Laff, M. (2009, September). The guiding hand: Mentoring women. *Talent Development, 63*(9), 32–35.

Levinson, D., Darrow, C., Klein, E., Levinson, M., & McKee, B. (1978). *The seasons of a man's life.* New York, NY: Alfred A. Knopf, Inc.

Liu Wong, M. (2015). *Dancing into the centers of the spiral labyrinth: Racial/ethnic minority women leaders in global Christian theological education.* (Unpublished doctoral dissertation). Teachers College, Columbia University, New York.

Lorde, A. (1988). *A burst of light, essays.* London, England: Sheba Feminist Publishers.

Marusic, A. (2012). Evidence base for mentoring women in academic medicine. *Journal of Graduate Medical Education, 4*(3), 389–390.

Merriam, S. C. (1983). Mentors and protégés: A critical review of literature. *Adult Education Quarterly, 35*(Spring), 161–173.

Mondo, N. (2014). *Pioneering women leaders in Kenya: Learning from experience.* (Unpublished doctoral dissertation). Teachers College, Columbia University, New York.

Ncube, L. B., & Washburn, M. H. (2010). Strategic collaboration and mentoring women entrepreneurs: A case study. *Academy of Entrepreneurship Journal, 16*(1), 71(23).

Parker, V. A., & Kram, K. E. (1993). Women mentoring women: Creating conditions for connection. *Business Horizons, 36*(2), 42–51

Perrow, C. (1970). *Organizational analysis: A sociological view.* Belmont, CA: Wadsworth.

Price-Sharps, J. L., Tillery, A. L., Giuliani, L. C., Poulsen, E. M., Bermio-Gonzalez, R. R., Vucovich-Cholakian, S., Newborg, E. M., & Roy-Pogutter, J. L. (2014). Mentoring women doctoral students to become community leaders. *Women & Therapy, 37,* 1–2.

Ragins, B. R., & Kram, K. E. (2007). *The handbook of mentoring at work: Theory, research, and practice.* Thousand Oaks, CA: Sage.

Ragins, B. R. (2012). Relational mentoring: A positive approach to mentoring at work. In K. S. Cameron & G. M. Spreitzer (Eds.), *The Oxford handbook of positive organizational scholarship* (pp. 519–536). Oxford, England: Oxford University Press.

Roper, J. M., & Shapira, J. (2000). *Ethnography in nursing research.* Thousand Oaks, CA: Sage.

Salazar, F., Crosby, R. A., & DiClemente, R. J. (2015). *Research methods in health promotion.* San Francisco, CA: Jossey-Bass.

Shapiro, S. A., Wasserman, I. L., & Gallegos, P. V. (2012). Group work and dialogue. Spaces and processes for transformative learning n relationships. In E. W. Taylor & P. Cranton and Associates (Eds.), *The handbook of transformative learning theory, research and practice* (pp. 355–372). San Francisco, CA: Jossey-Bass.

Schon, D. (1983). *The reflective practitioner: How professionals think in action.* New York, NY: Basic Books.

Tolar, M. H. (2012). Mentoring experiences of high-achieving women. *Advances in Developing Human Resources, 14*(2), 172–187.

Welsh, S. (2004). *Mentoring the future: A guide to building mentor programs that work.* Alberta, Canada: Global Book Publisher.

Yorks, L., & Kasl, E. (2002). Toward a theory and practice for whole-person learning: Reconceptualizing experience and the role of affect. *Adult Education Quarterly, 52*(3), 176–192.

ABOUT THE CONTRIBUTORS

Dr. Vonzell Agosto, PhD, is associate professor in the Department of Leadership, Counseling, Adult, Career and Workforce, and Higher Education at the University of South Florida, Tampa. Her research agenda engages theories of social oppression in connection to the concepts of culture, curriculum, and leadership. Her primary line of inquiry concerns how educators, administrators, and youth experience curriculum or influence it to be (more or less) oppressive with regard to race, gender, and dis/ability. Dr. Agosto has presented her research at major conferences including the American Education Research Association, Association for the Study of Higher Education, National Association of Multicultural Education, Association of Teacher Educators, Bergamo, and the University Council for Educational Administration. Her publications include handbook chapters and journal articles in *Race, Ethnicity and Education, Teachers College Record, Journal of Negro Education, Journal of School Leadership,* and the *Journal of Research on Leadership Education.*

Geleana Drew Alston, PhD, is an assistant professor in the Masters of Science in Adult Education Program at North Carolina A&T State University. She holds a PhD in Adult, Professional, and Community Education from Texas State University and a MS in Adult Education from North Carolina A&T State University. Her scholarship includes mentoring relationships and graduate adult learners, feminist grounded theory, (her)histories of African American adult educators, and women and minorities as adult learners. She formerly served as the Editorial Assistant for *Adult Education Quarterly* and Assistant to the Co-editor of *New Directions for Adult and Con-*

Mentoring in Formal and Informal Contexts, pages 321–335
Copyright © 2016 by Information Age Publishing
321

tinuing Education. She currently serves as the Social Media Coordinator for Adult Education Quarterly.

Shadi Aminololama-Shakeri, MD, is an Assistant Professor of Clinical Radiology at the University of California Davis where she is the Director of Breast Imaging Fellowship and Co-Director of Radiology Medical Student Education. She teaches third and fourth year medical students, radiology residents and fellows. Dr. Aminololama-Shakeri started her medical career as an internist. She completed her internal medicine residency at the University of Texas Southwestern-Parkland Hospital in Dallas, Texas and worked as a hospitalist physician in San Francisco, CA for a few years before pursuing a second career in radiology. After completing her radiology residency followed by fellowship training in breast imaging at the University of California Davis in Sacramento, California, Dr. Aminololama-Shakeri joined UC Davis Department of Radiology as a full time faculty member. In 2012, she was awarded the UC Davis Junior Faculty Radiology Teaching Excellence Award and was subsequently selected as a UC Davis Interprofessional Teaching Scholar in 2014. In her new role as the UC Davis American Medical Women's Association faculty advisor, she regularly mentors medical students and has developed workshops focusing on mentorship and leadership.

Carrie J. Boden-McGill, PhD is Professor and former Chair of the Department of Occupational, Workforce, and Leadership Studies at Texas State University. Dr. Boden-McGill's research is primarily focused in the areas of teaching and learning strategies, mentoring, transformative learning, and personal epistemological beliefs. She has presented papers in over 30 states and foreign countries and published articles in journals such as *Adult Learning Quarterly, The International Journal of Learning*, and *National Teacher Education Journal*. Her latest books are "Pathways to Transformation: Learning in Relationship", co-edited with Dr. Sola Kippers, "Conversations about Adult Learning in Our Complex World and Developing and Sustaining Adult Learners", co-edited with Dr. Kathleen P. King, "Building Sustainable Futures for Adult Learners" co-edited with Jennifer K. Holtz and Stephen B. Springer, and "Enhancing Writing Skills", co-edited with Oluwakemi Elufiede and Tina Murray. Dr. Boden-McGill serves as a Director on the AHEA Board and co-chairs the research and theory SIG of the Commission of Professors of Adult Education.

Ellen Brock, MD, MPH, Professor in the Department of Obstetrics and Gynecology at Virginia Commonwealth University, was appointed as the first Medical Director for the Center for Human Simulation and Patient Safety in 2008. Dr. Brock received the MD degree from the Medical University of South Carolina and completed residency training in Obstetrics and Gynecology at Virginia Commonwealth University. She received the MPH degree with a special interest in international health from VCU, and has worked internationally in health care delivery and education. Since 1987, Dr. Brock has served with distinction as faculty in the Department of Obstetrics and Gynecology, where she established a record of excellence in patient care, teaching, and service.

Teresa (Terry) Carter, EdD, is Associate Professor of Teaching and Learning and Associate Dean for Professional Instruction and Faculty Development in the School of Medicine at Virginia Commonwealth University. She directs the *Teaching in Medical Education Faculty Fellows Program, a* graduate certificate program developed in collaboration with the VCU School of Education for medical educators. Dr. Carter holds a Master's degree in Education and Human Development and a Doctor of Education degree in Adult and Organizational Learning from The George Washington University. Her scholarly publications and presentations focus on adult learning in professional work contexts and the scholarship of teaching and learning.

Dawn E. Chandler, PhD, is an Associate Professor of Management at Queens University of Charlotte where she teaches undergraduate, graduate, and Executive MBA programs. Prior to joining Queens, Dawn was an Assistant Professor of Management at California Polytechnic State University, San Luis Obispo. Her research centers on mentoring, career and adult development. She has published in a number of academic journals, including *Journal of Management, Academy of Management Annals, Journal of Vocational Behavior and Career Development International,* as well as in popular press outlets like the Wall Street Journal. She enjoys soccer and virtually all outdoor activities and spending time with her wife and daughter.

Nancy Feyl Chavkin, PhD, is the author of three books and more than a hundred publications on family/community involvement in education, program evaluation, and community partnerships. Dr. Chavkin currently serves as Regents' Professor of Social Work, University Distinguished Professor, and Director of the Center for Children and Families. Previously, she was the Director of the Richter Research Institute in the School of Social Work and Co-director of the Center for Children and Families. She has been the principal investigator of grants and contracts totaling more than $15 million dollars. Her evaluation experience spans two decades and includes work with grants from the US Department of Education, the Administration for Children and Families, foundations, and state and local agencies. Professor Chavkin has served on the steering committee for the National Center for Family and Community Connections with Schools, as a panel expert for National Household Survey on Early Childhood/Parent Involvement, and as a member of the National Parental Information and Resource Center Local Evaluation Panel. She has received Texas State University awards for excellence in scholarship and teaching and has been a mentor to both students and faculty.

Lori Ciccomascolo, PhD, has served as the University of Rhode Island's Interim Dean of the College of Human Science and Services since 2012 and the Dean of the College of Continuing Education since 2014. Prior to her administrative appointments, Dr. Ciccomascolo taught as a tenure track faculty member in the Department of Kinesiology and is currently a faculty member in the School of Education. Her research addresses areas of health and education including women and girls in sport and physical activity, health and physical education pedagogy, and best practices in leadership and mentoring. Dr. Ciccomascolo holds a doctorate in Curriculum and Teaching from Boston University and earned both her Master's degree in Exercise Science and Bachelor's degree in Corporate Communication from Southern Connecticut State University.

Xenia Coulter, PhD, is Professor Emeritus at the State University of New York Empire State College, currently part-time mentor in the Center for International Programs, where she works (largely online) with students in Lebanon. Her PhD from Princeton is in the area of Experimental Psychology, and she has published and presented mostly on issues of learning, teaching and mentoring, higher education, adult development, and prior learning assessments. In addition to a number of books reviews and articles, other recent publications, many with her colleague, Alan Mandell, are chapters in C. Paine (Ed.). *Information Technology and Constructivism in Higher Education*; C.J.B. McGill & K.P. King (Eds.), *21st Century Adult Learning in Our Complex World;* and M. Kappell, S. Reushle, & A. Antonio (Eds.), *Open Learning & Formal Credentialing in Higher Education.*

Theresa Criscitelli, EdD, RN, CNOR, is a doctorate prepared nurse with 28 years of experience. She spent 26 of those years in the operating room as a certified surgical technologist, staff registered nurse, assistant nurse manager, nurse educator, and then Director of Perioperative Education. Dr. Criscitelli is presently the Assistant Vice President, Administration of perioperative and procedural services at Winthrop-University Hospital, Mineola, New York. She also serves as an adjunct nursing professor at Adelphi University, Garden City, New York and at Empire State College School of Nursing Graduate Nursing program. She has published numerous articles and has conducted research that has been presented nationally and internationally. She has recently published a book for new and seasoned operating room nurses.

Maniphone S. Dickerson, PhD, completed her doctorate in Adult and Career Workforce Education at the University of South Florida. Her research interests include informal and formal mentoring for career development, gender and feminist studies, practices of adult education in community based environments, STEM pipeline for underrepresented populations, and equitable access to education and career opportunities. Dr. Dickerson is a member of the Adult Higher Education Association (AHEA), the Alpha Gamma Chapter of Omiron Tau Theta, and the American Association for Adult and Continuing Education (AAACE) where she also serves on the conference committee. She has presented research on mentoring and career workforce education at international and national conferences.

Sean L. Dickerson, MA, completed a Master's degree in Adult Education in 2012 and is currently pursuing a doctorate in Educational Leadership & Policy Studies at the University of South Florida. His research interests include mentoring programs, hip-hop pedagogy, disciplinary practices in K–12 educational environments, and community-school partnerships. Mr. Dickerson also serves as the managing editor for the *Journal of Cases in Educational Leadership*, a peer-reviewed publication for use in programs that prepare educational leaders. He has served as president for the 100 Black Men of Tampa Bay, a mentoring organization primarily focused on the improvement of outcomes for African American males and he has worked on the Hillsborough County Public Schools District 5 Task Force to address issues facing African American males in that district. He has presented at national conferences and has published in both the *eJournal of Education Policy* and *Curriculum and Teaching Dialogue*.

Michael Dove, MA, received a Master's degree in Adult Education from the University of South Florida and has been able to combine his corporate banking project management experience with his passion to improve communities through volunteer service. He is a 2010 recipient of the Bank of America Neighborhood Excellence Initiative, Volunteer Service Award and 2013 Florida Diversity Council Multicultural Leadership Award. As part of his commitment to community and service in the Tampa Bay area, Mr. Dove has served in leadership roles with Phi Beta Sigma Fraternity Inc., 100 Black Men of Tampa Bay, The Crescent Foundation, Inc. and the Tampa Heights Junior Civic Association—an organization dedicated to ensuring youth receive services to help them become strong leaders and good citizens. In 2013, he was selected to serve on the African American and Hispanic male Community Council of Hillsborough County whose purpose is to council the School Board and Administration in disciplinary policy issues within the school district. Currently serving as the Program Director for the Phi Sigma Beta Fraternity *Sigma Beta Club of Tampa*, Mr. Dove is a certified Collegiate Advisor and Membership Intake Program resource.

Frank A. Fulco, MD, RPh, is a graduate of the West Virginia University Schools of Pharmacy and Medicine. Dr. Fulco trained in Virginia Commonwealth University's combined internal medicine and pediatrics residency program and served as Chief Medical Resident in 2000–2001. He joined faculty as an assistant professor in Internal Medicine within VCU's Department of Internal Medicine and currently serves as an associate program director, site director, and academic hospitalist at the Hunter Holmes McGuire Veterans' Affairs Medical Center in Richmond, VA. Dr. Fulco has received numerous awards for teaching excellence in the Department of Internal Medicine, including the prestigious Irby-James Award for Excellence in Clinical Teaching in 2011. He is also a recent graduate of the Graduate Certificate Program in Medical Education from the School of Education at Virginia Commonwealth University.

Adam M. Garber, MD, is an Assistant Professor of Internal Medicine at Virginia Commonwealth University and Acting Intern Program Director for fourth year medical students in Internal Medicine at VCU. He received his undergraduate degree from the University of Virginia, graduated from the Virginia Commonwealth University School of Medicine in 2010, and completed his residency at Duke University Medical Center. Dr. Garber works as an academic hospitalist, teaches in the Principles of Clinical Medicine course, serves as a medical student advisor, and is a resident mentor in the Hospitalist Medicine program at VCU.

Catherine Hansman, EdD, is Professor of Adult Learning and Development at Cleveland State University. She was awarded the *Cyril O. Houle Emerging Scholar in Adult and Continuing Education Scholarship* and was bestowed a *Distinguished Faculty Award for Research* by Cleveland State University in 2005. Dr. Hansman is Past President of the *American Association for Adult and Continuing Education (AAACE),* and she also chaired the *Commission of Professors of Adult Education* (CPAE) and served on its executive committee for six years. Her research interests include learning in adulthood, higher education, mentoring, context-based learning, communities of practice, policies related to adult learners, qualitative research, and issues of diversity. Dr. Hansman teaches courses in adult education and qualitative research in the Master of Education in Adult Learning and Development and the PhD in Urban Education program (specialization in Adult, Continuing & Higher Education) at Cleveland State University. She is currently co-editor of the *Adult Education Quarterly.*

Reena H. Hemrajani, MD, is an Assistant Professor of Internal Medicine in General Medicine and Academic Hospitalist at Virginia Commonwealth University. She serves as an associate program director, focused on evaluation and competency-based medical education for the Internal Medicine

Residency Training program. Dr. Hemrajani is a 2006 graduate of the College of Medicine of Florida State University and a 2002 graduate of the University of Florida. She was board certified in Internal Medicine in 2010. Previously, Dr. Hemrajani was a faculty member at The George Washington University before she came back to VCU in 2013. She has received numerous awards for teaching excellence, including Attending of the Year at The George Washington University in 2012.

Monica C. Higgins, PhD, is the Kathleen McCartney Professor of Education Leadership at the Harvard Graduate School of Education. She joined the Harvard faculty in 1995 and spent 11 years on the Harvard Business School faculty in their Organizational Behavior unit before transitioning to the field of education. Her work centers on the subjects of leadership and organizational change, focusing in particular on the conditions that enable people to grow and develop in their careers. She has conducted research on mentoring and developmental networks in a variety of organizational contexts, including business, law, and education. In addition to her book, "Career Imprints: Creating Leaders Across an Industry", she has published in academic journals such as *Academy of Management Review, Organization Science, Journal of Education Change,* and *Strategic Management Journal.* She and her husband, Michael Higgins, enjoy spending time with their three daughters and live in Cambridge, Massachusetts.

Rita Kenahan, RN, EdD, is Group Manager of Professional Education at the DePuy Synthes Institute, a Johnson & Johnson company, where she manages a team of education specialists who develop and create learning programs for surgical healthcare professionals. She holds an EdD in Adult Learning and Leadership from Teachers College, Columbia University and a MEd in Instructional Design from the University of Massachusetts, Boston. Her scholarship focuses on the teaching and learning practices of surgeons who teach their peers in a medical device educational environment. She has written and presented on surgeon faculty development and professional development in the workplace. She focuses her energy on career development in the MD&D industry with a concentration on mentorship and professional competency models.

Kathleen P. King, EdD, is Professor and Program Coordinator of Higher Education, College of Education and Human Performance, University of Central Florida, Orlando, FL. Kathy's major areas of research and expertise include transformative learning, instructional technology innovations, leadership, international education, faculty development, and diversity. She has been a professor of adult and higher education for over 20 years at such institutions as Fordham University, New York, NY, and University of South Florida in Tampa, FL. Because of her outstanding contributions to adult and higher education, in 2011, Dr. King was inducted into The International Continuing and Adult Education Hall of Fame. As an award winning author who has published over 30 books, she is also a popular keynote conference speaker, mentor, and professor, she has designed and built several online learning portals, programs, and platform. Her on demand audio and video content has served over 7 million educators worldwide. Dr. King has been awarded the title International Distinguished Professor by foreign universities and is widely recognized for her research, teaching, service, and contributions to education by such associations as AERA, POD, NYACCE and UCEA. You may reach "Kathy" at Kathleen.King@UCF.edu

Kathy E. Kram, PhD, is the R.C. Shipley Professor in Management Emerita at Boston University. Her primary interests are in the areas of adult development, relational learning, mentoring and developmental networks, leadership development, and change processes in organizations. In addition to her book, "Mentoring at Work", she has published in a wide range of management and psychology journals. She is co-editor of *The Handbook of Mentoring at Work: Theory, Research and Practice* with Dr. Belle Rose Ragins. She is a founding member of the Center for Research on Emotional Intelligence in Organizations (CREIO). During 2000–2001, she served as a visiting scholar at the Center for Creative Leadership (CCL) when she completed a study of executive coaching and its role in developing emotional competence in leaders. She served as a member of the Center's Board of Governors from 2002-2009. Her most recent book "Strategic Relationships at Work: Creating your Circle of mentors, sponsors and peers for success in business and life" was co-authored with Prof. Wendy Murphy (Babson College). She and her husband, Peter Yeager, enjoy hiking, traveling, and listening to their musician son, Jason, perform in a variety of venues.

Arthur M. Langer, EdD, is the Director of the Center for Technology Management, Associate Chair of Faculty Affairs, Support, and Development, and Academic Director of the Executive Masters of Science in Technology Management at Columbia University. He also serves on the faculty of the Department of Organization and Leadership at the Graduate School of Education (Teachers College). Dr. Langer is also an elected member of the Executive Committee of the Columbia University Faculty Senate. He is the author of *Strategic IT: Best Practices for Managers and Executives* (2013 with Lyle Yorks), *Guide to Software Development: Designing & Managing the Life Cycle (2012), Information Technology and Organizational Learning* (2011), *Analysis and Design of Information Systems (2007), Applied Ecommerce* (2002), and *The Art of Analysis* (1997) and has numerous published articles and papers relating to service learning for underserved populations, IT organizational integration, mentoring and staff development. He consults with corporations and universities on information technology, staff development, management transformation, and curriculum development around the Globe. He is also the Chairman and Founder of Workforce Opportunity Services (www.wforce.org), a non-profit social venture that provides scholarships, mentoring and careers to underserved populations around the world.

Bennett B. Lee, MD, MPH, is an Associate Professor in the Division of General Internal Medicine within the Department of Internal Medicine at Virginia Commonwealth University. Dr. Lee is a 1988 graduate of Williams College and a 1994 graduate of the School of Medicine at Virginia Commonwealth University. In 2000, he earned a Master's degree in Public Health from Boston University, where he also completed fellowship training in General and Preventive Medicine in 2001. He served as Associate Residency Program Director and his research interests include medical education. Currently, Dr. Lee directs the third year medical student clerkship in Ambulatory Care in the VCU School of Medicine.

Rosie Lim-Williams, EdD, is a practitioner-scholar in the area of adult development and leadership training. She has worked at the Harvard Graduate School of Education as a Teaching Fellow and managed the Boston-Harvard Leadership Development Initiative, a collaborative program between Harvard and a dozen Boston Public Schools that focused on leading school reforms. Her Master's degree is from Harvard University and her doctorate from Teachers College, Columbia University. Rosie has co-published on the topic of adult learning and participated in research topics such as child development, collaborative learning, and in the area of women issues to address the problems that women face in the developing country of Madagascar. Her doctoral research was on social leadership in Singapore. Her research interests are in adult development and change, collaborative inquiry, action science and action research. She is the executive director of Thinking Heads Global, a leadership development consultancy.

Alan Mandell, PhD, is College Professor of Adult Learning and Mentoring, and was the first Susan Turben Chair in Mentoring at SUNY Empire State College. For the last four decades, Mandell has served as administrator, mentor in the social sciences, and director of the college's Mentoring Institute. He edits the journal, *All About Mentoring* and is also co-editor (with Nan Travers) of the on-line journal, *PLA Inside-Out.* Mandell regularly makes presentations at conferences, facilitates trainings on adult learning, mentoring and experiential learning, and has served as a consultant/reviewer on many projects. With Elana Michelson, Mandell is the author of "Portfolio Development and the Assessment of Prior Learning" (2nd edition, Stylus, 2004). He has written extensively with Lee Herman, including their book, "From Teaching to Mentoring: Principle and Practice, Dialogue and Life in Adult Education" (Routledge, 2004). Over the last several years,

Mandell and colleague, Xenia Coulter have regularly published on the state of adult learning today. In 2009, Mandell was honored by the Adult Higher Education Alliance with the Eugene Sullivan Award for Leadership in Adult Higher Education. He is the recipient of the Chancellor's Award for Excellence in Teaching (2001), the Chancellor's Award for Excellence in Professional Services (1991) and the Excellence in Mentoring Award (2000).

Elaine M. Silva Mangiante, PhD, is an assistant professor of teacher education at Salve Regina University. Formerly, Dr. Silva Mangiante served as a professional development specialist with The Education Alliance at Brown University for educational reform in high-poverty districts as well as a science specialist and mathematics curriculum coordinator for a K–8 school where she mentored early career teachers. Her current research includes examining effective teaching practices for science education in urban schools, elementary science pedagogy for critical thinking, purposeful ongoing mentoring, and teacher development from novice to expert. She is particularly interested in how teachers working in high-poverty school districts plan for reform-based science and create a collaborative climate for scientific discourse. Also, her interests include studying how teachers develop across their professional careers from novice to expert and how their planning shapes the form of instruction that students receive. Finally, she has been involved in developing a model for mentors to use in guiding mentees along the different stages from novice to expert. This model has been implemented not only with teachers, but also with medical faculty training residents/fellows to be surgeons.

Scott Matherly, MD, is Assistant Professor of Gastroenterology in the Department of Internal Medicine at Virginia Commonwealth University where he teaches in the Gastroenterology and Metabolism course for second year medical students. In 2014, Dr. Matherly was recognized with a teaching award for his work in the course. Dr. Matherly graduated from the University of South Carolina School of Medicine and completed his residency training at Johns Hopkins University in Baltimore, MD, before fellowship training at Virginia Commonwealth University. His specialties include gastroenterology, hepatology, and nutrition, with clinical expertise in end-stage liver disease, cirrhosis, hepatocellular cancer and liver transportation.

Elizabeth A. McAuliffe, EdD, is Associate Professor and Chair of the Department of Education at Salve Regina University. She holds a MAT in Chemistry from the University of New Hampshire and an EdD in Curriculum and Supervision from The Pennsylvania State University. Her research interests focus on teacher education and the education of women.

Emily R. Miller, Doctor of Osteopathy (DO), is a Fellow in Endocrinology and Metabolism within the Department of Pediatrics at Virginia Commonwealth University. Dr. Miller is a 2010 graduate of the Ohio University College of Osteopathic Medicine in Athens, Ohio. She completed her residency training in General Pediatrics at the University of Tennessee in 2013. Since then, she has been engaged in subspecialty training as a Fellow in Endrocrinology and Metabolism in the VCU School of Medicine. Dr. Miller has been board certified in Pediatrics since 2013. She teaches medical students and residents in her specialty, and sees pediatric patients with endocrine and metabolism disorders.

Naya Mondo, EdD, is an organizational leadership scholar and practitioner. She currently spends the majority of her time serving as Founder and President of Elerai Global Services LLC, an organization dedicated to providing Internet and solar solutions to rural and pastoral communities in Kenya and IGAD states, with the goal of providing access to lighting, education, agriculture and resources for all. She is also the Managing Partner at Management Solutions in Nairobi, Kenya a consulting firm, where she implements new business strategies, educational programs, leadership development and diversity training. Her research interests include leadership and gender, diversity, spirituality, African women and leadership and growth in Africa. She has published in the *International Boys Schools Coalition* (2010) and *IGI Handbook in Workforce Diversity* (2012).

Adam Moore, PhD, is an Assistant Professor of Special Education at the University of Rhode Island where he teaches and mentors special education teacher candidates in the graduate program. He holds a PhD in Education from the University of Rhode Island/Rhode Island College joint doctoral program, Master's of Education from the University of Massachusetts-Boston, and Bachelor's degree from Manchester College. A former Boston Public School special education teacher, his research interests include inclusive urban co-teaching and collaboration, disproportionality of students of color with special needs, cultural responsive teaching, inclusion as a social justice initiative, and family-centered practices.

Wendy Marcinkus Murphy, PhD, is an Associate Professor of Management at Babson College where she teaches organizational behavior for undergraduate students, managing talent in the MBA program, and custom programs for Executive Education. She also co-leads and teaches Foundations of Management and Entrepreneurship in which students create, launch and grow their own businesses. Her research is at the intersection of careers, mentoring, and work-life issues, with particular attention to nontraditional developmental relationships and learning. She has published her work in several journals, such as *Human Resource Management, Gender in Manage-*

ment, Journal of Management, and the *Journal of Vocational Behavior,* among others. Her book with Kathy Kram (Boston University), *Strategic Relationships at Work: Creating Your Circle of Mentors, Sponsors, and Peers for Success in Business and Life,* bridges mentoring scholarship and practice. She and her husband enjoy swimming and exploring the outdoors with their three young children.

Kathy Peno, PhD, is Professor of Adult Education at the University of Rhode Island. She prepares professional adult educators who teach in adult literacy, the military, higher education, corporations, and the health care fields. Her scholarship focuses on professional learning and skill development from novice to expert, with a focus on mentoring, in particular. She has written, consulted and presented extensively on workforce development, professional development and mentoring as a vehicle for continuous performance improvement in organizations. She serves on the Board of the Adult Higher Education Alliance (AHEA) and is Treasurer/Executive Committee Member of the Coalition of Lifelong Learning Organizations (COLLO). She holds a Master's and PhD in Adult Learning and Educational Studies from the University of Connecticut.

John G. Pierce, Jr., MD, is Associate Professor of Obstetrics and Gynecology at Virginia Commonwealth University School of Medicine. He is a 1991 graduate of the University of Florida College of Medicine and is board certified in Obstetrics and Gynecology and Internal Medicine. Dr. Pierce has extensive experience in education as the Obstetrics and Gynecology Clerkship Director for nine years and as the residency program director for three years. In July 2015, he will begin practicing in Lynchburg, VA with Women's Health Services of Central Virginia and will be the Director of Women's Health at Liberty University College of Medicine.

Amy Sedivy-Benton, PhD, is an Assistant Professor in the Teacher Education Department at the University of Arkansas at Little Rock. She holds a doctorate in Research Methodology from Loyola University of Chicago. Her research methodological expertise ranges from qualitative analysis to advanced statistical techniques including nested data and hierarchal linear modeling. Dr. Sedivy-Benton works extensively with graduate and undergraduate students in their continuing education to become teachers and administrators. Her research agenda focuses upon the career lifespan of teachers from teacher preparation throughout career retirement; these aspects are investigated through mentoring as well as informal learning environments. Her research interest areas have led to her involvement and work with multiple evaluation projects and extensive experience evaluating both program effectiveness and the impact of programs on student achievement. Her research and publications focus on policy and teacher preparation; the learning environment and access to education. She has presented at conferences both nationally and regionally and served on several journals as a consulting editor.

Anne Seitsinger, PhD, serves as the Interim Associate Dean for the College of Human Science and Services at the University of Rhode Island. In addition, she is a Professor in the School of Education and Director of the Center for School Improvement and Educational Policy. She holds a doctorate from the joint URI/Rhode Island College PhD in Education Program. She teaches courses for pre-service and in-service teachers. Her scholarship focuses on the critical conditions and practices related to school improvement, with a particular focus on family and community engagement in education. She has presented at regional, national and international conferences on education, psychology, and human development. Her publications appear in *The International Journal of Learner Diversity and Identities, Journal of School Psychology, Psychology in the Schools, Educational Psychologist,* and the *Journal of Educational Research.*

Catherine Semnoski, MEd, is a lecturer at the University of Rhode Island where she teaches students inclusive practices in the undergraduate program and supervises special education teacher candidates in the graduate program. She received her MEd in Special Education at The University of Mary Washington in Fredericksburg, Virginia and her Bachelors of Science in Elementary and Early Childhood Education at Bloomsburg University in Bloomsburg, Pennsylvania. She earned her Autism Certificate at Old Dominion University in Norfolk, Virginia. A former Chesapeake Public School special education teacher, her research interests include co-teaching and collaboration, student engagement, cultural responsive teaching, and family-centered practices.

Andreea Seritan, MD, is an Associate Professor of Clinical Psychiatry and Behavioral Sciences and Associate Dean for Student Wellness at the University of California, Davis School of Medicine. She completed her psychiatry residency training at Baylor College of Medicine in Houston, Texas, followed by a geriatric psychiatry fellowship at the University of California, Los Angeles. Dr. Seritan also pursued advanced training in psychodynamic psychotherapy, which she often applies in her clinical work. In her role as Associate Dean for Student Wellness, Dr. Seritan developed the student wellness program at the UC Davis School of Medicine, which she has been leading since July 2009. Her research focuses on the psychiatric and cognitive aspects of the fragile X-associated tremor/ataxia syndrome (FXTAS). Dr. Seritan is the recipient of the Frieda Fromm-Reichmann Award from the American Association of Directors of Psychiatry Residency Training, the Association for Academic Psychiatry Junior Faculty Award, and the UC Davis Chancellor's Achievement Award for Diversity and Community. In 2013, she was honored to be inducted into the Alpha Omega Alpha Honor Medical Society. Dr. Seritan actively mentors students, residents, and faculty colleagues and is the author or co-author of over 50 papers and book chapters.

Aimee Tiu-Wu is a higher education professional with experience in both student and academic affairs. She currently serves as Managing Partner for LearnLong Institute for Education and Learning Research (NFP), an independent educational think-tank informing individuals and the public about adult, higher, and continuing education. As a scholar practitioner, her research focuses on improving our quality of life by developing learning cities and educative societies for all; promoting cross-cultural consciousness, lifelong learning and leadership development for women; and exploring how mothers can manage their multiple life roles. As a multilingual adult educator, she is deeply passionate in the areas of collaborative and appreciative inquiry, higher education leadership, mentoring and diversity. Her recent academic work includes scholarly contributions in the fields of adult learning and leadership.

Connie Watson, EdD, is an Assistant Professor of Psychology at the Community College of Philadelphia where she teaches a variety of face-to-face and online Psychology and Leadership classes, and is the Co-Facilitator for the college's Faculty Center for Teaching and Learning. Her MS is in Industrial/Organizational Psychology and her Doctoral degree is in Adult Learning and Leadership. Connie facilitates the Leadership seminar for the Goldman Sachs 10,000 Small Businesses Initiative (in Philadelphia and with the National Cohort in Boston). She is also Co-Founder of GLOW Strategies, a consulting firm focused on growing businesses through leadership, operations, and workplace strategies. Lastly, Connie is a Managing Partner of a new think-tank, LearnLong Institute for Education and Learning Research. Her research interests include leadership development, global & multicultural education, action learning, and learning organizations and cities. She has published in the *IGI Handbook in Workforce Diversity* (2012), and in *New Directions in Adult and Continuing Education* (2015).

Maria Liu Wong, EdD, is the Dean of City Seminary of New York, and holds graduate degrees from Teachers College and Westminster Theological Seminary (in cooperation with City Seminary of New York). She has been an educator at the primary, adult and graduate levels for over 18 years. Maria trained teachers at Mercy College, Pace University, and Teachers College in New York City, and at the Gambella Teacher Education and Health Services College in Ethiopia. She also served on the Executive Board of *Bread & Water*, a non-profit organization fighting poverty in Asia and Africa. Her diverse research interests include women and leadership, adult learning, collaborative inquiry, faculty development, diversity, and urban theological education. She co-published a chapter in the *IGI Handbook in Workforce Diversity* (2012), and an article, "Christ in the Capital of the World," in *Christianity Today* (2013) with Mark Gornik. Forthcoming publications focus on racial/ethnic minority women, wisdom and leadership in Christian theological education in Africa, Asia and the United States, through portraiture and collaborative inquiry, and best practices in urban ministry and theological education.